D. CUSACK. 1984

IRISH CULTURE AND NATIONALISM, 1750–1950

The Humanities Research Centre/Macmillan Series

General editor: Professor Ian Donaldson, Director of the HRC

This series is designed for publications deriving from the Humanities Research Centre of the Australian National University, Canberra. The series, which is an occasional one, will include monographs by the academic staff and Visiting Fellows of the Humanities Research Centre, and collections of essays from the Centre's conferences and seminars.

Ian Donaldson (*editor*): JONSON AND SHAKESPEARE

Ian Donaldson (*editor*): TRANSFORMATIONS IN MODERN EUROPEAN DRAMA

J. E. Flower: LITERATURE AND THE LEFT IN FRANCE

Oliver MacDonagh, W. F. Mandle and Pauric Travers (*editors*): IRISH CULTURE AND NATIONALISM, 1750–1950

IRISH CULTURE AND NATIONALISM, 1750–1950

Edited by
Oliver MacDonagh, W. F. Mandle
and
Pauric Travers

in association with
Humanities Research Centre
Australian National University, Canberra

© Oliver MacDonagh 1983

All rights reserved. No part of this publication may be reproduced or transmitted, in any form or by any means, without permission

First published 1983 by
THE MACMILLAN PRESS LTD
*London and Basingstoke
Companies and representatives
throughout the world*

*Distributed in Australia by
Australian National University Press
PO Box 4, Canberra ACT 2600*

ISBN 0 333 32858 2

Printed and bound in Great Britain
at The Pitman Press, Bath

Contents

	Preface	vii
	Notes on the Contributors	ix
1	Burke, Ireland and the Empire J. C. Beckett	1
2	Problems Common to both Protestant and Catholic Churches in Eighteenth-century Ireland E. M. Johnston	14
3	Popular Recreation in Nineteenth-century Ireland Elizabeth Malcolm	40
4	Charles Gavan Duffy in Australia J. E. Parnaby	56
5	Irish Culture and Nationalism Translated: St Patrick's Day, 1888, in Australia Oliver MacDonagh	69
6	Irish Nationalism and the British Empire in the Late Nineteenth Century H. V. Brasted	83
7	The Gaelic Athletic Association and Popular Culture, 1884–1924 W. F. Mandle	104
8	Bernard Shaw's Other Island A. M. Gibbs	122
9	Imagination and Revolution: the Cuchulain Myth Patrick Rafroidi	137
10	Finland, Norway and the Easter Rising A. R. G. Griffiths	149
11	The Priest in Politics: the Case of Conscription Pauric Travers	161

CONTENTS

12 The Irish Republican Brotherhood in Australia: the 1918 Internments 182
    Patrick O'Farrell

13 Grafting Ireland onto Australia: some Literary Attempts 194
    Gerard Windsor

14 Yeats and the Anglo-Irish Twilight 212
    F. S. L. Lyons

15 The Anglo-Irish and the Historians, 1830-1980 239
    G. C. Bolton

16 Poetry and the Avoidance of Nationalism 258
    Vincent Buckley

Index 280

Preface

All the essays in this book originated as papers delivered to a conference on 'Irish Nationalism and Culture, 1750-1950', held at the Australian National University in Canberra in November 1980. The conference was jointly sponsored by the Humanities Research Centre at the University and the Australian Historical Association. It was organised by the editors of this volume.

The main purpose of the book (as of the conference whose offspring it is) was to help to define and establish, as well as to contribute to, Irish cultural history. 'Culture' was conceived of in a broad sense, to include popular as well as high, politics and sport as well as art, myth and religion. 'Irish' was also generously interpreted. Three of the papers dealt with Australian manifestations of Irish nationalism, two with its implications for the British Empire, and one with its Scandinavian counterparts and derivations. Both these extensive usages seem well-justified to the organiser-editors, and indeed indispensable if yet another narrow, isolated strip is not to be added to Irish studies. A secondary, but far from negligible, purpose of the book is to further Irish studies in Australia. The generating conference was the first such to be held there and this book is the first joint-fruit of the Irish research being carried out in Australia - as well, of course, as fruit of the work of the conference's distinguished visitors from Ireland, Professors Beckett and Lyons.

Our very warm thanks are due in the first place to the Humanities Research Centre and the Australian Historical Association for both financial help and general encouragement, and to the staff of the Humanities Research Centre, and most of all Miss Mary Theo, for their great organisational endeavours. We are also deeply grateful to the Irish Cultural Relations Committee for its support of the undertaking. Finally, we must pay tribute to the heroic labours of the secretarial staffs of the History Department, Research School of Social Sciences, Australian National University and of the Canberra College of Advanced Education, in typing various versions of papers at extraordinary speed and eventually mastering 'the new technology' by which this book has been produced.

The editors and publishers wish to thank the following who have kindly given permission for the use of copyright material:

R. Dardis Clarke, for the poem 'The Trial of Robert Emmet' by Austin Clarke.
Seamus Deane, for the poem 'After Derry, 30 January 1972', originally published in *Gradual Wars* by the Irish University Press.
Dolmen Press Ltd, for the poems 'When I Am Angry' from *The Rough Field* by John Montague, and 'The Young Fenians' by Padraic Fallon, included in the *Faber Book of Irish Verse*.
Faber and Faber Ltd, for extracts from the poems 'Punishment' and 'Summer 1969' from *North* by Seamus Heaney.
Macmillan Publishing Co. Inc., New York, and A. P. Watt Ltd, on behalf of M. W. Yeats and Anne Yeats, for the extract from the poem 'Sixteen Dead Men' by W. B. Yeats, from *Collected Poems of W. B. Yeats*.

Canberra   O. MacD., W.F.M.
July 1981   and P.T.

Notes on the Contributors

J. C. Beckett is Emeritus Professor of History at Queen's University, Belfast. He is the author of *A Short History of Ireland* (1952), *Confrontations* (1973) and *The Anglo-Irish Tradition* (1973).

G. C. Bolton is Professor of History at Murdoch University, Western Australia. His books include *The Passing of the Irish Act of Union* (1966), *Britain's Legacy Overseas* (1973) and *A Fine Country to Starve in* (1972).

H. V. Brasted is Lecturer in History at the University of New England. He is the author of articles on Indian nationalism, and is undertaking comparative research on Indian and Irish nationalism.

Vincent Buckley, poet and critic, is at present living in Ireland on extended leave from the University of Melbourne, where he holds a personal chair in the Department of English. Among his recent publications are *The Pattern* and *Late Winter Child* (1979).

A. M. Gibbs, Professor of English at Macquarie University, New South Wales, is the author of *Shaw* (1969) and *The Art and Mind of Shaw* (1983). He is now working on a two-volume study, *Shaw: Interviews and Recollections*.

A. R. G. Griffiths is Senior Lecturer in History at Flinders University, Adelaide. He is the author of *Contemporary Australia* (1977).

E. M. Johnston is Professor of History at Macquarie University, New South Wales. Among her books are *Great Britain and Ireland 1760-1800* (1963) and *Ireland in the Eighteenth Century* (1974).

F. S. L. Lyons is Professor of History at the University of Dublin, a Fellow and sometime Provost of Trinity College, Dublin. Among his publications are *Ireland since the Famine*

(1971), *Charles Stewart Parnell* (1977) and *Culture and Anarchy in Ireland 1890-1939* (1979).

Oliver MacDonagh is W. K. Hancock Professor of History at the Institute of Advanced Studies of the Australian National University. His publications include *Ireland: The Union and its Aftermath* (1968, rev. edn 1977), *Early Victorian Government* (1977) and *The Inspector General*, a life of Sir Jeremiah Fitzpatrick (1981).

Elizabeth Malcolm recently completed a doctorate on the nineteenth-century temperance movement in Ireland at Trinity College, Dublin. She is a graduate of the University of Sydney and contributed an essay to a volume of essays in honour of T. W. Moody, *Ireland under the Union* (ed. F. S. L. Lyons and R. A. J. Hawkins, 1980).

W. F. Mandle is Head of the School of Liberal Studies at the Canberra College of Advanced Education, and sometime Reader in History at the Australian National University. He is the author of numerous articles on sports history and of *Going it Alone: Australia's National Identity in the Twentieth Century* (1978).

Patrick O'Farrell holds a personal chair in History at the University of New South Wales. His books include *Ireland's English Question* (1971), *England and Ireland since 1800* (1975) and *The Catholic Church and Community in Australia* (1977).

J. E. Parnaby is a Senior Lecturer in History at the University of Melbourne. She has published several articles on Australian nineteenth-century political history and is currently working on a biography of Gavan Duffy.

Patrick Rafroidi is Professor of Modern and Contemporary English Literature and Director of the Centre d'Etudes et de Recherches Irlandaises at the University of Lille 3. During 1980/81 he held a Visiting Fellowship in the Humanities Research Centre, Canberra. Professor Rafroidi is Chairman of IASAIL, general editor of *Cahiers Irlandais* and *Etudes Irlandais*, and author of a two-volume history, *Irish Literature in English* (1980).

Pauric Travers has recently completed a doctorate at the Australian National University on 'The Last Years of Dublin Castle: the Administration of Ireland 1890-1921'. He is a graduate of University College, Dublin, where he was awarded his master's degree for a thesis on the conscription crisis in Ireland.

Gerard Windsor is a freelance critic, teacher and short-story writer who lives in Sydney. He wrote his doctoral dissertation on the literature of Easter Week.

1 Burke, Ireland and the Empire

J. C. BECKETT

Burke was born and educated in Ireland; but he moved to London when he was little more than twenty years of age and he made his career and his reputation in England. Though he continued throughout life to take an active interest in the affairs of his native country, there is nothing national, let alone nationalist about the policies he advocated for Ireland. Indeed, if we are to describe Burke as in any sense a 'nationalist' then he was an English (or perhaps one should say British), rather than an Irish, nationalist. Again, though it may be possible to find in his views on politics and society some elements that may reasonably be traced to his Irish background, his writings, taken as a whole, cannot be regarded as the product of a distinctively Irish culture.

Despite all this, a discussion of Burke's views on Ireland and on Anglo-Irish relations is relevant to the theme with which the conference is concerned. His thinking was essentially, even if not typically, that of his own day. His attitude on the 'Catholic Question' might seem, at first sight, a foreshadowing of nineteenth century liberalism; but closer investigation will show that it rested on quite different principles. There is often a good deal more in common between him and his opponents than appears on the surface. He was, for example, horrified at the constitutional claims put forward by Grattan on behalf of the Irish Parliament; but, in fact, both were aiming at the same end, though by different means. Burke reflected, though with the characteristic individuality of genius, the outlook of the pre-revolutionary era; and it is from this era that any study of 'nationalism and culture' must start. Neither term admits easily of a generally acceptable definition, and the nature of the relationship between them is even harder to establish precisely, though it can readily be illustrated by example. But we can safely say that, so far as the European world is concerned, the idea of nationalism, however defined, and its association with some distinctively national expression of cultural life, acquired a new significance under the influence of the French Revolution and the Romantic

Revival. What we might call Burke's 'Irish policy' - the changes he advocated in Ireland and the basis on which he thought Anglo-Irish relations should stand - was essentially a product of the pre-revolutionary age and provides a background against which ideas widely current in the nineteenth and twentieth centuries stand out in sharp contrast. Some understanding of that background will help us to see these ideas in their proper context and will act as a guard against too facile an interpretation.

On 20 July 1796 John Keogh, a member of the Catholic Committee in Dublin, wrote to Burke on the affairs of Ireland. He apologised for doing so, and continued: 'let it plead my apology that I know you are so uncourtly as to be a true Irishman - to Love your Country - may You live long its Ornament and Pride, the defender of Virtue, and of Ireland, and yet See her rise from her persecutions and persecutor's'.[1] Burke did not reply for some months; and when he did, on 17 November, he referred to this eulogy of Keogh's in the following terms:

> You do me Justice in saying in your Letter of July that I am 'a true Irishman'. Considering as I do England as my Country, of long habit, of long obligation and of establishment, and that my primary duties are here. I cannot conceive how a Man can be a genuine Englishman without being at the same time a true Irishman, tho' fortune should have made his birth on this side the water. I think the same Sentiments ought to be reciprocal on the part of Ireland, and if possible with much stronger reason. Ireland cannot be seperated one moment from England without losing every source of present prosperity, and even every hope of her future.[2]

Beside this extended exposition of his views may be set a much briefer comment from a letter of 1793, in which Burke refers to an act of the Irish Parliament, passed in that year, re-admitting Roman Catholics to the parliamentary franchise. This measure had his hearty approval; but it must, he says, be made 'subservient to the tranquillity of the country and the strength of the Empire'.

The letters from which these passages are taken were written during the last decade of Burke's life. But he had expressed similar sentiments at earlier periods also; and there is nothing to suggest that he ever varied in his opinion about the right policy to be followed in Ireland.

That policy rested on two principles, which in Burke's mind were closely related; the Catholics were to be conciliated by appropriate concessions and the links that bound Ireland to Great Britain were to be maintained and strengthened.

It would be unfair to Burke to suggest that his concern about the Catholics arose simply from a belief that it would be expedient to conciliate them; when he urged, as he constantly did, that their claims rested on grounds of abstract justice, he was perfectly sincere. But there can be no doubt that he regarded justice as the best policy; and in his writings on the Catholic Question the claims of justice and of policy are rarely separated. It would be unfair, also, to suggest that, maintaining that the Irish executive must always be controlled from London, he wished to subordinate the interests of Ireland to those of England. But his view of Anglo-Irish relations is less straightforward than his view of the Catholic Question and can be understood only in the light of his concept of the British Empire.

Here we must note that for Burke and his contemporaries the term 'British Empire' had a somewhat different connotation from that which it was to have less than a hundred years later. By the mid-nineteenth century, or perhaps even earlier, people in Britain, when they spoke of the 'Empire', were thinking primarily of the non-European possessions of the Crown. They could, and often did, speak of 'Britain *and* the Empire'. To Burke and his contemporaries this would have seemed a strange distinction. For them, the 'Empire' meant, first and foremost, the British Isles – Great Britain and Ireland.

In Burke's mind, then, Ireland was neither a colony, like those in North America, nor conquered territory, like Canada or British India, but an integral part of what might be called the 'heart-land' of the Empire. For this reason its administration must always be under direct and immediate control from London; and though he was content that it should have a Parliament of its own, that Parliament must always remain subject to Westminster. But Burke saw nothing unjust or unreasonable in this arrangement, which he regarded as equally advantageous to both countries. He was convinced that the interests of Ireland and Great Britain were not only compatible, but identical; and he believed that if there were advantage on either side it was on the side of Ireland. In a letter to Thomas Hussey, written in May 1795, he asserts that though Irish Catholics have legitimate grounds of grievance against Irish Protestants, Irishmen as a whole have no ground of complaint against Great Britain:

> For, in the name of God, what Grievance has Ireland, as Ireland, to complain of with regard to Great Britain? Unless the protection of the most powerful Country upon Earth, giving all her privileges without exception in common to Ireland, and reserving to her self only the painful preeminence of tenfold Burthens be a matter of complaint.[3]

The emphatic vigour of this passage no doubt owes something to the fact that it was written at a critical stage in the war with France, but the view that it takes of Anglo-Irish relations is one that Burke maintained throughout life.

Burke's views both on the Catholic Question and on Anglo-Irish relations differed widely from those most commonly held by that section of the population to which he belonged by birth and education. Irish Protestants long retained the suspicious fear of 'popery' inherited from the seventeenth-century wars; and it was only as those fears receded that the restrictions under which the Catholics laboured were gradually relaxed. But, even then, few Protestants were willing to trust them with any share of political power; and those who did support such a measure did so in the conviction that effective authority would still remain safely in Protestant hands. Burke's views were in marked contrast with all this. So far as Anglo-Irish relations were concerned Protestant opinion was less constantly alert. But there was a latent feeling, which could easily be stirred into activity, that Irish interests were constantly subordinated to those of England and that Irish rights were ignored and entrenched upon by the British Government and the British Parliament; and from the discontent thus engendered sprang a demand for legislative independence. Why, it may reasonably be asked, were Burke's views so radically different, in both respects, from those of his fellow-Protestants in Ireland?

It would be rash to assert that Burke's support of Catholic claims was a direct product of his family background; but the circumstances of his early life were certainly conducive to a tolerant outlook. His father was a Protestant, his mother a Roman Catholic; and in accordance with traditional practice, which survived until the early years of the present century, the sons followed the father, the daughters the mother. The liberal outlook encouraged by this early experience of the friendly co-existence of differing faiths was further strengthened by the influence of his schoolmaster, Abraham Shackleton, a broad-minded member of the Society of Friends. Burke always remained firmly attached to the established Church, but he was quite free of that dread of 'popery' and 'popish conspiracy' that was common among Irish Protestants and was by no means unknown in England and Scotland.

Burke's early training thus predisposed him to sympathy with the Catholic cause; and one may add, without being cynical, that his residence in England made it easier for him to give practical expression to that sympathy than if his career and his property had lain in Ireland. His English residence was also an important, perhaps the most important, factor in the formation of his view of Anglo-Irish relations. Having established himself in England, and seeking to make a career in British politics, it was natural that he should regard Ireland and Irish affairs from the point of view of London and Westminster. His mind, though capable of dealing with minute detail, was naturally attracted by large issues, and his major political concern was with the position and responsibilities of Britain as a great power - in his view, 'the most powerful country upon earth'. The zeal with which he championed the Catholics undoubtedly owed a good deal to his belief that they must, both on ground of conscience and in their own interest, share his view of the proper relationship between Ireland and Great Britain.[4]

Though Burke and the great majority of Irish Protestants differed so sharply in their attitudes to the Roman Catholics, they had at least one thing in common. Both sides misjudged the situation: the Protestants in their belief that they could maintain their dominant position indefinitely, despite the changes that were taking place in political, economic and social circumstances; Burke in his conviction that the Catholics, once admitted to political rights, would be permanently and firmly attached to the Crown and the British connection.

Burke's misreading of the future is, in the circumstances, understandable. In the early eighteenth century the Catholic leaders had looked to the British Government for protection against the more extreme measures advocated by Irish Protestants. In the 1780s and 1790s they looked to the same source to bring pressure on the Irish Parliament to remove or relax the restrictions under which they still suffered. Those of the Catholic leaders with whom Burke habitually corresponded were men of conservative outlook, who accepted, or appeared to accept, his view of Ireland's place in the Empire. The outbreak of the French Revolution made Burke even more urgent in his support of Catholic claims to political power, for he regarded the Roman Catholic Church as a major counter-revolutionary force. The admission of Irish Catholics to political rights would, in his view, strengthen the links between Ireland and Great Britain and act as a bulwark against revolution.

In advocating the cause of the Irish Catholics Burke was, from first to last, consistent. In his opposition to the constitutional claims put forward by the Irish Protestants he was obliged to temporise and, on one occasion, even to give formal approval to measures that were directly counter to his own principles. He was content that Ireland should have a Parliament of its own - he showed no interest in any proposal for a parliamentary union - but he was convinced that the Irish executive must always remain under direct British control, no more than a branch of the ministry in London. But the Irish executive could not govern unless it could ensure the passage of its measures, and especially of the money bills, through the House of Commons. To secure this end the executive depended heavily (as, indeed, did the ministry in contemporary Britain) on what the eighteenth century called 'management' and later generations have stigmatised as 'corruption'. Burke was convinced that the more dependent Irish MPs were on their constituents the more difficult it would be for the executive to maintain a safe majority; and for this reason he was absolutely opposed to any reform of the Irish parliamentary system. Even such a modest measure as the Octennial Act of 1768[5] seemed to him dangerous; and he condemned the more extensive reforms proposed in the 1790s, even though these were supported by the Irish allies of his own party.

Much more alarming, from Burke's point of view, than any proposal for parliamentary reform was the demand for legislative independence, which rested on the claim that Ireland was not an English dependency but a distinct kingdom, linked to England only by the fact that both had the same sovereign. This claim can be traced, though somewhat doubtfully, back to medieval times, but it did not emerge clearly until the seventeenth century. In the parliamentary debates of 1640-1 it was supported by an alliance of Protestant and recusant members. It was included in the programme of the Catholic Confederates of the 1640s. It was revived again in the 1690s. Swift expounded it in his allegorical *Story of the Injured Lady*, written in 1707, though not published at that time, and again, in plain terms, in his *Drapier's Letters*. But it was not until the later 1770s, when the formation of the Volunteers provided Grattan and his supporters in Parliament with the means of organising and directing popular opinion, that the issue became one of critical importance for British politicians.

The settlement that emerged, and Burke's share in it, cannot be understood in a purely Irish context, for much depended on the position of the parties at Westminster. While popular opinion in Ireland was pressing its demands Lord North's Government was growing steadily weaker under the attack of the Whig opposition, of which Burke was a prominent member. The Whigs, ready to use any weapon against North, supported the Irish demand that British acts restricting Ireland's overseas trade should be repealed; and North, in the hope of weakening the opposition, agreed. This was a concession of which Burke fully approved; for though he was convinced that the British Parliament had, and ought to have, authority to regulate the trade of every part of the Empire, at home or overseas, he did not regard the restrictions now to be removed as necessary, or even beneficial. But when the Whig leaders also gave their support to the Irish demand for legislative independence Burke was in an awkward position. For him, the supervising authority of the British Parliament over all the dominions of the Crown was essential to the unity of the Empire, and he was horrified at the claim put forward by Grattan - 'this madman', he called him[6] - that only the Irish Parliament could legislate for Ireland. Nevertheless, when North resigned, in March 1782, and Rockingham succeeded him, Burke accepted office in an administration committed to recognising the legislative independence of Ireland.

It may be said in his defence (if any defence be needed) that the leaders of his party, once in office, tried to persuade Grattan to negotiate a comprehensive settlement that would establish the rights of the Irish Parliament, while at the same time ensuring that the central direction of all matters of imperial concern would remain in London. But Grattan refused to negotiate and insisted on the immediate recognition of the sole right of the Irish Parliament to legislate for Ireland.[7] He had his way, and the so-called 'Constitution of 1782' gave Ireland, in theory at least, all that he had demanded. In these circumstances Burke kept his fears to himself, and he gave silent assent to a measure of which he heartily disapproved. What he really thought of the transaction is revealed in his comment that Ireland had now put herself outside the general protection of the Empire.

His disapproval seems to have been somewhat modified by the passage of time. In 1792 he could describe the concessions made to Ireland by the Rockingham ministry ten years earlier as an example of wise political generosity. And, having indicated the extent and importance of the changes then made, he could even add (what was certainly not true in his own case), 'This did not frighten any of us'.[8] But if he changed his mind the change was neither complete nor final. A few years later we find him reflecting again on the events of 1782, and in rather different terms:

> Ireland has derived some advantage from its independence on the parliament of this kingdom, or rather, it did derive advantage from the arrangements that were made at the time of the establishment of that independence. But human blessings are mixed, and I cannot but think that even these great blessings were bought dearly enough when along with the weight of authority they have totally lost all benefit from the superintendence of the British parliament.[9]

It is hard to escape the conclusion that in 1782 Burke allowed party considerations to outweigh conviction, and the impression is strengthened by his conduct a few years later. In 1784-5 Pitt put forward proposals for an Anglo-Irish commercial treaty which, if it had come into force, would have gone far to obviate the threat to imperial unity that Burke had professed to see in the legislation of 1782. But Burke was now in opposition; his overriding purpose was to drive Pitt from office, and to this end he was ready to condemn proposals which, had they been brought in by his own party, he would have defended as great and generous measures of imperial unity.

In the passage quoted above, where Burke is reflecting again, in 1796, on the effects of the constitutional settlement made in 1782, it is significant that he concerns himself solely with its effects upon Ireland. He says nothing now of that threat to the unity of the Empire which he had once considered to be the inevitable consequence of Irish legislative independence. Later events had shown that his fears, if not groundless, were certainly much exaggerated. Even the action of the Irish Parliament during the Regency crisis of 1789, which might on the surface appear to be an expression of Irish independence, was essentially a reflection of party rivalry at Westminster. Despite the changes made in 1782 the Irish executive remained, as before, under the direction of the ministry in London; and it was still able, by the traditional means, to maintain a majority in the Irish Parliament.

Even if things had been otherwise, even if the Irish

Parliament had been less amenable than it was to Government direction, it is very unlikely that Burke's fears would have been realised. The governing class in Ireland - the landlords and their allies - had no desire for separation from Britain, and they were prepared to share in the burdens as well as in the benefits of Empire. They had sympathised with the American colonists in their struggle for independence, but they had no intention of following their example. The policy of Grattan and his supporters is commonly described as 'colonial nationalism', but it was certainly not 'colonial' in the American sense. They did not rest their claims on general principles such as are found in the American Declaration of Independence, but on what they asserted to be the constitution and law of the kingdom of Ireland; and they could not deny or infringe upon the rights of the Crown without weakening, or even destroying, the basis on which their own claims rested.

This claim had, as we have seen, been put forward by the Confederate Catholics in the previous century, though they had sometimes found it difficult to reconcile their professions of loyalty to the Crown with the aims of their ecclesiastical policy. But the Protestant nationalists of the eighteenth century had no such problem; and in another way also it was easier for them than it had been for the Confederates to accept the limitations that this kind of nationalism involved. The social and cultural life of the upper and middle classes was closely linked with that of England. Education, in school and university, followed the same pattern as in corresponding English institutions. People read the same books, saw the same plays, listened to the same music as their English contemporaries. If we leave aside pamphlet literature, there is very little that is specifically Irish, either in subject-matter or in style, in the works of the Irish authors of the period. Though distinctive Irish styles can be traced in architecture, silver-work and glassware, these exceptions, and a few others of less importance, do little to modify the general picture. In short, the national self-consciousness of the eighteenth-century Irish Protestants expressed itself in political, but not in cultural, terms. An educated Irish Protestant felt himself to be a member of what might be called a 'cross-channel' society, within which there might indeed be local variations, but which had a cultural and social unity. There were, no doubt, some exceptions to this general pattern, but the Irish Protestants of the period, as a body, do not reveal any corporate sense of a distinctive and national cultural identity, such as certainly existed in contemporary Scotland. It is reasonable to argue that this state of affairs made it easy and natural for them to accept the limitations inherent in their constitutional principles and that there was much less danger than Burke seems to have feared that they would seek to extend their independence beyond the modest limits laid down by the 'Constitution of 1782'.

It is not unlikely that Burke himself came to realise this. Certainly by the 1790s, his anxiety about Ireland arose less from the conduct of Parliament than from the character of the executive. He was convinced that Pitt had failed to keep the Irish executive under proper control from London and, what was worse, that he had allowed effective control to pass into the hands of a group of Irish officials, whom Burke called, in contempt, the 'Junto' or the 'click'. It was the growing independence enjoyed, as he believed, by this group that now seemed to him to threaten the unity of the Empire. In September 1794 he wrote gloomily to the Duke of Portland: 'English government (if they are suffered to go on there [Ireland], as they have gone on), will not be left even the miserable shadow of authority which it now seems to possess.'[10] But here, again, Burke exaggerated the danger - if, indeed, it was anything more than a product of his own imagination. Pitt, even if he might sometimes leave the Irish executive to settle its own immediate problems, was always in effective control. And among the 'click' whom Burke suspected of seeking to weaken the British connection none was more prominent than Lord Clare who, at the time of Burke's letter to Portland, had already convinced himself that a parliamentary union between Ireland and Great Britain was a political necessity.

In considering Burke's view of Ireland's place in the Empire it is natural to take some account, by way of comparison, of his attitude to the North American colonies. He recognised that the colonies, unlike Ireland, were too far distant to be kept under constant supervision from London: 'Three thousand miles of ocean lie between you and them. No contrivance can prevent the effect of this distance in weakening government. Seas roll, and months pass, between the order and the execution; and the want of a speedy explanation of a single point is enough to defeat a whole system.'[11] He stuck firmly to the principle that in matters of imperial concern the British Government and the British Parliament should exercise final authority throughout the Empire; but he realised that the principle must be less rigorously applied on the other side of the Atlantic than on the other side of the Irish Sea.

The comparison here implied between the American colonies and Ireland, in their relationship to the British Government, was made at least twice by Burke himself. In a letter to an Irish correspondent in 1780, after the removal of the long-standing restrictions on Irish commerce imposed by the British Parliament, he wrote: 'Had the Crown pleased to retain the spirit with regard to Ireland which seems to be all directed to America we should have neglected our own immediate defence, and sent over the last man of our militia to fight with the last man of your volunteers.'[12] Though the concession referred to, by implication, in this passage had been granted by Lord North's Government, Burke was entitled to take some credit (as he seems half inclined to do here) for the relief granted to Ireland: the parliamentary pressure exerted by his party - the Rockingham Whigs - had had a powerful effect on North's conduct. But, all the same, the comparison Burke makes at this point is inept. The American issue was one of constitutional authority; the Irish issue, at this stage, was not. And, when it did develop into a challenge to the British Parliament, Burke, although he did (as we have seen) go along with his party in yielding, regarded the concession as a dangerous mistake.

Burke makes the same kind of comparison between the American and the Irish situations in another context also. In defending before the electors of Bristol his support of trade concessions to Ireland, despite their instructions to the contrary, he introduced the comparison in the following terms: 'To read what was approaching in Ireland, in the black and bloody characters of the American war, was a painful, but it was a necessary part of my public duty.'[13] Here the comparison may have more justification; but it would be hard to defend the use that Burke makes of it. He implies, in the first place, that if similar concessions had been made to the Americans war would have been averted; and, in the second place, that timely concessions to Ireland have averted the danger of further and more radical agitation there. Whether or not the former of these implications was justified is a matter for argument, but, so far as the latter is concerned, the granting of a free trade seems to have stimulated rather than allayed the Irish demand for legislative independence. Furthermore, this demand, even in its most extreme form, fell far short of that total separation from Great Britain for which the Americans were actually fighting as Burke addressed his audience in the Guildhall of Bristol.

Burke was not, of course, alone in suggesting that the Irish might go the way of the Americans. Many of his contemporaries, from George III downwards, thought along the same lines. But Burke's knowledge of Irish history and of the Irish society of his own day should have been enough to show him that such a development was, if not impossible, at least in the highest degree unlikely. It was, in fact, only under the influence of the French Revolution that the idea of a total break with England entered into the political thinking of Irishmen. In 1780 it was hardly even a theoretical speculation.

It is worthwhile, in conclusion, to consider Burke's view of Ireland and of Anglo-Irish relations in the light of what happened during the century-and-a-quarter that followed his death. The fear he expressed in the 1790s that the Roman Catholics, if not conciliated by admission to full political rights, would fall under the influence of revolutionary agitators was, at least in part, realised. We may reasonably doubt if they would, in any circumstances, have become firmly and permanently attached to the British connection, but this can be no more than a matter of conjecture. What is clear, beyond all conjecture, is that the Protestants became, though perhaps without knowing it, Burke's most ardent disciples. All that he said and wrote about the importance of England to Ireland and of Ireland to the Empire is to be found over and over again - more crudely expressed, but in essence the same - in the writings and speeches of Irish Unionist politicians; and probably the last man to give expression to these views at Westminster with the authority of great reputation and high office was Edward Carson.

Burke's assessment of Ireland's importance to Britain may well find a different and more disinterested kind of support at some date in the future. Though it is dangerous to prophesy, one may not unreasonably suppose that the scholar who, sooner or later, will sit down to write the History of the Decline and Fall of the British Empire will find his most natural starting-point in the events that led up to the Anglo-Irish treaty of 1921.

NOTES

1. Keogh to Burke, 20 July 1796, *Correspondence of Edmund Burke*, ed. Thomas W. Copeland (Cambridge, 1958-70) vol. ix, p. 59.

2. Burke to Keogh, 17 Nov. 1796, *Correspondence*, vol. ix, p. 113.
3. Burke to Thomas Hussey, 18 May 1795, *Correspondence*, vol. viii, p. 246.
4. See, for example, Burke to Samuel Span, 23 Apr. 1778, *Correspondence*, vol. iii, p. 434.
5. 7 Geo. III cap. 3. Prior to this act an Irish Parliament, like an English Parliament before the Triennial Act of 1694, lasted until it was dissolved by the Crown or until, by the demise of the Crown, it was dissolved automatically.
6. Burke to [unknown], *ante* 19 Apr. 1780, *Correspondence*, vol. iv, p. 231.
7. Shelburne to Portland, 18 May, 8 June 1782, PRO, HO 100/1, f. 218; ff. 7-8. See also J. C. Beckett, 'Anglo-Irish Constitutional Relations in the Later Eighteenth Century', in *Confrontations*, pp. 129-31.
8. Burke to Sir Hercules Langrishe, 3 Jan. 1792, *Edmund Burke on Irish Affairs*, ed. M. Arnold (London, 1881) p. 246.
9. Burke to Thomas Hussey, Dec. 1796, ibid., p. 424.
10. Burke to Portland, 14 Sept. 1794, *Correspondence*, vol. viii, p. 12.
11. *Select Works*, ed. E. J. Payne (Oxford, 1885) vol. i, p. 183.
12. Burke to Thomas Burgh, 1 Jan. 1780, Arnold, p. 293.
13. Arnold, p. 133.

2 Problems Common to both Protestant and Catholic Churches in Eighteenth-Century Ireland

E. M. JOHNSTON

The problems which confronted the Irish Church came from three different sources: the international problems created by the attack on Christianity itself inherent in the philosophies of the Age of Reason; the national problems created by a minority established Church and a country divided not only by religion but also by race and languages; while at a local level all the Churches were confronted with the persistence of pre-Christian beliefs and the hold which these exerted over the people.

Irish ecclesiastical history in the eighteenth century has been dominated by the impact and effects of the penal laws.[1] These laws perpetuated a racial division upon religious grounds and ensured the political, social and to an extent economic ascendancy of a small minority, whose privileges included a monopoly of higher education. Consequently both Catholic and Protestant non-conformist clergy had to be educated abroad. The former in Europe, particularly in France, and the latter in Scotland.

Eighteenth-century population statistics are notoriously unreliable and subject to continuous revision.[2] However, it has been estimated that in the course of the century the population rose from approximately 2.5 to 5.5 million and as the population rose the ratio of Catholics to Protestants increased. In 1731 it was about 3:1 but by the end of the century 4:1. The number of priests did not rise in proportion, as in 1731 there were estimated to be 1700 priests in the country and in 1801, 1800.[3] Until 1750 the balance between the regular and the secular clergy on the Irish mission had been approximately even. However, the regular clergy were particularly vulnerable to the anti-clericalism of the Age of Reason; between 1750 and 1800 the balance between the secular and the regular clergy was drastically altered and by 1800 only 400 of the 1800 clergy belonged to the regular orders.

CHURCH PROBLEMS IN THE EIGHTEENTH CENTURY

The clergy of the established Anglican Church were officially responsible for the spiritual welfare of the entire country but the Anglican population was probably about 1/8 of the population at the beginning of the century and 1/10 at its close. Thus their task was an impossible one. In 1742 Archbishop Hort of Tuam warned his clergy that:

> Coercive laws may restrain and disable those who avow principles that are destructive to the Church and State, and coercion in those cases is wise and necessary; but they never convince anybody: they may tie up men's hands and tongues, but never reach their hearts. . . .[4]

The lack of parishioners in many areas can be envisaged by Swift's rephrasing of the Prayer Book: 'Dearly beloved Roger, the Scripture moveth thee and me in sundry places',[5] or Lady Bessborough's description of her local church: 'our congregation consisted of eleven people! In a very large church with two clergymen officiating – to make up in piety I suppose what was lacking in numbers'.[6] For the many devout clergymen of the established Church this must have been a soul destroying life. And of these clergy there were never enough. In the 1720s Archbishop King and Primate Boulter estimated their numbers at about 600. In 1788 Grattan considered that the clergy of the established Church were about 900, and this figure is almost certainly an over-estimate. Thus at best the Anglican clergy were about half as numerous as their Catholic counterparts.[7]

The Anglicans possessed exclusive rights to higher education in Ireland, and Dublin University was officially closed to all who were not of this communion. Nevertheless, even the established clergy were not immune from the influence of foreign education, as of the 340 episcopal appointments and translations during this period 239 went to Englishmen and 101 to Irishmen; a ratio of 29:21 which remained fairly constant throughout the century.[8] As a simple head-count this statement requires modification, for Englishmen were usually appointed to the more influential and lucrative sees; thus, they were individually translated more often than their Irish counterparts. This in turn had an adverse impact upon the appointment of Irish clergy to positions at a lower level in the ecclesiastical hierarchy, as an episcopal appointment provoked a chain reaction which spread throughout the diocese: 'the Bishops sent to us from England follow the same track in many instances,' wrote Archbishop King in 1725, 'the Bishop of Derry since his translation to that see has given about 2,000 in benefices to his English friends and relations. . . . The Bishop of

Waterford has given all livings of value in his gift to his brothers and relations . . . though none of them reside in the kingdom'. In 1726 Swift wrote to the Earl of Peterborough commenting on the great discouragement which this system gave to the graduates of Dublin University.

The principal group of Protestant Dissenters was the Presbyterian Church in Ireland. Presbyterians were at least as numerous as the established Church, but largely concentrated in the north of the country. Until the nineteenth century Presbyterian clergy were trained in Scotland, mainly at the University of Glasgow. The short sea voyage between Scotland and the north of Ireland made communications easy and strengthened religious, linguistic and ethnic connections.[9] In 1709 they had approximately 130 ministers in the Synod of Ulster.[10] However, under the philosophical and theological pressures of the age the Presbyterians splintered and by the end of the century there were four main divisions: a liberal or 'new light' group in the Presbytery of Antrim, the main 'middle of the way' group in the Synod of Ulster, and then the progressively Calvinistic seceders who had divided themselves into the Burghers and the Anti-Burghers, taking their names from divisions in the parent Church of Scotland. A letter to Lord Castlereagh in 1799 contains details of 183 congregations in the Presbytery of Antrim and the Synod of Ulster; in addition there were 58 Burgher and 25 Anti-Burgher congregations, while in the south of Ireland there were a few Presbyterian congregations of English origin, and in the north some Covenanter or 'Reformed' congregations which had always been outside the Synod of Ulster. In all there were probably about 280 ministers in the different sections of the Presbyterian Church.[11]

Scattered through the country there were small groups of Quakers and French Huguenots. Some of the latter conformed but other congregations sent to Geneva for their pastors.[12] Finally, there were German Palatines and Moravians, small communities with overtones of Utopias and German pietism. For all of these groups 'conformity was made profitable and non-conformity easy'.[13] By comparison with the major denominations they were small, although both the Quakers and the Huguenots had a numerically disproportionate influence over the developing commerce and banking of the country. In the middle of the century Ireland was frequently visited by John Wesley[14] and as a result of his preaching tours Methodism made a considerable impact. It is probable that Wesley's charismatic popularity was increased by the fact that the informal preacher, as friar or minister, was familiar to both Catholic and Presbyterian. In the eighteenth century Methodism was officially within the Anglican community, although by 1800 its separatist tendencies were becoming increasingly marked.

Anti-clericalism in Ireland centred upon the control which the Church exercised, through the consistorial courts, over tithes and the matrimonial and testamentary aspects of everyday family life. At the same time the Anglican concept of the duality within the unity of Church and State is alien to the mind of both Catholic and Dissenter; for instance, in 1792 Edmund Burke pointed out that 'the Church and State . . .[were] one and the same thing, being different integral parts of the same whole . . .'.[15] In Ireland the Anglican Church became indissolubly linked to the politically exclusive ascendancy. Religion was the badge of race and ecclesiastical demands were resented accordingly.

Tithes were probably the greatest single element of disruption in Irish social life. Grattan outlined the problem in 1788 when he declared that:

> A tenth of your land, your labour, and your capital, to those who contribute in no shape whatsoever to the produce must be oppression. . . . But uncertainty aggravates that oppression . . . for it is the fixed proportion of a fluctuating quantity, and unless the high priest can give law to the winds, and ascertain the harvest, the tithe like the harvest must be uncertain. But this uncertainty is aggravated by the pernicious motives on which the tithe frequently rises and falls. It frequently rises on the poor, it falls in compliment to the rich.

A further problem with tithing was its regional variation; for example, potatoes were tithes in some areas and not in others. Finally, there were variations in methods of collection: sometimes they were collected in kind, sometimes commuted to a *modus* or cash payment. Similarly, the tithe could be collected directly by the clergyman or farmed through a proctor.

It is not surprising to find that tithes were a grievance in virtually every instance of social unrest throughout the century: 'combination is the defence of the laity, and partiality of the Church . . .' declared Grattan, 'the most sanguinary laws on your statute book are tithe bills; the Whiteboy act is a tithe bill'.[16] The House of Commons always reacted vociferously to tithes which they regarded either as a direct burden, especially in tithes of agistment,[17] or as a demand upon their tenantry which might endanger rents. In 1750 Nathaniel Nesbitt, Lord Abercorn's agent, calculated that Church demands in general 'amounts one way or other to one-fifth of the landlord's rent which is a very high tax on the country'.[18] Thus, between the landlord and the established clergy, the tenant paid 60 per cent of his income; with the remaining 40 per cent he had to support his family and maintain his own clergy.

The connection between tithes and terrorism added to the grievances of the gentry who greatly feared the breakdown of the rule of law: 'the Whiteboy should be hanged,' declared Grattan, 'but the tithe farmer should be restrained,' because 'murder was a greater offence than extortion'.[19] The Catholic hierarchy consistently denounced terrorism; for example in 1786 Dr Troy, then Bishop of Ossory, required the clergy of Kilkenny to emphasise once again to their parishioners:

> this doctrine of the Church concerning combination oaths in general, and declaring that they cannot be justified on any pretext whatsoever. . . . This has been our constant language, wherever a spirit of combination prevailed amongst Whiteboys, tradesmen or any other class of people.[20]

Finally, many of the leading positions in the established Church were held by Englishmen, who were often absent in London or in Great Britain. Also, the wealth of the Church was very unevenly divided; the revenue from the see of Derry was calculated to be £7000 in 1783, while in 1788 Grattan declared that the average clergyman's salary was 'forty or at most fifty pounds a year'.[21] A sum which was very similar to that of his Catholic or Presbyterian counterpart, as of the 183 Presbyterian ministers in the Presbytery of Antrim and the Synod of Ulster in 1801, 137 had incomes of between £30 and £60, 15 had less and 31 more; the highest salary was £200 and the lowest £10. Similar figures supplied to Lord Castlereagh for the Catholic clergy show them to be slightly better off.[22]

Incomes of these dimensions did not create anti-clericalism as a general rule, but the acute pressure on land caused by the swing from arable to pastoral farming in the middle of the century, and the unprecedented demographic expansion towards its close, produced economic pressures which erupted in local explosions. In these circumstances there were some examples of priests being given theatrical warnings about the consequences of overcharging ecclesiastical dues; for instance in 1786 a priest in Connacht was told to lower his fees or 'if not to have his coffin convenient'.[23] Presbyterian ministers occasionally became unpopular through renting farms wanted by their parishioners; for instance, this was an important element in the foundation of the first seceding congregation in Ulster at Lylehill in 1744, where the minister's son rented a farm which a prominent member of the congregation wished to secure for himself.[24] Many Presbyterian ministers were farmers' sons and farmed alongside their congregation. This mixture of farming and clerical activities is clearly shown in the diary kept by the Rev. John Kennedy.[25]

In the course of the eighteenth century all of the Churches were confronted with problems of discipline, either theological or hierarchical. Orthodoxy was a problem for the Protestant Churches, and hierarchical obedience for the Catholic Church. This latter problem was partly a national one created by the penal laws which encouraged malcontents by making ecclesiastical discipline difficult to enforce;[26] for instance, in 1751 Nicholas Sweetman, Bishop of Ferns, was examined by the Government on political charges laid against him by a disgruntled priest, and earlier there had been various charges of Jacobitism made against Catholic bishops by their recalcitrant clergy. There were often reports of disciplinary problems in the colleges overseas,[27] and the authorities considered that the novices had not been sufficiently rigorously trained before being professed. In the first half of the century novices had usually been professed in Ireland before proceeding to the continent for their studies and, during the penal era, this had led to some irregularities. Consequently, in 1751 it was decreed that novices for the Irish mission could only be ordained in the European convents of their order. In all the orders the numbers fell sharply, and, even after 1767 when this restriction was modified, they failed to recover their previous strength.[28]

Further difficulties were created by the 'enlightened' policies of the Emperor Joseph II who was suspicious of the power of the regular orders and dubious of their utility. More than half of the religious on the Irish mission belonged to the Franciscan Order and two of the three largest Franciscan colleges were at Prague and Louvain. In 1772 Joseph II extended his ban on the profession of novices before the age of twenty-five to include the Austrian Netherlands, and in 1786 he closed the Irish College at Prague. The gradual suppression, and in 1773 the dissolution, of the Society of Jesus severely affected not so much the actual mission, for there were very few Jesuits in Ireland, but the teaching staff of the Irish colleges throughout Europe.

After a European education the Catholic clergy returned home to be confronted with regional and even local problems.

Apart from small settlements of refugees which still retained their native languages at the beginning of the century, Irish was spoken throughout the country[29] with the exception of the area around Dublin, which had become Anglicised, and large parts of Ulster where the common speech was Lallans, a dialect of Lowland Scottish. Gaelic is a language with an essentially oral as opposed to a written tradition. In an illiterate peasant society, the proliferation of dialects meant that frequently the Gaelic speakers from the different provinces could not understand each other. Thus there was a problem of communication within Gaelic Ireland itself. Local dialects had to be remembered when the returned priests were assigned to their cures.

Regionalism and language were problems of sufficient importance to be featured in the Irish colleges in Europe. References to them are frequent; for example, a visitation by the Archbishop of Prague to the Irish Franciscan College learnt that 25-year old Francis Browne 'cannot study because of the dissentions in the convent and because, since he is from Munster, the lectors have no time for him';[30] similarly the Augustinian College at Lisbon was suspected of favouring students from Connacht, the Secular College at Bordeaux students from Munster, while the small college at Alcala, which was later incorporated into the college at Salamanca, catered solely for students from the north of Ireland. The two largest French colleges, the Secular Colleges at Paris and Nantes, made a point of accepting students from all provinces with careful impartiality.

The Lombard College was particularly aware of the linguistic problem and showed a special concern with teaching and encouraging the Irish language. Scholarships were available for Irish-speaking students and others were expected to become proficient Irish linguists; for example, in 1788 the Rector, Dr Kearney, wrote to the Bishop of Meath that a student from his diocese 'applies himself close to his study, of which one proof is that he knew no Irish some months ago; he has now got to be able to get [sic!] the whole Irish Catechism by heart'.[31] The college was instrumental in the publication of John O'Brien, Bishop of Cloyne's *Focaloir Gaoidhilge-Sax-Bhearla or Anglo-Irish Dictionary* in 1768. Bishop O'Brien had appealed to the Pope for a subsidy for its publication on the grounds that it was essential for the preservation of the faith that such a dictionary should be available for young priests.[32]

The Protestant denominations were also well aware of the necessity for the clergy to speak Irish if they were to have any success in proselytising the Gaelic-speaking peasantry. In the early years of the century Archbishop Marsh and his successor, Archbishop King, encouraged the students of Dublin University to study Irish. Archbishop Marsh, when Provost of Dublin University, had 80 students instructed in Irish at his own expense, and in 1715 Archbishop King wrote to Speaker Conolly: 'I send you a list of scholars taught to read Irish by Mr Linegar in the College. All of these are destined for the clergy being in number forty-five'.[33] In 1712 the Rev. John Richardson laid before Convocation a plan for the instruction of the clergy and the printing of books in the Irish language. Unfortunately, this scheme only received a nominal support. In the eighteenth century all of the Irish Churches were closely involved in the concerns of their brethren overseas, and at this juncture Convocation was preoccupied with the 'high' and 'low' Church disputes which had been transplanted from the English into the Irish Church. In 1733 the established Church turned to proselytisation through education and under Archbishop Boulter the Charter School system was developed to give instruction in the English language and Anglican theology conjointly.[34] Similarly, the Presbyterians' meeting in the Synod of Ulster in 1710, noting that seven of their ministers and three probationers could preach in Irish, began to plan a mission backed up with Bibles, confessions of faith and catechisms all in the vernacular.[35] However, shortly afterwards the Presbyterians were faced with persecution and then with schism; consequently this scheme lapsed until the nineteenth century.

Although John Richardson's scheme to provide Anglican instruction in the Irish language failed, he was an assiduous collector of 'heathen' Irish folk customs and superstitions, thereby focussing on another problem common to all the Churches, namely the survival of pre-Christian beliefs. The *Good Confessor*, written in 1743, enquires:

Did you make use of any superstitions, or vain observations, persuading yourselves that there are lucky and unlucky days: unlucky, if the first person you should meet in the morning should be red-haired, or if a hare should cross the way before you, or if a grave should be opened on a Tuesday, or if a marriage, or any bargain should be made on that day of the week, upon which Holy Innocents fell that year, or if 13 should be at table, etc., which are the remains of heathenism, vain and groundless remarks.

Did you make use of superstitious things for curing of diseases in men or cattle, which have, or can have, no natural connection with these effects, such as billets, certain words, prayers not approved by the Church, herbs gathered before sunrise or on certain days only, a little stone or flint-arrow dipped in milk, ale or water . . . had you recourse to magicians, sorcerers, or witches?[36]

At the other end of the theological spectrum, the Calvinist elders of the Presbyterian Church were charged to enquire of the heads of the households of their congregations:

Do they use any Charms on certain days as November 1st, or encourage spae-men and the like by consulting and giving heed to them?
Do they attend bonfires on Mid-Summer Eve?[37]

The Irish Church, born at the beginning of the Dark Ages, was left to develop in comparative isolation and in a long established pagan background. Under these circumstances, the Church's attempt to impose Christianity upon a complex and highly developed pagan foundation met with varying degrees of success. The continuity of rural society preserves traditions and Irish life in the eighteenth century was permeated with many examples of pre-Christian customs glossed over with a very thin veneer of Christianity. At the beginning of the nineteenth century, Wakefield noted that:

These people have many superstitious practices similar to those which prevailed in the days of ignorance and darkness, and which still partially exist. . . . On St John's eve they light fires in the middle of the roads, and imagine if they drive their cattle through them, they will be secured from accidents and prosper. They also swing their children over them for the like good end. This custom is supposed to be of very ancient origin and to have been derived from the idolatrous sacrifices to Baal.[38]

In fact this was the celebration of the old Celtic festival of Midsummer's Eve. The most important festivals of the Celtic year were Beltane and Samhain, corresponding to May-Eve and All Saints' Eve, and a rich pre-Christian culture gathered round these celebrations which heralded the coming of summer and the dying year. Various rites of passage, protection and fertility survived in games and customs for special occasions, such as weddings and wakes.[39]

The predominantly agrarian nature of Irish society encouraged a belief in magical properties associated with stone, wood and water. Stones could be used for beneficent or maleficent purposes.[40] In his *History of the Church of Ireland*, Mant deprecates these customs, but he also describes many of them. Included among these is the ritual associated with St Patrick's Well in the parish of Galloon, County Monaghan. At this place of pilgrimage, there was a stone which was reputed to bear the mark of the saint's knee, a cross he had erected and an alder tree which had sprung up upon the nearby ground which the saint had blessed. The ritual associated with this well involved the pilgrims kissing the stone and placing their knee in the indentation, saying various prayers on their knees and at intervals arising to bow to the cross, the stone and the alder tree. When the rite was complete, the water taken from the adjacent well would cure sick cattle.

The tales of William Carleton, written in the early nineteenth century, give many examples of this confusion between religion and magic; for example, in the *Midnight Mass* the unscrupulous tinker Darby More addresses the crowd assembling for the Christmas Mass as follows:

An' now, good Christians, you have an account o' the blessed carol I was singin' for yees. They're but hapuns apiece; an' anybody that has the grace to keep one o' these about them will never meet wid sudden deaths or accidents, sich as hangin', or drownin', or bein' taken suddenly wid a configuration inwardly . . . will any of yees take one? . . . An' now that Father Hoolaghan's comin', any of yees that 'ill want them 'ill find me here agin when mass is over - Oxis Doxis Glorioxis, Amin!

Later another character enquires: 'How did you larn all the prayers an' charms you have, Darby?' This mixture of prayers and charms was very common in cures for assorted ailments for man and beast.[41]

Throughout the eighteenth century these practices aroused a continual stream of condemnation from Catholic and Protestant clergy alike; for instance, in 1786, Archbishop Carpenter of Dublin caused a prohibition to be read from the altars admonishing the faithful against resorting 'to a place on the Circular Road, to which they give the name of St John's Well and there under pretext of devotion occasion many scandalous enormities not only disgraceful to religion but to civil society'.[42] Despite the censures of Church and State, pilgrimages were very popular. The clergy, suspicious of the often mixed motives of the pilgrims, deplored the fair-ground diversions which became attached to allegedly holy places, thereby encouraging both the back-sliding of the recently penitent and the profiteering of the unscrupulous, while the authorities were always nervous of large gatherings of people.

Outside even the far-flung mantle of the Church lay the

world of the fairies and leprechauns who inhabited ancient raths, forts and megalithic remains, and who frequently ventured forth to interfere, for good or ill, in the lives of mortals. The Irish peasant fervently believed that these supernatural beings exercised a potent force in his daily life, and stories about their activities are endless. Although they could perform beneficial acts for certain favoured mortals, they frequently displayed a disposition which was both spiteful and mischievous, while occasionally their reputed activities were actually malevolent. Much of their mischief had a domestic turn, they 'blinked' the cows to prevent them giving milk, stopped the butter coming for the churning housewife, and caused innumerable agricultural and domestic annoyances. More seriously, they could make cattle ill and they had even been known to substitute their own ill-natured and ill-favoured offspring for mortal children. Hence it was politic to placate them at every turn, and to speak of them with the utmost politeness, for example they were referred to as 'the gentle folk' and small offerings of food and drink were left for their refreshment. Thorn trees enjoyed their special protection and to this day in Ireland there are open fields with isolated thorn bushes standing in the middle of them.[43]

However, the major problem which confronted all the Churches in eighteenth-century Ireland was the attack on Christianity itself, mounted by the philosophical and theological views of the Age of Reason. These views came to Ireland by three routes, namely, from England, Scotland and the continent. The interpretation in all three cases was slightly different although their origins were the same, for they lay partly in the Renaissance, which had expanded man's knowledge of the earth and his idea of the universe; partly in the Reformation and Counter-Reformation, which had exalted the position and responsibilities of man in relation to God; and partly in the scientific revolution of the seventeenth century with its speculative basis in Francis Bacon and its mathematical foundation in Isaac Newton. By the late seventeenth century man's knowledge of the world had outstripped his philosophical and theological conception of the universe. Attempts to remedy this situation produced philosphical ideas which were to have important theological and political consequences. Not only was Ireland not isolated from this intellectual ferment, but she was an active contributor; for example, among the Irishmen involved were the scientists Robert Boyle (1627-91) and Joseph Black (1728-99), the philosophers George Berkeley (1685-1753) and Francis Hutcheson (1694-1746), while John Toland (?1670-1722) was a prominent figure in the evolution of

English deism.

The philosophical background of the period[44] stems from the work of the mathematician-philosopher Rene Descartes (1596-1650). Among Descartes' opponents was the English philosopher Thomas Hobbes. Hobbes's debates with John Bramwell, successively Bishop of Derry and Archbishop of Armagh, mark an early stage in both the utilitarian and theological debates which dominated eighteenth-century philosophy. In the England of Hobbes and Isaac Newton, Cartesian philosophy came under the critical review of John Locke (1632-1704), who held that the nature of the universe proves the existence of God. Among Locke's friends was William Molyneux, MP for Dublin University. Molyneux was an FRS and a man of wide philosophical and intellectual interests as well as a colonial politician; for instance, in 1698 he raised the question of colonial consent to indirect taxation imposed by the imperial government, declaring that: 'to tax me without consent is little better, if at all, than downright robbing me'.[45]

Both Descartes and Locke came under attack from Bishop Berkeley of Cloyne, who held that being is in perception and stabilised his system in the eternal perception of God. He was educated at Kilkenny College and Dublin University where, largely through Molyneux's influence in modernising the university curriculum, he had studied the writings of Descartes, Newton and Locke along with those of Hobbes, Malebranche and Liebniz. Thus, Descartes, Locke and Berkeley had all stabilised their philosophies on the existence of God, which they had postulated in different ways, in their attempt to reconcile philosophy and orthodox theology to the new scientific world.

Deism represented a less orthodox response to the same philosophical problems. In England it dates from the sixteenth century, but the political and scientific events of the seventeenth century increased its intellectual momentum. In the evolution of deist thought the position of John Toland is significant as his *Christianity not Mysterious* (1696) can claim to be the opening salvo in the deist *versus* orthodox debates of the eighteenth century. Toland was born in County Donegal about 1670 and he studied at the Universities of Glasgow, Edinburgh, Leyden and Oxford. In England he came into contact with Locke and although Locke denied Toland's deism nevertheless Locke's pupil, the 3rd Earl of Shaftesbury, was a noted figure among the leading deist thinkers at the turn of the century. On his return to Ireland in 1697 Toland's connection with Locke ensured his entrance into Molyneux's intellectual circle,[46] however, the unpopularity of his philosophical views soon made him an

unacceptable associate, for in 1697 the Irish Parliament
condemned *Christianity not Mysterious* and ordered it to be
burnt by the common hangman.[47] Nevertheless, deism
remained a strand in the philosophical and theological
debates of the century both in England and in Europe, and
Toland has been described as 'an internationalist of
consequence in the age of the enlightenment'.[48]

On the continent, Descartes' philosophy had come under
review by Spinoza (1632-77), Liebniz (1646-1716) and Bayle
(1647-1706). To Spinoza God was pure and infinite being, in
which all things existed. His thought was very influential
and it marks an obvious step on the road to deism. Liebniz,
on the other hand, attempted to harmonise the new scientific
world with Christian theology. He considered that the world
was a harmonious whole, produced by God to serve divine
ends. The popular empirical view was represented by Pierre
Bayle, who came from an area with a long history of dissent;
he was born in south-west France the son of a Huguenot
pastor. In his most celebrated work, the *Dictionnaire
Historique et Critique*, he used history to illustrate philosophy, giving historical examples of the irrationality of
mankind; Bayle's acutely critical and supremely rational
approach pointed to the inability of man to provide a complete and adequate answer to this type of problem.

In England among those influenced by Cartesian philosophy
and Newtonian science was Samuel Clarke (1675-1729). Like
Liebniz, Clarke wished to place Newton's scientific dis-
coveries within an acceptable theological context. He expressed his views in a treatise entitled: *A Discourse
concerning the Being and Attributes of God* . . ., in which
he attempted to answer the philosophical opinions of Spinoza
and Hobbes. Clarke's theology was tinged with Aryanism, for
he held in *The Scripture Doctrine of the Trinity* - published
in 1712 - that there was no scriptural proof of the doctrine
of the Trinity, and according to Voltaire the Bishop of
Lincoln, Edmund Gibson, prevented Clarke from becoming
Archbishop of Canterbury by informing the Princess of Wales
that, although an excellent man, he was not a Christian.
Nevertheless, Clarke's views enjoyed considerable vogue at
court, where Benjamin Hoadley, successively Bishop of Bangor,
Hereford, Salisbury and Winchester, was a prominent member
of Queen Caroline's intellectual circle. Bishop Hoadley was
the leader of the 'progressive' or Latitudinarian party; he
was also Clarke's friend, admirer and biographer.[49]

The dominant ecclesiastical figure of the early Hanoverian
period [50] was Edmund Gibson. As Bishop of London, from
1723, Gibson was the British Government's chief adviser on
ecclesiastical affairs until 1736. In this year he

quarrelled with the Government, but despite this
disagreement he continued to dominate the bench of bishops
until his death in 1748. Gibson was a consistent opponent of
the Latitudinarian wing of the Anglican Church and he
exerted all his powers to circumscribe the spread of
Hoadley's Latitudinarian views. To achieve these ends, there
is some evidence to suggest that Gibson was not averse to
using Irish patronage. The emoluments of a number of Irish
bishoprics compared very favourably with their English
counterparts, particularly the four archbishoprics and the
bishoprics of Derry and Clogher. Irish patronage at this
level and on this scale, combined with the support of formidable apologists such as Bishops Warburton of Gloucester and
Butler of Durham, enabled Gibson to mount a rearguard action
against Latitudinarianism in the Church of his day. Of the
Irish bishops appointed during Gibson's period of political
ascendancy, three had definitely been influenced by Samuel
Clarke and held heterodox views; they were Hoadley's
brother, John, who was successively Bishop of Ferns,
Archbishop of Dublin and Archbishop of Armagh; Thomas
Rundle, Bishop of Derry; and Robert Clayton, successively
Bishop of Killala, Cork and Clogher. These were key
appointments in the Irish Church, and invaluable assets in
Gibson's struggle to secure English orthodoxy.

In 1729 Benjamin Hoadley was exerting all his persuasive
influence at Court to be translated from Salisbury to
Durham; Gibson was endeavouring to prevent it. At this
juncture Archbishop King of Dublin died, and after a delay
of some months, John Hoadley was translated from Ferns to
Dublin, but Benjamin Hoadley was not translated to Durham.
At that time the Archbishop of Dublin was considered the
natural successor to the Primacy, and when Primate Boulter
died in 1742, John Hoadley became Archbishop of Armagh.
Primate Hoadley was a friend of the deist Thomas Chubb.

The case of Dr Thomas Rundle, who was appointed to the see
of Derry in 1735, was an even more blatant example and
something of a *cause célèbre* at the time. Dr Rundle was
Chaplain to the Chancellor, Lord Talbot, and both the
Chancellor and the Court exerted their influence to have
Rundle appointed Bishop of Gloucester. Gibson flatly refused
to countenance the nomination in view of Dr Rundle's
expressed Aryan views. In a quandary, Walpole and Newcastle
kept the see vacant until December 1734, when Gibson won his
point and another nomination resolved the deadlock, but in
January 1735 Dr Rundle was appointed Bishop of Derry. 'I
confess,' wrote Primate Boulter to the Duke of Newcastle,
'that I am very sorry to hear that the public service has
made it necessary to give the Bishopric of Derry to Dr

Rundle, because your Grace cannot but be sensible that it will give some clamour here.'[51]

The third representative of this group was the Anglo-Irish Robert Clayton. Born in Dublin, Dr Clayton had been educated at Westminster School and Dublin University. Subsequently he had been elected a Fellow of Trinity College, Dublin. His family connections linked him to Charlotte Clayton, Lady Sundon, who was a friend and confidante of both Queen Caroline and Benjamin Hoadley. In 1751 Dr Clayton set out his theological views in *An Essay on Spirit*. The views expressed were certainly confused; they ensured that in the following year he was not translated to the Archbishopric of Tuam. Nevertheless, the Bishop continued his theological works much to the concern of his wife and friends. His views grew less and less orthodox; for instance, in 1756 he made a speech in the Irish House of Lords, proposing the removal of the Nicene and Athanasian creeds from the liturgy. Finally, he was summoned to appear before the House of Lords to explain his views, but before this happened he collapsed, contracted a 'nervous fever' and died.[52]

The later eighteenth century saw the appointment of Frederick Augustus Hervey, successively Bishop of Cloyne and Derry, while in 1779 he succeeded his brother as 4th Earl of Bristol. Like Clayton, Hervey was educated at Westminster, and Lord Charlemont, who shared his enthusiasm for architecture and *objets d'art*, described him as 'a determined deist though a bishop and at times so indecently impious in his conversation as to shock the more reprobate'. Nevertheless, he managed to impress John Wesley, who considered that 'the Bishop is . . . exemplary in all parts of public worship, and plenteous in good works'.[53] Certainly, with an ecumenism which perhaps confirmed Charlemont's suspicions, he subscribed impartially to funds for the building of both Catholic and Presbyterian churches, in addition to improving those of his own denomination.

The views of Clarke also attracted the most influential Scottish divine of his generation, the Rev. John Simson, Professor of Divinity at the University of Glasgow from 1708 to 1729. Almost all of the Presbyterian clergy who had been trained during these years were students of Simson.[54] Simson had intellectual connections with the University of Leyden, where his brother, and possibly he himself, had been a student. One of the problems in Presbyterian theology is the doctrine of free will and the right, even the moral duty, of the individual to interpret the scriptures by the light of his or her conscience.[55] In the theological atmosphere of the early eighteenth century this was a recipe for schism. Simson's theological teaching encouraged the idea of man's free will, motivated by a divinely inspired natural illumination, and the tag 'new light' became attached to his followers.

From about 1712 Simson's views had been causing concern in the Scottish Church, and in 1715 they came under the consideration of a committee of the General Assembly, which reported in 1717 that Dr Simson had expressed some opinions 'not necessary to be taught in divinity'. Subsequently, Simson came under the influence of Clarke, and in 1726 he was again under pressure from the Church to explain his views. At this point his health, never very good, broke down and it was alleged that he brought Clarke, the early Church Fathers and the Council of Nicea – the scene of the early Church's debates on the Trinity – into all conversations. In 1729 the Scottish Assembly decided that it was not 'fit or safe' that Dr Simson should continue to teach divinity, and he was suspended from the functions of his Chair, but not from its emoluments.

The theological development of the early years of the eighteenth century had been followed with great interest by a group of influential Presbyterian ministers in Ulster. These ministers, who were associated with the Presbytery of Antrim, had formed a theological debating club called the Belfast Society. They became greatly interested in Simson's teaching, and in 1719 the Rev. John Abernethy preached a sermon on 'Religious Obedience founded on Personal Persuasion'. In an attempt to establish a commonly accepted theological basis, the Presbyterian Church had agreed on the doctrines expressed in the *Westminster Confession of Faith* (1647). The ministers of the Belfast Society now declared their reluctance to subscribe to any man-written confession of faith and their belief that every man should be guided by the light of his own conscience. In 1726 this group came to an amicable separation from the Synod of Ulster and formed the Non-subscribing Presbytery of Antrim.[56]

Among those influenced, though not entirely convinced by Clarke's arguments, was Simson's ablest student, Francis Hutcheson. The son and grandson of ministers of the Irish Presbyterian Church, Hutcheson was licensed to preach but never ordained. Instead, he opened a school in Dublin and in 1729 became Professor of Moral Philosophy at Glasgow. In 1738 he incurred the wrath of the Presbytery of Glasgow for teaching first, that we could have a knowledge of good and evil without a prior knowledge of God, and second, that the standard of moral goodness was the promotion of the happiness of others. In *The Enquiry Concerning Moral Good and Evil* published in 1726, Hutcheson coined the famous phrase 'the greatest happiness for the greatest numbers'.

Hutcheson attributed to man a social sense: 'a determination
to be pleased with the happiness of others and to be uneasy
at their misery'. Philosophically, he was a pivotal figure,
looking backwards to the philosopher 3rd Earl of
Shaftesbury, the pupil of Locke, and forward to the 'common
sense' and utilitarian philosophers.[57] The two most
influential Scottish philosophers of the eighteenth century,
Adam Smith (1723-90) and David Hume (1711-76), were both
influenced by him: he taught the former and corresponded
with the latter. Hume completed the divorce between theology
and philosophy as his sceptical mind, influenced by that of
Bayle, queried the postulation of God at all in the philosophical system of Descartes and his successors, particularly Locke and Berkeley.

On the continent, theological developments followed a
different path. In John Calvin, France had produced one of
the most uncompromising figures of the Reformation, and for
over a hundred years the Huguenots had been an able and
vociferous minority in the French state. It was perhaps
inevitable that some of the ideas of the Huguenots should
find a modified response within the Catholic Church in
France, particularly those ideas which had a common origin
in the teachings of the great North African bishop, St
Augustine of Hippo. Augustine's theories found an uncompromising interpretation in the doctrines promulgated by
Calvin and a gentler one in the writings of the French-
educated Dutch Bishop of Ypres, Cornelius Jansenius, whose
principal work was a treatise on St Augustine. However,
these views were unacceptable and in 1713, the bull
Unigenitus officially killed orthodox Jansenism.[58]

Nevertheless, the spirit of Jansenism was from its very
nature an attack upon the Latitudinarian theology of the
eighteenth century which its old enemy, the Jesuit Order,
was suspected of supporting, a suspicion which was particularly serious in view of the pre-eminent role of the
Jesuits in education. Inevitably, the dominance of the
Society of Jesus in both Church and State had created envy:
at the same time accusations of intrigue aroused the fears
of suspicious rulers. Nevertheless, the eventual dissolution
of the Jesuit Order weakened the entire *ultramontane*
position of the Church, as it weakened the position of all
of the regular clergy. Gallicanism, although it had existed
long before the reign of Louis XIV, had been refurbished and
given an even more nationalist impetus by the King's
ecclesiastical policies and financial necessities. In
eighteenth-century Ireland the difference between the
ultramontane attitude of the regular orders and the Gallican
instincts of the French-trained diocesan clergy, further

contributed to the bad relations between the secular and the regular clergy. Furthermore, in France the Irish secular clergy came into contact with the views of Edmund Richer, who sought to exalt the position of the priest in the government of the Church, thereby exacerbating problems of clerical discipline. At the same time Richer's views encouraged both lay anti-clericalism and further widened the division between the higher and lower clergy which was to be so fatal to the French Church during the Revolution.[59]

Censorship confronted the French Church with an officially suppressed theological debate. For instance, although Pierre Bayle influenced the formal development of the Scottish philosophical schools, his influence can also be seen in the numerous unorthodox tracts on religion, natural theology, problems of morality and politics which were circulated surreptitiously in early eighteenth-century France. In fact censorship probably had little effect either upon the spread or upon the restriction of ideas. In England the Licensing Act, which permitted the censorship of religious publications, expired in 1695. It was not renewed, and to this was attributed the great flood of pamphlet literature which accompanied the theological disputes of the early eighteenth century. Yet, although censorship might deny printed publication in France, it certainly did not prevent the spread of ideas. Instead it encouraged the rise of an underworld of copyists and their agents who frequented the cafes and sidewalks of towns peddling their goods. For example, in 1729, a French police report stated that:

Il y a à Paris de prétendeurs beaux-esprits qui parlent dans les cafés et ailleurs de la Religion comme d'une chimère. Entre autres, M. Boindin s'est signalé plus d'une fois dans le café de Conti, au coin de la rue Dauphine, et si l'on n'y met ordre le nombre des athées ou déistes augmentera et bien des gens se feront une religion à leur mode, comme en Angleterre.

This deposition was taken from the examination of a *colporteur*:

qui loge dans un café . . . débite et vend des copies de plusieurs ouvrages remplis d'impiétés et de maximes contraires à l'existence de Dieu, à la divinité et à la morale de J. C. Bien des gens abbés et autres lui achètent fort cher des copies de ses ouvrages. [60]

Evidence has been found for the widespread circulation of over a hundred of these tracts in early eighteenth-century

France. Many show the influence of Bayle, Gallicanism, Jansenism or the anti-clericalism of the Richéristes. Among the most influential of these pamphlets was Pierre Cuppé's *Le Ciel Ouvert à Tous les Hommes* . . . Cuppé reacted against the exclusionism of Jansenism: he could not reconcile the goodness of God with the salvation of an elected few. Cuppe maintained that all would attain salvation through the goodness of God, regardless of baptism, condition or religion. He maintained that man's moral conduct did not depend upon the threat of eternal damnation. When this work was first published, in 1716, it created a sensation among his colleagues and it figured prominently in contemporary clerical libraries. Shortly after its publication, Cuppe renounced his errors of doctrine, but despite his recantation, he continued to revise his treatise and subsequent editions appeared both before and after his death in 1744. It was still in circulation in 1790 when the Librarian of the Sorbonne admitted that the library had three copies while declaring that since 1768 '*il est tombé dans un juste mépris*'.

About 1711 the anonymous Le Militaire Philosophe began to circulate his *Difficultés sur la religion* . . . which contains a clear and unequivocal statement of deism, in a work which shows the influence of Bayle while it looks forward to Voltaire, Rousseau and Montesquieu. Possibly one of the most influential works written during this period was the *Testament* of the embittered Jean Meslier, the parish priest of Etrépigny, who calls so vividly to mind the advice of Job's wife: 'Dost thou still retain thine integrity? Curse God and die'. For, unlike Job, that is exactly what, in 1729, Meslier did, leaving behind him three copies of his *Testament*. In it he declared with fanatical zeal that all religions, and the Christian religion in particular, were false. At the same time he propounded a social philosophy which condemned, amid other things, the institution of indissoluble marriage, taxation and ownership of property. He felt that man was terrorised by man, and that the various orders of society prey upon each other - in particular the higher clergy upon the lower.[61]

In the 1730s the Archbishop of Armagh was sufficiently concerned about the doctrines which were reputed to be current in the University of Paris to wish to prohibit Irish students from going there.[62] The orthodoxy of the Lombard College was not in dispute, but the students who went there took some of their courses in the university. On this, the Archbishop was overruled by his episcopal colleagues; nevertheless, in 1739, the numbers attending this, the most popular of the French colleges, fell substantially. In 1778 similar fears were expressed by the Rev. Nicholas Lynch, who wrote from Paris to warn the Rev. Augustine Kirwin that:

> Mr Mannin has finished his time and consequently will be obliged to quit the College next year, for which reason the Warden should do his utmost to place and call him home next season while he is in his purity, for fear that the air and maxims of Paris should corrupt him. He is an excellent subject and now full fit for the mission.[63]

In 1792 Dr Troy, the Archbishop of Dublin, was writing to the Warden of Galway: 'to inform you that the French Assembly doctrines respecting the Church had affected many of my flock, and even some ignorant lukewarm or temporising clergy of whom we have unhappily too many'.[64] Nevertheless, when it came to the 1798 Rebellion the number of clergy involved was surprisingly small: Madden in *The United Irishmen* lists only fourteen as being implicated or accused of being concerned in the 1798 Rebellion; of these six were executed - not a great number out of a clerical establishment of 'upwards of 1,800'. In a parallel list he gives the names of thirteen Presbyterian clergy, similarly accused and of these three were executed - a much higher percentage.[65] The Presbyterian historian Reid comments that 'a large proportion of the members of the Synod of Ulster, who were concerned in the Rebellion, were noted abettors of New-Light principles'.[66]

In conclusion, it is perhaps worth looking at the impact of this ferment upon the laity. Throughout the eighteenth century the *Journals* of the British and Irish Parliaments reflected the theological conservatism of the overwhelming majority of the nation who clearly considered that an outward conformity to the established religion was, at the very least, an essential element in the maintenance of social order and good government; for instance, Toland's *Christianity not Mysterious* was condemned by the Irish Parliament in 1697, and in 1737 the Irish House of Lords condemned in the strongest terms the activities of Peter Lens, a declared votary of the devil, who had founded a society called The Blasters - an Irish equivalent of the notorious English Hell-Fire Club. They requested that Lens be prosecuted 'with the utmost severity of the law'. At the same time the Lord Lieutenant was asked to request the judges on circuit to charge the magistrates to 'put the laws into execution against immorality and profane cursing, swearing and gaming, and to inquire into atheistical and blasphemous clubs'.[67]

The climate of the century encouraged the development of

secular societies both open and secret.[68] These represented a wide variety of motives and involved a wide cross-section of society. Among the most enduring of the secret societies was the Freemasons, who became prominent among 'free-thinking' sections, first of the British and Irish and then of the European nobility. Among their members was James, 1st Duke of Leinster whose Duchess wished to install Rousseau as tutor to their children.[69] By the end of the century the egalitarian overtones in masonry had encouraged its spread through society and, at least in Ulster, it began to be regarded as a possible alleviator of sectarian bitterness; James Orr, the Ballycarry weaver, mason and former United Irishman, specifically praised its non-sectarian basis.[70] The most prominent of the political clubs was the United Irishmen, many of whose members had close intellectual and social connections with France; for instance, Arthur O'Connor married the daughter of the Marquis de Condorcet who, even on the steps of the guillotine, contemplated a society free from the tyranny of priest or dictator whose citizens would, in a rational manner, enjoy liberty and the pursuit of happiness. Among the literate middle and poorer classes Reading Societies were popular, particularly in Ulster, and through them radical and other opinions were quickly disseminated for wider discussion; for instance Wolfe Tone described Paine's *Rights of Man* as the 'Koran' of Belfast. The authorities regarded these societies as politically dangerous, a belief confirmed when Thomas Russell, a friend of Tone and the librarian of the Belfast Reading Society (the Linen Hall Library), was implicated in Emmet's Rebellion and executed.[71]

In all of the Churches there was frequently a considerable split between the theological views of the clergy and those of the laity, who did not always hold with what they considered to be new-fangled views and unnecessary complexities. For instance, as a young man Hutcheson preached to his father's congregation at Armagh. He emptied the church, as the disapproving members departed in the middle of the sermon. Subsequently, one of the elders informed his father that 'your silly son Frank has been babbling this hour about a good and benevolent God, and that the souls of the heathen themselves will gang to heaven if they follow the light of their own consciences. Not a word . . . about the good old comfortable doctrines of election, reprobation, original sin and faith'.[72]

Emerging from the theological and social turmoil of the eighteenth century and common to both the European and British debates was a contemplation of the connection between conduct and religion. On the one hand there emerged the belief that man was inherently virtuous and naturally endowed with a social sense which ensured that he would be 'moral' without the 'restraints' or the 'rewards' of religion. Certain aspects of the French Revolution added a cautionary note to this optimism. In Scotland the philosophical reaction took a characteristically practical turn. Thomas Reid (1710-96), one of Hutcheson's academic successors, attempted in *An Inquiry into the Human Mind on the Principles of Common Sense* to answer Hume by declaring that philosophers had been led to promulgate ideas which were contrary to common sense. Common sense was interpreted as the opinions held by rational people and the Common Sense School held that by this criterion philosophy had reached a *reductio ad absurdum*. Finally there was the evangelical reaction triggered off by men like John Wesley, who substituted faith and belief in divine grace for the fallibility of human reason.

The great theological-philosophical debates of the eighteenth century had very different consequences in Britain and Europe. The British debate, which often led and encouraged the European one, resulted in the peaceful evangelical reconstruction of theology accompanied by humanitarian and utilitarian developments in politics. The continental debate erupted in a violent destruction of the traditional structure of society. Ireland reacted to both traditions. Much of the legislation of the Irish Parliament shows evidence of both humanitarianism and utilitarianism; on the other hand, Irish nationalism in its modern sense was born in the social explosion of the 1798 Rebellion and the political, economic and demographic pressures which both preceded and succeeded it.

From the conflicts of the eighteenth century none of the Irish Churches emerged unscathed, and the reaction of all three of the major denominations to this challenge has had a lasting effect upon the development of Irish nationalism. All the Churches adopted an entrenched defensive position. The foundation of Maynooth created a fortress for Irish Catholicism, introspective and safe from the problems and the corruptions of continental Catholicism. The Ulster Presbyterians sought security from their theological confusion in an often rigid and excessively narrow interpretation of Calvinism, while the Anglicans, always the most ecclesiastically vulnerable, found what proved to be a short lived haven in the political-ecclesiastical solution enshrined in the Act of Union.

NOTES

1. See M. Wall, *The Penal Laws* (Dublin, 1967); also W. E. H. Lecky, *A History of Ireland in the Eighteenth Century* (London, 1902-6) vol. ii, pp. 272-3.
2. See K. H. Connell, *The Population of Ireland 1750-1845* (Oxford, 1950); for the ensuing debate see *Economic History Review*: M. Drake, 'Marriage and Population Growth in Ireland, 1750-1845', vol. xvi (1963-4) pp. 301-13; J. Lee, 'Marriage and Population in Pre-Famine Ireland', vol. xxi (1968) pp. 283-95; and G. S. L. Tucker, 'Irish Fertility Ratios before the Famine', vol. xxiii (1970) pp. 267-84.
3. H. Fenning, *The Undoing of the Friars of Ireland* (Louvain, 1972) p. 40; P. J. Corish, *The Irish Church under the Penal Code* (Dublin, 1971) pp. 40-1; *Castlereagh Correspondence*, ed. C. W. Vane (London, 1848-53) vol. iv, p. 99.
4. J. Hort, *Instructions to the Clergy* (Carlisle, 1742) pp. 23-4: these instructions contain very basic everyday advice.
5. Quoted in E. Wakefield, *An Account of Ireland, Statistical and Political* (London, 1812) vol. ii, p. 623.
6. *Letters of Lord Granville Leveson Gower*, ed. C. Granville (London, 1916) vol. ii, p. 341.
7. C. S. King, *A Great Archbishop of Dublin, William King D. D. 1650-1729* (London, 1906); H. Boulter, *Letters* (Oxford, 1769) vol. i, p. 223, but see also p. 210 where he gives the number at 800 - possibly the smaller figure is for beneficed clergy; D. O. Madden, *The Speeches of the Rt. Hon. Henry Grattan* (London, 1853) p. 119.
8. R. Mant, *A History of the Church of Ireland* (London, 1840) vol. ii, pp. 781-91.
9. Lecky, *A History of Ireland*, vol. i, pp. 430-1, gives some of the reasons for the antipathy between the Protestant denominations.
10. W. D. Killen, *Ecclesiastical History of Ireland* (London, 1875) vol. ii, p. 214.
11. *Castlereagh Correspondence*, vol. iii, pp. 167-71; D. Stewart, *The Seceders in Ireland* (Belfast, 1950) pp. 271ff.
12. J. S. Burn, *History of the French, Walloon, Dutch and Other Foreign Protestants in England* (London, 1846) p. 248.
13. J. C. Beckett, *Protestant Dissent in Ireland 1689-1780* (London, 1948) p. 128; Mant, *A History of the Church of Ireland*, vol. ii, p. 56.

14. See *Wesley's Journals* (London, 1903).
15. E. Burke, *Works* (London, 1792-1827) vol. v, p. 353, quoted in E. N. Williams, *The Eighteenth Century Constitution* (Cambridge, 1960) p. 319.
16. Madden, *Grattan Speeches*, p. 107.
17. Lecky, *A History of Ireland*, vol. i, p. 201.
18. PRONI, Abercorn mss T2541/1A1/4.
19. Madden, *Grattan Speeches*, pp. 110, 136.
20. *Analecta Hibernica*, vol. xiv (1944) p. 58.
21. Madden, *Grattan Speeches*, p. 127; see also E. M. Johnston, *Ireland in the Eighteenth Century* (Dublin, 1974) pp. 49, 51.
22. *Castlereagh Correspondence*, vol. iv, pp. 97ff.
23. Quoted in G. C. Lewis, *On Local Disturbances in Ireland* (London, 1836) p. 34.
24. J. M. Barkley, *Short History of the Presbyterian Church in Ireland* (Belfast, 1959) p. 31.
25. This diary is printed in J. Stevenson, *Two Centuries of Life in Down, 1600-1800* (Belfast, 1920) pp. 359-63.
26. Fenning, *The Undoing of the Friars of Ireland*, p. 35.
27. *Analecta Hibernica*, vol. xiv (1944) p. 46.
28. W. P. Burke, *The Irish Priest in the Penal Times 1600-1760* (Waterford, 1914) pp. 252, 257.
29. Wakefield, *Account of Ireland*, vol. ii, pp. 754, 766.
30. Fenning, *The Undoing of the Friars of Ireland*, p. 73.
31. P. Boyle, 'The Irish College in Paris 1578-1901', *Irish Ecclesiastical Record*, vols xi-xii (1902); see also T. J. Walsh, *The Irish Continental College Movement* (Dublin, 1973).
32. Wall, *The Penal Laws*, p. 7; Donlevy's *Irish-English Cathecism* (1742) was also published in Paris.
33. See Killen, *Ecclesiastical History of Ireland*, vol. ii, p. 165, n. 5.
34. *Reports from the Commissioners of the Board of Education in Ireland*, House of Commons 1809 (142) vol. vii, 3rd Report, p. 24.
35. *Record of the General Synod of Ulster 1691-1820* (Belfast, 1898) p. 211.
36. Quoted in Corish, *The Irish Church under the Penal Code*, pp. 79-80.
37. Barkley, *Short History of the Presbyterian Church*, p. 99; Stewart, *The Seceders in Ireland*, p. 423.
38. Wakefield, *Account of Ireland*, vol. ii, p. 610.
39. See K. Danaher, *The Year in Ireland* (Cork, 1972); E. E. Evans, *Irish Folk Ways* (London, 1957) esp. pp. 267-94.
40. Evans, *Irish Folk Ways*, p. 30.
41. Carleton, *Midnight Mass*, Mercier Press edn (Cork, 1973) pp. 110, 124.

42. *Repertorium Novum*, vol. ii, p. 171; J. Brady, *Catholics and Catholicism in the Eighteenth Century Press* (Maynooth, 1965) p. 85.
43. Evans, *Irish Folk Ways*, pp. 297ff.; also E. E. Evans, *Irish Heritage: the Landscape, the People and their Work* (Dundalk, 1942) pp. 163-78.
44. The literature on the philosophical background is immense. Those who wish to pursue the topic will find suggestions in : L. Stephen, *English Thought in the Eighteenth Century* (London, 1876); P. Hazard, *European Thought in the Eighteenth Century* (London, 1954); G. R. Cragg, *The Church in the Age of Reason* (London, 1962).
45. W. Molyneux, *The Case for Ireland . . . Stated* (London, 1698).
46. For some of the ramifications of this circle see B. E. Mansfield, *Phoenix of his Age* (Toronto, 1979) pp. 161-2.
47. *Journals of the Irish House of Commons*, vol. ii, p. 190.
48. P. Edwards (ed.), *The Encyclopedia of Philosophy* (London, 1967) vol. vii, p. 142; Gaelic was among the ten languages to which he laid claim. See *Dictionary of National Biography*.
49. Hogarth's painting of Hoadley in the Tate Gallery is a magnificent comment on an eighteenth-century Latitudinarian bishop.
50. For the ecclesiastical politics of the period see N. Sykes, *Church and State in England in the Eighteenth Century* (London, 1934) and *Edmund Gibson, Bishop of London* (London, 1926); for the Irish side see King, *A Great Archbishop of Dublin*, and Boulter, *Letters*.
51. Boulter, *Letters*; see also Killen, *Ecclesiastical History of Ireland*, vol. ii, pp. 256-8.
52. For the impact of Clayton's writings, see A. Llanover (ed.), *The Autobiography and Correspondence of Mary Granville, Mrs Delany* (London, 1861) ser. i, vol. iii, Mrs Delany to Mrs Dewes, 17 May 1753 and 4 Mar. 1760; also PRONI, O'Hara mss T2812/10/16, 17, 24 and Abercorn mss T2541/1A1/119.
53. *H. M. C. Charlemont Manuscripts and Correspondence*, ed. J. T. Gilbert (London, 1891) vol. i, p. 122; *Wesley's Journals*, 6 June 1775.
54. J. S. Reid, *History of the Presbyterian Church in Ireland* (Belfast, 1867) vol. iii, p. 293; Stewart, *The Seceders in Ireland*, p. 35.
55. This important problem is considered in detail in R. Allen, 'The Principle of Non-Subscription in Irish Presbyterianism' (unpublished Ph.D. thesis, Queen's University, Belfast).

56. Barkley, *Short History of the Presbyterian Church*, p. 28.
57. See Stephen, *English Thought in the Eighteenth Century* (Harbinger edn, 1962) vol. ii, pp. 47ff.
58. A visual impact of the nature and austerity of Jansenism can be felt in some of the paintings of Philippe de Champaigne, whose daughter was a nun at the great Jansenist Convent of Port Roy.
59. J. McManners, *French Ecclesiastical Society under the Ancien Regime* (Manchester, 1960) especially pp. 10-11. This study of Angers is particularly relevant in view of its proximity to the Irish Colleges at Nantes, Poitiers and Rouen. See also McManners, *The French Revolution and the Church* (London, 1969).
60. Quoted in I. O. Wade, *The Clandestine Organisation and Diffusion of Ideas From France from 1700 to 1750* (Princeton, 1938) p. 5.
61. These views are summarised in Wade, ibid., pp. 33ff., 54-64; and Hazard, *European Thought in the Eighteenth Century*, pp. 66-8.
62. C. Giblin, *Irish Exiles in Europe* (Dublin, 1971) p. 17. This fascicle is published with Corish, *The Irish Church under the Penal Code*.
63. *Analecta Hibernica*, vol. xiv (1944) p. 48. The warden was the leading ecclesiastic in Galway.
64. Ibid., 3 Oct. 1792.
65. R. R. Madden, *The United Irishmen* (London, 1842-6) vol. i, App. x, p. 586.
66. Reid, *History of the Presbyterian Church*, vol. iii, p. 396, especially n. 45 and n. 46.
67. See *Journals of the House of Lords*, vol. iii, p. 414, 10 Mar. 1737/8, Report from the Lords Committee for Religion; and Lecky, *A History of Ireland*, vol. i, pp. 323-4.
68. J. M. Roberts, *The Mythology of Secret Societies* (London, 1972) pp. 41-2, 60, 105; for the reaction of the Catholic Church, see p. 83. See also R. Jacob, *The Rise of the United Irishmen* (London, 1937) p. 187.
69. *Delany Correspondence*, ser. ii, vol. i, pp. 76-7, 4 Sept. 1766; *I. M. C. Leinster Correspondence*, ed. B. Fitzgerald (Dublin, 1949) vol. iii, p. 446, n. 2.
70. D. H. Akenson and W. H. Crawford, *James Orr, the Bard of Ballycarry* (Belfast, 1978).
71. J. R. R. Adams, 'Reading Societies in Ulster', *Ulster Folklife*, vol. xxvi (1980) pp. 56-64.
72. Reid, *History of the Presbyterian Church*, vol. iii, p. 294, n. 22.

3 Popular Recreation in Nineteenth-Century Ireland

ELIZABETH MALCOLM

In 1852 Sir William Wilde in his delightful little book, *Irish Popular Superstitions*, lamented the recent disappearance of many traditional beliefs, customs and recreations. 'The old forms and customs . . . are becoming obliterated,' wrote Wilde,

> the festivals are unobserved, and the rustic festivities neglected or forgotten . . . [the peasants' balls and routs], do not often take place when starvation and pestilence stalk over a country. . . . The faction-fights, the hurlings, and the mains of cocks that used to be fought at Shrovetide and Easter . . . are past and gone these twenty years. . . . It was only, however, within those three years that the *waits* ceased to go their rounds upon the cold frosty mornings in our native village at Christmas. . . . The native humour of the people is not so rich and racy as in days of yore. . . . Well-honoured be the name of Theobald Mathew – but, after all, a power of fun went away with the whiskey. . . . The pilgrimages formerly undertaken to holy wells and sacred shrines for cures and penances have been strenuously interdicted. . . . The fairies, the whole pantheon of Irish demigods are retiring, one by one, from the habitations of man to the distant islands where the wild waves of the Atlantic raise their foaming crests, to render their fastnesses inaccessible to the schoolmaster and the railroad engineer . . . [1]

But by no means all observers joined Wilde in lamenting the passing of traditional customs. The travellers, Mr and Mrs S. C. Hall, writing more than ten years before him, had recognised the same phenomenon, but their attitude was altogether different and probably more typical of their class.

> Happily, customs that are equally opposed to reason and religion are rapidly removing before the advancing spirit of improvement – and its gigantic ally, Education – and as the Roman Catholic clergy are, at length, convinced that

it is in their own true interest to discourage or suppress
them, they will no doubt, be noted, ere long, only among
histories of gone-by evils and absurdities - to which
Ireland has been of late years, so extensive a contributor.[2]

While their attitudes were different, however, Wilde and
the Halls did agree that in recent decades traditional
religious customs, festivals and recreations had been
disappearing rapidly. The Halls, as quoted, identified
education, the 'spirit of improvement' - what we would
perhaps call modernisation - and the opposition of the
Catholic clergy as primarily responsible for this development. Wilde also mentions the spread of education and
clerical opposition, adding the growth of railways, Father
Mathew's total abstinence crusade and last, but hardly
least, the Famine. Historians today would probably agree
that the 'modernisation of Irish society', as it has been
called, proceeded apace during the 1830s and 1840s.[3] One
would certainly want to add to these contemporary catalogues
of modernising influences, for instance, the establishment
of the Royal Irish Constabulary in the late 1830s.[4]

In this chapter, however, I want to focus on the popular
recreations and customs referred to by Wilde and the Halls:
first, to describe some of the major characteristics of
traditional recreations, showing that they were by no means
exclusive to Ireland, but rather reflected a European
pattern; secondly, to look briefly at when and how these
practices underwent drastic change; and finally, to explore
the relationship between such changes in recreation and the
nationalist movements of the period.

Traditional or non-modern European societies have displayed certain characteristic forms of recreation, perhaps
the most striking being the festival. Festivals could take a
variety of forms: family festivals, like weddings; community
festivals, like feasts of local patron saints; seasonal-cum-religious festivals like May Day, Midsummer or All
Saints' Day; and in large parts of Europe there was the
Carnival. Peter Burke in his recent book, *Popular Culture in
Early Modern Europe*, provides a stimulating analysis of such
festivals, in particular of Carnival. Burke detects three
major themes, real and symbolic, in the Carnival
festivities: food, sex and violence.[5] Heavy consumption of
meat generally took place, as did a great deal of drinking.
Carnival was also a time of particularly intense sexual
activity and many of the traditional Carnival plays and
games had obvious sexual overtones. Carnival was also a
festival of aggression. This aggression was often ritualised

in mock battles or in violent games, like football. But aggression could also be direct and open. Carnival provided an opportunity to pay off old grudges, so rioting and violent death frequently occurred.[6] Carnival was set in opposition not merely to Lent, which it preceded, but to everyday life in general. Carnival was the 'world turned upside down': a world in which the normal social and moral constraints were abandoned.[7]

But Carnival did not have the same importance over the whole of Europe. It was most prevalent in the Mediterranean area, in Italy, Spain and France, common in central Europe, but little known in Britain and Scandinavia, perhaps because the weather there discouraged an elaborate outdoor festival during the late winter or spring. But, where Carnival was weakest, other festivals with similar characteristics were held at different times of the year. In England Burke notes especially the celebrations connected with May Day, with Midsummer or St John's Day (24 June) and with St Bartholomew's Day (24 August) as being most 'carnivalesque'.[8]

In Ireland one of the most important events in the traditional calendar, both rural and urban, was the fair. The fair of course had great economic significance, but it was also the focus of much festivity and recreation, and associated with other celebrations as well. Weddings were often arranged at fairs, which provided opportunities both for young people to meet and for their families to bargain.[9] Fairs were frequently held in conjunction with patterns, feasts of local patron saints or religious holydays. Seasonal activities like sowing and harvesting were also marked by fairs. This is not to say that recreations and sports were restricted to fair times. Many observers remarked that Sunday afternoons and evenings were popular times for drinking, games and dancing. Also there were family festivals, like wakes and christenings, which were not connected with fairs.[10] But the Irish fair and its associated patterns, festivals and games, was similar in many respects to the European Carnival, sharing the themes of food, sex and violence, and providing a focus for much popular recreation.

Many of the major traditional Irish fairs developed from *'aenachs'* or ritual assemblies held on hilltops at fixed times, marking the beginnings of the Celtic seasons. Thus, the quarter days, 1 May and 1 November and also 1 February and 1 August, were the favoured dates for these gatherings, which usually lasted some fifteen days. Commerce was conducted during the first days, while the last were given over to games and sports.[11] These assemblies celebrated recurring rural activities. Later, when the Christian liturgical calendar was superimposed upon the old agricultural calendar, they marked religious holydays. Such occasions seem from the beginning to have been recognised as times of special licence. They were accompanied by a strong spirit of revelry and a temporary slackening of the moral code.[12] The Normans also established fairs, often intended to supplant the old Irish gatherings. The most notorious was Donnybrook Fair, established by royal charter early in the thirteenth century. It began on 26 August, following St Bartholomew's Day, and originally lasted for fifteen days.[13] The seventeenth and eighteenth centuries also saw the appearance of many new fairs, usually held on days with existing religious associations. These were intended to be one- or two-day events, restricted to business, but country people continued to regard the fair as a major social and recreational event.[14] The flavour of Donnybrook is clearly conveyed by a French traveller, who visited the Fair in 1828.

I rode out today, for the first time, to see the Fair at Donnybrook, near Dublin, which is a kind of popular festival. Nothing, indeed, can be more national! The poverty, the dirt, and the wild tumult, were as great as the glee and merriment with which the cheapest pleasures were enjoyed. I saw things eaten and drunk with delight, which forced me to turn my head quickly away, to remain master of my disgust. Heat and dust, crowd and stench made it impossible to stay longer; but these do not annoy the natives. There were many hundred tents, all ragged like the people, and adorned with tawdry rags instead of flags. . . . The lowest sort of rope-dancers and posture-masters exercised their toilsome vocation on stages of planks, and dressed in shabby finery, dancing and grimacing in the dreadful heat till they were completely exhausted. A third part of the public lay or rather rolled about drunk; others ate, screamed, shouted and fought.[15]

Fairs were often associated with celebrations of the feasts of local patron saints: patrons or patterns, as they were called. Patterns, despite their religious significance, resembled fairs in that they generaly involved much drinking and violence. It has been suggested that popular religious observances, like patterns and pilgrimages, may in fact have become more prevalent in the seventeenth and eighteenth centuries due to the persecution of the Catholic Church.[16] But by the beginning of the nineteenth century patterns were under attack from both the Church and the civil authorities because of their accompanying excesses. In 1813 Thomas Crofton Croker visited the famous pattern held at Gougane

Barra on St John's Eve (23 June). While pilgrims prayed in the chapels and around the holy well on the island, others celebrated in the numerous tents which lined the lake's shore. According to Croker:

> The tents are generally so crowded that the dancers have scarcely room for their performance: from twenty to thirty men and women are often huddled together in each, and the circulation of porter and whiskey amongst the various groups is soon evident in its effects. All become actors - none spectators - rebellious songs, in the Irish language, are loudly vociferated, and received with yells of applause: towards evening the tumult increases, and intoxication becomes almost universal. Cudgels are brandished, the shrieks of women and the piercing cry of children thrill painfully upon the ear in the riot and uproar of the scene; indeed the distraction and tumult of a patron cannot be described. At midnight the assembly become somewhat less noisy and confused, but the chapels were still crowded . . . the washing and bathing in the well still continued, and the dancing, drinking, roaring, and singing were, in some degree, kept up throughout the night.[17]

Observers from at least the sixteenth century had noted this tendency to indulge in periodic drunken and violent orgies.[18] Thomas Newenham for instance remarked in 1805 that the Irish reputation for drunkenness essentially arose from the towns. But in the country, it was otherwise. 'Except at fairs, patrons, wakes and weddings, those who dwell in the single-hearth houses . . . are scarcely ever seen intoxicated, and never use spirits at their meals.'[19] In 1835 the Bishop in Carlow expressed a similar view to de Tocqueville, when he said that the Irish people were 'gentle, polite and hospitable'. However, 'when the chance of a drunken orgy offers, they do not know how to resist it. They become turbulent and often violent and disorderly'.[20]

All seemed agreed that fighting was an integral part of these periodic orgies. Such fights were not chance affairs; they were ritualised faction fights. The Halls described faction fighting as the 'necessary epilogue to a fair', while John Barrow saw it as a 'pastime', a form of entertainment.[21] William Carleton, who, in his two stories, 'The Battle of the Factions' and 'The Party Fight and the Funeral', provided a detailed contemporary account of faction fighting, shared Barrow's assessment. In both these stories, Carleton was at pains to distinguish between faction fights and party fights, the latter being what we would today call sectarian riots. The atmosphere during the two fights was altogether different. Party fights were dangerous, bad-tempered conflicts. But according to Carleton,

> a faction fight doesn't resemble this, at all at all. Paddy's at home here; all song, dance, good-humour, and affection. His cheek is flushed with delight, which, indeed, may derive assistance from the consciousness of having no bayonets or loaded carbines to contend with: but, anyhow he's at home - his eye is lit with real glee - he tosses his hat in the air, in the height of mirth. . . . If he meets his sweetheart, he will give her a kiss and a hug, and that with double kindness, because he is on his way to thrash her father or brother. . . . To be sure, skulls and bones are broken, and lives lost; but they are lost in pleasant fighting - they are the consequences of the sport.[22]

It should be noted that Carleton writes with considerable irony, for his stories show the consequences of both forms of fighting to be tragic; the faction fight perhaps more so as it divides families and friends.

Faction fighting closely resembled the mock battles that Burke describes as an essential element of Carnival.[23] The ritualistic nature of faction fighting is clear from the fact that the participants seldom knew why they were fighting, or only had the vaguest of rationalisations. Moreover, fights generally conformed to a set pattern. A ritualised challenge was issued, frequently taking the form of a 'coat trailing'. The fight was brief, seldom involved fatalities, and the contending parties were usually friends again immediately afterwards. Henry Inglis in 1834 described a fight at a pattern in the Joyce Country, County Galway. The fight only lasted ten minutes and after it: 'Some, who had been opposed to each other, shook hands and kissed; and appeared as good friends as before'.[24]

Thus, prior to the Famine, the Irish found much of their recreation in religious and seasonal festivals. Such celebrations were the antithesis of everyday life and even in supposedly religious festivals, like patterns, the conventional Christian morality was abandoned. Excess was the hallmark of these celebrations: excess in eating, drinking and in fighting. The sexual side of Irish festivals is much less well documented, though this may be due rather to the reticence of middle-class writers than to an absence of such activity. Croker, for instance, did observe that there were many 'depraved women' drinking and dancing in the tents at Gougane Barra. Moreover, as characteristic of the 'world turned upside down', it was the women at Gougane Barra who asked the men to dance.[25]

The oppressed and weakened Catholic Church of the seventeenth and early eighteenth centuries may have been prepared to allow popular religious festivals to flourish, but as it gained strength it came increasingly to challenge such practices. In Kerry as early as the 1740s the Bishop attempted to abolish patterns, though it was not till after 1798, when the Archbishop of Cashel moved against them, that any significant decline occurred.[26] The Ordnance Survey letters of the 1830s and 1840s are full of references to the disappearance of religious festivals. John O'Donovan's letters from County Waterford in 1841, for instance, refer repeatedly to patterns suppressed by the clergy from the 1790s onwards.[27] In 1836 O'Donovan had visited Telltown in County Meath, site of the most famous of the August harvest festivals, where games and sports had been held for centuries and observed that the celebrations had been suppressed by clergy and magistrates about thirty years previously.[28] The number of holydays had also been progressively reduced, from over thirty in 1700 to ten in 1830.[29] Between the 1790s and the 1840s, the clergy were thus very much to the fore in the campaign to destroy popular religious practices. David Miller has seen the Famine as the prime factor in the discrediting of what he terms 'customary' religious practices.[30] The Famine was doubtless important, but it should perhaps be seen simply as the final blow to celebrations that were already in serious decline. As noted, the Halls were happily anticipating the total disappearance of 'customs that are equally opposed to reason and religion' in the late 1830s.

With regard to fairs the situation is more complex. The number held in Ireland seems to have increased during the nineteenth century. An examination of the fairs listed in *Thom's Directory* for the years 1845 and 1900 shows an increase of some 700 — from nearly 5000 to a little over 5700.[31] But, during this period, the distribution of fairs throughout the year changed significantly. The number of fairs which were held monthly increased from 34.4 per cent in 1845 to 64.2 per cent in 1900. In 1845 May, November and August were by far the most popular months for fairs. In 1900 these same three months were still at the top of the list, but only marginally so. In other words, the traditional seasonal pattern of fairs was disappearing. Athlone, an important commercial centre, provides a good example of what was happening. In the eighteenth century four fairs were held there, in January, March, May and August. All lasted three days and were linked with holydays. However, by 1900 Athlone fairs had become monthly and were one-day events except for the January and September fairs, which lasted for two days. What had happened was that, partly as a result of improved transport facilities, fairs in the smaller towns around Athlone had died out and business had become concentrated there.[32] The nature of fairs also changed drastically, the recreational element giving way increasingly to more serious commercial purposes. Donnybrook Fair was suppressed in the 1850s by the clergy and Dublin civic authorities and in the 1860s a church dedicated to the Sacred Heart was built on the old fairground.[33] Other fairs, which survived, came to concentrate more and more on the livestock trade. By 1900 the selling of food, rural crafts and clothes at fairs was declining, the ballad singers and storytellers were seldom to be seen, while the faction fights and bull-baiting had long ago been suppressed. The fair was well on the way to becoming the livestock mart that we know today.

The change in the recreational pattern that occurred between the 1790s and the 1840s was drastic. In 1812 Edward Wakefield had calculated that 'one-third at least of the time of the labouring classes in Ireland, is wasted in holydays, funerals, weddings, christenings, fairs, patterns, races, and other recreations'.[34] But, scarcely thirty years later, the Halls thought that there were 'no people in the world who have so few amusements as the Irish; now that drinking and fighting are done away with, they can be scarcely said to have any; for dancing and hurling seem to be equally neglected, the absence of the accompanying stimulus having induced indifference towards them.'[35] We have already noted that the 1830s and 1840s were decades of accelerated modernisation; a time when the decline of traditional recreations was becoming obvious to outside observers. An interesting issue is the relationship between this decline and the success, during this same period, of mass movements, like Father Mathew's total abstinence crusade, O'Connell's Repeal campaign and Young Ireland. These movements, whatever their serious political and social purposes, did have significant recreational elements, which their leaders sought to foster. Were people more ready to join such movements, with their strong social and emotional appeals, during a time of change and uncertainty, when traditional religious and recreational practices were in decline?

Drink was clearly a vital ingredient of traditional recreation. Wilde thought that 'a power of fun went away with the whiskey'. However, Father Mathew was keenly aware of the need to provide social and recreational substitutes for drinking. In 1843 the German traveller, J. G. Kohl, was in Kilrush when the town was visited by Mathew. What struck Kohl most forcefully was the 'extravagance' and the 'intemperance' of this so-called temperance movement. 'Their music is loud and without taste,' wrote Kohl 'the speeches declamatory and vaunting, the meetings often continue till the night is far advanced, and, by the temperance people, are concluded with dancing and noise.'[36] In the intervals between speeches and toasts, music and songs were performed and when Mathew left around midnight a dance began, which lasted till daylight. Kohl heard the temperance band playing their music through the streets as they returned home at dawn. The meeting, though sober, was clearly far from sedate. Kohl in fact concluded that the chief aim of the Irish temperance movement was to infuse 'into the people a taste for a description of pleasure and enjoyments widely differing from those they formerly enjoyed in the whisky-shops'.[37] In other words, Father Mathew's crusade was primarily a form of recreation, substituted for the old entertainments associated with drink.

The Young Irelanders were also very conscious of the need to introduce new forms of recreation to match the new sober mood of the country. The recreations they envisaged, however, were ones which would complement, if not further, the nationalist cause. Gavan Duffy, writing in the *Nation* in December 1842, claimed that:

> Teetotalism has taken from the People their *only* enjoyment. They are altogether without public amusement. . . . *They need some stimulant*. We are a social, lively, enjoying People, and we must have excitement. Here is an opportunity to give it, of the purest and most healthy character — if it be not given, the People will find it for themselves.[38]

Duffy clearly feared a return to the drunken festivals of the past unless new forms of entertainment were provided. But it is questionable whether his idea of exciting amusement would have had much appeal, for he recommended principally 'THE ESTABLISHMENT OF LITERARY AND SCIENTIFIC INSTITUTIONS IN CONNEXION WITH TEETOTAL SOCIETIES IN EVERY CONSIDERABLE TOWN IN IRELAND'.[39] Davis also urged the introduction of rational and uplifting recreation, in particular reading rooms, museums, public gardens, lectures and music.[40] With the possible exception of music, the forms of recreation mentioned by Duffy and Davis were largely educational. To them recreation was not just frivolous amusement, but an important weapon in the struggle to liberate the Irish people from both ignorance and oppression. There were other Young Irelanders who anticipated the Gaelic Athletic Association (GAA) in seeking to revive traditional Irish sports. In 1848, for instance, Thomas Francis Meagher attempted to revive hurling in Waterford City.[41]

Although O'Connell does not seem to have been consciously concerned about recreation in the way Father Mathew and the Young Irelanders were, his Repeal movement nevertheless had important recreational aspects. O'Connell made great use of processions, music, costumes, mass meetings, banquets, concerts, to say nothing of Repeal reading rooms. These all certainly served political purposes, but at the same time afforded a great deal of recreation and amusement. Would it be going too far to suggest a parallel between O'Connell's mass meetings and the old fairs and patterns, also held at significant religious and historic sites? One subsequent imaginative writer, noting that only a tiny fraction of the vast audience at Tara in August 1843 could have heard O'Connell's speech, drew attention to the recreational elements apparent at the meeting, likening it to 'some popular festival, or some sportive occasion like a race meeting'.[42] Although amazement is often expressed at the size of O'Connell's meetings, the Irish in fact were a people used to travelling substantial distances to historic sites in order to attend great outdoor festivals.[43] Moreover, the Tara meeting was held in August, traditionally the most popular month for festivals and sports. The major difference between O'Connell's meetings and the old festivals was the soberness of the former. This perhaps, more than the size of the meetings themselves, was the most novel aspect, reflecting Father Mathew's remarkable successes.

These speculations about the popular movements of the 1830s and 1840s suggest that nationalism, from this time onwards, was not merely a political ideology, but also a form of recreation. Thus, even before the establishment of the GAA, Irish nationalist movements provided important recreational outlets for a people largely deprived of their traditional amusements. In other words, historians should not see the appeal of Repeal or Fenianism, or even teetotalism, purely in ideological terms. One cannot assume that the people who travelled to Tara, or other mass meetings, in 1843 and did not hear or even see O'Connell were necessarily disappointed.

Nationalists had long used sporting occasions to disguise illegal meetings. In the 1660s there were reports of 'rebellious Irish papists' meeting in Tipperary 'under pretence of a match of hurling'.[44] In his novel *Roddy the*

Rover, Carleton portrays Ribbonmen in Tyrone using hurling and football matches as covers for recruiting activities.[45] The Fenians were notorious for using recreational occasions in this way. Public houses were favourite hunting grounds for Fenian recruiters.[46] As well, there were numerous instances of cricket and football matches, races and even dances being used to conceal Fenian gatherings.[47] The authorities were well aware of this connection between sport and nationalism. Writing in the *Irish People* in October 1864, under the heading 'National Sports', Charles Kickham defended hurling, football and dancing, which he said were being discouraged by police and magistrates. If a score or two of young men and women met on a Sunday afternoon, complained Kickham, they were likely to be interrupted, if not dispersed, by the police.[48]

However, it was not simply a matter of recreation being subordinated to political purposes. There were also instances in which the social and recreational aspects of gatherings clearly took precedence over the political. On a Sunday in October 1864, for example, some 400 people gathered for a cricket match and picnic at the village of Dunnamaggin in County Kilkenny. The local constabulary noted a number of Fenian leaders in the group, which only seemed intent on drawing attention to itself by playing nationalist music and wearing green ribbons and hatbands.[49] Rather than serving the Fenians' secret political aims, such a gathering imperilled them and one can only conclude that the recreational appeal of such an occasion outweighed the political dangers involved. Observers in the 1860s and 1870s frequently remarked on the lack of recreation available to the young in both town and country. A Tipperary magistrate in 1868, for instance, said that men were largely without amusement when the public houses were closed. They just walked about, read newspapers and tried to organise dances.[50] Similarly, in 1877 the Recorder of Dublin, lamenting the fact that cricket was not widely popular in Ireland, said he thought the Irish 'the most ignorant people in respect to . . . the way of amusing themselves . . . that exist in the civilised world'.[51] Although doubtless somewhat exaggerated,[52] these, and similar, comments do point to the fact that in the middle years of the century recreational opportunities, particularly for the young, were contracting. The old sports and festivals were in decline, while the new games, like cricket and rugby football, had not proved as popular in Ireland as they had in England.[53] In this context it is easy to see that the appeal of Fenianism was strongly social and recreational, as well as political.

In the 1880s, the establishment of the GAA saw the beginning of an explicit alliance between nationalism and sport. This alliance was not new. It had existed, though in a less clearly defined form, for many years. Ireland, perhaps more than most countries, demonstrates the futility of attempting to separate sport from politics.

The opposition of clergy and magistrates, the spread of national education, the coming of the railway, the introduction of effective policing, the suppression of illicit distillation and the Famine were all factors contributing to the decline in traditional popular recreation. This decline was evident from the late eighteenth century, but seems to have accelerated in the 1830s and 1840s. Fairs, patterns, pilgrimages, holydays, wakes, calendar customs and Gaelic games were either disappearing or being radically transformed. Deprived of many of their traditional gatherings and festivals, people were naturally attracted by the marches, the meetings and the music offered by reformist crusades. Repeal, teetotalism and Fenianism certainly appealed to their respective adherents on political or ideological grounds - one could hardly deny that - but these were not the only grounds of appeal. Thus, in seeking reasons for the popularity of these various movements, historians should not overlook the simple need for entertainment and recreation in a society undergoing the painful process of modernisation.

NOTES

1. W.R. Wilde, *Irish Popular Superstitions* (Dublin, 1852) pp. 14-16.
2. S.C. and A.M. Hall, *Ireland: its Scenery, Character, &c.* (London, 1841) vol. i, p. 279.
3. See, for example, the outline of modernising factors given in Joseph Lee, *The Modernisation of Irish Society, 1848-1918* (Dublin, 1973) pp. 1-35.
4. For the background to the establishment of the Royal Irish Constabulary, see Galen Broeker, *Rural Disorder and Police Reform in Ireland, 1812-36* (London and Toronto, 1970).
5. Peter Burke, *Popular Culture in Early Modern Europe* (London, 1978) p. 186.
6. Ibid., pp. 187-8.
7. Ibid., pp. 188-91.
8. Ibid., pp. 194-9; for a more detailed description of holyday festivities in England, see R. W. Malcolmson,

Popular Recreations in English Society, 1700-1850 (Cambridge, 1973) pp. 15-33, and Christina Hole, *English Sports and Pastimes* (London, 1949) pp. 95-132.

9. Anon., 'An Irish Wedding, by One Who Has Seen Many', *Dublin University Magazine*, vol. lx, no. 257 (Sept. 1862) pp. 359-76; Anon., 'Weddings and Wakes', *Dublin University Magazine*, vol. lxxxviii, no. 525 (Sept. 1876) pp. 292-6.
10. Folklore Commission Archives (Folklore Department, UCD, ms 107, pp. 57-60); John Carr, *The Stranger in Ireland; or, a Tour in the Southern and Western Parts of that Country, in the Year 1805* (London, 1806) pp. 257-9; Edward Wakefield, *An Account of Ireland, Statistical and Political* (London, 1812) vol. ii, p. 776.
11. E. E. Evans, *Irish Heritage: the Landscape, the People and their Work* (Dundalk, 1942) pp. 157-8; E. E. Evans, *Irish Folk Ways* (London, 1957) pp. 253-66; Máire MacNeill, *The Festival of Lughnasa: a Study of the Celtic Festival of the Beginning of the Harvest* (London, 1962) pp. 309-10.
12. Evans, *Irish Heritage*, p. 161; M. A. Murray, 'Puck Fair of Kilorglin', *Folk-lore*, vol. lxiv, no. 2 (June 1953) pp. 351-4.
13. R. J. Kerry, 'Donnybrook Fair', *Journal of the Royal Society of Antiquaries of Ireland*, vol. xlix (1919) pp. 136-48; Laurence O'Dea, 'The Fair of Donnybrook', *Dublin Historical Record*, vol. xv, no. 1 (Oct. 1958) pp. 11-12.
14. MacNeill, *The Festival of Lughnasa*, p. 310; Jeremiah Sheehan, *South Westmeath: Farm and Folk* (Dublin, 1978) pp. 256-7.
15. Quoted in O'Dea, 'The Fair of Donnybrook', p. 16.
16. MacNeill, *The Festival of Lughnasa*, p. 78; for contemporary descriptions of patterns at Croagh Patrick, County Mayo, and Ardmore, County Waterford, see M. A. Titmarsh [W. M. Thackeray], *The Irish Sketch-book* (London, 1843) vol. ii, pp. 99-102 and the Halls, *Ireland: its Scenery, Character, &c.*, vol. i, pp. 282-5.
17. T. Crofton Croker, *Researches in the South of Ireland, Illustrative of the Scenery, Architectural Remains, and the Manners and Superstitions of the Peasantry; with an Appendix Containing a Private Narrative of the Rebellion of 1798* (London, 1824) p. 281.
18. See, for example, Fynes Moryson's remarks of 1617, quoted in D. B. Quinn, *The Elizabethans and the Irish* (Ithaca, NY, 1966) p. 78.
19. Thomas Newenham, *A Statistical and Historical Inquiry into the Progress and Magnitude of the Population of*

19. *Ireland* (London, 1805) p. 233.
20. Alexis de Tocqueville, *Journeys to England and Ireland*, ed. J. P. Mayer (London, 1958) p. 131.
21. The Halls, *Ireland: its Scenery, Character, &c.*, vol. i, p. 425; John Barrow, *A Tour round Ireland, through the Sea-Coast Counties, in the Autumn of 1835* (London, 1836) pp. 348-9.
22. William Carleton, 'The Battle of the Factions', *Traits and Stories of the Irish Peasantry* (London, n.d.) p. 129; for an interesting discussion of this story, see Maurice Harmon, 'Cobwebs before the Wind: Aspects of the Peasantry in Irish Literature from 1800 to 1916', in *Views of the Irish Peasantry, 1800-1916*, eds D. J. Casey and R. E. Rhodes (Hamden, Conn., 1977) pp. 136-40.
23. Burke, *Popular Culture*, pp. 187-8.
24. H. D. Inglis, *Ireland in 1834: a Journey throughout Ireland, during the Spring, Summer and Autumn of 1834* (London, 1834) vol. i, pp. 51-2; for a general, popular examination of faction fighting, see Patrick O'Donnell, *The Irish Faction Fighters of the 19th Century* (Dublin, 1975); for further interesting contemporary accounts of faction fights, see James Hall, *Tour through Ireland; particularly the Interior and Least Known Parts . . .* (London, 1813) vol. ii, p. 100 and Asenath Nicholson, *Ireland's Welcome to a Stranger: or, Excursions through Ireland, 1844 and 1845, for the Purpose of Personally Investigating the Condition of the Poor* (London, 1847) p.318.
25. Croker, *Researches in the South of Ireland*, p. 280.
26. Wakefield, *An Account of Ireland*, vol. ii, p. 662.
27. 'Letters Containing Information Relative to the Antiquities of the County Waterford, Collected during the Progress of the Ordnance Survey in 1841' (National Library of Ireland (hereafter NLI), typescript (1928) pp. 29, 49-50, 63, 87).
28. 'Letters Containing Information Relative to the Antiquities of the County Meath, Collected during the Progress of the Ordnance Survey in 1836' (NLI, typescript (1927) pp. 4-5); MacNeill, *The Festival of Lughnasa*, pp. 336-9.
29. *Personal Recollections of the Life and Times, with Extracts from the Correspondence of Valentine, Lord Cloncurry*, 2nd edn (Dublin, 1850) pp. 258-60; Kevin Danaher, *The Year in Ireland* (Cork, 1972) pp. 265-7.
30. David Miller, 'Irish Catholicism and the Great Famine', *Journal of Social History*, vol. ix, no. 1 (Sept. 1975) pp. 81-98.

31. *Thom's Directory* (1845) pp. 44-52; (1900) pp. 35-41. I would like to thank Dr Hoy Lee of the CSIRO, Sydney, for helping me to analyse these figures.
32. Ibid., (1845) p. 52; (1900), p. 40; Sheehan, *South Westmeath*, pp. 257-62.
33. O'Dea, 'The Fair of Donnybrook', p. 20.
34. Wakefield, *An Account of Ireland*, vol. ii, p. 810.
35. The Halls, *Ireland: its Scenery, Character, &c.*, vol. iii, p. 422.
36. J. G. Kohl, *Travels in Ireland* (London, 1844) pp. 100-1; for further descriptions of temperance celebrations, see *Freeman's Journal*, 30 Mar. 1842, and Reports of Temperance Enquiry (SPO, Miscellaneous Papers, 1799-1868, nos 2-10 (1799-1840) IA/76/3).
37. Kohl, *Travels in Ireland*, p. 102; for an interesting new analysis of the significance of Father Mathew's crusade, see H. F. Kearney, 'Fr Mathew: Apostle of Modernisation', in *Studies in Irish History, Presented to R. Dudley Edwards*, eds Art Cosgrove and Donal McCartney (Dublin, 1979) pp. 164-75.
38. *Nation*, 10 Dec. 1842.
39. Ibid.; Duffy pursued this theme further in another article on 31 Dec. 1842.
40. Ibid., 18 Feb. 1843; interesting extracts from Davis's writings on recreation and education can be found in *Prose Writings: Essays on Ireland, by Thomas Davis*, ed. T. W. Rolleston (London, 1889) pp. 208-16.
41. Seamus Ó Ceallaigh, *Story of the G. A. A.* (Limerick, 1977) p. 13.
42. Sean O'Faolain, *King of the Beggars* (London, 1938) pp. 340-1; for a contemporary description of the Tara meeting, see Charles Gavan Duffy, *Young Ireland: a Fragment of Irish History, 1840-5* (London, 1880) pp. 344-7.
43. In 1834, for example, Henry Inglis visited Lough Derg and estimated that during the pilgrimage season, from 1 June to 15 August, some 500 people per day made the rounds on the island. Many travelled from as far away as Waterford and Kerry. Inglis thought the round trip would have taken five to six weeks and, as it was harvest time, some pilgrims would have forfeited at least 22 shillings in wages. (Inglis, *Ireland in 1834*, vol. ii, pp. 178-9). For other contemporary comments on the crowds attending patterns, see the Halls, *Ireland: Its Scenery, Character, &c.*, vol. i, p. 284, and Croker, *Researches in the South of Ireland*, pp. 277-8.
44. Quoted in Art Ó Maolfabhail, *Camán: Two Thousand Years of Hurling in Ireland* (Dundalk, 1973) p. 40.

45. William Carleton, *Roddy the Rover* (Dublin, 1845) p. 84.
46. See the account of the life of a Fenian recruiter in John Devoy, *Recollections of an Irish Rebel* (New York, 1929) pp. 63-4.
47. R. V. Comerford, 'Irish Nationalist Politics, 1858-70' (unpublished Ph.D. thesis, Trinity College, Dublin, 1976) pp. 212-15. I would like to thank Dr Comerford for allowing me to make use of his unpublished work on the social and recreational aspects of Fenianism.
48. *Irish People*, 15 Oct. 1864.
49. Comerford, 'Irish Nationalist Politics', pp. 208-10; instances of similar behaviour are discussed in ibid., pp. 211-15.
50. *Report from the Select Committee on the Sale of Liquors on Sunday (Ireland) Bill*, p. 8, H. C. 1867-8 (280) vol. xiv.
51. *Report from the Select Committee on the Sale of Intoxicating Liquors on Sunday (Ireland) Bill*, p. 69, H. C. 1877 (198) vol. xvi.
52. The Archives of the Irish Folklore Commission in fact contain a wealth of information on games and sports which were played in Ireland in the latter half of the nineteenth century; see Folklore Commission Archives (Folklore Department, UCD, ms 1162).
53. For accounts of the introduction of cricket and rugby to Ireland, see Arthur Samuels, *Early Cricket in Ireland: a Paper Read before the Kingstown Literary and Debating Society on the 22nd February, 1888* (Dublin, 1888); W. P. Hone, *Cricket in Ireland* (Tralee, 1956); Ó Ceallaigh, *Story of the G. A. A.*, pp. 14-15; Sean Diffley, *The Men in Green: the Story of Irish Rugby* (London, 1973) pp. 13-43.

4 Charles Gavan Duffy in Australia

J. E. PARNABY

When Charles Gavan Duffy landed in Melbourne in 1856 at the age of forty, he was mature, a man of definite convictions and ideas. A leading Young Irelander, editor of the *Nation*, he had spent the formative years of his life in devoted service to his native country in an effort to 'raise up Ireland morally, socially and politically and put the sceptre of self government in her hands'.[1] He looked on this purpose as the only one which could give meaning to his life and he tended to regard his stay in Victoria as an episode in a life of service to Ireland.

He left Victoria in 1880 and in the remaining twenty-three years of his life continued the histories of Young Ireland, the League of North and South, Four Years of Irish History, Thomas Davis, was prominent in the Irish literary revival, and lobbied actively for Home Rule. I am interested to see how his life in Victoria was influenced by his earlier career and how in turn the experience of his Victorian career was woven into his arguments for Home Rule.

He was an unusual migrant and he came to an unusual colony, a colony peopled by two rushes, the land rush of the 1830s and the gold rush of the 1850s. All its settlers were recent migrants from neighbouring colonies or from overseas, and after a bare twenty years of settlement it had achieved self-government. The pioneers of the land rush had not had time to establish their political and economic supremacy, but faced a political struggle with the gold rush migrants which continued for some twenty-five years - the period which coincided with Duffy's stay in the colony.

The freedom and scope of this society had great appeal for Duffy who had been interested in the passage through the House of Commons of its draft constitution. He believed in the possibility of building a society in the new world which would be free from the evils and prejudices of the old. He told the deputation which met his ship:

I recognise perfectly that this is not Ireland, but
Australia where there is fair play for all . . . where no
nationality need stand on the defensive because none is
assailed. In such a land I could be what . . . nature
intended me to be if national injustice and fraud had not
turned my blood into gall, a man who lent a willing and
cheerful obedience to the laws.

But he added 'Let me not be misunderstood. I am not here to
repudiate or apologise for any part of my past life. I am
still an Irish rebel to the backbone and to the spinal
marrow.'[2] This last statement, referring to his connection
with 1848, as a result of which Smith O'Brien, Mitchel and
others were sent as convicts to Van Diemen's Land, was often
repeated by his opponents. It gave a misleading impression
of Duffy. He was above all else a liberal and a moderate,
believing that parliamentary methods were the best for
achieving reform. 'Force was the last resource, long evaded,
long postponed. . . .'[3] He believed in the steady progress
of liberty, and education was the key to freedom: 'Educate
that you may be free.' Parliamentary government was 'the
most perfect system of liberty in the world'.[4] Through
Parliament, Ireland would share in this boon of freedom.

Parliament was at the centre of his reform programme, both
as a means and as an end. In the 1840s he wanted the
Confederacy to build up a strong independent parliamentary
party, able to employ the tactic of independent opposition
as the Tenant League hoped to do, when Duffy sat for three
years as a League representative in the House of Commons.
Parliament remained at the centre of his life in Victoria,
where he was in turn Member, Minister, Premier and Speaker,
and when he returned to Europe the colonial Parliament was
the model for an Irish Parliament under Home Rule.

In the repeal agitation inaugurated by O'Connell, Duffy
had been at the centre of a group of young men who developed
a romantic notion of nationality. In 1842, together with
Davis and Dillon, he founded the *Nation*, a weekly which
sought to foster a sense of national unity and to educate
the Irish people, aiming to change the mind of their generation and so to change its institutions. Mind-making and
propagandist, it was designed 'to teach the people that they
had a history as harmonious as an epic poem',[5] to inspire

Nationality which will not only raise our people from
their poverty, by securing for them the blessings of a
Domestic Legislation, but inflame and purify them with a
lofty and heroic love of country - a Nationality of the
spirit . . . a Nationality which may embrace Protestant,

Catholic and Dissenter – Milesian and Cromwellian – the Irishman of a hundred generations and the stranger who is within our gates.[6]

This was indeed a vision of reconciliation and unity. Ireland's divisions were to be transcended by an awareness of a common heritage. Behind this idealist vision, the competent organisation of Duffy raised the circulation of the paper to 11,000 copies in two years, and produced books of ballad poetry, creating a 'tumult of enthusiasm. The People loved and pitied their country – that they might honour and worship it was a revelation.'[7]

The contributors to the *Nation* formed a circle of friends, the Young Irelanders, who roamed the countryside to visit historic sites and who met for supper on Saturdays to hammer out their ideas, listening to readings from *Sartor Resartus*; 'Tea and Thomas' they called it. Duffy recalls the first time he read Carlyle: 'his daring theories moved me like electric shocks'.[8] In 1845, Duffy sought to enlist his pen in the Irish cause, taking him, after the Famine, for a tour of the disaster areas. Their friendship developed when Duffy was a member of the House of Commons and they continued to meet and correspond until Carlyle died. Duffy published his *Conversations with Carlyle* in 1892.

Here then to the new colony came this liberal and prophet of Irish nationalism. He was welcomed with great enthusiasm in Melbourne and Sydney as a recruit to the liberal cause as well as a champion of certain groups of the Irish population. He settled in Melbourne, which he described as the capital of Australia, where the popular element was strong and triumphant,[9] was given a house as part of a property qualification to enable him to stand for the first Parliament about to be elected. He thus entered Parliament on the liberal side at the beginning of a contest between pioneer squatter, merchant and banking interests entrenched in the Legislative Council, and the gold rush migrants, who came to dominate the Legislative Assembly.

To many Irish colonists, Duffy appeared as a folk hero, to opponents as an Irish ogre, a demagogue of the reddest school. It was confusing to find that the man who took such pride in describing himself as an Irish rebel should appear in the new Parliament as a rather wearisome parliamentary schoolmaster, seeking to organise procedure on the English model, assuming this role because he was the only member who had sat in the House of Commons. It was confusing for Duffy who thought of himself as an advanced liberal to find a society so radical and democratic as to possess vote by ballot and a wide franchise. But letters written home within the first few months of arrival show his great enthusiasm for the new society and its possibilities. He wrote to George Henry Moore in May 1856:

> We are making a newer and better America. All is growth and progress and sense of life that imparts itself to all who are handling public affairs. The seed is sown and grown and reaped in a span. You propose work and it is done. You expose an abuse and it is abandoned. I am not idealising but reporting nakedly my experience – a sort of experience that belongs only to new countries . . .[10]

To Bishop Moriarty he wrote with a different emphasis

> There is as much bigotry here as at home; but nevertheless there is no place on the face of the earth where Irish Catholics are so independent as a body or as individuals . . . it would be the salvation of the bodies and souls of our people to send such as must emigrate where religious freedom and material prosperity await them . . .[11]

Duffy's arrival acted as a catalyst in a society where first-generation migrants were likely to cling to their nationality and their religion as they faced bewildering new circumstances. Here the settlers from England, Scotland and Ireland lived in closer proximity than in their homelands, the Irish minority was a large one – the Irish born were 16.5 per cent in 1854 – and in the absence of establishment the churches were competing for position and converts. His welcome was so exuberant that it alienated many English and Scottish settlers and it brought to the surface divisions among the Irish settlers, between the Protestant Anglo-Irish, some of whom were members of the pioneer squatter, merchant and banker groups and the poorer Roman Catholic migrants, and between O'Connellites and Young Irelanders. The leading Catholic layman in politics, John O'Shanassy, a successful migrant of peasant background, was an O'Connellite who never trusted Duffy, the middle-class intellectual and Young Irelander, although Duffy became a member of a Ministry led by O'Shannassy in 1857. This Ministry was short-lived, overthrown by what Duffy called, a 'No Popery howl'. He wrote of this to Bishop Moriarty,

> A curious fate and experience mine have been . . . to be howled at in both ends of the earth by parties more asunder than the Antipodes on diametrically opposite grounds of complaint. Yonder for betraying the interests of religion; here for being its slave and missionary. I

wonder if I had stopped at the Equator would they have done me the justice . . . of admitting that I belong to neither Antipodes of opinion.[12]

In Ireland it was Cardinal Cullen who led the attack on Duffy for betraying the interests of religion, convinced that Duffy was an Irish Mazzini.

Nationalism, liberalism and religion were interwoven in Duffy's activities in Ireland and in Victoria. In Victoria he was welcomed, not only as a national patriot, but also as a recruit to the liberal cause in the conflict of pioneer and migrant which centred in the new Parliament. The most pressing issue in this conflict of interests was over land use, how to regulate the tenure of the squatters but also allow men with capital to set up small farms, to reconcile the interests of sheep and of homesteads.

On the land issue Duffy was on home ground. He felt that his work for the Tenant League gave him special expertise and he was enthusiastic about the possibility of making small areas of land available for the type of prosperous farmers he had met in his electorate - Irish farmers who could neither read nor write but who showed him a healthy balance in their bank books. However, when it came to translating popular demands into legislation, Duffy's own Land Act, a compromise measure giving squatters time to buy land and selectors the opportunity to peg claims only in surveyed areas, was found to have legal loopholes which enabled squatters to use dummies to buy up large areas of freehold. One interesting feature of Duffy's Act was the encouragement of experimental crops, for Duffy had a vision not only of prosperous Irish farmers, but of a variety of crops. He saw how closely parts of Victoria resembled the French wine-producing areas and wanted to encourage the establishment here of vineyards, as well as olives, tobacco, etc. - ideas only realised a century later. This capacity to think in large terms also led him to begin work immediately for Australian federation, chairing select committees and writing reports, but with no immediate success.

Land for the people was the first plank of the liberal programme. The second was protection for native industry, both of which were designed to anchor the gold field migrants in the colony. Duffy was enthusiastic about the first, but not the second. A free-trader by conviction, he rationalised his unwilling acquiescence in the growing pressure for protective duties by arguing that he needed to stay in politics to secure equity in other areas, in particular with regard to education. This was an issue on which liberalism, nationalism and religion were again

closely interwoven and in which Duffy was to become a
leading spokesman of Catholic interests. In Ireland Duffy
had worked with Protestants for an all-embracing nationalism
which would unite Protestant and Catholic, but it was a
unity to be based on equality. In Victoria he was determined
to make Catholic Emancipation a reality. On the voyage out
he had insisted that prayers should be read for Roman
Catholic passengers. In the new Parliament he introduced the
bill which abolished oaths of office, he claims to have
appointed Roman Catholics to the public service 'as a policy
proclaimed and defended, not by stealth'[13] and he argued
with another Irish-born liberal, George Higinbotham, a
lawyer from Trinity College, Dublin, about representation of
Catholics in Parliament in closer proportion to their
numbers in the colony. The central issue in this search for
freedom and equality was education. In Parliament Duffy
prefaced a speech on education with his reason for taking
for the first time in the colony a political stance
representing one section of the community - the Irish
Catholic. 'In every country in the old and the new world we
are labouring in some of the humblest, most laborious
employments for the reason that we have been debarred from
education by the iniquitous laws in our own country.'[14]
The Bishop and O'Shanassy were both out of the colony and it
fell to Duffy to marshall Catholic opposition to the 1867
Bill which provided for common religious instruction in
state schools, and in February 1868 he helped to found the
Advocate, a Catholic lay journal, writing the first
editorial, 'What shall we do in the pending elections?' The
1867 Education Bill was defeated amid great sectarian
bitterness, and the issue was still unresolved when Duffy
became Premier in 1871. Despite the prayer of David Syme,
editor of the liberal *Age*, that he keep the Pope and the
Irish out of his road, his twelve months as Premier
heightened national and religious prejudice which had been
aroused by the education question. In addition the attempted
assassination of the Duke of Edinburgh in 1868 had
stimulated rumours of Fenian conspiracy. Other factors
militated against Catholic leadership - the Pope's
denunciation of liberalism in the Syllabus of 1864, the
publication of the doctrine of Infallibility in 1870, and
nearer home, the strong line taken by the hierarchy on
education, and the results of the 1871 census which showed
an increase in the proportion of Roman Catholics in the
colony from 20.3 per cent in 1861 to 23.3 per cent in 1871.
In this setting Duffy's Ministry could be made to appear a
serious political danger. This is the version which Duffy
gives: 'They hated the ministry mainly because I was an

Irishman and a Roman Catholic.'[15] He does say mainly, but the free-traders of the squatter, merchant, banker alliance hated it because it brought in a definite protectionist tariff. The Cabinet was divided on the education issue and so brought forward no new proposals. Duffy himself was not a popular leader with strong support. He was brusque and aggressive in debate. A doctor who treated him in 1858 wrote of him as 'sincere, straight and honest, but . . . a man whose temper had been soured by adversity'.[16] By 1872 Duffy was losing touch with the main current of liberalism which was moving strongly towards higher protective tariffs.

The great lesson which Duffy and others underlined from his Victorian career was the ability of the Irish to govern. An article in the London *Spectator* in September 1871 stressed this theme:

> If anyone wishes to know what the empire loses by English inability to conciliate Irish affection, let him read the speech . . . of Mr. Gavan Duffy, the new Premier of Victoria. Mr. Duffy is an Irishman, Catholic and a rebel, a typical man of the class which we English say can neither govern nor be governed; but he speaks like the man for whom the Tories are sighing, the born administrator, utterly free of flummery and buncombe.[17]

Carlyle read the speech and wrote with enthusiasm 'Few British men have such a bit of work on hand. You seem to me to be . . . modelling the first elements of mighty nations over yonder . . . . Stand to your work hero like . . . be wise, be diligent, patient, faithful.'[18] After 1872 Duffy retired from active politics. He accepted a knighthood, and from 1877 to 1880 was Speaker in the stormy years of conflict between Assembly and Council which marked the end of the pioneer migrant conflict. He had built up a seaside estate at Sorrento, and he had a pension for life of £1000 a year, one of the four lucky ministers to qualify for this before the provision was revoked. This looks like a success story, but in Duffy's version it has the quality of second-best about it: 'If I could love my work as well as the work of old and love my associates half as well, this would be a heaven upon earth.'[19] Nostalgia and homesickness in the early years became mingled with disillusion in the 1870s in the tradition of the disappointed liberal. Duffy's public utterances are of Irish migrant success, but disillusion and weariness appear in his private letters. 'I am weary of new countries and long for the green pastures where we wandered of old.'[20] He wrote to Henry Parkes in Sydney 'We have lost our way here'.[21] 'I feel a strong distaste for the bitterness and the meanness and the pettiness of Colonial politics.'[22] 'We shall not create a new Arcadia in these pastoral lands, labour we ever so zealously.'[23]

When he returned to Europe in 1880 the sons who had grown up in Australia stayed behind; one, Frank, became Chief Justice of Australia. The children of his third marriage grew up in Europe and settled in Ireland. George, a member of the Peace Delegation to London in 1921, became President of the High Court, two other sons became missionary priests, and his favourite daughter, Louise, set up a progressive school in Dublin. It seems fitting that this 'man of two hemispheres' should have distinguished descendants in both Ireland and Australia. Duffy retired to the south of France, visiting London and Ireland from time to time, and became involved in three fields of activity - writing the history of the movements of the 1840s and 1850s in which he had been involved, taking an active part in the Irish literary revival, and giving enthusiastic support for Home Rule by writing persuasive articles and by lobbying. It was in this last field that his colonial experience was most clearly expressed. He returned to Europe in the new guise of a colonial statesman with the trappings of success - in English eyes at least - a knighthood and economic security. Sometimes, in true colonial fashion, he called himself a 'benighted colonist'. He brought with him a positive, constructive message which he hammered home in articles published mainly in the *Contemporary Review*, and in the Irish press between 1885 and 1891. 'Self government worked well in the great colonies. Human liberty is nowhere established on a broader or more secure basis, and nowhere answers more promptly to the ascertained will of the community, than in the great colonies enjoying responsible government.'[24] This was a restatement of that defence of colonial self-government which had been mounted by liberals such as C. H. Pearson and Duffy in the 1860s.

In these free societies, the Irish have proved that they could govern. 'They have proved their right and capacity to govern by governing.'[25] 'Men of Irish birth or blood have held the supreme offices of government in all the great possessions of the empire.'[26] The Irish have also proved that they can become prosperous. 'They have become good and prosperous citizens everywhere but in Ireland, a fact which writes the cause of their misery in characters of light.'[27] Where they have been given 'fair play' - one of Duffy's favourite phrases - they have become loyal. The Sudan expedition was organised by the Australian son of an Irish Catholic. Duffy's own life story and that of D'Arcy

McGee in Canada were cited to prove this point by both liberal and conservative in England. In his speech on the second reading of the first Home Rule Bill, Gladstone declared: 'Sir Charles Gavan Duffy exhibits in his own person as vividly as anybody the transition from a discontented to a loyal subject.'[28] These conclusions – given freedom, the Irish could govern, become prosperous and loyal citizens – were used by Duffy looking back, to justify the agitation of the 1840s and 1850s, and looking forward, as arguments for Home Rule in the 1880s.

Only self-government would satisfy Ireland. She must share in this great experiment of freedom. The colonies 'govern themselves and they are content. This was the price of peace in the colonies; it is the price of peace in Ireland and it cannot be had a fraction cheaper.'[29] 'Human nature has the same spiritual warp and woof in the Old World as in the New, and what made Irish Catholics contented and loyal on the banks of the Parramatta and the Yarra Yarra would make them contented and loyal on the banks of the Liffey.'[30] From his own experience, Duffy was aware of the sadness of exile, of migration as banishment, of the hollowness of economic security far from one's homeland. 'I long to see the energy which is conquering the Prairie and the Bush . . . let loose on our own soil. Irishmen are sometimes prosperous in other countries, but they are contented and happy I think, only in the land God gave them as a birthright and an inheritance.'[31] Canada was the pioneer of this great liberal experiment of self-government and she had the same difficulties which existed in Ireland in governing 'on the same soil, two races divided by religion and historic memories'.[32] 'She did not get Home Rule because she was loyal and friendly, but she is loyal and friendly because she got Home Rule.'[33] This sentence of Duffy's was also cited by Gladstone in his second reading speech on the first Home Rule Bill.

The Irish Question had begun to take on a new dimension. Not only were colonial examples cited to prove the value of self-government, but the Irish issue had become interwoven with one concerning all the colonies. 'Home Rule for Ireland was the first step towards the essential work of federating the Empire',[34] a task in Duffy's view which must be achieved within, at most, ten years. It was even suggested that provision should be made in an Irish constitution for the powers to be reserved for a Parliament of the Empire. A general scheme of this kind had been in Duffy's mind since at least 1874 when he visited Carnarvon, then the Colonial Secretary. At that stage, he seems to have planned for parliaments on the colonial model for each of the political divisions of the British Isles, and a grand Imperial Congress for imperial affairs.

It is interesting to see how Duffy had become more and more involved in colonial issues. He had joined the Imperial Federation League, and came to stress the urgency of some closer union. In 1890 he wrote 'I am for confederation of the Empire, and as speedily as possible under the strong conviction that if it be postponed till after a foreign fleet has bombarded Sydney, Melbourne and Cape Town, there will be only broken fragments of our colonial possessions left to federate.'[35] His arguments for Home Rule for Ireland as part of a wider scheme of federation came at a time of generally increased interest in the colonies and their relations with the mother country, and when colonial initiatives were being taken on the subject. In 1882 the Canadian Parliament voted an address to the Queen to grant Ireland Canadian Home Rule.

Those who feared and opposed Home Rule challenged the validity of this colonial parallel, in particular, A. V. Dicey. He might regard Duffy as 'by far the ablest among the Irish advocates of Home Rule',[36] but he stressed the differences between the colonial and the Irish situation, the subordination rather than the independence of the colonial Parliaments, and Gladstone again in his second reading speech on the first Home Rule Bill was careful to indicate that the Canadian case was not parallel with that of Ireland, but analagous. Duffy also had been aware of one of the great differences between the colonies and Ireland. When he arrived in Victoria, he told the colonists that they had been helped in their struggle for self-government by two potent allies — the Atlantic and the Pacific.

Thus the ideas which Duffy put forward in the 1880s were neither new nor unchallenged, but his prestige as a colonial statesman, his persistent and eloquent advocacy and his personal lobbying with some of the leading liberals and conservatives gave them considerable weight. He brought all the pressure he could muster on Lord Carnarvon whom he had visited in 1874, and Lord Ripon who had entered the House of Commons in 1852 at the same time as Duffy. Discussions with Carnarvon prompted his article in the *National Review* in 1885, 'An Appeal to the Conservative Party', and when Carnarvon became Lord Lieutenant, he published a letter to him in the *Freeman's Journal*, 'The Price of Peace in Ireland'.

From his general argument for Ireland sharing in the colonial experiment of freedom, Duffy went on to make more specific suggestions for an Irish constitution. He regarded himself, and came to be regarded, as something of an authority on this field — it is interesting that he dismissed Parnell as 'someone who had probably never read a consititution in his life time'.[37] In 1885 he published a series of articles in the *Freeman's Journal* on colonial constitutions, and in 1887 a 'Fair Constitution for Ireland' in the *Contemporary Review*. Here the constitutional provisions which he advocated or wished to avoid were rooted in his Victorian experience. He wanted a bicameral parliament, of reasonably small size, the upper house to be nominated. He was wary of an elected upper house as he had witnessed the challenge of an elected upper house to the supremacy of the lower house in Victoria. He recommended payment of members and he felt that the functions of the Lord Lieutenant 'cannot be made too closely identical with those of the Governor of a great colony'.[38] Not only the provisions but also the procedure had a colonial basis. Like the Australian colonists, the Irish must themselves take the largest share in framing the constitution. This was one of his grounds for dissatisfaction with both Gladstone's Home Rule Bills, although he had been asked for advice by Bryce on some details of the second Bill. It is interesting to note that in 1885 Bryce had suggested to Gladstone that the head of government ought if possible to be an Irishman in sympathy with the nationalist sentiments, such a person as Sir Charles Gavan Duffy.[39]

This colonial statesman who had found his way back to the Old World and who pronounced on constitutional issues was still a liberal and a moderate. He writes of *sober, ordered* liberty, of equal justice and fair play. He reminds his readers of the 'Ireland of whom none of you know much — just, moderate and national in a sense that embraces the whole nation'.[40] From this Ireland 'a substantial force of moderate, well informed, conscientious opinion . . . will make itself felt in an Irish Parliament, which does not desire separation any more than English liberals desire a republic'.[41] The moderate constitutionalist and liberal is here, but also the man whose rhetoric in the *Nation* inspired national consciousness. A letter of 1881 to Canon Doyle in praise of the Land Act is full of this same rhetoric.

> What just man will honour less the flag which for seven centuries has been lifted up anew after every defeat, which, though it was stained by the blood of its defenders, and soiled by the dust of obscure hiding places, still flies boldly on three continents, and can no more be plucked from its place than a star from the firmament . . . [42]

In reply, Canon Doyle wrote to him a few days later

In your beautiful and eloquent language you give expression to the sentiment of every Irishman deserving the name. If I mistake not, some of those soul stirring sentences will be printed in gold and flung aloft on green banners to the breeze in our future national processions.[43]

I wonder how much the unity which Duffy wove about the three periods of his life was also part of the rhetoric. Certainly behind the publicly proclaimed success story there was a disappointed and disillusioned man. So too, in retirement, he was pleased to appear as the successful ex-colonist, the living proof that given freedom and scope the Irish rebel can become a leading citizen. But again we find the sadness and resigned despair of a man growing old away from his homeland. In 1899 he wrote to a friend, 'My 84th year will commence in a few days. I am weary with the thought that my life will end without seeing the promised land.'[44]

NOTES

1. C. G. Duffy, *Thomas Davis* (London, 1890) p. 72.
2. *Age* (Melbourne), 5 Feb. 1856.
3. 'Tocsin of Ireland', cited in C. G. Duffy, *My Life in Two Hemispheres* (London, 1898) vol. i, p. 288.
4. C. G. Duffy, 'A Fair Constitution for Ireland', *Contemporary Review*, Sept. 1887, p. 311.
5. Duffy, *Thomas Davis*, p. 139.
6. Prospectus of the *Nation*, cited in Duffy, *Thomas Davis*, p. 84.
7. Duffy, *Thomas Davis*, p. 139.
8. Duffy, *My Life*, vol. i, p. 820.
9. Duffy to Parkes, 3 Apr. 1857 (Mitchell Library, Parkes Correspondence).
10. Duffy to G. H. Moore, 1 May 1856, quoted in M. C. Moore, *G. H. Moore: An Irish Gentleman* (London, 1913) p. 257.
11. Duffy to Moriarty, 12 Apr. 1856 (NLI, Monsell Papers, ms 8319).
12. Ibid., 13 Sept. 1857.
13. Duffy, *My Life*, vol. ii, p. 308.
14. *Victorian Parliamentary Debates*, vol. 8, 1869, 1830.
15. J. F. Hogan, *The Irish In Australia* (Melbourne, 1888) p. 283.
16. Motherwell to O'Brien, 14 Oct. 1858 (NLI, O'Brien Papers, ms 3073, vol. 446).
17. *Spectator*, 9 Sept. 1871.

18. Carlyle to Duffy, 28 May 1872, *My Life*, vol. ii, p. 336.
19. Duffy, *My Life*, vol. ii, p. 242.
20. Ibid., p. 378.
21. Duffy to Parkes, 27 Feb. 1877 (ML, PC).
22. Duffy to Parkes, 23 Sept. 1874 (ML, PC).
23. Duffy to Parkes, 18 Apr. 1877 (ML, PC).
24. Duffy, 'Colonial Constitutions 1', *Freeman's Journal*, 28 Aug. 1885.
25. Duffy, 'An Australian Example', *Contemporary Review*, Jan. 1888, p. 27.
26. Duffy, 'Mr. Gladstone's Irish Constitution', *Contemporary Review*, May 1886, p. 612.
27. Duffy, 'An Appeal to the Conservative Party', *National Review*, Feb. 1885, p. 74.
28. Parliamentary Debates: House of Commons Debates, ser. iii, cccv, p. 587.
29. Duffy, 'How Ireland Ought to Receive the Land Act', *Freeman's Journal*, 22 Aug. 1881.
30. Duffy, 'The Price of Peace in Ireland', *Freeman's Journal*, 22 July 1885.
31. Duffy, 'How Ireland Ought to Receive the Land Act'.
32. Duffy, 'A Fair Constitution', p. 316.
33. Duffy, 'Mr. Gladstone's Irish Constitution', p. 610.
34. Duffy, 'After the Battle', *Contemporary Review*, Aug. 1886, p. 161.
35. Duffy, 'Some Fruits of Federation', *Speaker*, 25 Jan. 1890, p. 87.
36. A. V. Dicey, *England's Case Against Home Rule* (London, 1886) p. 189.
37. Duffy, 'The Humble Remonstrance of an Irish Nationalist', *Contemporary Review*, May 1891, p. 662.
38. Duffy, 'A Fair Constitution', p. 318.
39. Bryce Memo, 11 Dec. 1885 (BL, Gladstone Papers, 44770, ff. 5-16).
40. Duffy to Ripon, 5 Aug. 1886 (BL, Ripon Papers, lv, 43545).
41. Ibid., 18 Jan. 1886.
42. Duffy, 'How Ireland Ought to Receive the Land Act'.
43. *Freeman's Journal*, 26 Aug. 1881.
44. Duffy to Sullivan, 27 Mar. 1899 (NLI, McCarthy Papers, 5937).

5 Irish Culture and Nationalism Translated: St Patrick's Day, 1888, in Australia

OLIVER MACDONAGH

Ambiguity is inherent in the political process, and perhaps most of all where, as in the Anglo-Irish case in the eighteenth and nineteenth centuries, there was a masked colonialism at play.[1] Of course, the existence of an ostensibly independent Irish Parliament before 1800, and participation in an ostensibly unitary Parliament, thereafter, forced double-thought and double-language upon the controlling power. It is not with this but with Irish nationalist ambiguity, in its constitutional form, that I am here concerned. None the less, the interaction should never be forgotten. It was British opinion, and in the last resort British opinion working in British domestic politics, which produced political change in Ireland. From stage to stage, the form of Irish pressure altered, from mollification to violence or outrage, and back again, and intermingled. But the strategic iron law – that all words and actions were ultimately to be evaluated in terms of their effects upon neighbouring opinion – endured. Thus the exterior set of ambivalences deeply affected the internal. Similarly, Irish nationalism in Australia had to accommodate itself to the dominant self-images in the colonial communities.

Let us take as an early and classic instance of the internal ambiguity in Ireland, O'Connell's campaign for repeal of the Act of Union. Strictly interpreted, repeal was politically nonsensical. The 'Grattan's Parliament' of 1782 which was being sought had rested on the basis of British political control, which had in turn depended on parliamentary corruption, and on the Protestant engrossment of local power and office. By 1830 both, in their pre-1800 forms, lay in the dustbin of history. Why, then, hope for so improbable a concession as repeal? The answer is (I think) that O'Connell did not intend it as a specific proposition or demand. It was rather, in lawyer's language, an invitation to treat, an attempt to *elicit* a proposition from the British Government. Repeal was only *apparently* a demand. In reality it represented the sloganising of pressure designed to force out a counter-offer, as is apparent in this strange passage at the close of the speech in which he launched his great popular movement in 1843: 'I will never ask for . . . any other save an independent legislative, but if others offer me a subordinate parliament, I will close with any such authorized offer and accept that offer.'[2] In short, Janus-facing both his own people and Westminster, his demand was expressed in apparently precise and precedented, but essentially empty, abstractions.

Parnell and Home Rule was the evening performance of O'Connell and repeal. Carved deep into the granite of the Parnell monument in Dublin are Parnell's best remembered words, 'No man had a right to set a boundary to the march of a nation'. But no carved words record that this characteristic sibylline threat-promise had been immediately preceded by a very specific limitation of Home Rule, for the present age, to the principles and system of 1782. A few moments earlier Parnell had asked for 'the restitution of that which was stolen from us towards the close of the last century'. 'We cannot,' he went on, 'ask for less than restitution of Grattan's Parliament, with its important privileges and wide and far-reaching constitution. We cannot under the British Constitution ask for more than the restitution of Grattan's Parliament.'[3] 'Restitution' was the incantation of Home Rule. It even opened the constitution of the Irish National League, whose first objective was declared to be 'the restitution of . . . [the Irish] parliament'. The Irish reverberations of '1782' were quite sufficient for the building of a popular front. The revolutionary potential in the idea of legislative independence was counteracted by the preservative concept of restoration; while the cruel reality of Irish sectarian hatred was masked by the association of Protestantism and patriotism implicit in the resurrection of Grattan. Meanwhile, under cover of a seeming political demand, other fundamental purposes of Home Rule in Ireland, the re-creation of national self-regard after two decades of abasement, and the fusion of the disparate native elements of power into a single aggressive unit, might be pursued.

Thus, ambiguity reigned, and had to reign, at the very apex of the nineteenth-century constitutional movements. Lower in the pyramid, however, the ambiguity was rather different in character, though no less pervasive in extent. In the nature of things, the Parliamentary Party and especially its leadership had to shape their words and actions in terms of the likely British reactions - not solely in these terms of course, but to a very considerable extent. The ordinary nationalist follower shaped his, rather, in terms of the indigenous separatist and revolutionary tradition. He had to find a way between, on the one hand, his instinctive sympathies and, on the other their apparent impracticability and the danger of venting them openly, even to himself. The difference between top and bottom was one of degree not kind, for the constitutional leadership could not altogether repudiate the violent heritage, if indeed it wished to. Still, even a difference of degree, in such a matter, has its interest.

How did the ordinary Irish nationalist try to hold the uneasy balance? By, I think, an emphasis on the past and on the personal. First, as particular manifestations of nationalistic violence receded in time so might they be the more safely sanctioned. By 1848 the Wexford rising of 1798, though execrated and repudiated by almost the entire Irish episcopate in its own day, was being held up as a noble contrast to the irresponsible vapouring of the Young Irelanders. Yet eighteen years later, when the Church was in full cry in denouncing Fenianism, the open 'nobility' of Young Ireland was made to stand in bold relief to the dark and squalid machinations of the new conspirators. In turn, in 1887, a Nenagh priest condemning the left-wing capture of the Gaelic Athletic Association, was to declare 'I have mentioned them [the Fenians] and I ask you to give a cheer for their names. I admire those men, I know they were honest and true.'[4] Meanwhile, the hagiography of the Irish revolutionary tradition was becoming a settled thing, enshrined in particular in the Sullivans' stirring compilation, *Speeches from the Dock (1867)*, and the Parnellites of the future were being reared in the classic perorations of heroic violence, from Robert Emmet's 'When my country takes her place among the nations of the earth, *then* and *not till then* let my epitaph be written' to the 'God Save Ireland' of the Manchester Martyrs.

Secondly, humanitarianism afforded an escape. Perhaps humanitarianism is not the exact word: what one really needs is a compound embracing sympathy with suffering, the distinction between a man and his beliefs, and elemental tribal identification. The Manchester executions provided a characteristic and most important opening for this form of dualism, in the flood of funeral processions, mourning demonstrations and requiem services which it released in 1868. 'For the first time during years,' wrote A. M. Sullivan, 'the distinction between Fenian and non-Fenian Nationalists seemed to disappear.'[5] Still more characteristic perhaps was the general participation in the Amnesty Association during the next two years, in prisoners' aid subscriptions and in the getting up of petitions for the pardoning of particular 'unwise but afflicted' IRB men. In this particular nationalistic genre, old age and, later, death were the great blurrers of offences. When, for example, James Stephens, the begetter of Fenianism, returned to Ireland in 1885, impoverished and rejected by the French republicans, many priests presided over the meetings of sympathy, and many contributed to the fund for Stephens's relief. As always the well-poised Archbishop Croke struck the perfect balance. In subscribing 5 to the relief fund, he eulogised Stephens's selfless patriotism, adding however that he had ever been 'a deluded lover of his country'.[6]

So much for the setting of the stage: let us now turn to what was said and done in Australia on St Patrick's Day 1888. The centenary year was peculiarly favourable to political convergence in the southern colonies. Gladstone's recent conversion to Home Rule had transformed the standing of Irish nationalism there. For the first time, it could be plausibly presented as supportive of instead of inimical to the Empire. Moreover, by 1888 the sectarian passions in the colonies over the education issue had been largely spent, while those to be fired by the rise of labour were not yet manifest. All this means, of course, that 1888 was quite extraordinary. But the uncommon harmony will, it is hoped, throw into better relief more than one element which might stay otherwise concealed.

The staple of St Patrick's Day celebrations was the athletic sports meeting. In Victoria alone such meetings were held in Melbourne, Ballarat, Bendigo, Echucha, Geelong, Rochester, Benalla, Wangaratta, and doubtless many smaller places. Horse-races - St Patrick's Day meetings - were also common. But unless the horse-racing itself, or the number of protests, be so accounted, it is difficult to see these as peculiarly Irish, apart from such trivia as green race cards or a profusion of green gowns, harmonising, as the *Age* once reported, with the grass.[7] There were some distinctive Irish items at the athletic meetings. Hurling matches took place at the 1888 meetings in Brisbane, Sydney, Melbourne and Ballarat, with the winning team placed first and the loser second. Here and there, there was 'Irish' wrestling, distinctive enough at least, to have puzzled Cornishmen.[8] The reel and jig contests were indubitably Irish, although their accompaniment, at Melbourne, by two brass bands instead of fiddles was scarcely 'native'; and *Scottish* dancing was included in several programmes. But generally the sports - bicycle and track-races, pole-vaults, high-jump and shot-putting - were the run-of-the-mill events of the 1880s. They were, moreover, the target of semi-professional athletes, and a magnet for gambling and swindles. At Rochester the favourite, Egan, was so jostled that a race-off against all comers was arranged after an inquiry by the stewards; in Melbourne one competitor, Bloxham, was challenged as running - and being handicapped - under a false name; and throughout Victoria there were disputes as to whether the contests conformed to the then-fashionable Sheffield rules. Besides, the sports meetings were often of interest to less than half the spectators. *Al fresco* dancing, picnicking and fun-fairs might take place side by side with the athletics. The 'gigantic picnic' in which the Geelong sports were embedded in 1888 was praised as a striking innovation; and the report from Corowa spent less space on its cricket, football and athletic contests than on the 'undergrowth abounding [which] afforded ample room for lovers to bill and coo while the open spaces were availed of for dancing, kiss in the ring, tip cat etc.'. Only in Sydney were speeches an added feature of the entertainment. But then the Sydney celebrations had a much more decidedly political air than any other.[9]

Who organised these programmes? Most commonly, the Hibernian (more fully the Hibernian Australian Catholic Benefit) Society, a 'friendly' association, some forty years old,[10] with branches throughout the continent, and several in each of the larger cities. Often they worked in harness with the local St Patrick's Societies, quasi-political organisations, so far as I can tell, to some extent overlapping with the branches of the Irish National League. In one or two cases, Geelong for instance, what appears to have been a Catholic parish club also played a part. Sydney was unusual in that five years before the Hibernian had been displaced as organiser by the United Irish Societies, the Shamrock and St Patrick's, with a consequent heavy list towards Irish nationalism. But the widespread Hibernian Society predominance meant a general stress on good citizenship in the colonies, and had some importance in drawing in non-Irish support. In Brisbane, for example, most of the other friendly societies joined in the celebration; and elsewhere 'alien' speakers singled out the Hibernian for praise as a community venture in self-help.[11]

Most of the celebrations made money, with an interesting variety of destinations. In Sydney and Adelaide, all takings (and in Sydney they were very large) went to the Irish

Evicted Tenants Fund; in Perth to West Australian flood relief; in Bendigo to the local Catholic schools; and in Melbourne to an unspecified charity and a parish hall. Brisbane boxed the compass. The main celebration there, the sports-cum-communal picnic, contributed to essentially cross-communal and humanitarian purposes. But a second collection was taken up for the Evicted Tenants Fund, which, given the Irish circumstances of the day, was an unadulterated political cause. Finally, the proceeds of another Brisbane celebration, the steamer excursions up the river, were directed to a local charity, the Brisbane Hospital. This medley of purposes epitomises the heterogeneity, not to say ambivalence, in the country as a whole.[12]

What topped and tailed the main St Patrick's Day event? In three places at least there were St Patrick's Eve festivities, that at Perth taking the bizarre form of a Grand Walking Tournament which ended in a Royal Irish Ball. Universal however were the special masses and sermons with which the feast day opened. St Patrick's Day had been 'retrenched' as a holyday of obligation for Australian Catholics, but they were most strongly urged to attend church as a matter of all sorts of piety. How many did so, or how they related mass to other celebrations is necessarily unknown. All we *can* say is that the processions were timed to fit the ending of the religious services. Processions to the sports grounds were very general. In some places such as Adelaide and Ballarat they began at the Catholic Cathedral. In several the schoolchildren (Catholic presumably) were dragooned into the march: Ballarat had the sad addition of a squadron from the Orphan Asylum. The two largest processions, at Sydney and Melbourne, are worth a closer scrutiny. The Sydney cortege, several thousand strong, marched from St Benedict's church to the tramways terminal, led by one O'Farrell on horseback 'emblazoned in . . . green and gold' and Sergeant Donovan 'of mounted sword combat fame'. At the head of the parade proper marched the Highland pipers - this ecumenical gesture was warmly welcomed later - playing 'Bonnie Dundee'. Lower down the line, the Burwood and the Fife and Drum Bands responded antiphonally with Irish airs. Somewhere in the middle the Irish National League officers rode in a jaunting car, all emerald in trappings; many of the marchers wore 'Remember Mitchelstown' badges, and mementoes of William O'Brien; 'Remember Tullamore' (from which prison O'Brien had been released on 20 January) was emblazoned on one flag, carried by a little boy attired entirely in green velvet; among the other 'banners and regalia' were those of the Holy Australian Catholic Guilds, the Sacred Heart Literary

Society and the Sydney Hurlers; and at the rear of all sat the officers of the Shamrock Club displayed upon a huge green dray. As the procession passed the Town Hall 'three Irish cheers' were given for Harris, the first Irish lord mayor of the city.[13]

The reports of the Melbourne procession give no suggestion of an Irish political demonstration. The ten banners of the branches of the Hibernian Society were noted only for their depiction of the saint and 'great beauty of design'. All told, Melbourne seems to have been a rather dispirited affair. The weather was cold, gloomy and wet; the crowd was smaller and less green-decked than usual; and the tramways would not halt their services for the quarter hour necessary for the procession to cross the tracks, nor the police intervene on behalf of the marchers, so that the procession was halted repeatedly.[14]

Finally, let us see one small march, at Bendigo, without retrospective intrusion - 'just as real', to apply Hawthorne's encomium of 1860 on Trollope's novels, 'as if some giant had hewn a great lump out of the earth and put it under a glass case, with all the inhabitants going about their daily business, and not suspecting that they were made a show of.'[15] On 19 March, the *Bendigo Advertiser* reported:

It was eleven o'clock before Marshal Flood got his forces into processional array, and a start was made. First came Northcott's band playing 'St. Patrick's Day in the morning', then followed the Bishop's carriage containing Coadjutor Bishop Reville, Revs. Fathers Barry, Crane, and Murphy; a carriage containing the mayor (Mr. T. J. Connelly), Crs. Carolin, Hayes, O'Neill, Bailes, Sterry, and Dr. Quick; a buggy containing Mr. D. O'Keefe, and Father Landy, of Castlemaine; the children of St. Kilian's and the other Catholic schools, who were dressed in white and wore green sashes; a lorry, on which was placed the handsome banner of the H. C. A. B. Society; a Highland piper, in full costume, playing 'The Wearin' of the green', (present no doubt, out of compliment to the fact that the gentleman whose day they were celebrating was born near Dumbarton, in Scotland); the members of the society wearing their regalia; the Myer's Flat and Sandhurst hurling clubs, the latter of whom had their 'sticks' painted blue and green, scarcely an artistic combination, but withal effective; last but not least, came Mr. P. Maher with a drag containing a few of the most decrepit of the asylum inmates. On the box seat of the drag was seated Considine, the Irish piper, who played the

'Boyne water' very gently for the benefit of these lingerers on life's threshold.

The evening entertainments were more socially and culturally divided than the sports or the processions. The music halls in the capitals, the Bijous and the Tivolis, put on some Irish items, or in one case at least an entire Irish night. Higher in the scale was the ubiquitous National Concert. In the smaller places the 'National' tended to be diluted. At Ballarat for instance all the performers seem to have been solidly Anglo-Saxon in name, at least: 'Mr. Woodcock rose to the occasion; he was in splendid voice, and rarely has been heard to better advantage than . . . in "Molly Asthore". . . . It is always unnecessary to say that Mrs. Carter sang well'; and Master Gude on the violin received a similar, though more happily phrased, accolade. The jewel of the evening at Ballarat appears to have been 'Lesbia hath a Beaming Eye'.[16] With corresponding catholicity, Hobart opened with the overture to *Il Trovatore* rendered by the Federal Band.[17]

All the items at the Hibernian Hall Concert in Melbourne were claimed to be - shades of the *Nation* and Young Ireland! - 'racy of the soil'. Perhaps: but Moore's Melodies predominated, and even these were 'interspersed with comic songs and step-dancing'. The selections at the Sydney National Concert were, without exception, Irish. But they combined traditional airs, such as the 'The Coulin'; the inevitable Moore's Melodies - repeatedly; '98 ballads with the 'Shan Van Vocht'; Fenian songs, such as 'The Rising of the Moon'; and plain tin-pan alley in 'The Dear Little Shamrock' and similar effusions. 'The Wearing of the Green' brought down the house, but with a new final verse:

At least we know each other's hearts
What foe does come between?
We'll weave the Shamrock with the Rose
And wear the Red and Green.

To complete the gallimaufry, the evening ended with audience and performers singing together 'God Save Ireland',[18] by now the alternative anthem of Irish nationalism.

At the apex of the night festivities stood the formal banquet, with its roll of toasts and speeches. In several places, the banquet was capped by a ball; generally the ladies watched the eating, or ate more delicately, in the galleries, although at Melbourne they enjoyed, or endured, full parity. Two of the main objectives (and indeed annual anxieties) of the organisers of these climactic events were to muster as many as possible of the prominent Irish or Catholics in the colony, and to entice as many as possible of the colony's leading men, especially politicians, to grace the table and move the toasts.

The evening oratory takes us a little deeper in ambiguity. Perhaps its most interesting expression was an address delivered by Carr, the newly appointed Catholic Archbishop, in the Melbourne Town Hall on 'the story of Ireland as told in her songs'. The occasion was as ecumenical as could well be arranged; and Carr insisted that the celebration was not exclusively Irish, let alone aggressive, and that the 'broad liberality' manifested by the Mayor's attendance was a most joyous sign. Carr's was a skilful performance, nicely catholic in every sense. Curiously enough perhaps, Davis, Mangan and the *Nation* school constituted the main frame of reference and recipients of praise for 'not only a faithful reflection of the past, but also the strongest stimulus to exertion in the future'. But the ballads selected for particular consideration celebrated Owen Roe O'Neill and Brian Boru, the two 'patriots' who might most plausibly be represented as Catholic and Irish warriors in one. Moreover, Carr continued, although the *Nation* balladeers recalled essentially the centuries of 'bondage and oppression', Ireland was now being 'gradually resurrected from this tomb'; and even the bondage and oppression might indeed be part of God's dispensation in scattering the Irish across the world 'to be the salt and the seasoning of the nations amongst whom they have settled'. Carr ended by calling on the Irish Australians to show 'magnanimous forgiveness of past wrongs' in their new country, and 'practical sympathy' for their motherland 'in her present distress'.[19] The balance was held between the words and the deeds of Young Ireland, between nationality and religion, between glorious violence in the past and present pacific agitation, between the sustenance derived from the recollection of former wrongs and their irrelevance to present action.

The Melbourne crop of notabilities for Carr's meeting and the Hibernian and St Patrick's Society's banquets was thin indeed. Between them, the three events drew only Colman O'Loghlen, John Gavan Duffy and one other 'Irish' member of the Legislative Assembly; Nicholas Fitzgerald from the Council; the Mayor, Alderman Benjamin; Mr Justice Quinlan; and the two radical politicians, Gaunson and Mirams. The Catholic *Advocate* was reduced to adding an ex-mayor of St Kilda to the list. The speeches were correspondingly anodyne. Only O'Loghlen sounded the faintest note of Irish nationalism, glancing at 1798 only to say that the modern equivalent of the oppression of that year was the Coercion

Acts - which he then invited the audience to imagine in operation in Victoria. But Home Rule as imperial strength, and adulation of Gladstone and Morley, were his leading themes. Fitzgerald was still more compliant to his surroundings. After approving St Patrick for a conquest of Ireland 'unstained by one drop of martyr's blood', he concluded, amid warm applause, that the Irish yielded 'to no section of their fellow colonists in their fond desire ... to maintain the fame, and promote the unity, strength and honour of the Empire'.[20]

Things were rather different at Sydney. There, if I may so put it, genuine ambiguity held the field. The sports meeting speeches read primarily like an annual report for 1887 on the Irish struggle. Progress and the change wrought by the conversion of Gladstone's Liberals to Home Rule were certainly acknowledged. But the land war itself, the greed and cruelty of the proprietors and the suffering of the political prisoners were mainly emphasised. At the same time, even Freehill himself, the ardent President of the Irish National League, went out of his way to repudiate hostility to Britain: Home Rule was in no way 'inimical to the well-being of the British Empire'; and the cheers which closed the meeting were for - in descending order - the Queen, Mr Gladstone, William O'Brien, T. D. Sullivan, Mr Blunt and Father McFadden, an imprisoned priest.[21]

The Sydney banquets were much more successful, qualitatively as well as numerically, than Melbourne's. The St Patrick's dinner was attended not only by the Lord Mayor and numerous local mayors and aldermen, but also by the former Premier, Sir John Robertson, Mr Justice Stephen, the Archbishop, Moran, nine members of the Legislative Assembly, eleven doctors and four army officers; and even the Governor and the Anglican primate sent formal apologies for absence. In these circumstances, it was important that no loyalist should be put to the blush. By the repeated assertion that the Home Rule sought for Ireland was precisely what New South Wales already enjoyed, even Stephen was set at ease. He toasted Ireland as a nation, he said, but not with any idea that she should be dismembered from the Empire. He had determined to leave had he heard the shadow of a sentiment to which a loyal subject of the Queen could not listen; but no such shadow had fallen[22] - yet Emmet, Arthur O'Connor and 'that group of young Athenians', the Young Irelanders, were among those lauded on the night!

The president of the Shamrock Club, John McGuinness, in moving 'Ireland a nation' at his dinner, traced the line of martyrs directly and exclusively in the armed revolutionary tradition from 1798 to 1867. But then the gear changed.

Whereas, he concluded, 'each thrilling epoch' to the present had been 'sanctified' by a rising, the current heroes were those jailed for land agitation at Tullamore, and the 'gallant Englishmen', Gladstone, Morley and Scawen Blunt. Another orator, W. P. Cawley, struck the precise note of vapid bellicosity: 'Sometimes we have felt the old warlike spirit arise in us, but we have consoled ourselves with the belief that the cause of our country will be won by peaceable means.' Home Rule would come because the Irish were united under leaders they would 'follow to the battle field if necessary. We will never cease . . . until the old green flag that has been carried to victory so often over many a bloody battlefield is once more planted in the Old House [of Commons] in College Green.'[23] This stirring flight ended somewhat lamely with thanks to Messrs Toohey, the Sydney brewers for a donation of 20 towards prizes for the sporting events! But James Toohey's own turn at banquet eloquence had soared far above the material by proclaiming the attachment of all Irish-Australians to the 'dying words' of their 'darling patriot' - and Emmet's speech from the dock was aired yet again. But, Toohey continued, the day was almost upon them when Ireland would 'be reverenced by England as a sister, and not humbled as a slave' - significant if simple imagery. Perhaps it can be all summed up in that the first three toasts were to the Queen, the Prince of Wales and the royal family, before Toohey's speech caused the entire company to rise to 'God Save Ireland', the dying words of other darling patriots at Manchester.[24]

As even this outline of what was done and said suggests, the Australian role of St Patrick's Day was complex. Setting the larger matters of ideology and identification momentarily aside, it seems clear that the celebration of 1888 had - not solely perhaps but substantially - a cohesive function in the colonies. It could scarcely be exclusive. The very effort to mobilise that indistinct category, 'the Irish', enforced a wide and loose view of Hibernicity upon the organisers. Moreover, Irish-Australia had been formed much too early for the concept of cultural and linguistic separatism, only now beginning to emerge at home, ever to take root in the new soil. Further, political radicalism was still in suspense in Ireland; no serious challenge to 'the Party' was yet practicable. In these circumstances, the notion, 'Irishness', was capable of virtually indefinite expansion in the colonies, and Irish and Australian loyalties and political goals could be colourably presented as compatible, indeed positively convergent. In its turn, this must surely have opened a way for traffic with the Australian community at large, and contributed to forming patterns or sequences of general social ritual and community mobilisation in a new land. Especially was this the case in the smaller places: the report from Ararat[25] that many 'Saxons' celebrated the festival as fervently as the Irish 'out of compliment to their fellow citizens' could be multiplied. It seems to me no coincidence that - to pick apparently trivial but, I think, telling instances - the pivotal celebration of the Australian St Patrick's Day was the sports meeting, or that the little concerts should have been general town affairs, or that Moore (of all Irishmen) should have been called upon most often, and in speech as well as song, to symbolise and epitomise the day.

At the deeper level of allegiance, the whole superficially bewildering spectacle of political ambivalence and contrariety is not, I think, really difficult to comprehend or empathise with. For to return to our starting point, we are dealing with a doubly colonial condition in the case of Irish nationalist expatriates of whom confessions of imperial faith were, almost ritualistically, demanded. Even at the extremity of Australian Irish nationalism - and this was very far from being extreme in 1888 - the colonial condition enjoined a considerable measure of conformity as well as of defiance, conformity being necessary for social survival, defiance for self-regard. The two might even meet in the desire for parity of esteem in the new society.

Perhaps we can understand this phenomenon most clearly if we look for a moment at the dichotomy in the Irish-American *avant garde* between the idealistic, rebel and working-class strain and its opposite, the drive towards achievement, success, conformity, and the satisfaction of social aspiration. These did not necessarily form antithetical groups within a movement. The very same persons might be driven alternately by either impulse; and, as the ultimate refinement in ambiguity, it might be possible for them to exploit to this end their very dilemma itself. If (the argument might run) the Irish were victims of the same imperial system as had debased the thirteen colonies; if they were seeking to establish the same democratic, egalitarian and republican principles in Ireland which Americans supposed themselves to enjoy at home - then were they not on a level, in aspiration and civic virtue, with the rest? 'Dual allegiance' had thus an interior dualism of its own.[26] Albeit in paler form, this serves to explain the uses of such a concept as Home Rule in the Australian colonies in the late 1880s.

But doubtless the majority of Irish-born, or Irish-derived, colonists felt small need of even this degree of subtlety. For them, St Patrick's Day may have had a much simpler, Australianising function. The colonial press, at its most kindly, took an assimilationist line. On an earlier occasion, the Brisbane *Courier* having lauded St Patrick as an opponent of violence and friend of mutual toleration, went on to describe the mental revolution which Irishmen underwent upon Australian soil. 'They search in vain for the oppressor and sanguinary tyrant, the hereditary foe of their race whose misdeeds have been the stock theme of patriotic agitators. The hereditary bondsman now sees him as only a friend with outstretched hands welcoming him as a fellow citizen and countryman.'[27] Similarly, the *South Australian Register* observed on 17 March 1888, that 'There is no harm done if the observances of distinct nationalities do not interfere with the progress of that national spirit which changed climates and altered conditions bring. . . . Australia looks kindly upon such manifestations as to-day's celebration. . . .' But, as we have seen, if there an assimilative process at work, it was neither one-directional nor simple. Clearly, in favourable circumstances, such as those of 1888, the festival had a socialising rather than a separating function, most strikingly in the outback and the smaller towns. But if it provided the Irish with bridges into the larger community, it was also helping to transfer Irish cultural elements, crude and derivative as well as genuinely traditional, to the emergent Australian patterns, especially the patterns of style, sentiment and recreation. Simultaneously, if paradoxically, it may have eased the supersession of Irish by Australian identification. In short, St Patrick's Day 1888 may be seen as - among many other things - a celebration of the rites of passage.

NOTES

1. This paper extends the arguments of O. MacDonagh, 'Ambiguity in Nationalism - the Case of Ireland', *Historical Studies* (Melbourne) vol. xix, no. 76 (Apr. 1981) pp. 337-52, especially in section I.
2. *A Full and Revised Report of the Three Days' Discussion in the Corporation of Dublin on the Repeal of the Union* . . ., ed. J. Levy (Dublin, 1843) pp. 191-2.
3. *Freeman's Journal* (Dublin), 18 Oct. 1882; see also F. S. L. Lyons, *Charles Stewart Parnell* (London, 1977) pp. 235-6.

4. *Tipperary Advocate*, 26 Nov. 1887, quoted in J. P. P. O'Shea, 'The Priest and Politics in County Tipperary 1850-1891', Ph.D. thesis, NUI (1979) p. 201.
5. A. M. Sullivan, *New Ireland: Political Sketches and Personal Reminiscences*, 5th edn (London, 1878) vol. ii, p. 203.
6. *Freeman's Journal* (Dublin), 2 Jan. 1887.
7. *Age* (Melbourne), 18 Mar. 1880.
8. Ibid.
9. *Age, Argus* (Melbourne), *Ballarat Courier, Courier* (Brisbane), *Sydney Morning Herald*, 19 Mar. 1888; *Albury Border Post and Wodonga Advertiser*, 23 Mar. 1888; *Advocate* (Melbourne), *Freeman's Journal* (Sydney), 24 Mar. 1888.
10. The Society, in its 1888 form, may have been a more recent foundation, but its antecedents lie in the 1840s
11. *Advocate*, 10 Mar. 1888; *Sydney Morning Herald*, 17 Mar. 1888; *Argus*, 17 and 19 Mar. 1888; *Age*, 19 Mar. 1888; P. Ford, *Cardinal Moran and the ALP* (Melbourne, 1966) p. 184.
12. *West Australian* (Perth), 16 Mar. 1888; *Argus, Bendigo Advertiser, Courier* (Brisbane), *South Australian Register* (Adelaide), *Sydney Morning Herald*, 19 Mar. 1888.
13. *West Australian*, 16 Mar. 1888; *Sydney Morning Herald*, 19 Mar. 1888; *Advocate Freeman's Journal* (Sydney), 24 Mar. 1888.
14. *Advocate*, 24 Mar. 1888.
15. M. Sadlier, *Trollope: a Commentary*, new edn (London, 1945) p. 240, n. 1.
16. *Courier* (Brisbane), 18 Mar. 1880; report from *Ballarat Star* in *Advocate*, 24 Mar. 1888.
17. *Mercury* (Hobart), 20 Mar. 1888.
18. *Sydney Morning Herald*, 19 Mar. 1888; *Advocate*, 24 Mar. 1888.
19. *Advocate*, 24 Mar. 1888.
20. Ibid.
21. *Sydney Morning Herald*, 19 Mar. 1888; *Freeman's Journal* (Sydney), 24 Mar. 1888.
22. *Sydney Morning Herald*, 19 Mar. 1888.
23. *Freeman's Journal* (Sydney), 24 Mar. 1888.
24. Ibid.
25. *Ararat Advertiser*, 20 Mar. 1880.
26. For a development of this argument, see O. MacDonagh, 'The Irish Famine Migration to the United States', in D. Fleming and B. Bailyn (eds), *Perspectives in American History*, vol. x (Harvard, 1976) pp. 437-46.
27. 17 Mar. 1880.

6 Irish Nationalism and the British Empire in the Late Nineteenth Century

H. V. BRASTED

In the historiography of Irish nationalism in the late nineteenth century the emphasis is less on the ideological content and complexities of nationalist thought than on its political expression. That is to do less than justice, perhaps, to the brief sallies by L. McCaffrey on Isaac Butt's 'federalism'[1] and F. S. L. Lyons on Charles Stewart Parnell's economic ideas[2] and, certainly, to the more substantial *Ireland's English Question* by Patrick O'Farrell.[3] Richard Davis' exploration of the infusion of new intellectual concepts to Irish nationalism in *Arthur Griffith and Non-Violent Sinn Fein* might be similarly excepted.[4] None the less, it remains substantially true that, apart from N. Mansergh's *The Irish Question 1840-1921*, [5] there has been very little investigation of nationalist ideas and their influence particularly in the time of Butt and Parnell. A generation of historians led by Conor Cruise O'Brien has tended to concentrate on defining the political context in which nationalists were forced to act and to explain their political behaviour in terms of that context. For the immensely influential O'Brien the strength of Parnellism, for example, lies not so much in the evolution of a coherent and rational philosophy of nationalism as its leader's grasp of and response to the 'great forces' making for political change.[6] The result has been if not to ignore the role of ideology in promoting political action at least, in part, to discount it.

The purpose of this paper is to throw some light on the connection between ideological perspectives and nationalist responses, taking Irish attitudes to the British Empire in the late nineteenth century as a case study. Specifically, it is hoped to show that these attitudes served to clarify the nationalist impulse and the politics it governed. A growing awareness of Ireland's position within the British imperial framework launched Irishmen into a reappraisal of nationalist goals and the principles on which they were founded. Both were subjected by the factor of empire to more stringent tests of acceptability. In the process not only was a new code of behaviour established but new solutions to the Irish Question were arrived at. Irish nationalism itself underwent significant redefinition and enrichment.

According to Mansergh, in Ireland, as elsewhere, the 'purpose of nationality' was invariably 'forgotten in the immediate struggle for independence'. The predominant outlook was basically insular;[7] not so when the intrusion of the British Empire widened the dimension of nationalist discussion. By the 1870s, nationalists were becoming increasingly aware that the context in which the Irish Question was debated was being subtly altered by non-parochial considerations. First, the legacy of the Famine and the migration of an 'unending exodus of a permanently antagonised population' especially to the United States, and to a lesser extent to Canada, Australia and New Zealand, elevated the condition of Ireland to the level of an international issue.[8] Secondly, English statesmen, Liberals as well as Conservatives, responded to the challenge of Home Rule by treating it as a threat to imperial integrity. Here was a case of the English for once changing the question in order to forestall local remedy. The exact nexus between Home Rule and imperial security was spelled out in a Victorian 'domino theory' by Lord Salisbury, its leading proponent. In 1883 he presented the argument that if the forces of nationalism and revolution were allowed to triumph on the doorstep of the imperial centre, they must triumph in the far-flung Empire where British power was fragmented. Should Irish aspirations be met, then the Empire would disintegrate 'step by step' as if set off by a 'chain reaction'.[9] For Salisbury and the 'dominoists' the tide of Irish nationalism could be swept back not by appeasement but only through 'a courageous maintenance of the rights' of empire.[10] As Michael Davitt recalled, Englishmen began to be schooled in the faith that the very existence of the British Empire depended on the maintenance of a single Parliament for Great Britain and Ireland.[11]

Broadly speaking, the British Empire was incorporated into Irish nationalist thinking in three distinct ways. At one extreme imperial partnership was advocated as a solution to the Irish Question. This approach was favoured by the Buttites who opted for a type of federalism achievable within the confines of simple local adjustment. At the other extreme were descendants of the republican tradition with their emphasis on imperial destruction through violent means as the appropriate objective. Coming somewhere in between was the Parnellite programme of Irish freedom based in part on imperial metamorphosis, or the transformation of empire into commonwealth.

The first Home Rule conference of November 1873 has been adopted as the point of departure, because it sets the scene for the struggles that are to follow under Isaac Butt and Charles Stewart Parnell, marking out the conflicting positions of moderate and activist parliamentary nationalists on the nature of the imperial connection and on suitable methods to secure its modification. The attitude stamped by Isaac Butt in a pamphlet on federalism [12] before the conference and at the Rotunda, where it was held, was symptomatic of a large body of conservative opinion. Basically, Home Rule as outlined by Butt was designed, as McCaffrey puts it, to secure Ireland most of the advantages of self-government without sacrificing any of the benefits of British association.[13] 'The true solution', he affirmed, was neither separation nor simple repeal which would be hopeless and injurious, but the 'federation of the Empire on the basis of self-governed nations'.[14] If, as David Thornley has stated, these federal proposals looked ahead to an entire system of imperial devolution,[15] it is certain that Butt himself did not have the prescience to include the coloured colonies and dependencies in his scheme. On the contrary he specifically excluded them. Satisfaction for Ireland, he frequently reassured Parliament, would in no way affect Britain's imperial prerogatives. In essence Butt saw Irish Home Rule as a unique phenomenon conditioned by the special relationship between Britain and Ireland, and therefore unlikely to have repercussions in the empire at large. Indeed, a liberated Ireland under Butt's arrangement would pull its weight as an imperial partner.[16]

From the very start imperialism was a fundamental plank on which Butt built his nationalist platform. In his opening address to the conference he linked the two together in support of his federal interpretation of Home Rule. In a manner reminiscent more of a colonial oppressor than of a leading advocate of the constitutional parliamentary tradition, he argued that Ireland was entitled to her blood money:

> The United Kingdom of which Ireland is now a part, has vast foreign and colonial possessions. Many of these possessions have been acquired during the period of our disastrous partnership of seventy years. Heaven knows we have paid dearly enough for them. We are entitled to our share in them . . . . [17]

There was no trace here of any notion of universal liberty. The rights Butt appealed to were those of the conquerors.

The greatest empire that Europe had ever seen had been won since the Union of 1801 with the aid of 'Irish valour' and the sacrifice of Irish wealth. In short, the Empire belonged to Ireland as much as it did to England. But only federalism, by preserving the opportunities of imperial employment, could secure Ireland's just inheritance. Separation would automatically jeopardise it.[18] As Mitchell Henry candidly put it, India supplied 'too many openings' for even Irishmen 'to be indifferent to it'.[19] The seventh resolution which he moved was passed unanimously: 'That in the opinion of this Conference, a Federal arrangement based upon these principles, would consolidate the strength and maintain the integrity of the Empire, and add to the dignity and power of the Imperial Crown.'[20] Thus expressed, Home Rule meant Ireland for the Irish but also the rest of the Empire into the bargain.

Although Butt carried the conference his views on federalism and its concomitant of an Irish involvement in the maintenance and growth of the Empire did not receive an unequivocal stamp of approval. W. J. O'Neill Daunt, an old repealer, gave firm warning that although delegates acquiesced in federalism their continued support was conditional on substantial and immediate results. Should the present system of 'nominal incorporation with England' be prolonged, he promised that the words 'British Empire' would be rendered hateful to Irishmen and the British connection would emerge a 'galling' chain.[21] While Daunt was no rebel to the Crown and no advocate of separation,[22] he realised that the factor of Union gave Ireland a not incongruous stake in either the preservation or destruction of the Empire: 'It [the Union] gives Ireland a certain interest in the overthrow of the Empire on the same principle that prisoners in the hold of a slave-ship would welcome shipwreck as affording them a desperate chance of escaping from their bondage.'[23] If federalism offered the empire the co-operation and the partnership of Irishmen, its rejection guaranteed their non-co-operation and the progression to complete severance.

In practice Buttite Home Rule made very little headway. The party which was elected to Parliament in 1874 was simply not geared to undertake a strong, independent, Irish line. In keeping with an occasional pressure-group its membership was both scattered and indistinct in the House of Commons. Allegiance, in effect, meant voting for an annual Home Rule motion but otherwise according to individual inclination and former habit. To this institutional weakness was added tactical impotence. Butt's policy was one of conciliation, of convincing the English mind by reasoned argument and impeccable manners that Irish government could be safely devolved on Irish gentlemen.[24] Obstruction and belligerency were always ruled out and contentious issues were avoided for fear that they might impair the disposition of Englishmen to give Irish demands a just hearing. According to William O'Brien there was nothing now for an Irish member to do 'except drink himself to death'.[25]

The fatal flaw of Buttite nationalism ultimately lay in its ideological vagueness. For a start, the implications of Home Rule and the particular means by which it was to be attained were never clearly thought out. Home Rule simply proclaimed the political philosophy of self-determination. But the birth of this phase did not cause the death of a traditional frame of mind. If the inalienable right of Ireland to be restored her Parliament was insisted upon, almost nothing else was or could be. Conservative elements, whose commitment to Home Rule must even be doubted, were thus able to infiltrate the party.[26] The price of their reconciliation to Home Rule was the persistence of imperialist loyalties and indifferent allegiance to Irish interests.

Significantly, it was an issue bound up with the welfare of the British Empire that undermined Buttite nationalism and led to its purification and refinement. In August 1878, ignoring a rare party decision to vote as a critical unit on the Government's Eastern policy, Butt indulged instead in an unashamed panegyric on imperialism. Supporting the Disraeli-Salisbury line on the delimitation of the Balkans he argued that it was England's providential mission to thwart Russian ambitions in the region.[27] His speech foreshadowed the very best Kipling sentiments and served to destroy the personal affection of the Irish for Butt, which the complete failure of his policy had not done. Suddenly, he and fifteen Home Rulers who voted with him were subjected to impassioned condemnation. All were accused of selling out to the enemy, of betraying the principles of their party, and of working towards its disintegration.[28] Treason was the predominant charge. The *Nation* for example, was outraged that Butt especially could talk such 'rampant Britonism as would have beseemed the most thoroughbred Saxon in the whole assembly'.[29] For the first time in the history of the Home Rule movement, nationalism was determined on the basis of imperial attitudes, and on this criterion Butt and his fellow conservatives had failed the acid test. Their nationalism was considered counterfeit, a gross misrepresentation of the genuine feeling of the Irish people.[30] Whatever the Buttites might say about Russian despotism the choice before them had been one between the advocacy of independence and British power as the solution of the Balkan problem.[31] It was as British citizens rather than Irish patriots that they had been seen to opt for the latter.[32]

Daunt's prophecy had in fact come true. The concept of imperial partnership was jettisoned as ideologically unsuitable and politically bankrupt. Excessive attachment to the Empire had done nothing to advance the Home Rule cause and was becoming untenable to nationalists in general. Even the *Freeman's Journal*, a firm supporter of moderation in the past, could muster no enthusiasm for this approach while the English remained indifferent to Irish demands.[33] Buttite federalism was thus thrown back into the melting pot.

The most extreme reappraisal of Irish nationalist requirements emanated from outside the constitutional parliamentary tradition. The solution progressively advanced by American Fenians and their most distinctive institution Clan na Gael was almost the exact antithesis of Butt's. They sought complete separation for Ireland by means of imperial dissolution. The classic expression of this outlook was articulated by Patrick Ford,[34] the editor and proprietor of the influential *Irish World* of New York, for a number of years the official mouthpiece of Clan na Gael. Purveyed through the proselytising columns of the *Irish World* Irish-American nationalism constituted a frothy mixture of global terrorism against the British Empire and christian service to downtrodden humanity. In its most volatile form it sought to synchronise Irish insurrection with a strategy of guerrilla warfare against British colonial possessions. But it also involved distinct moral and idealistic duties. Ford constantly preached to nationalists in Ireland that if they sought justice on the principle of self-determination they must learn to apply it universally rather than merely parochially.

From its inception federalism was treated disdainfully by Ford as an inferior expression of Irish will. As early as 1875 he warned Butt that it could never enable Ireland to rise 'to the true dignity of her nationhood'. [35] The ambivalence of Irish attitudes towards the British connection and the various statements of unashamed reverence for the Empire eventually provoked Ford to fulminate against the 'criminal' inconsistency of the Irish case. He was particularly pained by Butt's frequent assurances in Parliament [36] that an essential part of his duty was to consider how far he could gratify the spirit of nationality without endangering the Empire. To Ford, nationality was absolute and could only be compromised in this way: 'If the people of Ireland have a right to their country, the people of India have as just a claim to theirs; if it is wrong to plunder the Irish, it is also wrong to plunder the Hindoos.'[37] He ended this outburst with the significant motto: 'Liberty not Power, Nationality not Empire', which was to do long service as a statement of Irish-American attitudes to British imperialism.

For Ford himself, empire was not only the enemy of nationality, it also infringed the law of God. In a remarkable series of open letters to W. E. Gladstone,[38] 'Minister-in-Chief of the British Empire' in 1881, Ford summoned England to the 'bar of Christendom' to answer the gravest charges known to mankind. In terms biblical rather than legal, the *Irish World* indicted England for the crime of apostasy.[39] In the first letter, published on 2 April 1881, the Empire was variously described as 'a work of the devil', a 'system of diabolism' and a 'modern Babylon'.[40] Ford subsequently exhorted all the 'victims of this infernal system' - the Chinese who had opium forced down their throats, the Indians emaciated by English-made famines,[41] the Zulus sullenly nursing their wrath - to combine with the Irish 'in a holy crusade' to lay it in ruins.[42] In advocating violent retribution the *Irish World* argued that it was simply doing 'God's work upon earth'.[43]

The British Empire, as the object of this resurrected crusading ideal, thus figured crucially in Ford's recipe of Irish freedom. He was convinced that if Home Rule was to have any chance of fulfilment, then it had to capture the imagination not only of the Irish race but of the human race as well. Ireland had to effect contacts with fellow-travellers throughout the world though particularly throughout the Empire. This was not a difficult task. Besides the Irish, 'scores of other peoples' who were downtrodden by English rule had cause to hate it. The Indians especially were looked upon as the natural allies of Irish nationalists.[44] They were constantly referred to in the *Irish World* as 'fellow subjects' and 'fellow sufferers' of English misgovernment. They were subjected to the same grievances: to an iniquitous land system [45] and to the complete tyranny of 'castle' government.[46] The concept of Indians as brown Irishmen, as discontented and as revolutionary-minded as themselves, was a basic tenet of Ford's strategy. Nothing was clearer in his mind than that because of their shared experience Ireland and India had a joint interest to foment rebellion whenever the opportunity presented itself.

The part of Patrick Ford's gospel on nationalism that most appealed to American Fenians was his call to strike at England indirectly through a vulnerable empire. An Ireland writ large in the east, resistant to pacification, might ideally launch the process of disintegration. The *Irish World* looked to the 'soldier Fenians' in the Indian army to play their part. The 'Sepoy' mutiny had almost overwhelmed the Raj in 1857; an Irish mutiny could possibly destroy it.[47] Certainly John Devoy, pre-eminent among the leaders of Clan na Gael, accepted the Ford line on this. He defined the British Empire as a 'vast agglomeration of hostile races', which was 'filled with inflammable material within and beset with powerful and watchful enemies without'.[48]

With the international situation charged with conflict, it was confidently assumed that sooner or later England would be involved in a war, in Europe or in Asia, that could prelude an armed uprising in Ireland. While England was distracted by military engagement at a number of weak points, Ireland could sue for independence.[49] This is what had seemingly happened in 1782 when England had conceded an Irish Parliament while fighting the American colonies.[50] Hopes were pinned this time on an Anglo-Russian conflict over Afghanistan,[51] although the possibility of a Spanish-Irish raid on Gibraltar was not discounted.[52] While Russian connivance was desired most of all, attention shifted to Zululand in 1879 [53] and to Egypt in 1882 [54] when they also threatened to become trouble-spots of some potential.[55]

Dr Thomas Brown correctly dismisses subterranean activity of this kind as mostly 'building castles in the air'. It is true that a 'skirmishing fund' was established to finance the work of imperial destruction, but it was mainly used to 'subsidise propaganda' rather than the 'terrorism' of specially trained *agents provocateurs*.[56] Contact was also made with the Russian [57] and Spanish [58] Governments to enlist their co-operation and Clan delegations were apparently 'well received' in Washington and St Petersburg. They were unable, however, to convince their hosts that a sufficently strong nationalist feeling antagonistic to the Union existed in Ireland.[59] Without a firm guarantee of Irish uprising, such Clan intrigue was inevitably rebuffed, and on the whole produced little tangible effect. Certainly, the British Government did not take the threat of Empire-wide espionage very seriously, although they periodically advised colonial Governments to take precautions just in case.[60] Most reports about likely Fenian raids were considered 'utterly unworthy of belief'.[61]

Imperial dissolution was no more than imperial partnership at the time a practical route to Irish independence. The Clan could neither deliver Ireland into the fold of 'physical force',[62] nor promote an Anglo-European war. By December 1877 the roving Clan spy, General Millen, was inclined to concede that without Russian participation they must 'despair of doing anything in the present generation'.[63] Later attempts to damage England through submarine activity [64] and by dynamiting public buildings simply confirmed this judgement.[65] The British Empire was not vulnerable to bizarre attacks of this kind. [66]

John Devoy, amongst others, soon realised that more reliable allies were needed as well as a more united and realistic campaign to undermine British imperialism. On 25 October 1878 he offered activist Home Rulers led by Parnell the conditional support of the American movement based on a five-point programme.[67] In this 'New Departure' focus is usually placed on the land issue, which was soon to overtake Irish politics. It should, perhaps, still be seen within the ambit of Irish-American intrigues against the British Empire. This much is suggested by Devoy's follow-up letter to the *Freeman's Journal* on 11 December. He urged the 'adoption of a broad and comprehensive public policy' which nationalists of all persuasions could support 'without sacrifice of principle', less because of the coming land war than of imminent imperial decline. As the Empire was on the slope leading 'inevitably' to ruin, Irishmen should be on their guard; it was their turn now and their watchwords should be: 'patience, prudence, courage and sleepless vigilance'.[68] The 'great events' which Devoy predicted, and for which he wished to prepare Ireland, were logically an Anglo-Russian confrontation arising out of the Afghan war. From this angle the 'New Departure' looks like the culmination of the Irish-American policy of imperial dissolution rather than a preparation for agrarian upheaval.[69]

Ideologically and tactically the most realistic response to the factor of empire was demonstrated by the Parnellite wing of the Home Rule party. In essence Parnellism [70] represented a compromise between the flagrant imperial perspective of Butt and the frenetic anti-English approach of American Fenians. The Empire might remain intact but as a commonwealth of free and equal nations. Irish freedom was considered compatible with this new arrangement.

Within the Home Rule party the most comprehensive and coherent redefinition of Ireland's relationship with the British Empire was formulated by Frank Hugh O'Donnell. At first, like other activists irritated by British intransigence, O'Donnell recommended that Home Rulers take an interest in imperial affairs as an act of retaliation.[71] But in its final form, his policy of 'intervention' consisted of three basic canons of anti- imperial belief:

one, that Irishmen were specially qualified to postulate cures for imperial disorders;
two, that Home Rulers were the natural representatives in Parliament of the unenfranchised empire;
three, that nationalists in Ireland should form an

alliance with nationalists in Asia and Africa to
achieve the mutual goal of self-government.

The first canon was derived from experimental intervention
over the Bengal Famine of 1874 and the 'annexation' of the
Transvaal in 1877. On both occasions O'Donnell's criticism
of the nature of British rule posited the same principles as
Patrick Ford, but independently of him. He stated that Irish
misgovernment was mirrored wherever the British raised their
standard of civilisation on conquered or weaker races. Thus
the case of Ireland was only 'the instance close at hand of
evils rampant from Cork to Cairo and Calcutta'.[72] Again,
there was the sharing of similar experience. Irish history
was repeating itself in India [73] through the creation of
another famine tradition and in South Africa with the
revocation of independence by confederation, an equivalent
of Union. Such thinking projected the Parnellite shift in
attitude to the imperial connection. It ran in channels
contrary to that of the less advanced Home Rulers, and
conflicted with the Buttite notion that British misrule in
Ireland was a unique phenomenon requiring a unique solution.

O'Donnell's portayal of Ireland as a victim of English
imperialism led to his second canon: that Home Rulers
constituted the 'natural representatives and spokesmen of
the unrepresented nationalities of the Empire'.[74] The
presence of Irishmen in the House of Commons simply affirmed
the special position of Ireland, but did not contradict the
subordinate status.[75] O'Donnell understood that by giving
a voice at Westminster to the unprivileged and unprotected
within the Empire[76] Home Rulers would acquire a symbolic
significance that far outweighed their numerical strength.
It lay within their power to become the pioneers of social
and imperial change. Besides, as O'Donnell put the case,
Ireland had a distinct moral duty to come to the aid of
subject nations. In a fourteen-point memorandum to the
Chairman of the Clan Executive, Dr Carroll, on the virtues
of constitutional agitation, O'Donnell presented a significant variation of Butt's 1873 theme about Irish claims on
empire.[77] The emphasis was away from the materialistic
rights of Ireland stressed at the Home Rule conference, more
towards an obligation of atonement for wrongs committed. As
Irishmen in the past had helped deprive India, for example,
of her independence it was just that they now do all in
their power to restore it.[78]

The third canon exhorting an anti-imperial alliance
completed the rationale of intervention. In two open
letters, to the *Freeman's Journal* on 13 August 1878 and to
the *Nation* on 24 August 1878, he outlined his policy of

'Power in the Empire and Outside'.[79] Declaring his faith in a federal solution of Home Rule, O'Donnell rejected the view that Ireland's withdrawal from the Empire was any preparation for the resumption of her place in the world of nations. Despite puzzling references to an imperial Ireland, he conjured up an alliance geared not to the maintenance of English hegemony, but to the attainment of national independence within the Empire. In her struggle for 'life and freedom' Ireland could call upon the help of England's other victims, whose instinct for liberty was as strong as Ireland's. He addressed the same message from Parliament a few years later: as the British Empire was a 'veritable slave empire', there Home Rulers should 'find allies, and they should take up an attitude of defence commensurate with the area of the tyranny'.[80] In such a combination 'Ireland was marked out as the natural leader of the imperial majority' and could direct it against the twenty-seven millions of England if they remained obdurate on Home Rule.[81] O'Donnell was convinced that the English Government confronted by a well-co-ordinated agitation for independence in Ireland, India and South Africa, could not muster sufficient force to stem the tide of nationalism.

This exposition failed to silence O'Donnell's critics and simply confirmed their worst fears that he was tainted with imperialism,[82] a myth perpetuated by history. Yet, despite an admiration for the concept of empire that occasionally infused his writings and speeches, O'Donnell always held that the 'nations' ruled by England had both a right and a duty to consider their own interests quite independently of hers.[83] Not even in his ambitious vision of a paternal Ireland giving the lead to fledgling states could he be accused of anti-national tendencies. If Ireland rather than England was to be the hub of a new radiating empire it was an empire based on a confederation of independent if filial states.[84] In effect O'Donnell was moving towards an ideal of commonwealth and must be considered one of the first exponents of this solution to the Irish problem. It was his misfortune and Ireland's that commonwealth was politically in advance of its time.[85] Ireland was perhaps ready for it, but the rest of the Empire was not.

The other main contributor to the theory of imperial metamorphosis was the founder and philosopher of the Land League, Michael Davitt. Rejecting mendicancy or crime as panaceas of Irish freedom, he recommended in December 1882 that faith instead be placed on 'moral dynamite', on 'ideas alone'.[86] Davitt's flash of insight was to see landlordism and imperialism as related manifestations of the order suppressing Ireland. The way to undermine both was to attack the monopoly of political power exercised by the aristocratic and propertied classes by taking away their control of land. Not surprisingly, he came to uphold land, the lowest common denominator of shared experience, as the direct link binding the enemies of England together. It followed that because Ireland, India, and to a lesser extent, Africa, were united in similar grievance, so they might resort to similar remedy.[87] Davitt's plan of campaign, therefore, included the transformation of the Empire preferably by means of land reform, but by land war if necessary. The 'No Rent' manifesto, which issued from Kilmainham on 18 October 1881, was looked to not only to propel Ireland along the path of social revolution, but to convulse the Empire as well. Indeed, the *Irish World* confidently acclaimed it as the solvent of empire. Its cable despatches from India carried the comforting news that the 'Light' had spread there and that 'No Rent' was being taken up in the nationalist press.[88]

Davitt's focus, then, was essentially international. His concern for the welfare of the Irish people always spilled over into a concern for people at large. As O'Donnell put it Davitt 'had a call to preach a covenant'.[89] This involved a moral crusade against all forms of British imperialism, which he looked upon as the 'greatest curse' imaginable.[90] It became an inseparable aspect of his faith, that Ireland's role in the world, when not being 'dragooned or otherwise persecuted by England', was that of the 'nursery of missionary ideas and ideals'.[91]

While O'Donnell and Davitt did not persuade every Home Ruler that the destiny of Ireland and the destiny of the Empire were intricately linked, they helped form new habits of mind concerning national duty and the rights of man. Even if both at times had their credentials as genuine nationalists questioned,[92] the universalism which they promoted in their different ways managed to secure the solid adherence of an influential coterie of Home Rulers who were committed to the spread of anti-imperial aspirations.

The finest example was Alfred Webb, the untiring treasurer of the Irish National League, and a Home Ruler of unchallenged orthodoxy. Initially a separatist, [93] it was because of his conception of Ireland's humanitarian duty of protecting the weaker races within the Empire [94] that Webb was won over to the O'Donnell-Davitt formula of imperial metamorphosis.[95] While he hated the idea of empire, Devoy's 'New Departure' did not attract him because, although it might hurt England, it did not necessarily help Ireland.[96] 'Is a man a whole man who thinks only of his own affairs?', he inquired of the *Freeman's Journal* in

December 1885: 'Does his nature not become dwarfed and narrowed, and is not the world becoming more like one federation - one family with reciprocal rights and duties? And should we have any right knowingly to shut ourselves out from this communion?'[97] Like an apostle Webb was 'ready to go to any land whenever ordered'.[98] In 1894 he accepted an invitation to go to India as President of the Indian National Congress.[99] On his return he dismissed Kipling's theory of the 'white-man's burden' as 'unadulterated cant'[100] and declared that the connection between 'vast continent' and 'petty island' was 'so close that if both [did] not rise both must fall together'.[101]

The majority of Parnellites, however, were not prepared to go so far. Most accepted 'universalism', but only so long as it was practical politics and demonstrably served Ireland's cause. Parnell himself falls into this category. His pronounced dislike of England made him a willing opponent of her acquisition of empire, but not necessarily a committed crusader for nationalism outside Ireland. His imprimatur for ambitious schemes hung ultimately on the criterion of their utility to Home Rule. This partly explains his rejection of a lucrative Indian alliance in 1878 [102] and his hesitancy in setting aside an Irish seat for the Indian nationalist, Dadabhai Naoroji, in 1883.[103] Not that his use of interventionist rhetoric was thereby insincere. Irrespective of whether he was playing to an extremist gallery,[104] Parnell rose to prominence less as the scourge of Butt than as the advocate of justice to the Boers, the opponent of flogging in the armed services, and the enemy of imperialism. The financial inducement of imperial service which had tempted Butt found Parnell totally unmoved. He instructed that if Irishmen were to be sent abroad mainly to carry on 'cruel and unjust' wars, he would rather they eschew English employment altogether.[105] J. L. Garvin's argument that Parnell was deep down an imperialist himself and that had Gladstone carried the day in 1886 he 'would have become at once an imperial force as strong as Mr. Rhodes', is rather too plausible.[106] Parnell wanted equality with England, but he was not averse to securing Home Rule all round. Interviewed about his attitude to India's future he replied that he would have 'all component parts of the empire manage their own internal affairs'.[107] Simply, Parnell was not prepared to subordinate everything to the theory of imperial metamorphosis. Where it fell within his own programme of 'parliamentary pressure'[108] it was taken up, but not otherwise.

To a degree, then, the growth of anti-imperialism in the Home Rule movement was motivated by changing political requirements as well as a change of heart. While the Parnellite inquest into empire reflected the assertion of a distinct Irish nationality,[109] it also satisfied the parliamentary imperative of taking on the English enemy. The frame of mind was aptly expressed by William O'Brien when he updated O'Neill Daunt's peace terms: 'In 1902 and in 1870, the message to England,' he wrote, is '"friends, if you will let us; Rebels, if you will drive us".'[110] Like many Parnellites, O'Brien envisaged intervention at Westminster as a kind of offensive activity, a manifestation of war rather than a positive exercise of parliamentary investigation. Taking over from Patrick Ford as the British Empire's prophet of doom, his constant theme in *United Ireland*, which he edited, and on National League platforms, became 'England's difficulty, Ireland's opportunity'.[111] This old slogan held a strong fascination for many Home Rulers and was always an effective rallying cry for action. Even Parnell was susceptible to its appeal. A. M. Sullivan recalled his desire in 1880 to keep Beasconsfield in power because he would 'infallibly bring England into some disastrous European complication'.[112]

Much of this, of course, was simply designed to bolster Irish morale. If violence was talked it was essentially rhetorical. Parnell conceded this much in his last parliamentary speech. 'No one now wished to blow up the British Empire with dynamite,' he confessed,'an idea which has passed out of the view of the most extreme Irishman.'[113] Nevertheless, it is possible to see Parnellite responses to 'universalism' and the factor of empire as divergent. To some like William O'Brien, for example, the Empire seems to have been rendered anathema less because it was the antithesis of nation than because it failed to afford any sign of English bounty.[114] The priority was to 'tear it to pieces' rather than liberate the peoples it governed.[115] Still, the old Buttite talk about enjoying the fruits of empire was considered inappropriate in a struggle for independence and a new dialogue of responsibility and concern for the welfare of dependent peoples was progressively substituted. 'Universalism', in short, had its vices as well as its virtues.

Of the three approaches to the British Empire, that of the Parnellites contributed most to the development of Irish nationalism by going some way to purge it of ideological ambiguity. This the Buttites clearly failed to do. With their goal of imperial partnership conservative Home Rulers were much too fond of English imitation and thus ultimately hedged on the claim of distinct Irish nationality. For their part, the American Fenians managed to broaden the horizon of

Irish nationalist perspective but, with the notable exception of Patrick Ford, were not motivated by any broad love of humanity. While they were interested in the progress of nationalism throughout the Empire, it was primarily with an eye to the fight that could be put up against it. Imperial dissolution was promulgated as a solution to cripple England instead of, necessarily, to elevate India, South Africa or, for that matter, Ireland. By contrast, the Parnellite concept of linking Home Rule to the transformation of the Empire helped to discard the 'insularity' that Mansergh noted and placed the Irish struggle for freedom firmly within the context of a universal and historic process. Even if many Home Rulers continued to look on the Empire with 'pride and enthusiasm',[116] and few loathed it sufficiently to 'let it go to pot', they understood that it was an impediment to full national expression, and made adjustments as has been shown.

If 'universalism' naturally did not gain mastery of the Irish Question and did not hold priority over Irish issues, it did become for a time an integral part of Irish parliamentary policy and establish a programme of action that was broadly acceptable to diverse nationalist groups. Under Parnell's direction the Home Rule party was unchallenged as the most aggressive and vocal advocate of liberty within the Empire. Between 1877 and 1886 especially, it dominated question time on imperial matters and conducted the most thorough investigation of imperial government.[117] It is true that without Parnell the party tended to sink back into the old habits of inaction and anonymity. What remained of it after the 1891 'split' became thoroughly dependent on the Liberals and was unable to retrieve independence and objectivity in its Parnellite form.[118] Although unity was re-established, significantly through common opposition to the Boer War, John Redmond seemed too willing to return to the Buttite position of keeping Ireland a subordinate part of the Empire.[119] Little wonder that Alfred Webb was constrained to lament in 1906 that Home Rule had lost its way again. 'Effective Home Rule', he reminded Redmond, was necessary for the good of Ireland and for the 'good of humanity'. But in the form of some 'contemptible devolutionary measure', it was 'unacceptable'.[120]

Nevertheless, 'universalism' bequeathed many positive features. It did attract world attention and secure allies for Ireland. It did spread the idea of nationality, in particular, to India,[121] and began to persuade the English that nationalism was not a vile Irish disease but a natural and irresistible phenomenon. Above all, it held in check the 'self-centred' and 'chauvinist' interpretations that Mitchel and, to a lesser extent, Griffith attempted to impose on

Irish nationalism. The founder of Sinn Fein initially had no patience with sentimental ideals of 'national brotherhood'. 'The right of the Irish to political independence,' he once laid down, 'never was, is not, and never can be dependent upon the admission of equal right in all other peoples': '... it is independent of theories of government and doctrines of philanthropy and Universalism.'[122] But even Griffith in the end conceded that Ireland was not alone and did not have to go it alone. 'Universalism' had left a legacy.

NOTES

1. L. J. McCaffrey, 'Irish Federalism in the 1870s: a Study in Conservative Nationalism', *Transactions of the American Philosophical Society*, new series, vol. 52, pt 6 (1962) pp. 1-58.
2. F. S. L. Lyons, 'The Economic Ideas of Parnell', in M. Roberts (ed.), *Historical Studies*, vol. ii (1959) pp. 60-78.
3. P. O'Farrell, *Ireland's English Question: Anglo-Irish Relations 1534-1970* (London, 1971).
4. R. P. Davis, *Arthur Griffith and Non-Violent Sinn Féin* (Dublin, 1974).
5. N. Mansergh, *The Irish Question 1840-1921*, 3rd edn (London, 1975). This volume was originally published in 1940 under the title *Ireland in the Age of Reform and Revolution*.
6. C. C. O'Brien, *Parnell and his Party 1880-90* (London, 1968) pp. 7-8.
7. Mansergh, *The Irish Question*, pp. 80-100.
8. F. S. L. Lyons, *Ireland since the Famine* (London, 1971) p. 4.
9. See L. P. Curtis, *Coercion and Conciliation in Ireland* (Princeton, NJ, 1963) pp. 427-32.
10. Salisbury outlined his theory in 'Disintegration', *Quarterly Review*, vol. 156 (Oct. 1883) pp. 559-95, and during a speech at Newport on 7 Oct. 1885. See also Lady Gwendolen Cecil, *Life of Robert Marquis of Salisbury* (London, 1931) vol. iii, pp. 270, 294.
11. M. Davitt, *The Fall of Feudalism in Ireland* (London, 1904) p. 499.
12. See I. Butt, *Home Government for Ireland, Irish Federalism: its Meaning, its Objects and its Hopes*, 4th edn (Dublin, 1874).
13. McCaffrey, 'Irish Federalism in the 1870s', p. 4.

14. Butt quoted in F.H. O'Donnell, *A History of the Irish Parliamentary Party* (London, 1910) vol. i, p. 47.
15. D. Thornley, *Isaac Butt and Home Rule* (London, 1964) p. 99.
16. Butt, *Home Government for Ireland*, p. 29.
17. Irish Home Rule League, *Proceedings of the Home Rule Conference* (Dublin, 1874) p. 27. (Hereafter cited as *Proceedings*.)
18. Ibid., pp. 27-8.
19. Henry to Butt, Butt Papers (n.d., ms 832, NLI). Butt's son, George Butt (1842-79) had been employed in the Bengal Civil Service since 1863 (*India List*, 1879).
20. *Proceedings*, p. 127.
21. Ibid., pp. 132 ff.
22. W. J. O'Neill Daunt, *Eighty-Five Years of Irish History, 1800-1885* (London, 1896) vol. i, p. 268.
23. *Proceedings*, p. 133.
24. *Nation*, 11 Apr. 1874.
25. W. O'Brien, *Recollections* (London, 1905) p. 144.
26. See E. Strauss, *Irish Nationalism and British Democracy* (London, 1951) p. 155; and Butt, *Home Government for Ireland*, p. 39.
27. H. C. Debates, ser. iii, vol. 242, 2 Aug. 1878, cols 1084-91. See also Butt to Beach, 11 Feb. 1878, Butt Papers (ms 832, NLI).
28. *Freeman's Journal*, 5 Aug. 1878.
29. *Nation*, 10 Aug. 1878.
30. This, at least, was the reaction in America. See T. W. Moody, 'The New Departure in Irish Politics, 1878-79', in H. A. Cronne, T. W. Moody and D. B. Quinn (eds), *Essays in British and Irish History in Honour of James Eadie Todd* (London, 1949) p. 319.
31. H. C. Debates, ser. iii, vol. 242, 2 Aug. 1878, col. 111.
32. *The Times*, 10 Aug. 1878.
33. *Freeman's Journal*, 30 Nov.; 2, 6 Dec. 1879.
34. See *Dictionary of American Biography* (London, 1929-58) vol. vi, p. 518.
35. Ford to Butt, 6 Jan. 1875, Butt Papers (ms 10415, NLI).
36. H.C. Debates, ser iii, vol 230, 30 June 1876, col. 748.
37. *Irish World*, 12 Aug. 1877.
38. These letters were subsequently published in book form under the title *The Criminal History of the British Empire* (London, 1915).
39. Ford, *Criminal History*, p. 9.
40. *Irish World*, 2 Apr. 1881; Ford, *Criminal History*, pp. 7-11.
41. *Irish World*, 30 Apr. 1881; Ford, *Criminal History*,

pp. 43-5.
42. *Irish World*, 23 Apr. 1881; Ford, *Criminal History*, pp. 13, 27.
43. Ford, *Criminal History*, p. 63.
44. *Irish World*, 13 June 1877.
45. Ibid., 17 Mar. 1877.
46. Ford, *Criminal History*, p. 44.
47. *Irish World*, 25 Aug. 1877.
48. P. H. Bagenal, *The Irish Agitator in Parliament and on the Platform: A Complete History of Irish Politics for the year 1879* (Dublin, 1880) Appendix A, p. 130.
49. Enclosure I, Copy of Report of Military Agent (General F. F. Millen), in Desp. Secret no. 131, Thornton to Salisbury, 26 Apr. 1880, FO5 Papers, vol. 1745, PRO. This document can also be found among the Fenian papers in the State Paper Office, Dublin: Fenian Papers 1858-83, A Files, Box 5, A621.
50. McCaffrey, 'Irish Federalism in the 1870s', p. 46.
51. See Carroll to Devoy, 8 Feb. 1876, in W. O'Brien and D. Ryan (eds), *Devoy's Post Bag 1871-1880* (Dublin, 1948) vol. i, pp. 133-5, 207ff.
52. Desp. Political no. 4, Archibald to Salisbury, 17 Oct. 1879, FO5 Papers, vol. 1707.
53. O'Kelly to Davitt, 10 Mar. 1876, *Devoy's Post Bag*, vol. i, pp. 408-11. This letter was in fact sent to Devoy. See also Carroll to Devoy, 11 Mar. 1879, ibid., pp. 412-14.
54. See Edwards to Granville, 8 and 16 Aug., 11 Sept., 1882, FO5 Papers, vols 1819, 1820.
55. See Clipperton to Thornton, 24 Jan. 1881, Fenian Papers 1858-83, A Files, Box 5, A645.
56. T. N. Brown, *Irish-American Nationalism 1870-1890* (Philadelphia and New York, 1966) pp. 66-70.
57. Enclosure I in Desp. Secret no. 90, Thornton to Salisbury, 8 Apr. 1878, FO5 Papers, vol. 1706. See also Henri le Caron, *Twenty-Five Years in the Secret Service* (London, 1892) pp. 139-41.
58. See Desp. Political no. 4, Archibald to Salisbury, 17 Oct. 1879, FO5 Papers, vol. 1707; O'Kelly to Devoy, 23 Dec. 1877, *Devoy's Post Bag*, vol. i, pp. 60, 293-4.
59. Brown, *Irish-American Nationalism 1870-1890*, pp. 66-7; *Devoy's Post Bag*, vol i, p. 209.
60. See Circular Desp., Secret and Confidential, Colonial Office to Foreign Office, 28 June 1877, FO5 Papers, vol. 1599.
61. Desp. no. 121, Thornton to Salisbury, 6 May 1878, FO5 Papers, vol. 1707.
62. Carroll to Devoy, 19 Jan. 1878, *Devoy's Post Bag*,

vol. i, p. 296. See also instructions from Dr Carroll to Millen, enclosure in Desp., Thornton to Granville, 26 Apr. 1880, Fenian papers 1858-83, A Files, Box 4.
63. Millen to Supreme Council, IRB, 23 Dec. 1877, *Devoy's Post Bag*, vol. i, p.288.
64. This was to take the form of armed 'submersibles', a species of torpedo.
65. See Desp. Secret no. 66, Archibald to Granville, 28 Dec. 1882, FO5 Papers, vol. 1820; and Desp. Political no. 12, Clipperton to Granville, 8 May 1883, FO5 Papers, vol. 1861.
66. Most of this activity was verbal anyway. See D. Ryan, 'Stephens, Devoy, Tom Clarke', in C. C. O'Brien (ed.), *The Shaping of Modern Ireland* (London, 1960) p. 35.
67. The 'New Departure' telegram was first published in the *New York Herald* on 26 Oct., and reprinted in the *Freeman's Journal* on 11 Nov. 1878.
68. *Freeman's Journal*, 11 Dec. 1878. This letter is also printed as Appendix A in Bagenal, *The Irish Agitator in Parliament*, pp. 115ff.
69. The fourth head of the 'New Departure' telegram urged Home Rulers to vote together on all imperial and Irish questions. The fifth head reiterated a principle of long standing upheld by the *Irish World;* namely the 'advocacy of all struggling nationalities in the British Empire and elsewhere'.
70. The term 'Parnellite' is used here to denote not only the pledged supporters of Parnell, but also those independent-minded Home Rulers, such as F. H. O'Donnell, who shared similar views on most issues and generally voted with the former.
71. O'Donnell, *History*, vol. i, pp. 176-80; *Irish Home Rule League, Proceedings*, pp. 104-5; see also F. H. O'Donnell, *How Home Rule was Wrecked* (Dublin, 1895).
72. O'Donnell, *History*, vol. ii, p. 471.
73. H. C. Debates, ser. iii, vol. 218, 24 Apr. 1874, cols 1067-72.
74. Ibid., vol. 266, 17 Feb. 1882, pp. 1065-6.
75. See Strauss, *Irish Nationalism and British Democracy*, pp. 2, 187.
76. *Nation*, 24 Mar. 1883; *The Times*, 20 Mar. 1883.
77. Accounts of the meeting between revolutionary and parliamentary nationalists in March 1878 can be found in O'Donnell, *History*, vol. i, pp. 270-85; and R. B. O'Brien, *The Life of Charles Stewart Parnell* (London, 1899) vol. i, pp. 158-60.
78. See point 14 of O'Donnell's memorandum in O'Donnell, *History*, vol. i, pp. 275-8.

79. O'Donnell to J. E. Redmond, 20 May 1904, Redmond Papers (ms 15216, NLI).
80. H. C. Debates, vol. 285, 15 Mar. 1884, col. 1766.
81. *Nation*, 24 Aug. 1878.
82. See *Irish World*, 1 Feb. 1879; O'Donnell, *History*, vol. i, p. 93; Carroll to Devoy, 14 Aug. 1878, *Devoy's Post Bag*, vol. i, pp. 344-5.
83. *Nation*, 24 Aug. 1878.
84. O'Donnell, *History*, vol. ii, p.472.
85. See C. J. O'Donnell, *The Lordship of the World, the British Empire, the United States and Germany*, 3rd edn (London, 1924) p. 156.
86. *The Times*, 23 Dec. 1882.
87. *Freeman's Journal*, 23 Aug. 1881.
88. *Irish World*, 17 Dec. 1881; 14 Jan., 4 Feb. 1882. O'Donnell 'triumphantly' addressed the same message to a gathering of Land Leaguers in January 1882. *Freeman's Journal*, 23 Jan. 1882.
89. O'Donnell, *History*, vol. i, p. 452.
90. Davitt to anon., 18 July 1898, Davitt Papers (ms 2159, NLI).
91. Davitt, *Feudalism*, p. 446.
92. *Nation*, 2 July 1880. T. M. Healy was partly responsible for spreading the rumour that O'Donnell was really of dubious Scottish ancestry and had therefore no right to pose as a bona fide nationalist. See O'Donnell to J. Redmond, 9 May 1885, Redmond Papers (ms 15216, NLI). See also P. Bew, *Land and the National Question in Ireland, 1858-82* (Dublin, 1978) pp. 229-31. Strangely, O'Donnell himself remembered Davitt as a sort of Lancashire radical with 'Hibernian varnish'. O'Donnell, *History*, vol. i, p. 372.
93. Webb to editor of *Freeman's Journal*, 21 Oct. 1878, Webb Papers (ms 1745, NLI).
94. Webb in *Freeman's Journal*, 26 Dec. 1885.
95. See article, 'The Duty of an Irishman', ibid., 29 Mar. 1880.
96. Webb to editor of *New York Herald*, dated 20 Nov. 1878, Webb Papers (ms 1745, NLI).
97. *Freeman's Journal*, 26 Dec. 1885.
98. *Speeches by Alfred Webb* (Bombay, 1895); Webb Papers (ms 1746, NLI).
99. See H. V. Brasted and G. Douds, 'Passages to India: Peripatetic MPs on the Grand Indian Tour 1870-1940', *South Asia*, vol. ii (March and Sept. 1879) pp. 95-6.
100. *Hindu*, 30 Mar. 1899; *Madras Standard*, 3 Apr. 1899.
101. Webb, 'England's Imperial Despotism: Indian Portents', *Weekly Freeman*, 17 July 1897.

102. O'Donnell, *History*, vol. ii, pp. 428-9; *Freeman's Journal*, 13 Aug. 1878.
103. Davitt, *Feudalism*, p. 447.
104. C. C. O'Brien, *Parnell*, p. 23.
105. H. C. Debates, ser. iii, vol. 244, 17 Mar. 1879, cols 1077-9, 1082-5, 1090-2.
106. J. L. Garvin, 'Parnell and his Power', *Fortnightly Review*, vol. lxiv (1898) p. 882. Gladstone was also inclined to the opinion that 'imperial patriotism' could be salvaged if 'local patriotism were satisfied in time' (H. C. Debates, ser. iii, vol. 304, 8 Apr. 1886, col. 1082).
107. *Bengalee*, Nov. 1886, p. 543.
108. C. C. O'Brien, *Parnell*, p. 26n.
109. H. C. Debates, ser. iii, vol. 243, 5 Dec. 1878, cols 164-6.
110. W. O'Brien, *Recollections*, p. 95.
111. Police Reports 1848-1921, Box no. 3; see selection of speeches by O'Brien on 2 Sept., 30 Oct. 1883; 8, 13 Feb., 12 Apr. 1885.
112. A. M. Sullivan quoted in M. MacDonagh, *The Home Rule Movement* (London, 1920) p. 256.
113. H. C. Debates, ser. iii, vol. 333, 3 Aug. 1891, col. 206.
114. Report of speech by W. O'Brien, 2 Sept. 1883, Police Reports 1848-1921, Box 3.
115. Report of speech by T. Mayne MP, 20 Sept. 1885, ibid.
116. A. O'Day, *The English Face of Irish Nationalism* (Dublin, 1972) p. 163.
117. Statistics of questions asked by Irish MPs can be found in I. M. Cumpston, 'Some Early Nationalists and their Allies in the British Parliament, 1851-1906', *English Historical Review*, vol. lxxvi (1961) p. 285; and O'Day, *The English Face of Irish Nationalism*, p. 161.
118. F. S. L. Lyons, *The Irish Parliamentary Party, 1890-1910* (London, 1951) p. 259.
119. Davis, *Arthur Griffith*, p. 107.
120. Webb to Redmond, 26 June 1906; 4, 29 May 1907, Redmond Papers (ms 15231, NLI).
121. See H. V. Brasted, 'Indian Nationalist Development and the Influence of Irish Home Rule, 1870-1886', *Modern Asian Studies*, vol. 14, no. 1 (1980) pp. 37-63.
122. Griffith quoted in O. D. Edwards, 'Ireland', in O. D. Edwards, G. Evans, J. Rhys and A. MacDiarmid, *Celtic Nationalism* (London, 1968) pp. 127-8.

7 The Gaelic Athletic Association and Popular Culture, 1884–1924

W. F. MANDLE

At present it is historiographically fashionable to see nineteenth-century Ireland in the context of its being part of Victorian Britain. As one writer has put it, 'the *Victorian* context of Irish culture in mid-century (and after) has been neglected in favour – on occasion – of an exclusivist attention to "the national tradition" '.[1] This statement would be more true of the GAA than of any other manifestation of Irish culture – popular or otherwise.

When dealing with the GAA and its relation to popular culture in Ireland, three main aspects require attention. First, the place of the GAA in the tradition of Irish nationalism, a tradition that took many forms: of Catholicism; of the secret societies; of the language movement; of ascribed peasant virtue; and of increasing political and social resentment of the English. To introduce such political matters into the concept of popular culture is, in an Irish context, justified. Few cultures, at the popular as well as at higher levels, were as politicised as was that of Ireland in the period under review. Secondly, the GAA was an example of a sporting organisation operating at the time of the birth of modern sport, one of the most striking phenomena of modern popular culture. Thirdly, the GAA illustrates a characteristic of popular culture, that of communicating through rhetoric (albeit often of a debased or a tendentious nature) a justificatory philosophy that tries to engage a necessary popular response. For this purpose the GAA drew upon something more than the nationalist tradition.

The GAA's nationalist credentials, often of the most extreme sort, were never in doubt. Nationalism was central to its popular cultural role. The Irish Republican Brotherhood was largely instrumental in its foundation, and for lengthy periods was in control of the GAA.[2] Even when not demonstrably members of the Irish Republican Brotherhood its leadership was always strongly nationalist, and few organisations of the time were as consistently outspoken against Britain, or so willing to make actions, as in the case of the Ban, speak as loudly as words.

But not even the GAA, founded, manipulated, and sustained, first by the IRB, later by the nationalist movement as a whole, could escape the wider influences that came from its being located within the United Kingdom. The sports revolution that codified and organised so many traditional games, and invented new ones, was a British, even an English phenomenon.[3] No sporting development anywhere in the world in the nineteenth century could avoid the impress of the original English methodology. The games might vary, but their relation to society, their philosophy, their very progress followed principles laid down, almost copyrighted, by the English. Sport, to become popular, and the GAA sought popularity for the very nationalist ends it espoused, had to become a mass entertainment. To do so it had to follow the rules of the game. Profound social and economic forces, connected with the effects of the growth of western capitalism, lay behind this process. The result, as far as sport was concerned, was to transform sport from rustic play into urban display; from recreation into organised competition; from unwatched (and largely unwatchable) exercise into spectacle geared to the turnstile. No matter how deeply imbued with expression of national identity, Gaelic games, like baseball in Japan, rugby football in New Zealand, cricket in Australia, had to conform to the principles of the new sport that transgressed all national boundaries.[4]

Furthermore, the English had not been content to let the new sports speak for themselves. They were surrounded with a high sounding but none the less important rhetoric that was intended to invest games with high moral purpose. This ethic was first and foremost the creation of Victorian England, and was applied, with national variations, wherever the new sport was taken up.[5]

I will take first the political role of the GAA. It might be argued that culture, both high and popular, was in fact largely political in those forty years. Politics impinged ineluctably upon literature and language, upon farming and upon religion, upon urban life and even upon the everyday purchasing of goods. The GAA, given its founders' purposes and its continuing interest, was avowedly political, so much so that at times its commitment outran popular feeling, or offended powerful minorities. It is true that at its inception it seemed that all Ireland had been awaiting its advent. It scarcely mattered that its foundation meeting at Thurles saw only eight in attendance, albeit in possession of messages of support from Croke and Davitt.[6] Within nine months scores of athletics meetings had been held throughout Ireland, one of them, at Tralee, deliberately opposed to the

British-dominated Irish Amateur Athletic Association, attracting an attendance of nearly 15,000.[7] By February 1885 Gaelic athletics, football and hurling had been codified;[8] by August the GAA had a membership of 'hundreds' of clubs,[9] and the ascribed dream of the GAA, to see an Ireland 'dotted all over with miniature armies of hurlers, bowlers, jumpers, weight-throwers, merry dancers and joyous singers',[10] was closer to reality than parody.

This initial success was achieved by utilising a combination of the factors touched upon in the opening section of this paper. There was an undoubted appeal to nationalism: rhetoric was anti-English; club names were evocative; deliberate challenge was made to west Britonism; the green flag with gold harp was raised. The precursor of the famous Ban was instituted as early as January 1885.[11] There was also recognition of the needs of a modern sport. The codification of the rules was almost immediate. Both football and hurling remained rough-and-tumble, but initial laws had been drawn up, nationally applicable if not always adhered to. A competition was instituted, its basic structure, involving club, county and province, remaining to this day.[12] The links with local loyalties, so essential to the games people played in England and Australia, New Zealand and Wales, were at once established. A master-stroke was to introduce the one parish, one club rule.[13] By this decision not only nationalism, but the Catholic tradition and the place of the priest in society were brought to the aid of the GAA. Latter-day historians have spent much time analysing the factors essential to the establishment of modern sport. The founders and officials of that first GAA went straight to the heart of the matter with uncanny perception. By accident and design they had created what must have been the most speedily and extensively established sporting organisation in the world.

For its mentors, the IRB, who just as rapidly took over the direction of the GAA at local and central level, the temptation to outrun popular feeling was irresistible. The 1880s was a decade of high expectation and of a high level of co-operation between the driving forces of Irish nationalism. Priest and politician were in alliance, and the revolutionary wing benefited, as the GAA itself showed. But to use the GAA blatantly for the recruitment of Fenians, and to interpret the startling growth of the Association as a manifestation of widespread support for extension was a mistake.

At the famous convention of 1887 the facade of unity was shattered: effectively the GAA was split into clerical and Fenian factions, still popular, but suddenly without the impetus that had resulted in so startling a growth in its first few years.[14] That the Fenian faction in the GAA chose to support Parnell in 1891 compounded the error. By the early 1890s the GAA was all but dead.[15]

It remained moribund until the early years of the twentieth century. The social and political exhaustion that seemed to have settled upon Ireland after the heady, almost orgiastic, excitements of the years that coincided with the career and ended with the death of Parnell affected one of the most notable creations of those years, the GAA. It was still run by the IRB - a secretary, Blake who was not of the Brotherhood and who tried to exorcise its influence, was in 1898 given short shrift.[16] Despite changes to the rules, reduction of the number of players in teams, and relaxation of the Ban, and dogged continuation of the championships the GAA did no more than barely survive.[17]

Some nice questions of the relation of sport to society are posed. The GAA was as nationalistic as ever: but this was a time of slack enthusiasm. The GAA was as well organised as ever: but it lacked resources, and because it could not engender popular appeal its resources remained diminished. The peculiar dichotomy of the GAA is perhaps best revealed at this time of its lowest fortunes. Without widespread popular nationalist support it could not embark upon the measures needed to widen that support further by appealing to those who wanted merely to be entertained. A nationalist breeze was needed to stir the sails, then, the vessel in motion again, stronger winds might be engaged.

The turn of the century saw that first essential quickening in most areas of Irish nationalism: in literature, in the language movement, in the Irish industrial movement, in politics itself, with the Parliamentary Party reunited with Redmond, and, at the other political extreme, the feud between the IRB and the INB resolved.[18] In religion there was a growing militancy and concern;[19] in sport the GAA, under the new leaders, began an expansion comparable with its first successful phase.

The new leaders, among them Nowlan, J. J. Walsh and O'Toole were not, according to official GAA historian Marcus Bourke, members of the IRB although he agrees there is doubt on the matter and I remain convinced that they were.[20] Be that as it may, it is clear that they were extreme nationalists, as their later careers, in and out of prison, testify. They were much warier than their IRB predecessors in office. They sought a *rapprochement* with the clergy;[21] they were reconciled with the Parliamentary Party;[22] they tried to cultivate co-operation with the Gaelic League, many of them being prominent in the language movement.[23] Above all, they tried to restore the finances of the GAA and make of it a successful sporting movement.

The success of the GAA as a sporting organisation reacted upon and with its nationalist endeavours. The Ban, all but officially abandoned in the 1890s, returned with renewed vigour in the 1900s. It was extended to police and jailers and rigorously applied to servicemen, even as spectators.[24] There were new strident calls for the use of the Irish language on Gaelic fields and in Gaelic committee rooms;[25] and calls for trophies and equipment to be of Irish manufacture, with dire penalties for those found wanting.[26] Long before the outbreak of the First World War, and of the eventual conscription crisis of 1918, elements in the GAA were conducting an anti-recruitment campaign.[27] When the Volunteer movement came to southern Ireland in 1913 it was wholeheartedly espoused by the GAA at club level, although not officially by the Association itself.[28]

This refusal by the GAA, as a body, to endorse the Volunteer movement in 1914 indicated how circumspect it had become, and of how its very success as a sporting organisation caused its leadership to place considerable importance on that sporting role. The GAA's claim, entrenched in its constitution since 1895, to be a non-political body had been more honoured in the breach than in the observance. Now its officials were not prepared to endanger the carefully built up success of the GAA as a sporting body by open political commitment. Again, immediately following the 1916 Rising, the GAA approached the British military authorities disclaiming any official connection with that Rising and rejecting the assertions to the contrary made before the Royal Commission of Inquiry.[29]

Only during the conscription crisis of the summer of 1918 did the GAA take up a political cause, and even then its argument was more against the authorities proscribing Gaelic games than against conscription itself. That is not to say that the GAA did not wholly oppose conscription: it did and it said so, but the so-called Gaelic Sunday of 4 August 1918 was (as well as being unnecessary) specifically a protest by a sporting body against a perceived unjust interference with sporting activity.[30]

That the GAA, unlike the Gaelic League and of course unlike the Sinn Fein movement itself, was never proclaimed indicates that its message had got across to British authority. Certainly its officials were constantly being arrested, harassed and interned, but as individuals not as members of the GAA. It was true that a substantial proportion of those who fought and were gaoled at the time of the Rising, were members of the GAA, true also that it has been alleged that the bulk of the Irish republican forces came from the ranks of the GAA.[31] It would be surprising if it had not been so, and the close connection between Eoin O'Duffy, the GAA and the army testifies that it was so.[32]

But it is also fair to say that the GAA saw itself as having a wider responsibility: to itself as a popular sporting organisation. The War of Independence did not test this feeling fully: the Civil War did. During the War of Independence the GAA's political credentials, and its sporting role could remain accepted. It could be at one with the Ballybriggan Creamery and Cash & Co. of Cork in suffering the reprisal of Bloody Sunday.[33] There was no chance that its political declaration could be other than for independence, but it no longer needed to be a spearhead of resistance. Moreover it was proper that it should endeavour to carry on its games and sports (although Cork thought such activity inappropriate in time of war).[34]

The Civil War posed more difficult questions. Links between pro-Treaty politicians and soldiers, and the GAA executive were close, and were to remain so until the mid-1930s. The pro-Treaty section of the leadership of the IRB had long-standing connections with the GAA.[35] Yet it is fair to say that just as the majority of the rank-and-file of the Army was against the Treaty, so too was the majority of the rank-and-file of the GAA.[36] Aware of the deep division in Irish society, and within itself, the GAA chose to avoid choice. The lesson of 1890 had been well learned. The GAA, as Ireland's most important sporting organisation, put sport above politics. Its effort was directed to keeping the Association functioning as a national organisation. Only in Clare did it fail to maintain at least the facade of unity. There the execution of two county officials by the Free State forces precipitated the formation of a rival county board - a situation reminiscent of clerical-Fenian feud days of a generation before.[37] Elsewhere there were close calls, and the football championships due to be played off in 1924 had initially to be abandoned because first Kerry in the football, then Leix and Limerick in the hurling, and Offaly and Cork in the junior hurling refused to play until republican internees, among them Austin Stack of the Kerry GAA, were released.[38]

One indication of the GAA's shift in emphasis was the way in which pro- and anti-Treaty debate was transferred to dispute over the continuation of the Ban. As MacLua has written, debates within the GAA 'weren't in the main, about the Ban at all. They were really miniature Treaty debates.'[39] That the Ban was retained after some bitter argument in the years 1922-4 was an indication of the pro-republican strength in the GAA at large, for much of the leadership was in favour of its abandonment now that the British had gone. Yet the anti-Banner, McCarthy was elected, and the pro-Banner Clifford defeated for the Presidency whilst their causes were being separately resolved, a sign of the coming to terms with priorities.[40] Less productive of controversy, although there was some criticism from extreme republicans, was the GAA's espousal of the Tailteann Games. In October 1921 de Valera had conceived the idea of their revival. During this festival of arts and athleticism, held, it was claimed, annually for over 1500 years after 632 BC, 'all trivial and personal discord was suspended and man associated with man in the halcyon garden of peace'. [41] The Games had stopped in the year of the Norman invasion of Ireland, so it seemed appropriate to de Valera that they should be resumed now that the descendants of the invader were about to depart. August was the traditional month of meeting, so J. J. Walsh, a former official of the GAA, was put in charge of a committee, to plan an Irish Olympic (a name rapidly changed to Aonach Tailteann) centred on Dublin and particularly upon Croke Park for August 1922.[42] 'It was an admitted fact,' said Walsh 'that Irishmen are more prominent in athletics than any other race.' The Tailteann Games were to be a demonstration of this fact; in addition, 'nothing was to unite the Irish people more'.[43]

Originally, events were to be confined to 'items strictly common to the Greek Olympics, embracing the Gaelic race at home and abroad', but soon the almost comic began to supervene. Proposals were entertained for contests remote from either the Greek or Irish past. There was to be clay-bird shooting and motorboat racing; the Phoenix Park was to be turned over to motorcycle racing; rounders, claimed to be an old Irish game fallen into disuse in the last century but revived in prison camps; tennis 'played in Ireland for centuries', chess and golf, yachting and swimming, ordinary cycle racing, even billiards, were to be played.[44]

In July 1921, with the outbreak of war, it all fell apart. There were attempts to keep the Games going; they 'would help to relieve the present tension' it was said, but the destruction of four major hotels in Dublin, together with American dismay at the news from Dublin forced the announcement on 16 July of postponement for a year, a postponement extended for a further year the following July.

In January 1924 the ebullient Walsh was on the move again: the Games were to go ahead that August, and plans were put in train to bring John McCormack the great Irish tenor back for the occasion, to bring for some extraordinary reason Prince Ranjitsinhji to the opening, and, for more comprehensible reasons, John Devoy, the American-based Fenian, to deliver an opening speech.

The Games were, at least in the early stages, well attended, and total attendances at the week's events were estimated at about 140,000, a far cry from half a million, but gratifying none the less.

As a healing exercise it is not to be disdained. Although close examination reveals certain discordances, and closer examination might reveal more, the Games' success and their purported meaning passed rapidly into the folklore of the GAA.[45] They became, properly, a symbol of the GAA's contribution to Irish nationalism and Irish reconciliation.

The GAA had, by 1924, moved close to the centre of popular Irish nationalism. It had always been at its most powerful when it identified with the prevailing nationalist mood, at its weakest when it espoused the extremist fringes. It came to recognise this fact, incurring the hostility of many, in both 1916 and during the Civil War. As an indicator of where the centre of gravity reposed in Irish nationalism the GAA is unequalled in these forty years - precisely one might argue because it was the only genuine popular cultural organisation that existed. But its popular appeal was based upon more than an uncanny identification with the political mood of the majority of nationalists.

Gaelic football, like all pre-codified folk football in the nineteenth century, would be, to the modern eye, an unstructured shambles. It was a rough-and-tumble game in which wrestling and tripping were allowed. Even the first Gaelic football rules allowed individual wrestling to occur whilst the game proceeded. Not until 1887 was 'handigrips' as it was termed abolished.[46] Style and tactics were geared to close, rushed ground play, there was much fly-kicking and little catching. The ball, larger and heavier in the 1880s and 1890s, was struck with the forearm if it bounced in the air. [47] Some elements of skill were practised: Dublin sides played a primitive kick-and-catch with position play even in the 1880s, and two of its missionaries, Dublin teachers, led Killorglin to a victory over the 'bunched' Ballymagellicot side in Tralee.[48]

For much of the 1880s and 1890s even the introduction of rules did little to relieve congestion and encourage skilful open play. The scoring system took time to be perfected. Points, or near misses through side posts as in Australian Rules football, had no goal equivalents until in 1892 five points were made equal to a goal, the reduction to the present three points equivalent coming in 1896.[49] A cross-bar for the goal as well as side-posts existed from 1892, the side-posts finally going in 1909 with a point being scored for a shot over the bar between elongated rugby-type goal-posts.[50] In 1910 goal-nets were introduced for provincial and all-Ireland championships.[51]

More important than scoring changes was the introduction of a cleared area, which became known as the parallelogram, in front of goal. This rid the game of 'the whips' who stood by and harassed the goalkeeper.[52] Kerry with kick-and-catch, Kildare with hand-passing, and northern counties with ground foot-passing in soccer style made of Gaelic football by 1914 an attractive open game. [53] Attendances grew – not to English soccer heights, but in proportion to population substantial enough. In 1907 nearly 20,000 watched Kerry play Kildare at Thurles; in 1913 the highly successful Croke Cup tournament final was played first before 26,000, then the replay before 50,000 'in sweltering heat' at Jones's Road ground, soon to be named Croke Park.[54]

Hurling partook of the new trend towards open play. From the turn of the century, hurleys were made lighter, a smaller ball was used, and although some deplored the new 'air work' in the game, the crowds responded, though not as readily as to Gaelic football.[55]

The study of the effects of rule, style and equipment changes in the history of sport is a neglected backwater. It should not be, for the appeal of popular cultural phenomena depends greatly upon changes in technology and approach. In effect Gaelic games were doing, ten or fifteen years later, what soccer and rugby had been doing in Britain in the closing decades of the nineteenth century. Professionalism was the spur for some counties, but not for all.[56] Even so, all sports organisations began to see their purpose as entertainment as well as character-building. Even rugby union football, *par excellence* a players' game, modified its style to attract large crowds to its major games, becoming in Wales the most popular football code.

The GAA was certainly pursuing ends other than sports popularity, but one of its functions was to encourage the spread of Gaelic games, and another to make a profit. It did both, which in turn assisted its major purpose.

With popular success in the field there developed all the parerga of modern commercialised sport. Individual champions 'with names like Homeric heroes – Walsh of Portnascully, Davins of Deerpark, Shanahan of Kilfinane' emerged.[57] 'Tyler' Mackey, the Limerick hurler, was presented with a purse of a hundred sovereigns for his play in 1910;[58] Dick Fitzgerald of Kerry was perhaps Ireland's most famous footballer prior to the First World War. As was customary in all football codes, teams as well as individuals became stars, among them the Kerry footballers of 1903 and 1904, those of Dublin 1906-8, and the Kilkenny hurlers who dominated the game in the early years of the century, winning seven all-Ireland titles in eleven years.

A successful Gaelic sports paper, the *Gaelic Athlete* was at last achieved. The forerunners, the *Celtic Times* and the *Gael* of 1887 had soon perished, unhappily without trace, and the *Champion* lasted only a few months in 1903-4. The *Gaelic Athlete*, begun in 1912, flourished until the 1916 Rising dealt it a mortal blow.[59]

This great Edwardian burgeoning of Gaelic games as popular pastimes and as popular spectator sports paralleled precisely the English experience. The Victorian prescription for sporting popularity extended into the Edwardian years. Gaelic games were able to maintain their exclusive amateurism (although not entirely Simon-pure) but in all other respects - rule changes, provision for spectators, the star system and the development of skills, the British model was faithfully followed, if perhaps unconsciously and certainly, in view of the Ban and other attendant anti-Britishry, ironically. Elements common to popular culture in both societies were exercising their effect: Irish popular culture was more than solely nationalistic.

Finally, we must look at the Irish adoption and adaptation of the Victorian cult of manliness, of 'pluck, loyalty, and the rest, the idea of life as sport'.[60]

The ascription of a moral worth, over and above the physical benefit to be derived from sport, was as evident in Gaelic games as in English. Much of the rhetoric about manliness, the need for vigour, self-reliance and self-control was an echo of English statements. 'Gaelic football . . . [was] . . . a test, not merely of footwork, but of the entire man and his physique'[61] wrote one clergyman. Others wrote of 'the ideal Gael - a matchless athlete, sober, pure in mind, speech and deed, self-possessed, self-reliant, self-respecting, loving his religion and his country with a deep and resistless love, earnest in thought and effective in action' [62] or 'the Irish Celt is distinguished among the races, for height and strength, manly vigour . . . despite wars, and domestic disabilities, the stamina of the race has survived almost in its pristine perfection.'[63] There was, in addition to the inevitable chauvinistic strain, which claimed unique powers and unmatched ancestry for Irish games, an emphasis upon the rural peasant virtues. This was not unusual in the eulogising of games - the rural tradition of English cricket was constantly being emphasised - but the romanticism of the vision of Irish peasant life, with strong overtones of religious observance, was given added point by the essentially rural nature of the GAA.

O'Farrell has noted that in both the literary and

religious revivals that took place in Ireland at about the same time as the GAA was developing, there was a strong tendency to set 'the peasantry, their culture and religion' against a modernism linked with the English.[64] It was a reactionary movement in both senses of the word; it was also romantic. The idealisation of Irish rural life was challenged at one's peril, as the Abbey Theatre demonstrations of 1907 showed; and it might be thought the artificial glow cast upon Gaelic games bears little relation to the realities of squabble and drunkenness, fights and injury, that attended so many fixtures, and indeed official meetings.

Yet in myth the games were linked to Ireland's rural strength. The peasantry was praised for its strength of sinew, '. . . tougher than the twanging Yew with strengthening nuts and good Potatoes fed'.[65] It was always sportsmanlike and obedient: 'No people in the world are more amenable to order and discipline',[66] it was claimed, and in early accounts of GAA matches there was a constant reiteration of the good humour and good temper of the players, partly no doubt a riposte to the received opinion of the English about the Irish, but also an affirmation of the basic moral worth of the peasantry.[67]

The links with rural religion were also emphasised. Once Mass was over, the sturdy peasantry met to run and jump and throw weights and the imagery in this beatific description in praise of Irish athletes is evocative in the extreme:

> The kind heavens be thanked for this communion of past and present, of youth and age, of a race that is fated not to die, diffusing the tenderness of an evening Angelus bell and the loneliness of a golden sunset fading behind the eternal hills, recalling the dear ones who consecrated the long ago, but did not live to see the coming glory of their sacrifices.[68]

The antiquity of the Irish games tradition was emphasised, bypassing the English and going straight to Greece, or even to the caveman: 'What more natural play for the lusty son of a caveman than to kick with his foot any spherical fruit or semi-round planthead that lay in his hunting path! He learnt the rudiments - toe down, drive with the instep!'[69]

The eventual need for the hurling men to lay aside their camans for even deadlier weapons was frequently present in the poetry of the GAA. The Rev. Dollard was a prolific versifier:

> Ye noble Gaels of Ireland

Fair Bansha needs you all;
Stand by your suffering sireland
And wait your battle-call.
Then may your peaceful weapons
Be changed to shimmering steel,
And from your bristling vanguard
Dismayed oppression reel![70]

Through Gaelic games Gaelic manhood was apotheosised into heroes who displayed not only 'Spartan strength' but revered 'truth, virtue and patriotism'.[71]

There was, inevitably, a particularly Irish dimension to this philosophic heightening of the meaning of games, but the moralising, at all levels, save perhaps the specifically Catholic, was in the Victorian English tradition. Victorian England praised manliness and sobriety, good temper and conformity to the rules. The reminder that games might well be merely preparation for sterner contests was constant in English rhetoric, and, after all, the concept of muscular Christianity was an English invention that need not necessarily be limited to reformed Churches.[72]

The sanctification of games, if we may pursue the metaphor, was an essential concomitant to their social acceptance by all classes. In each country where the sports revolution took hold a particular local twist was imparted to the mythology; but the basic emphases remained the same as they had been in the originating society, that of Victorian England. Naturally, in Ireland, and by an organisation devoted to the eradication of all things English, the attendant mythology was coloured by that hostility. It is true that, as Lyons has recently written,'every cultural initiative . . . was liable to be judged by a single criterion — whether it helped or hindered the breaking of the English connection'[73] but, as he also points out in his study of the higher cultural aspects of the period, those criteria had to be defined in relation to 'the English culture under whose shadow they existed and to which they had always to respond'.[74]

Response in the case of the GAA took the form of unconsciously imitative hostility. Much of what the GAA regarded as distinctive about the meaning and development of its games, and of their morality was, to only slightly overstate the case, merely substituting the word Ireland for the word England. Popular culture everywhere made strikingly similar demands of its games, and elicited strikingly similar responses that had particular national variations but an unchanging basic core.

This chapter has intended to suggest how the GAA might be

viewed as something more than a manifestation of Irish nationalism. Few if any aspects of Irish life escaped the consequences of centuries of English rule: literature, politics, language among them, even religion. It is not being disloyal to the myths of Irish nationalism to consider those effects. That the GAA, to many that most uncompromising symbol of Irish nationalist integrity, can be seen to have been as affected as any is no slur upon its nationality, but it is an indication of the complexity of the Irish cultural heritage.

NOTES

1. Letter of W. J. McCormack, *TLS*, 4 July 1980. See also his *Sheridan Le Fanu and Victorian Ireland* (Oxford, 1980) F. S. L. Lyons, *Culture and Anarchy in Ireland 1890-1939* (Oxford, 1979), can also be accounted part of a trend which began perhaps with P. O'Farrell, *Ireland's English Question* (London, 1971).
2. See, for example, my own two articles 'The IRB and the Beginnings of the Gaelic Athletic Association', *Irish Historical Studies*, vol. xx (1977) pp. 418-38, and 'Sport as Politics: the Gaelic Athletic Association 1884-1916' in R. Cashman and M. McKernan (eds), *Sport in History* (Brisbane, 1979) pp. 99-123; also M. Bourke, 'The Early GAA in South Ulster', *Clogher Record*, vol. vii (1969) pp. 5-26.
3. For the codification of soccer and of rugby see, for example, N. Mason, *Football!* (London, 1976). For developments in cricket see, for example, R. Bowen, *Cricket* (London, 1970) chs 5-8. Hockey (codified in the 1870s), boxing (given the Queensberry Rules in 1867) and horse-racing (regulated in 1830s) are further examples. There were also 'invented' games, such as lawn tennis (1873). For details on these and other sports see J. Arlott (ed.) *The Oxford Companion to Sport and Games* (Oxford, 1975) and J. A. Cuddon, *The Macmillan Dictionary of Sports and Games* (London, 1980).
4. For baseball in Japan see D. Roden, 'Baseball and the Quest for National Dignity in Meiji Japan', *American Historical Review*, vol. lxxxv (June 1980) pp. 511-34; for cricket in Australia my articles 'Games People Played . . .', *Historical Studies*, vol. xv (1973) pp. 511-35, and 'Cricket and Australian Nationalism in the Nineteenth Century', *Journal of the Royal*

Australian Historical Society, vol. lix (1973) pp. 225-46; for rugby in New Zealand (not yet well served in this respect) W. J. Morgan and G. Nicholson, *Report on Rugby* (London, 1959).

5. Roden, 'Baseball and the Quest for National Dignity', pp. 530-2, notes the infusion of particularly Japanese militarism, and of anti-American resentment into baseball's ethical stance. Australian cricket was given an indigenous twist, see, for example, Mandle, 'Cricket and Australian Nationalism', pp. 241-2 and 'Games People Played', p. 533. See also for a reverse development J. Rosselli, 'The Self-Image of Effeteness: Physical Education and Nationalism in Nineteenth-Century Bengal', *Past and Present*, vol. lxxxvi (1980) pp. 121-48.
6. *Freeman's Journal* and *Cork Examiner*, 3 Nov. 1884; see also Mandle, 'IRB and the Beginnings of the GAA', pp. 419-20.
7. T. S. O'Sullivan Papers (ms 15385, NLI) *United Ireland*, 30 May, 13 and 27 June 1885.
8. *United Ireland*, 7, 14 and 21 Feb. 1885.
9. *United Ireland*, 6 Aug. 1885, but see Mandle, 'IRB and the Beginnings of the GAA', p. 423.
10. *United Ireland*, 5 Sept. 1885.
11. For anti-Englishry, see, for example, Archbishop Croke's letter of support to the GAA, *United Ireland*, 27 Dec. 1884, and Michael Cusack in ibid., 3 Jan. 1885. Among club names were Young Ireland, Kickham's, Emmet's, Davitt's, Parnell's; see Mandle, 'IRB and the Beginnings of the GAA', p. 425 and note; and for the green flag, *United Ireland*, 26 Sept. 1885. The first Ban was against GAA athletes competing under any other rules from 17 Mar. 1885 (see *United Ireland*, 24 Jan. 1885).
12. The first competitions involving parish club teams competing against each other to win through to a final in which they met as representatives of their respective provinces were begun in 1887. In 1923 provincial selections replaced club sides.
13. The first executive committee meeting of the GAA, held 17 Jan. 1885, passed this resolution (*United Ireland*, 24 Jan. 1885).
14. The story of the 1887 convention at Thurles is told in detail in Mandle, 'IRB and the Beginnings of the GAA', pp. 432-7, where additional references to newspapers and police reports may be found.
15. There were over 1000 clubs, Fenian, clerical and unattached in 1890. By 1892 there were only 220 and

only three counties sent delegates to the Annual Convention in 1893, see Mandle, 'Sport as Politics', pp. 104, 106.
16. For Blake's own account see his *How the G.A.A. Was Grabbed* (n.p., 1900). For Dublin Castle's version see State Paper Office, Dublin Castle (hereafter SPO), Home Office Precis on Secret Societies, RIC Precis 11 Aug. and 5 Oct. 1895, 8 and 17 July 1897, 18 Jan. 1898. For the GAA's version, see T. F. O'Sullivan, *Story of the G.A.A.* (Dublin, 1916) pp. 133-4.
17. Rule changes in the 1890s included a reduction in the number of players to seventeen (1892), three 'points' to equal a goal (1896), and the lowering of the crossbar to eight feet from ten feet six inches (1896). The championships continued, but were completed two years in arrears. Not until 1912 did they come back fully into line. As for the Ban, in 1893 members of the Royal Irish Constabulary were allowed to join the GAA, and in 1896 the playing of other games was permitted.
18. The dispute between the IRB, and the Irish National Brotherhood (INB) which necessarily involved the GAA is told in L. O'Broin, *Revolutionary Underground* (Dublin, 1976) pp. 60-95, and its effects on the GAA in Mandle, 'Sport as Politics', pp. 106-9.
19. See O'Farrell, *Ireland's English Question*, pp. 224-40.
20. I am deeply indebted to Mr Marcus Bourke, both for allowing me access to the manuscript of his official history of the GAA, and for facilitating my access to the record of the GAA at Croke Park. I cannot agree with his opinion that the leaders of the GAA early in the twentieth century were not members of the IRB: the evidence from police files is overwhelming. On Nowlan see, for example, SPO, Home Office Secret Society Precis, 16 Oct. 1901, reporting that he attended an IRB meeting immediately after his election as President, also ibid., 14 Apr. and 17 Sept. 1902. He was named as IRB secretary in Callan, County Kilkenny in ibid., 19 Oct. 1899. O'Sullivan, O'Toole and Dooley (another GAA executive member) were named as IRB men in ibid., 14 Apr. 1902. For O'Toole see also 19 Jan. and 20 Feb. 1903. J. J. Walsh's own memoirs *Recollections of a Rebel* (Tralee, 1944) and in S. O Ceallaigh (ed.), *Gaelic Athletic Memories* (Dublin, 1945) especially p. 21 give rise to suspicion. Study of the file quoted, and of the Monthly Confidential Reports in the SPO shows that virtually every official of importance in the GAA, at central and county level, was an IRB man, and this some years before the accepted date of revival

of the Brotherhood prior to 1910.
21. See Mandle, 'Sport as Politics', p. 114.
22. Irish MPs Sexton, Duffy, Willie Redmond, McKillip and J. P. Hayden gave trophies and medals to GAA county associations (Bourke, unpub. ms).
23. See, for example, the Gaelic League being responsible for the revival of the GAA in Donegal from 1905 (*Irish Press GAA Golden Jubilee Supplement*, 14 Apr. 1934, p. 40) and a joint feis in Wicklow in 1906 (G. M. Byrne and P. J. Noonan, *50 Years of G.A.A. in Co. Wicklow* (Wicklow, 1935) p. 128). See also Douglas Hyde's preface to the *Gaelic Athletic Annual 1908-9* cited in O'Sullivan, *Story of the G.A.A.*, pp. 196-8, and P. O'Neill, *History of the G.A.A. 1910-1930* (Kilkenny, 1931) pp. 26-7.
24. B. MacLua, *The Steadfast Rule* (Dublin, 1967) pp. 43-4.
25. *The Gaelic Athletic Annual and County Directory* (Dublin, 1967) pp. 43-4.
26. *Gaelic Athlete*, 13 Jan. 1912; *Sport*, 24 Feb. 1917; P. O'Neill, *History of the G.A.A.*, p. 6.
27. See, for example, *Annual 1908-9*, p. 7; CO 904/11, 17 June 1905; CO 904/11, Divisional Inspector's Report, Sept. 1905, in Public Record Office, London.
28. *Gaelic Athlete*, 6 and 20 Dec. 1913. For example of club participation see: for Galway, PRO CO 904/14, Mar. 1914; for Waterford, PRO CO 904/93, May 1914; for other areas *Irish Volunteer*, 18 Apr. and 2 May 1914. The GAA's 1914 convention decision is reported in *Gaelic Athlete*, 18 Apr. 1914 and *Freeman's Journal*, 13 Apr. 1914.
29. The accusations are in *Royal Commission on the Rebellion in Ireland, Evidence* (1916) pp. 3, 18, 82. The GAA's demand was sent in a message to the Royal Commission, see GAA Control Council Minutes, 28 May 1916 (Croke Park, access by kind permission of the Secretary), also *Sport*, 3 June 1916. This, and other attempts to revive Gaelic games engendered resentment in later years. See, for example, Bourke's unpub. ms on the closed 1918 Annual Congress where James Boland's motion of censure on the delegates to Dublin Castle and London was passed 27 votes to 25. The issue was often revived during Ban debates in the Civil War period.
30. For 'Gaelic Sunday' see *Freeman's Journal*, 5, 8, 9, 10, 11, 13, 15, 22, 24, 27, 30, 31 July, 2, 3, 4, 5 Aug. 1918.
31. 'The Irish army from 1916 to 1921 had been almost exclusively recruited from the GAA' (Bourke, unpub. ms).

32. E. O'Duffy in O Ceallaigh (ed.), *Memories*, p. 181.
33. There is an extensive literature on 'Bloody Sunday' 21 Nov. 1920. See J. Gleeson, *Bloody Sunday* (London, 1962); T. Bowden, 'Bloody Sunday - a Reappraisal', *European Studies Review*, vol. ii (1972) pp. 25-42. Full newspaper reports are in *Freeman's Journal*, 22 Nov. 1920ff; see also the official British report PRO CO 904/168. See also C. Townshend, *The British Campaign in Ireland 1919-1921* (Oxford, 1975) pp. 129-31.
34. J. P. Power, *A Story of Champions* (Cork, 1941) p. 28.
35. J. O'Beirne-Ranelagh, 'The I.R.B. from the Treaty to 1924', *Irish Historical Studies*, vol. xx (1976) p. 27.
36. Ibid., p. 33 for the IRA; M. Bourke, unpub. ms and personal communication.
37. *Clare Champion*, 20, 27 Jan., 10 Feb. 1925; Bourke, unpub. ms.
38. *Freeman's Journal*, 12, 19, 28 and 30 June, 11 Aug. 1924; *Kerryman*, 7 and 28 June, 16 Aug. 1924; *Cork Examiner*, 30 June and 2 July 1924; *Sport*, 28 June and 5 July 1924.
39. MacLua, *That Steadfast Rule*, p. 59.
40. *Irish Independent*, 2 Apr. 1923; *Freeman's Journal*, 21 Apr. 1924.
41. S. O Ceallaigh, *Story of the G.A.A.* (Limerick, 1977) p. 83; *Sport*, 10 Dec. 1921.
42. *Freeman's Journal*, 3 Feb., 2 Mar. 1922.
43. Ibid., 22 Apr. 1922.
44. Ibid., 3, 9, 16 Mar., 22 Apr. 1922.
45. Ibid., 18 Aug. 1924 for attendances; for folklore see, for example, O Ceallaigh, *Story of the G.A.A.* pp. 81-3.
46. 'Carbery' (P. D. Mehigan), *Gaelic Football* (Dublin, 1941) p. 15; 'P. F.' (Patrick Foley), *Kerry's Football Story* (Tralee, 1945) p. 169.
47. 'Carbery', *Gaelic Football*, p. 19.
48. *GAA Official Brochure Jubilee Commemoration March, September 1934* (Longford, 1934) p. 76; 'P. F.', *Kerry's Football Story*, pp. 132-3.
49. See, for example, 'Carbery', *Gaelic Football*, p. 21.
50. Ibid.
51. *Annual 1907-8*, p. 27; *Sport*, 2 Feb. 1907 registered but their introduction was not until five years later, see *Sixty Glorious Years of the GAA: A History of National Achievement* (Dublin, 1947) p. 59.
52. R. Smith, *Decades of Glory* (Dublin, 1966) p. 73; *Sixty Years*, p. 60; 'Carbery', *Gaelic Football*, p. 41.
53. *Official Brochure*, p. 79, for Kerry and Kildare. The north's 'semi-soccer' style, as played by Louth and

Antrim was noted, and frowned upon, see *Gaelic Athlete*, 20 Jan. and 31 Aug. 1912, 5 July 1913, 4 July 1914.
54. For allowances see *Sport*, 22 June 1907; *Sixty Years*, pp. 63-4. The GAA made a profit of £1900 on the Croke Memorial Tournament (*Sport*, 5 July 1913).
55. O Ceallaigh, *Memories*, p. 141; *Sport*, 1 Jan. 1910.
56. Professionalism entered British soccer in the 1880s, British rugby, as rugby league, in the 1890s; in Australia professionalism was frowned upon, both in cricket and Australian Rules (see Mandle, 'Games People Played', pp. 531-4); in New Zealand and South Africa rugby stayed amateur.
57. *The Gaelic Athletic Annual and County Directory for 1907-8* (Dublin, 1907) pp. 18-19.
58. S. O Ceallaigh, *Story of the G.A.A.*, p. 119.
59. The *Gael* was the GAA's official newspaper in 1887, the *Celtic Times* Michael Cusack's. No copies of either have survived, although there are cuttings from the *Gael* in SPO, CBS 126/S. The *Champion* (1903) has also vanished, but a copy of its first issue is in SPO, CBS 29/88S.
60. F. Aloya in review of W. S. Peterson, 'Browning's Trumpeter', in *Victorian Studies*, vol. xxiii (1980) p. 512.
61. O Ceallaigh, *Memories*, p. 93.
62. *Annual 1907-8*, p. 16.
63. Ibid., p. 11.
64. O'Farrell, *Ireland's English Question*, p. 239.
65. 'Carbery', *Gaelic Football*, p. 148.
66. *United Ireland*, 8 May 1886.
67. See, for example, *United Ireland*, 28 Mar., 16 and 23 May 1885, and 20 Feb. 1886.
68. O Ceallaigh, *Memories*, p. 41, an advertisement on behalf of the Munster Council of the GAA.
69. 'Carbery', *Gaelic Football*, p. 13.
70. O'Sullivan, *Story of the G.A.A.*, p. 41.
71. Byrne and Noonan, *50 Years of G.A.A.*, pp. 49-50; 'Carbery', *Gaelic Football*, p. 109.
72. The literature on the relationship between Victorian sport and society is vast. For introduction and further reference see Haley, *The Healthy Body and Victorian Culture*, D. Newsome, *Godliness and Good Learning* (London, 1961), and two of my articles, 'Games People Played' and 'W. G. Grace as a Victorian Hero', *Historical Studies* (Melbourne) vol. xix (Apr. 1981) pp. 353-69.
73. Lyons, *Culture and Anarchy*, p. 82.
74. Ibid., p. 7.

8 Bernard Shaw's Other Island

A. M. GIBBS

The decision of the Corporation of Dublin in 1946 to offer Mr Bernard Shaw the Honorary Freedom of the City was not arrived at unanimously. One councillor declared Shaw to be not a fit mentor for either the youth or the adults of Ireland. Another complained that all he could find that Shaw had done for Ireland was to send 'an occasional long-distance wisecrack'.[1] Other compatriots of Shaw were more generous in their recognition of his achievement and more discerning in their understanding of his relations with Ireland. But even today there are those who, like the councillor in 1946, think of Shaw as having almost completely cast off his connections with Ireland, and even find themselves able to describe him as 'not very Irish'.[2] He is often omitted from critical books on Anglo-Irish literature, a fate he does not deserve, despite the fact that he was wont to deny the existence of the species Anglo-Irish.

Shaw's attitude towards Ireland was certainly complex. He described himself as 'a Supernationalist',[3] and in the Preface to *John Bull's Other Island* (written three years after the play, in 1907) declared that 'nationalism stands between Ireland and the light of the world'.[4] But such remarks can be quite misleading if they are taken as a summary of Shaw's attitude towards Ireland. Shaw did dissociate himself from chauvinist nationalism. But it is not difficult to reconcile that with his description of himself in a speech to the Fabian Society in 1919 as 'a patriotic Irishman',[5] or with a later comment that, in spite of reason and commonsense, he shared the conviction of the Irish that they are 'The Chosen Race'.[6] Very late in his life - at that time when, for many people, some simple but fundamental truths and self-discoveries come to the surface - Shaw wrote of Ireland and his connections with it:

> Eternal is the fact that the human creature born in Ireland and brought up in its air is Irish. . . . I have lived for twenty years in Ireland and for seventy-two in England; but the twenty came first, and in Britain I am still a foreigner and shall die one.[7]

If the seventy-four years he spent in England makes us think of the land of his birth as Bernard Shaw's other island, it was 'other' only in a physical, not in a spiritual, sense.

One part of the story of those first twenty years in Ireland which has had less than its due of attention from biographers was the family decision, taken when Shaw was ten, to move out of Dublin to a cottage on nearby Dalkey Hill, a largely rural area of furze-covered hills and splendid views of sea and sky. Very late in his life Shaw said in an interview that 'It is the beauty of Ireland that has made us what we are. I am a product of Dalkey's outlook'.[8] Shaw regarded the move to Dalkey as, along with his self-education in music and art, one of the great liberating experiences of his childhood. It was an escape from various prisons of the soul in Dublin, from Sunday church-going in a Protestant congregation of 'set faces, pale with the malignant rigidity produced by the suppression of all expression',[9] and from a series of schools, beginning with Wesley College and ending with the Dublin English Scientific and Commercial Day School, all of which Shaw hated. But if, in one sense, Dalkey was a liberating experience, it also seems to have been, more than anything else, what established Shaw's bondage with Ireland. In *Sixteen Self Sketches* he writes of that time in this way:

> I had one moment of ecstatic happiness in my childhood when my mother told me that we were going to live in Dalkey. I had only to open my eyes there to see such pictures as no painter could make for me. I could not believe that such skies existed anywhere else in the world until I read Shakespeare's 'this majestical roof fretted with golden fire', and wondered where he could have seen it if not from Torca Cottage.
>
> The joy of it has remained with me all my life.[10]

The essentially Irish character of Shaw's genius was recognised by his literary contemporaries both in Ireland and England. George Russell described him as 'a romantic, a true descendant of the writers of the Old Irish Sagas' who had 'decided when he was young that he would hide the leprechaun in himself under civilised clothing'.[11] Shaw's friend, Lady Gregory, was also reminded by Shaw of the old writings when she compared him to the Great Jester in the history of the ancient gods who, 'for all his quips and mischief . . . came when he was needed to the help of Finn and Fianna, and gave good teaching to the boy-hero Cuchulain'.[12] W. B. Yeats, in his essay 'J. M. Synge and the Ireland of his Time', links Shaw with Oscar Wilde and

Synge in some suggestive comments about the Irish literary imagination:

> Our minds, being sufficient to themselves, do not wish for victory but are content to elaborate our extravagance, if fortune aid, into wit or lyric beauty. . . . This habit of the mind has made Oscar Wilde and Mr. Bernard Shaw the most celebrated makers of comedy to our time . . . in Synge's plays also, fantasy gives the form and not the thought.[13]

In England, Max Beerbohm and G. K. Chesterton were amongst those who recognised the significance of Shaw's Irish background.

A selection of Shaw's non-dramatic writings on the subjects of Ireland and Irish nationalism was gathered together in 1962 in a volume entitled *The Matter with Ireland*. Ranging in date from 1886 to 1950, the essays, speeches, letters and other writings included in this volume amply demonstrate Shaw's continuing and lively engagement with Irish political and cultural issues and causes throughout his career. The personal pronouns he habitually employs in referring to the Irish are 'we' and 'us'.

The primary orientation of his attitude towards nationalism is established in a book review published in 1888 in which Shaw said, 'Nationalism is surely an incident of organic growth, not an invention. A man discusses whether he shall introduce a roasting jack into his kitchen but not whether he shall introduce an eye tooth into his son's mouth or lengthen him as he grows older.'[14] Shaw saw Ireland's self-determination as a 'natural right'[15] and as part of an 'inevitable order of social growth'.[16] He described the gaining of national liberty as the second phase in an ultimately irresistible process which begins with the gaining of personal liberty from feudal systems, slave-holding oligarchies and the like, and ends with the formation of international federations. In his pre-1923 comments on nationalism in Ireland, Shaw insists on the need for national self-determination, but at the same time takes a strongly critical view of nationalism as a cultural and social phenomenon. In a section of the Preface to *John Bull's Other Island* entitled 'The Curse of Nationalism', Shaw describes nationalist movements in general as 'the agonizing symptoms of a suppressed natural function'.[17] A country which is without national self-determination is like a man with a broken bone, who can think of nothing else until the bone is set. In Shaw's view, rabid nationalism, as distinct from naturally assumed national identity, is a manifestation of a fundamental disorder in the body politic. Until that disorder is righted all the evils of nationalism - the windbaggery and tub-thumping, the callousness and rancour, the stifling parochialism, the false sentimentality - will flourish. This sharply critical attitude of Shaw's towards Irish nationalism needs to be seen in the context of other aspects of his commentary on Irish affairs, such as his defences of Parnell (at the time of his fall) and of Roger Casement, his passionate protest at the summary execution of the leaders of the Easter Rising, or his trenchant arguments against the policy of devolution. Shaw's thinking about the kind of relation which he believed ought to exist between Ireland and England is well illustrated in his 1919 attack on devolution:

> To a nation seeking its freedom Devolution means no more than 'Good doggie! you may carry my stick.' It leaves all the residual powers with England, and puts upon Ireland the burden of such legislative jobs as the London House of Commons is too busy or too lazy or too stupid to find time for. It is rather like profit-sharing in the industrial world: an ingenious method of making the worker sweat himself to save his employer trouble. . . .
> If we are to remain in the British Commonwealth voluntarily, we will remain on exactly the same terms as England. First, we must be free as England is free: that is, we shall order our national life in our own way to our own taste over the whole range of it that is not touched by our treaty with the Commonwealth. That treaty will bind us, as it will bind England and the Dominions, to do certain specified things, and to accept a certain specified division of labor in public work between the States of the Commonwealth in matters affecting the whole organism. Outside that contract our relation to England will be that of France to England or the United States to Switzerland: that is, the relation of one grown-up man to another. What it will be inside the contract will depend on the covenants; but it will be like the relation established by the Australian contract as distinguished from that established by the original Canadian contract in respect of the residual powers.
> And so, Devolution, goodbye. Please dont call again.[18]

But if such comments reveal a great deal of sympathy with the struggle for self-determination in Ireland, they do not imply that Shaw could have agreed with the aim of the Irish National Literary Society to 'unite literature to the great passion of patriotism and ennoble both thereby'.[19] With

Edith Cavell, Shaw believed that 'patriotism is not enough'. Only in terms of what David Krause, in a discussion of Sean O'Casey, has called the 'higher nationalism', a nationalism which involves not only patriotic concern but 'the search for the truth about man, the quintessential nature of his character and his world',[20] could Shaw have endorsed such a manifesto.

Shaw's view of the Irish Question was also conditioned by his early allegiance to the wider cause of socialism. He saw the oppression of Ireland as part of a larger pattern of economic and political oppression which had its evil effects in the very country under whose yoke Ireland itself was suffering. The Irish, he urged, needed to perceive the fundamental similarities between their own situation and that of the oppressed classes in England. Writing to the *Irish Times* on the eve of the Civil War in 1922, he addressed the narrow nationalists among his fellow-countrymen as follows:

> I am a Supernationalist and a Socialist; and all I have to say to an Irish carpenter (for instance) is that as long as he hates an English carpenter he will be a slave, no matter what flag he flies. I cannot stand the stale romance that passes for politics in Ireland. I cannot imagine why people bother so much about us: I am sure we dont deserve it. Look at Russia: now there is a really interesting country politically. The bottom has fallen out of the centre of Europe, and England is on the brink of the abyss. But what matter if for Ireland dear we fall! It is too silly: I must hurry back to London. The lunatics there are comparatively harmless.[21]

Further illustrations of Shaw's ambivalent and critical, but not alien-minded, attitude towards Ireland and the Irish national character is provided by his treatment of these themes in the plays. Two of his full-length plays and one of the one-acters are set in Ireland, and Irish characters play significant roles in works set elsewhere. The fact that the matter of Ireland does not loom large in quantitative terms in Shaw's plays does not diminish its symbolic significance. Some of the essential qualities of his outlook and sensibility are defined in his treatment of this subject.

The extremes of Shaw's treatment of the Irish character are presented in his portrayal of two female characters, in the one-act plays *O'Flaherty VC* and *Press Cuttings*. The most fervent nationalist in all of Shaw's plays is the mother of the hero of *O'Flaherty VC*, Mrs O'Flaherty, who believes that Shakespeare was born in Cork, that Venus arose out of the sea in Killiney Bay, and that Lazarus was buried in Glasnevin. O'Flaherty is in trouble with his mother because she was tricked into believing that he was going to fight against, rather than with, the English. O'Flaherty's report of his mother's response to this deception is: 'And sure the poor woman kissed me and went about the house singing in her old cracky voice that the French was on the sea, and theyd be here without delay, and the Orange will decay, says the Shan van Vocht.' *O'Flaherty VC* carries the ironical sub-title *A Recruiting Pamphlet*, and in the play Irish nationalist fervour is brought into the play's general satire on patriotism, and protest against war. In the middle of the play, O'Flaherty, a reluctant and sceptical instrument of the recruiting campaign in Ireland, declares, no doubt thinking of his own kith and kin as much as anything else, that 'Youll never have a quiet world until you knock the patriotism out of the human race.'

Press Cuttings is a topical sketch on the Women's War in 1909. In a letter at the time, Shaw said that 'the only really sympathetic woman in the play is the Charwoman'.[22] The charwoman is Mrs Farrell, whose only women rivals for sympathy in the play are the dangerous Egeria, Lady Corinthia Fanshawe, and the militant and distinctly masculine secretary of the Anti-Suffraget League, Mrs Banger. Mrs Farrell is a survivor of a marriage which produced eight children (acquired in such numbers because her husband used to argue that controlling himself was against his religion) and is now in the employ of the play's principal male character, General Mitchener. Although it is only a minor role in a minor, though splendidly funny, play, Mrs Farrell epitomises Shaw's conception of the Irish national character at its best. Mrs Farrell is shrewd, sharply observant, verbally resourceful and a natural wit, a woman of both common and uncommon sense. She knows what goes on beneath the exterior of male pomposity and pretentiousness as well as she knows 'the seamy side o General Sandstone's uniform, where his flask rubs agen the buckle of his braces'. Defeated in verbal combat with Mrs Farrell about the relative risks of bearing 'livin people into the world' and 'blow[ing] dhem out of it', General Mitchener can only fall back on acknowledging her to be 'a woman of very powerful mind'. In a typical example of upward social mobility in Shavian comedy, Mrs Farrell eventually condescends to accept his offer of marriage.

In its overall span of time and space, Shaw's post-First World War play cycle, *Back to Methuselah*, departs from the classical unities almost as far as possible. The first play is set in the Garden of Eden and the last in a sunlit glade in an unspecified country in the year 31,920 AD. But far as the plays wander in their temporal and spatial journeys they also bear a close relation to the period in which they were written, and, in one play especially, to the contemporary history of Ireland.

The fourth play of the *Back to Methuselah* cycle, *Tragedy of an Elderly Gentleman*, is set on Burrin pier on the south shore of Galway Bay, in the year 3000 AD. The Elderly Gentleman, a world traveller, has come on a pilgrimage to the British Isles: 'I turn, with a hungry heart, to the mystery and beauty of these haunted islands, thronged with spectres from a magic past, made holy by the footsteps of the wise men of the West.' Unexpectedly, he finds himself in an utterly alien society, and in the custody of two rather horrendous products of evolution - a woman, Zoo, and a man, Zozim - creatures who have completely lost touch with spiritual and metaphysical concepts. Their topical relevance is underlined by the Elderly Gentleman's reference to Zoo as 'a primary flapper'. Amongst these people the Elderly Gentleman is rather in the position of a pathetic stray from the Savage Reservation of Huxley's *Brave New World*. Between him and his custodians there are insurmountable linguistic and cultural barriers. Zoo is unable to comprehend any other than the literal meaning of expressions such as 'blood is thicker than water', and mistakes the phrase 'a pious pilgrimage' for a reference to a new means of transport. Primitive marital and parental relations have completely gone, words such as 'father', 'Miss' and 'Mrs' have fallen out of polite use and blushing is unknown.

Back to Methuselah is not a successful work. In the final play Shaw resolves too facilely the real issues in more of a dystopian than utopian fable. But in the fourth part convincing tensions are established, the setting, and the Elderly Gentleman's reflections on Ireland and its people, play an essential part in the dialectical argument. By the year 3000 AD the Irish and the Jews are vanished races, and the world has become 'a tame dull place'. Before making that declaration the Elderly Gentleman looks back on Irish history after the granting of independence from England. Robbed of their main purpose in life, the Irish emigrate to various other countries where there was still a nationalist question:

> Hardly two hundred years had elapsed when the claims of nationality were so universally conceded that there was no longer a single country on the face of the earth with a national grievance or a national movement. Think of the position of the Irish, who had lost all their political faculties by disuse except that of nationalist agitation,

and who owed their position as the most interesting race on earth solely to their sufferings! The very countries they had helped to set free boycotted them as intolerable bores. The communities which had once idolized them as the incarnation of all that is adorable in the warm heart and witty brain, fled from them as from a pestilence.

Despite the severity of this speech, its positive notes are strongly sounded. A land of mystery, beauty and holiness, peopled by a race adored for its 'warm heart and witty brain' - this image of Ireland's past is an essential part of the argument directed in this play against the soulless, humourless and ruthless materialism of the brave new world of Zoo and Zozim, which is also, of course, the brave new world of post-First World War Europe. But Shaw allows Zoo one profound piece of advice to the Elderly Gentleman, which is also no doubt directed at contemporary Ireland: 'How often must I tell you that we are made wise not by the recollections of our past, but by the responsibilities of our future.'

In some ways, *Tragedy of an Elderly Gentleman* is a return to territory which Shaw had explored sixteen years before in *John Bull's Other Island*. *John Bull's Other Island* is Shaw's most extensive and comprehensive treatment of Irish themes in the plays and full justice can be done to it only in a separate discussion. But here perhaps I can briefly indicate some of the ways in which it fits into this general account of Shaw's engagement with the matter of Ireland.

The portrayal of Ireland and its material and spiritual problems in *John Bull's Other Island* is both entertaining and perceptive. It is a portrait born out of love and hate, and executed with a fine, pugnacious wit. Although Shaw is always skilful in his selection and evocation of the locale of his plays, perhaps none other in the canon gives us such a strong sense of place as *John Bull's Other Island*. W. B. Yeats remarked that it was the first of Shaw's plays to have a 'geographical conscience'.[23] The prosaic box set of Act I, part of the office of Doyle and Broadbent's civil engineering firm in London, effectively sets off the tranquil '*hillside of granite rock*', the '*round tower*' and the '*great breadths of silken green in the Irish sky*' of the scene at sunset with which Act II begins. But this has been verbally anticipated in a speech of Doyle's in Act I so as to place its soft, melancholy charm in a critical light. It is an indication of Shaw's dread of sentimentality that this passage, one of the very few of his writings where a landscape is sharply and sensuously evoked, should be set in the context of a fierce denunciation of Ireland:

But your wits cant thicken in that soft moist air, on
those white springy roads, in those misty rushes and brown
bogs, on those hillsides of granite rocks and magenta
heather. Youve no such colors in the sky, no such lure in
the distances, no such sadness in the evenings.

The stage directions make demands of specificity unusual
even for Shaw. Larry Doyle has to scream with laughter, at
one point, '*in the falsetto Irish register unused for that
purpose in England*'; the garden of Cornelius Doyle's should
contain the remnant of a plaster statue of a Roman lady such
as '*grow naturally in Irish gardens*'; the car which appears
in Act II should be a Bianconi. Yeats's fears that the
play's technical demands might prove too great for the Abbey
Theatre were possibly well-founded, though probably there
were other reasons for not going ahead with its production.[24]

John Bull's Other Island is at once a highly critical and
deeply sympathetic portrayal of Ireland. It is a mistaken
approach to the play to try to identify any one of the three
principal male characters Broadbent, Keegan and Doyle as the
spokesman for Shaw's own views. In a recent London production,
the producer had Larry Doyle, the cynical, dyspeptic
Irishman who has taken up residence in London, wander
down to the front of the stage from time to time and deliver
his speeches as though he were the voice of the oracle. But
Doyle is a character in a play, and he is eventually seen in
the play as, despite his intelligence and insights, an
ineffectual and destructive critic and an inadequate human
being. As Father Keegan points out late in the play, it is
Irishmen such as Doyle who turn Ireland into 'a Land of
Derision'. It is more true to say that the three major
characters in the play reflect conflicting impulses in
Shaw's mind and temperament which were never quite synthesised,
except perhaps temporarily in the triumvirate of
spirit, intelligence and material force which is formed at
the end of *Major Barbara*.

In his presentation of the local inhabitants of Rosscullen
in *John Bull's Other Island*, Shaw provides a deft,
intimately knowledgeable portrait in miniature of Irish
village life. A far cry from the Irishmen of sentimental
comedies such as *Finnucane's Rainbow* or *The Colleen Bawn* are
Shaw's seedy ex-land agent Cornelius Doyle, the disgruntled
and quarrelsome small-time landlord farmer, Matt Haffigan,
the sturdy, but unimaginative and limited Catholic priest,
Father Dempsey, the superstitious Patsy Farrell, the red-headed,
loutish Doran, the commonsensical Aunt Judy, and the
wan, emotionally starved Nora. In the depressed economy

caused by a combination of exploitative landlords, local and absentee, inefficient farming, and apathy, the village is ripe for takeover by the all-conquering incarnation of John Bull, Broadbent. Not even their perception of his ignorance and absurdity can prevent the local Irish from being drawn into the wake of Broadbent's bustling energy, as he comes to Ireland with his head full of Gladstonian ideals, and develops his plans for turning Rosscullen into a tourist resort, with himself as the chief beneficiary.

Early on, Larry Doyle delivers a passionately critical denunciation of Ireland as a nation paralysed by imagination, dreaming and sentimentality. The Irishman, he says,

> cant be religious. The inspired Churchman that teaches him the sanctity of life and the importance of conduct is sent away empty; while the poor village priest that gives him a miracle or a sentimental story of a saint, has cathedrals built for him out of the pennies of the poor. He cant be intelligently political: he dreams of what the Shan Van Vocht said in ninetyeight. If you want to interest him in Ireland youve got to call the unfortunate island Kathleen ni Hoolihan and pretend she's a little old woman. It saves thinking.

But there is another image of Ireland in the play which provides us with the measure of what Broadbent and his 'foolish dream of efficiency' will destroy. For Father Keegan, Broadbent, for all his good nature and good intentions, is the ass of Mammon, 'mighty in mischief, skilful in ruin, heroic in destruction', who has come to browse in Ireland 'without knowing that the soil his hoof touches is holy ground'. Through Keegan's eyes, Ireland is seen as a place sanctified by its ancient religious traditions, but betrayed in its finer aspirations by its own servants of Mammon. Keegan is a powerful opponent of Broadbent. But in the end all he can do is to submit, and retreat to Rosscullen's Round Tower and break his heart 'uselessly in the curtained gloaming over the dead heart and blinded soul of the island of the saints'.

Shaw's description of *John Bull's Other Island* in the first sentence of the Preface as a 'patriotic' play was only partly a jest. His play is a challenge to, not simply a satirical attack upon, contemporary Ireland. In this play, as more generally in his work, the upholders of sweetness and light command our primary allegiance and sympathy. But perhaps more successfully than any other writer of his time Shaw was able to reveal, in his portrayal of characters such as Ramsden in *Man and Superman* Broadbent in *John Bull's*

Other Island and Undershaft in *Major Barbara*, the nature of those forces in society which are pitted against sweetness and light. In *John Bull's Other Island*, the passionate utterances of Father Keegan tend to be simply swallowed up in the enormous ocean of Broadbent's bland geniality, or to come up against the wall of his invincible pragmatism. Commenting on one of Father Keegan's speeches, in which he expresses his allegiance to a truly universal Catholicism, Broadbent says: 'these things cannot be said too often: they keep up the moral tone of the community'. As Keegan goes off to his Round Tower at the end of the play after delivering an inspired speech about his dream of a totally unified human culture, Broadbent watches him out and muses on his possibilities as a tourist attraction.

> Broadbent: [*looking after him affectionately*]
> What a regular old Church and State Tory he is: He's a character: he'll be an attraction here. Really almost equal to Ruskin and Carlyle.

The last scene of the play is constructed in such a way as to bring the Broadbent and Keegan themes to their final point of development almost simultaneously. Keegan's account of his dream of heaven, delivered from a position upstage and above Doyle and Broadbent, forms part of a delicately constructed and effective coda to the last movement of discussion in Act IV. The elevated rhetoric of Keegan's dream - the speech has a strongly marked, liturgical rhythm - is prepared for in his arresting line as he turns to face the two below him, 'Every dream is a prophecy: every jest is an earnest in the womb of Time'. The tension created by this line is momentarily released by the conversational tone of the prose in Broadbent's next speech about his dream of heaven; but this provides a springboard for the measured, hieratic diction of:

> In my dreams it is a country where the State is the Church and the Church the people: three in one and one in three. It is a commonwealth in which work is play and play is life: three in one and one in three. It is a temple in which the priest is the worshipper and the worshipper the worshipped: three in one and one in three. It is a god-head in which all life is human and all humanity divine: three in one and one in three. It is, in short, the dream of a madman. [*He goes away across the hill.*]

This vision, of a state in which the distinction between divine and human natures is dissolved; a society in which

State and Church are identical institutions, embodied not in remote groups of politicians or priests, but in the whole population; a commonwealth in which work is play and play the business of life, harmonises with Shaw's own outlook as expressed in non-dramatic contexts. Religious, political, cultural, economic pursuits should not, he believed, be regarded as stemming from distinct and separable human impulses and concerns. He once remarked to Hesketh Pearson: 'You are still a bit in the nineteenth-century in respect to arranging religion, politics, science, and art in braintight compartments, mostly incompatible and exclusive. . . . They don't exist that way at all.'[25] But there is something of a paradox here since the nineteenth century offers some remarkably close parallels to Shaw's ideas in this regard. The notion that humanity itself should be an object of religious worship, for example, might well have been suggested to Shaw by the positivist system of Auguste Comte, and William Morris and Ruskin anticipate Father Keegan's ideas about work and play.

Father Keegan's dream belongs in essence to a tradition of romantic thought which M. H. Abrams, borrowing a phrase from Carlyle, has called 'natural supernaturalism'.[26] The notion of a state in which 'all humanity [is] divine' epitomises the romantic quest for a religious faith centred not on concepts of the supernatural but on humanity and the natural world. T. E. Hulme's description of romanticism as 'spilt religion' is peculiarly appropriate to the vision of Father Keegan, a character whose position as a religious figure Shaw has deliberately surrounded with ambiguity. He is a priest but not a priest. His outlook is religious but not ecclesiastical. Patsy Farrell has trouble with his name as a result: 'Arra, hwat am I to call you? Father Dempsey sez youre not a priest; n we all know youre not a man: n how do we know what ud happen to us if we shewed any disrespect to you?' Keegan's dream is cast in a deeply ironic light by Broadbent's remarks at the end of Act IV. We realise that Keegan's utopian dream has been dreamed before and that Broadbent's twentieth-century 'progressive' bustle will almost certainly keep it firmly in its place as a dream. Keegan is echoing the lost causes of the previous century. But if in one way the comic anticlimax here works against Keegan, reducing him, in the debasing perspective of Broadbent's business eye, to a mere tourist attraction, it is clear that Broadbent is victorious in only limited senses. Keegan's dream and his declaration about dreams as prophecy, with its reminder of the evolutionary thought of *Man and Superman*, to some degree balances the more sceptical aspects at the end. It is very much to the point of the argument of this paper that Shaw should choose Ireland as the setting for one of his most searching explorations of themes which continued to preoccupy him throughout his career.

Some time ago Mr Angus Wilson delivered a lecture in Australia with the title 'The Artist As Your Enemy Is Your Only Friend'.[27] The notion of the artist as a friendly enemy, as one courageous enough 'to reveal his hostilities to the very full' and yet who serves man by enriching his imagination and bringing him to confrontation with his true self, and forcibly, in Sir Philip Sidney's sense, recalling fundamental human values, provides an apt description of Shaw in his relation with Ireland. It also suggests one way in which Shaw can be linked with other Irish writers of his time: with J. M. Synge, 'that rooted man' as Yeats called him, whose *Playboy of the Western World* presented such an unflattering picture of Ireland as to cause a riot; with Sean O'Casey who in plays such as *Juno and the Paycock* and *The Plough and the Stars* forcefully attacks the 'murtherin hate' and false sentiment which he saw as undermining the very humanity of his countrymen; and even with W. B. Yeats who in the poems 'September 1913' and 'Nineteen Hundred and Nineteen' meditates on a race which has degenerated from its best self, and lost touch with its best traditions, a race which now fumbles in a greasy till and traffics in mockery.

Shaw was aware of the need for that kind of relation to exist between the artist and society in a national culture. Commenting on the Irish Players in 1911, he said,

> In a modern Irish play the hero doesnt sing that 'Ould Ireland' is his country and his name it is Molloy; he pours forth all his bitterness on it like the prophets of old.
>
> The last time I saw an Irish play in Dublin, the line on which the hero made his most effective exit was 'I hate Ireland'. Even in the plays of Lady Gregory, penetrated as they are by . . . intense love of Ireland . . . there is no flattery of the Irish; she writes about the Irish as Moliere wrote about the French.[28]

It is that double relation which Shaw describes here of hostility and amity in the writer's stance, which is surely one of the primary conditions of a vital national culture.

When Prospero first came to his island in Shakespeare's *The Tempest*, he found Ariel confined fast into a cloven pine:

> within which rift
> Imprison'd thou didst painfully remain

A dozen years.

Shaw's 'cloven pine' was Dublin. In order to realise his powers, Shaw needed, as did James Joyce, to get out of Dublin, and to get out of Ireland. But he did not repudiate his national origins, and he contributed very much more than the 'occasional long distance wisecrack' to the national culture of Ireland in his time.

NOTES

1. Bernard Shaw, *The Matter with Ireland*, ed. David H. Greene and Dan H. Laurence (London, 1962) pp. 292-3.
2. Henry Summerfield, 'AE as a Literary Critic', in Joseph Ronsley (ed.), *Myth and Reality in Irish Literature* (Ontario, 1977) p. 58. Cf. Daniel Corkery's remarks on expatriate Irish writers: 'Some of them, of course, have cut away their own land as summarily as Henry James did his. Shaw, Ervine, Munro, others, are of the class', in *Synge and Anglo-Irish Literature* (Cork, 1931) p. 5.
3. *The Matter with Ireland*, p. 257.
4. Bernard Shaw, *Collected Plays with their Prefaces*, ed. Dan H. Laurence, 7 vols (London, 1970-4) vol. ii, p. 842.
5. *The Matter with Ireland*, p. 257.
6. Ibid., p. 296.
7. These comments appear in an essay contributed by Shaw to the *New Statesman* on 30 Oct. 1948, entitled 'Ireland Eternal and External' (reprinted in *The Matter with Ireland*, pp. 294-5).
8. *The Matter with Ireland*, p. 291.
9. *Shaw: An Autobiography, 1856-1889* (selected from his writings by Stanley Weintraub (London, 1970) p. 31.
10. Bernard Shaw, *Sixteen Self Sketches* (London, 1949) p. 72.
11. Review of Gwladys Evan Morris's *Tales from Bernard Shaw*, in *Irish Statesman*, 14 Sept. 1929, pp. 38-9, cited by Summerfield, 'AE as a Literary Critic', p. 58.
12. Lady Gregory, note to *The Jester*, in *The Collected Plays of Lady Gregory*, ed. Ann Saddlemyer, 4 vols (London, 1971) vol. iii, p. 379, cited by Herbert Howarth, *The Irish Writers, 1880-1940* (London, 1958) p. 18.
13. W. B. Yeats, *Essays and Introductions* (London, 1961) pp. 338-9.

14. *The Matter with Ireland*, p. 21.
15. *Collected Plays*, vol. ii, p. 844.
16. *The Matter with Ireland*, p. 23.
17. *Collected Plays*, vol. ii, p. 843.
18. *The Matter with Ireland*, pp. 198-9.
19. W. B. Yeats, 'The Irish National Literary Society', in A. Norman Jeffares (ed.), *W. B. Yeats: Selected Criticism* (London, 1964) p. 18.
20. David Krause, 'Sean O'Casey and the Higher Nationalism: the Desecration of Ireland's Household Gods', in Robert O'Driscoll (ed.), *Theatre and Nationalism in Twentieth-Century Ireland* (London, 1971) p. 115.
21. *The Matter with Ireland*, p. 257.
22. *Bernard Shaw: Collected Letters, 1889-1910* (London, 1972) p. 843.
23. Cited by M. J. Sidnell, *'John Bull's Other Island - Yeats and Shaw'*, PMLA, vol. lxxxii (1967) p. 546.
24. See A. M. Gibbs, 'Yeats, Shaw and Unity of Culture', *Southern Review* (Australia) vol. vi (1973) pp. 194-5.
25. Hesketh Pearson, *G. B. S: A Postscript* (New York, 1950) p. 61.
26. M. H. Abrams, *Natural Supernaturalism: Tradition and Revolution in Romantic Literature* (London, 1971).
27. *Southern Review* (Australia) vol. ii (1966) pp. 101-14.
28. *The Matter with Ireland*, p. 65.

9 Imagination and Revolution: the Cuchulain Myth

PATRICK RAFROIDI

In the Dublin General Post Office, the headquarters of the 1916 Revolution, Oliver Sheppard's bronze memorial to the men who started the struggle and sacrificed their lives represents the Celtic warrior Cuchulain - the main hero of the Ulster cycle - tied to a stone pillar facing his enemies, with the raven goddess of war perched on his shoulder, a reminder of whom the revolutionary leader Patrick Pearse 'summoned to his side'[1] and an apt symbol of the strange marriage which it is our task to try and describe here in the background of, essentially, the first quarter of the twentieth century in Ireland.

Like most Gaelic figures - some of whom had remained alive in the tales which the Gaeltacht still cherished in the original tongue, though, not this one[2] - Cuchulain is a rediscovery of the Romantic period, Macpherson's first and then Charlotte Brooke's: in her *Reliques* of 1789 are found such pieces as 'Conloch', or 'the Lamentation of Cucullin over the body of his son Conloch' and the Hound of Ulster reappeared in the poetical works of several writers of the first and second generations: Aubrey Thomas De Vere,[3] Denis Florence MacCarthy,[4] and Samuel Ferguson.[5]

It is noticeable, that such authors laid stress on the more 'sentimental' episodes of the saga and tended to blur both the energy and the tragic intensity of the hero - a trap some later adapters would not avoid any better, witness Eva Gore-Booth's ecological ejaculations of the type: 'My heart is like a haunted forest glade!'[6] We are far at once from the original and from its re-creation by a great modern poet like Austin Clarke:

> Terrible within the West!
> Flaming among those kingdomless sea-mountains,
> And bound by storm against stupendous cliffs,
> Cuchullin shone![7]

The great romantic Irish myths, down to John Millington Synge, could only be female: Roisin Dubh, Kathleen ni Houlihan or Deirdre of the Sorrows.

For Cuchulain to come to his own again required a wider and more profound knowledge and a popularisation of his high deeds, together with an adequation of his destiny to the tendencies, experiences and needs of a different generation.

Knowledge and popularisation came through the exertions firstly of Standish James O'Grady who came across, quite by chance, Sylvester O'Halloran's unreliable history of Ireland, then delved into Eugene O'Curry's more learned material, enthusiastically set upon the task: 'I desire', he wrote, 'to make this heroic period once again a portion of the imagination of the country, and its chief characters as familiar in the minds of our people as they once were'[8], and succeeded, not in recapturing the real spirit of the past, but (so Yeats thought) in making 'the old Irish heroes, Fion and Oisin, and *Cuchullan* alive again'.[9] He succeeded beyond his hopes and desires, for this Irish Unionist who hated the mob was no revolutionary and wanted even less than Yeats to send out certain men the English shot, and yet had foreseen as early as 1899 he would do so: 'We have now a literary movement, it is not very important; it will be followed by a political movement, that will not be very important; then must come a military movement, that will be important indeed.'[10] Besides, his pioneer work was propped up by other endeavours starting with Eleanor Hull's in 1898. Her introduction to *The Cuchillin Saga* may perhaps detain us a second:

> A recent American essayist, Mr Godkin, has said that 'no country retains the hearty affection of its educated classes which does not feed their imagination'. Patriotism, that is to say, does not rest to any large degree upon a natural pride in the physical beauty of the country that gave us birth, nor yet on a legitimate satisfaction in its commercial or industrial prosperity; it rests upon what we may call *the historic imagination*.

Then, there came Lady Gregory's (whose seminal *Cuchulain of Muirthemne* (1902) added to the presentation of the legend the notation, or invention of an Irish form of English, the Kiltartan dialect) and Windisch's authoritative text in 1905.

Also, the times were ripe. Overshadowed by imperial England, Ireland was ready for the Cuchulain myth just as Germany, overshadowed by cosmopolitan France, had been ready for the Siegfried one. Sick of being considered as the buffoons of the Empire, Irishmen were eager to embrace any representation that restored their self-respect. Thus AE (George Russell) reacted to the rediscovery of Cuchulain and his knights, he said, like a man 'who suddenly feels ancient memories rushing at him, and knows he was born in a royal house, that he had mixed with the mighty of heaven and earth and had the very noblest companions.'[11]

Action and revolution, rather than grief and moaning, were becoming the cry of the day, even if it should entail fighting one's only son (like Cuchulain's Conloch) or one's best friend (like Ferdiad) - the hazards of civil war.

Heroism was needed; devotion to the cause, be it until the ultimate sacrifice; decorum and a religious dimension also, which would hardly be found *solely* in a creed whose kingdom was not of this world, and here it was that Cuchulain on his rock and Jesus on his cross could be fused into one, in a sort of Jewish rather than Christian messianism, in a nativistic as well as a Catholic outlook.

This, at least, was the feeling of Patrick Pearse whose ideal Irishman was, in Stephen MacKenna's phrase[12] 'a Cuchulain baptized' and for whom the boy Christ who had confounded the learned doctors and the boy warrior of Gaelic legend who had confounded the skilled knights of the Red Branch were not opposed any more than the Gospel and the antique Irish evangel:

We must re-create and perpetuate in Ireland the knightly tradition of Cuchulainn, 'better is short life with honour than long life with dishonour'; 'I care not though I were to live but one day and one night, if only my fame and my deeds live after me'; the noble tradition of the Fianna, 'we, the Fianna, never told a lie, falsehood was never imputed to us'; 'strength in our hands, truth on our lips, and cleanness in our hearts'; the Christ-like tradition of Colmcille, 'if I die it shall be from the excess of love I bear the Gael'.[13]

A similar fusion of Christian and native elements occurs in the very Declaration of the Irish Republic by Pearse: 'In the name of God and of the dead generations from which she receives her old tradition of nationhood, Ireland, through us, summons her children . . .' and elsewhere, and before - particularly in the piece written in November 1913 and entitled 'The Coming Revolution' - the double origin of Pearse's vision had been clearly at work:

the people itself will perhaps be its own Messiah, the people labouring, scourged, crowned with thorns, agonising and dying, to rise again immortal and impassible. For peoples are divine and are the only things that can properly be spoken of under figures drawn from the divine epos.

Even more so in the concluding words of the article: 'Bloodshed is a cleansing and a sanctifying thing, and the nation which regards it as the final horror has lost its manhood. There are many things more horrible than bloodshed; and slavery is one of them.'[14]

Such statements have been held against the man who uttered them - as if he had been the only one in his time to nurture these beliefs including the socialists that a later generation would visualise in opposition to Pearse. This is a mistake Yeats did not make in 'The Rose Tree', where Connolly seems to agree with the other leader:

'But where can we draw water,'
Said Pearse to Connolly,
'When all the wells are parched away?
O plain as plain can be
There's nothing but our own red blood
Can make a right Rose Tree'.[15]

Sean O'Casey in *The Plough and the Stars* quotes verbatim the passage on 'bloodshed', or rather puts its very words into the mouth of the tall dark man of Act II whose war-like injunctions are indirectly condemned by Nora's sufferings and directly ridiculed by the comments of vulgar personae such as Rosie the prostitute: 'It's th' sacred truth, mind you, what that man's afther sayin'; the barman: 'If I was only a little younger, I'd be plungin' mad into th' middle of it';[16] or Fluther, the stage-Irishman:

Jammed as I was in th' crowd, I listened to th' speeches patterin' on th' people's head, like rain fallin' on th' corn; every derogatory thought went out o' me mind, an' I said to meself, 'You can die now, Fluther, for you've seen th' shadow-dhreams of th' past leppin' to life in th' bodies of livin' men that show, if we were without a titther o' courage for centuries, we're vice versa now!' Looka here. [*He stretches out his arm . . . and rolls up his sleeve*] The blood was BOILIN' in me veins![17]

Peter's answer, 'I was burnin' to dhraw me sword, an' wave an' wave it over me' [18] refers to yet another familiar phrase of Pearse's also to be found in 'The Coming Revolution':[19] 'Whenever Dr. Hyde . . . has produced his dove of peace, I have always been careful to produce my sword.'

As for Patrick Pearse's love of myth and his poetic gifts, they have been used to emphasise his dreaminess and lack of practical ability - an accusation which the recent publication of his correspondence[20] should easily dismiss, however. Witness the mention of his 'archaistic visions' in Iris Murdoch's *The Red and the Green* [21] or the following remark by one of the characters in the novel: 'The man [Pearse] . . . romanticized Ireland's heroic past, which he peopled not only with Red Branch Knights but also ghosts and fairies and leprechauns.' And this is also the place, probably, to recall an instructive dialogue in Mervyn Wall's *Leaves for the Burning* (1946):

– 'I must admit that I've always had a certain sympathy for fools. Our rebellion in 1916 and our whole national movement was started by fools who expected nothing out of it for themselves.'
– 'Men of vision, I would rather call them,' said the County Manager softly.
– 'Men of vision me eye,' ejaculated the Senator, 'fellows that wrote poetry, and the like. . . . We're the men of vision. We're the ones that did well for ourselves out of their sacrifice.'[22]

It is highly ironical that one of Pearse's best known poems should be called, precisely, 'The Fool'. Lucidity at least cannot be denied him:

The lawyers have sat in council, the men with the
  keen, long faces,
And said, 'This man is a fool', and others have
  said, 'He blasphemeth';
And the wise have pitied the fool that hath
  striven to give a life
In the world of time and space among the bulks of
  actual things,
To a dream that was dreamed in the heart,
  and that only the heart could hold.

O wise men, riddle me this: what if the dream
  come true?
What if the dream come true and if millions unborn
  shall dwell
In the house that I shaped in my heart, the noble
  house of my thought? . . .[23]

The dream, as we know, did come true – in parts, which is enough to assert that in the case of Pearse as in the case of many of his Irish contemporaries, the usual dichotomy between imagination and action is as useless as it is irrelevant, one of those false *'idées reçues'* which would greatly benefit by a Flaubertian treatment.

We are not suggesting that the prime function of literary myth is not to operate within its own circle, i.e. act as an image that yet fresh images begets to be judged according to their new originality, stylistic value and adequacy to express the writer's self - what Cuchulain does for Yeats whose dramas devoted to the archetypal hero 'appear at particular critical periods of his life' as Birgit Bjersby (Bramsback) noted[24] and display 'a fascinating pattern of his own emotions and experiences'.

But there can already be a link between personal aspirations and the aspirations of an age or poetical aspirations and the aspirations of men of action. Thus did Yeats reinvent Cuchulain not only for self-expression but *also* as the ritual of a lost faith, in the hope of re-creating an heroic age for Ireland and resuscitating an all-round, Parnell-like chief: 'warrior, aristocrat, political leader and visionary',[25] the equation between the legendary and the historical figure being all the easier as Yeats was used to portraying the uncrowned king as 'tragic Cuchullain disdainful of the ignoble Firbolgs by whom he was dragged down and torn apart'.[26]

A similar occurrence took place with the master of St Enda's, a school where - according to Desmond Ryan, also a teacher there, like Thomas MacDonagh - Cuchulain was 'an invisible but important member of the staff'. The difference with Yeats is that Pearse finally identified himself with the hero *in action* instead of merely indulging a nostalgic mood, thus transmuting myth into an active, present force; before being 'changed, changed utterly' through martyrdom, he went perhaps even further. The main character in *The Scythe and the Sunset* which is Denis Johnston's response to *The Plough and the Stars* just as his *Moon in the Yellow River* is his own distorted echo of *Juno and the Paycock* is Pearse in disguise under the name of Sean Tetley. Towards the end of the play he takes part in an interesting dialogue with a woman called, typically enough, Emer, and a military, Palliser:

> *Tetley*: There's a better use I can make of the last few days of my life than by being burnt to death like a rat. So we're going to surrender.
> *Emer*: [*horrified*] Surrender! But if you do that they'll only hang you!
> *Tetley* [*with grave simplicity*]: Yes I hope I can face up to it. I think I can.
> *Palliser*: [*disturbed*] That's not a soldier's end.

Tetley: Then may be you were right, Captain. Maybe I'm not much of a soldier after all. [*Then with a slight smile.*] Perhaps I'M SOMETHING MORE SIGNIFICANT.[27]

Would it be too far-fetched, I wonder, to remark on the choice of two poems arranged from older versions, one modernised by Yeats, the other translated by Pearse. Yeats's is the well-known:

'I am *of* Ireland, [our italics]
And the Holy Land of Ireland
And time runs on' cried she,
'Come out of charity,
Come dance with me in Ireland'[28]

Pearse's is:

I am Ireland
I am older than the old woman of Beare.

Great my glory
I that bore Cuchulainn.[29]

We need not, perhaps, go as far as William Irwin Thompson when he states that 'the Irish revolutionaries lived as if they were in a work of art', adding that 'this inability to tell the difference between sober reality and the realm of imagination is perhaps one very important characteristic of a revolutionary'.[30] But we may undoubtedly follow him when, adapting Jean Piaget's and Heinz Werner's theories to a different field, he asserts that 'as language is responsible for the growth of a consciousness of self by articulating the diffuse thought of a child, art is responsible for the growth of society's consciousness of itself'.[31] And we can accept Peter Costello's statement: 'The cultural revival made possible the political revolution by creating a new ideal of Ireland, and the literature of the revival provides what might almost be called "the secret history" of the Irish revolution'.[32]

There remains a last question: what of the Cuchulain myth since 1916? Of course, as we all know, myths never die, being rooted in the eternity of the human and cosmic tendencies that gave them birth, and Cuchulain, the son of the Sun-God Lug, is no exception.

Yet, in the foul rag-and-bone shop of the heart, each generation re-creates what suits it best and Cuchulain seems to stand a chance in the present one only as a regret, or as a standard by which to measure the mediocrity of our age. This

is, at any rate, the impression his introduction in Eimar
O'Duffy's *King Goshawk and the Birds*[33] leaves, although he
- Cuchulain - has, indeed, kept fit:

> You should have seen Cuchulain playing tennis with the
> gentry and ladies of the Bon Ton suburb. He learnt the
> whole art and skill of the game in ten minutes, and
> straightway beat the champion of all Ireland six-love,
> six-love and six-love. Never had such strength and agility
> been seen before. He could cross the court in one leap, he
> never served a fault, and none but the champion ever ret-
> urned his service; he would take any stroke on the volley;
> and at the net his smash invariably burst the ball.

As a literary impetus, Synge had already discarded him: 'I
do not believe in the possibility of a purely fantastic,
unmodern, ideal, breezy springdayish, Cuchulainoid National
Theatre . . .' he wrote in 1904, and it is without glory he
appears in the pages of the sneering author of *The Shadow
of a Gunman* in praise of a pair of braces: 'They'd do
Cuchullian, they're so strong'[34], which doesn't prevent
them, of course, from breaking.

Since then, although he has recovered his dignity when he
appears, such appearances, down to Thomas Kinsella's
Tain,[35] have been limited to retellings of the ancient
saga, without any identification of the teller to the hero
of old, and without any obvious 'lesson' to be drawn.

Our contemporaries cannot reactuate the Cuchulain myth
without feeling guilty of a double sin which they are no
longer willing to commit: the first being the un-Irish sin
of pompousness - taking oneself seriously; the second, per-
version of the role of the artist - and the critic - as now
conceived, rightly or wrongly, by those who belong to these
confraternities in the western world.

Insofar as the artist is concerned, Yeats had already
sensed and expressed the danger; Shaw had denounced it. More
recently Francis Stuart, in a meditation on Marcuse, recalled, to indicate agreement with them, the philosopher's
statements:

> Art must never lose its negative and alienating power
> . . . . To lose this power is, in effect, to eliminate the
> (necessary) tension between art and reality. . . . Art
> cannot submit to the actual requirements of the revolution
> without denying itself.[36]

As for criticism, it is obvious it cannot use as relevant
criteria good intentions and conformity to an ideal other

than aesthetic. Thus has it come to dismiss most of the heroic writings of a previous period, as Patrick Kavanagh did, in his usual blunt way: 'The important thing about this idea of literature, was how Irish was it. No matter what sort of trash it was, if it had the Irish quality'[37] and it is not ready to embark upon a similar venture for the future.

In actual life - whether or not it is also conveyed through literature - Cuchulain does not fare much better as scepticism concerning war and who profits by it keeps growing, as the cult of personality is looked down upon, nothing seems to justify the loss of a human life, and efficiency becomes more praiseworthy than honour.

The Cuchulain myth can operate only in an heroic period that fosters admiration and a degree of imitation for the warrior who serves and struggles for the motherland even though the majority of the others undergo the kind of debility that the Ulstermen of the beginning of the Christian era are said to have suffered: like women, they were stricken as with pangs of child birth - probably a symbol for what was once called the sensual life and could now be described as the stigma of affluent society.

In such a period Cuchulain's appeal could work beyond his usual battlefields. He had already moved from North to South. A writer like Francis Ledwidge who, in his *Songs of the Fields* (1915) had devoted several poems to him, could carry him to France and Belgium where he was killed on 31 July 1917, fighting 'neither for a principle, nor a people, nor a law, but for the fields along the Boyne, for the birds and the blue sky over them'.[38]

Times have changed. Of the year 1923, Frank O'Connor, who was to give us *Guests of the Nation*, but who, earlier on, had owed a nationalist vocation to Standish O'Grady (like his elders: AE, Stephens, Yeats, and like many of his contemporaries) could already write:

At the age of 20 I was released from an internment camp, without money or job. . . . I had taken the losers' side . . . . I set out for Dublin on my way to the West, like Cu Chulainn setting out for Armagh at the age of seven, though I was fourteen years older and had nothing of the heroic Spirit.[39]

The age of heroes seems to be now past, and if any remained, he would be likely to meet a worse death than at the hand of a coward, like Yeats's Cuchulain, slain by a blind old beggar acting for a paltry reward - in the anonymous butchery of a car-accident, a plane-crash, an IRA or UDA raid, or an atom-bomb - not very strong incentives.

Not even the Ulster troubles, to which we have briefly alluded, seem likely to change the face of the earth. To quote a passage from James Simmons which we shall use both as unavoidable anti-climax and conclusion:

> Nationality preoccupies a people when it is contested. . . . By Beckett's time the sense of nationality is secure enough to be ignored. Northern writers must still be confused in this area whether they are in favour of the political link with Dublin or London. The problem can seem at the same time trivial and inescapable. One can hardly be drawn towards either political set-up very strongly. Any solution that would stop the killing would suit, perhaps; but that sort of feeling can hardly speak with 'passionate intensity'. There is no unjust monster to be endured and resisted; but the uncomfortable knowledge that we and our immediate ancestors have burnt our collective backside, and we must sit on the blister.[40]

NOTES

1. W. B. Yeats, 'The Statues', *Last Poems 1936-1939*; *Collected Poems* (London, 1958), p. 375:

    When Pearse summoned Cuchulain to his side,
    What stalked through the Post Office?

2. See Robin Flower, *The Irish Tradition* (Oxford, 1947) p. 104.
3. Aubrey Thomas De Vere, *The Foray of Queen Maeve and Other Legends of Ireland's Heroic Age* (London, 1882).
4. Denis Florence MacCarthy, *Ferdiah* (Dublin, 1882).
5. Samuel Ferguson, 'The Tain-Quest', *Lays of the Western Gael* (Dublin, 1888).
6. Eva Gore-Booth, *Unseen Kings* (London, 1904) p. 10.
7. Austin Clarke, *The Sword of the West* (Dublin and London, 1921), p. 94. For references of other poetic adaptations and a fairly complete list of plays based on the Cuchulain myth, see Raymonde Popot, 'The Hero's Light' in P. Rafroidi, R. Popot and W. Parker (eds), *Aspects of the Irish Theatre* (Paris, 1972) pp. 173-212. I take this opportunity of thanking Miss Popot not only for allowing me freely to borrow from her paper but for kindly giving me access to her rich Cuchulain file and a later article of hers: *'Mythes et Nationalisme:*

l'exemple irlandais' (*Gaeliana* Université de Caen, 1979) pp. 39-61.
8. Quoted in Hugh Art O'Grady, *Standish James O'Grady, the Man and the Work* (Dublin, 1929) p. 64.
9. W. B. Yeats, *Autobiographies* (London, 1961) p. 220.
10. A speech reported by Yeats, ibid., p. 424. O'Grady's contributions to the rediscovery of the Cuchulain myth are the following: *History of Ireland: The Heroic Period* (Dublin and London, 1878); *History of Ireland: Cuculain and his Contemporaries* (Dublin and London, 1880); *History of Ireland: Critical and Philosophical* (Dublin and London, 1881); *Cuculain: An Epic* (Dublin and London, 1882); *The Comming of Cuculain* (London, 1894); *In the Gates of the North* (Kilkenny, 1901); *The Triumph and Passing of Cuculain* (London and Dublin, 1920).
11. Quoted in Phillip L. Marcus, *Yeats and the Beginning of the Irish Renaissance* (Ithaca, NY, 1970) p. 235.
12. Stephen MacKenna, *Memories of the Dead* (Dublin, n.d.).
13. *Collected Works of Padraic H. Pearse: Political Writings and Speeches* (Dublin and London, 1922) pp. 38-9.
14. Ibid., pp. 91-2, 99.
15. W. B. Yeats, *Michael Robartes and the Dancer* (1921); *Collected Poems*, p. 206.
16. Sean O'Casey, *The Plough and the Stars* (1926) in *Three Plays* (London, 1957) p. 162.
17. Ibid., p. 163.
18. Ibid., p. 164.
19. MacKenna, *Memories of the Dead*, pp. 95-6.
20. *The Letters of P. H. Pearse*, ed. S. O'Buachalla (Gerrards Cross, Bucks, 1980).
21. Iris Murdoch, *The Red and the Green* (London, 1965) p. 87.
22. Mervyn Wall, *Leaves for the Burning* (London, 1946) p. 207.
23. *Collected Works of Padraic H. Pearse: Plays, Stories, Poems* (Dublin and London, 1917) p. 335.
24. Birgit Bjersby, *The Interpretation of the Cuchulain Legend in the Works of W. B. Yeats* (Dublin, 1950) p. 14.
25. Alex Zwerdling, *Yeats and the Heroic Ideal* (New York, 1965) p. 25.
26. Malcolm Brown, *The Politics of Irish Literature from Thomas Davis to W. B. Yeats* (London, 1972) p. 242.
27. Denis Johnston, *The Scythe and the Sunset* (1958) in *Collected Plays*, vol. i (London, 1969) p. 93.
28. W. B. Yeats, 'Words for Music Perhaps', *The Winding Stair* (1933); *Collected Poems*, p. 303.

29. *Collected Works of Pearse: Plays, Stories, Poems,* p. 323.
30. William Irwin Thompson, *The Imagination of an Insurrection: Dublin, Easter 1961* (New York, 1967) p. ix.
31. Ibid., p. 236.
32. Peter Costello, *The Heart Grown Brutal: The Irish Revolution in Literature, from Parnell to the Death of Yeats, 1891-1939* (Dublin, 1977) p. xi. A similar conclusion had been reached by Joan Towey Mitchell in 'Yeats, Pearse and Cuchulain', *Eire-Ireland*, vol. xi, (Winter 1976) pp. 51-65.
33. Eimar O'Duffy, *King Goshawk and the Birds* (London, 1926).
34. Sean O'Casey, *The Shadow of a Gunman* (1925) in *Three Plays*, p. 83.
35. *Tain* (Dublin, 1969).
36. Francis Stuart, 'Politics and the Modern Irish Writer', in P. Rafroidi and P. Joannon (eds), *Ireland at the Crossroads* (Lille, 1979) p. 46.
37. Quoted in Alan Warner, *Clay is the Word* (Dublin, 1973) p. 28.
38. Quoted in *DNB: 1912-1921*, p. 328.
39. Frank O'Connor, *My Father's Son* (Dublin, 1968) pp. 11-13.
40. James Simmons (ed.), *Ten Irish Poets* (Cheadle, 1974) introduction, p. 9.

10 Finland, Norway and the Easter Rising

A. R. G. GRIFFITHS

The flagship of the small flotilla which sailed to Ireland at Easter 1916 was called by the planners of the expedition the *Aud*. The *Aud*'s first baptismal launching name was evocative; it was christened the *Castro*. It was owned by the Wilson line of Hull and was almost new when taken as a prize by German destoyers early in the war. The *Castro* was renamed by its captors the *Libau* (a port in Latvia) and at Lübeck was fitted out for its voyage to Ireland under Lieutenant Karl Spindler. The cover story which Spindler spread in Lübeck was that he was going 'to take aboard troops in Libau which were to carry out a "coup" in Finland. That sounded quite credible'.[1] After the *Libau* slipped through Danish coastal waters the crew painted out *Libau* and wrote in letters a yard and a half long *Aud-Norvege*. The Finnish coup, credible indeed, was carried out in 1917 with the help of the German bayonets of General Von Der Goltz, but in 1916 the Finns had to stand behind the Irish in the queue for German help. Karl Spindler and the *Aud* raced with Casement's submarine to land a cargo of Russian weapons (seized perhaps by Finnish Jägers fighting on the Eastern front) with which to arm the Irish volunteers.[2] Spindler and his crew were not only disguised in Norwegian merchant sailors' clothing but, with characteristic German planning, carried old sardine tins, Christiania (Oslo) newspapers and photos of Norwegian girl friends and letters in Norwegian to establish their bona fides if challenged. The symbolism of a Germano-Norwegian assault on British hegemony in Ireland was unappreciated at the time, although there were those among the Irish revolutionaries who recognised that the Norwegian flag was chosen partly because Norway had one of the world's largest merchant navies, but also because in Norwegian historical experience there lay not only a parallel series of analogous conditions, but a cause and effect element as well.[3]

The general connection between Irish and European history has long been recognised, and historians have traced the relationship between the Irish and the continental mind. Professor Mansergh, for example, has pointed out, how, after the failure of the United Irishmen, the Irish people were but little moved by the revolts against imperial domination in partitioned Poland, in Italy, Hungary and the Balkans.[4] By the twentieth century, however, Arthur Griffith showed many of the Irish revolutionary leaders that concepts of Irish nationalism, and the relationship of Ireland to the British Empire, could be defined by looking at the Austro-Hungarian parallels.[5] There were other parallels (Constance Markievicz, for example, found inspiration tramping around the Ukraine with Casimir) and some Irishmen looked north to Scandinavia. The interest in Scandinavia encompassed a wide spectrum of Irish society.

It was based, in the first instance, on shared common experiences. Both areas in the nineteenth century suffered poverty, disease, alcoholism, famine and emigration. The great constitutional changes of the Napoleonic era affected both Ireland and Scandinavia in a similar way. The democratic ideals of the Enlightenment and the devastating forces generated by the French Revolution had broadly similar effects on both regions. The revolution of 1798 in Ireland was abetted by the French and led to the decision of the British Parliament to pass the Act of Union which was only undone, and partly at that, by revolution. A similar impression of alien culture fell upon both the Finns and Norwegians in the carve-up of Europe which followed the defeat of Napoleon and the Congress of Vienna and the Treaty of Tilsit. The Finns in 1809 found themselves in the power of the Russians and the Irish in the grip of the English, with no consideration of the cultural differences between metropolitan and colonial power given or expected. Similarly, the Danes were deprived of Norway, which was given to Sweden by an Act of Union in 1814 which was to last for nearly a century. The result of the constitutional rearrangements was a state of cultural shock which staggered the liberal intelligentsia and the rural population alike. The changes were so intrinsically unnatural that despite the efforts of Alexander II to improve the condition of Finland, and the wishes of such enlightened British statesmen as Gladstone to steer through Irish Home Rule, a wave of protest was generated which eventually swept away the old imperial order with as much devastation as that which accompanied the French Revolution.

The whole pressure for constitutional change was, in both Scandinavia and Ireland, largely cultural in inspiration. The basic objection which the Norwegians had to the Swedes was not that they were in a position of sovereign power over them, but that they were fantastic and foreign. After all, Norwegians had been happy to be governed by the Danes since the Kalmar Union in 1397.

At the centre of the campaign for national sovereignty was the idea of a national language. The national language was identified with the lower classes, so that 'ruling class - ruling language' was a basic assumption of Scandinavian and Irish nationalists. Norwegian, Swedish and Danish are of course closely related and quite different from Finnish. For the five hundred years before the Treaty of Kiel, Denmark governed Norway and Danish was the language of the towns, while in the isolated cut of hinterland dialects were spoken. During the 1830s Henrik Wergeland began a campaign to modify Danish by slow degrees into *riksmål* (the language of the state). At the same time, Ivar Åsen produced a form of written Norwegian *(landsmål)* collected from the western districts, and based, to some extent, on Old Norse. Since 1907 orthographic reforms have gradually reduced the differences between *landsmål (nynorsk)* and *riksmål (bokmål)*, but at the turn of the nineteenth century the conflict between the two modes of expression was a bone of contention between rival nationalists, and mirrored in its intensity the political struggle between the Fennomen and the Svencomen in Finland for leadership in the battle against Russian domination of the Grand Duchy's affairs.

The battleground of the protagonists in Finland, Ireland and Norway was the theatre. In 1851 a young student, Henrik Ibsen, was engaged as dramatic author at the Bergen Theatre, and for six years struggled to bring Norwegian themes before an audience expecting a traditional diet of French farces and plays in Danish. The Bergen Theatre's regulations were so chauvinistic that not only the actors and instructors but even the prompter had to be of Norwegian birth. Ibsen left Bergen for Oslo in 1857, and completed his masterpiece *The Vikings at Helgeland* in the national capital, making an explicit attack on the Danish establishment there. *The Vikings at Helgeland* stressed the heroic feats and national characteristics of ancient Norway, at that time regarded with positive approbation, and was part of the movement led by P. A. Munch to encourage popular respect for the nation's traditions, rooted as they were in peasant traditions.

This trend was not without its critics. Just as the Gaelic enthusiasts and Sinn Feiners were ridiculed (by James Joyce) as 'their intensities', and disparaged as a back-to-the-bogs movement, no less a nationalist than Edvard Grieg described Ibsen's over-emphasis on the rural virtues of the national romantic movement as 'full of cow turds, norse-norsehood, and to be thyself enoughness'. There were many other examples of the folk-rooted revolution. Edvard Grieg himself for example, created his musical reputation out of the fiddle folk songs of the Hardanger fjord. Although he wrote (against his inclinations) incidental music to *Peer Gynt* he could not gainsay the impact Peer Gynt had on public opinion. In the contemporary setting of the Schleswig-Holstein crisis Peer Gynt, with his empty bragging, personified the Norwegian nation which stood by and saw its small brother beaten by a Prussian bully.

In Finland, an analogous development took place. Under the Treaty of Tilsit Finland was taken from Sweden and given to Russia. The language of government in Helsinki however remained Swedish until the Russification period at the turn of the nineteenth century, and since the Russian Governor-General did not understand Swedish he understandably stayed away from meetings which discussed the Grand Duchy's affairs. The Swedes had governed Finland since 1154 and the liaison of Napoleon and Alexander made little difference to the lives of peasants living in remote areas. In much the same way as the peasants of Kerry spoke Gaelic before and after the Act of Union, the Finnish peasant farmers conducted their lives in Finnish. Hence it became a priority of the national romantics in Finland to get rid not only of Russian but Swedish also, thus they began their struggle for independence on the Karelian frontier (between Finland and Russia), collecting the folk history of the *Kalevala* and composing a Finnish grammar and dictionary. It was taken as axiomatic that the national identity resided in the breasts of the simple Karelians speaking the Finnish language and upholding their national history in their day-to-day struggle for subsistence.

A Scandinavian analogy was evident not only in the Irish domestic situation and in literature, but in foreign policy as well. During the period 1886-1925 foreign policy relationships between European powers manifest a kaleidoscope of changes. So far as both Ireland and Scandinavia were concerned young men beginning nationalist activities in 1886 saw a different Europe forty years later. Old alliances had crumbled, new ones had been forged, and a whole series of issues (in which social democracy was one) had a primacy entirely lacking to earlier generations. There was, however, not only change but continuity, and the fixed stars by which independence-seeking Scandinavians and Irishmen navigated were located in London and Berlin. One fixed theme, common to both societies, was the way in which the nationalist revolutionaries were sponsored by Governments hostile to the metropolitan powers. The most notorious (or one should perhaps say consistent) advocates of clandestine operations were the Germans. They helped both the nationalist Irish against the British during the First World War, and the nationalist Finns against the Russians after the 1917 revolution. The Germans and the British were not the only foreign powers to interfere in the domestic affairs of Scandinavia and Ireland with a view to hastening the collapse of enemy Governments. Even the Japanese (in 1905) were engaged in clandestine operations in Europe.[6]

In the first two decades of the twentieth century the revolutionaries were successful. Although the Swedes and Norwegians play the violent element down, the peaceful transition in 1905 to Norwegian independence was not inevitable, and both nations armed themselves and prepared for bloodshed.[7] Finland was given its independence by the Bolsheviks after the 1917 revolution, but it took a civil war to ratify the agreement between Lenin and the head of the Finnish provincial government.[8] A similar process took place in Ireland. Nor could national independence be equated with national progress. There were fascist midwives at the birth of all the embryo nations in Scandinavia and Ireland. Norwegian patriotism moved with Vidkun Quisling's Hird into an area of repression only matched by Fritz Clausen's Danish Nazis, and their German and Italian mentors. *The New Totalitarians* of the Swedish Welfare State emerged with the triumph of social democracy in Stockholm in 1925. In Finland the Communist Party was banned and for years right wing radicalism threatened to take over the State and destroy its democratic institutions. Neither in the Irish case, nor in the Scandinavian one, was the emergence of parliamentary democracy the inevitable result of the success of the independence movement, although fortunately for Ireland General Eoin O'Duffy's Blueshirts were a pale reflection of their nordic cousins.

Scandinavian and Irish history exhibited not only a conjunction of similar problems and similar solutions, but a cause and effect element as well. Although the consumers of Guinness did not know it (and probably would not have cared even if they did) the subtle alchemy of the brewing industry in Dublin was the product of collaboration on the frontiers of science between Irish and Danish brewers. The Guinness brewers T. B. Case and L. McMullen studied in Copenhagen in Jorgensen's experimental laboratory at the Carlsberg brewery.[9] And one could take more sober examples of the links between Scandinavian and Irish history. The battle for Irish independence was carried out in the theatres as well as the pubs. The theatrical revolution which reflected and caused the national revolution demanded a set of metaphors and images. But what is not as well known is the extent to which many of the Irish cultural and political leaders, and the rank and file who followed them, were in the grip of enthusiasm for Nordic thought. A personal, national and social revolution were all implied in the writing of Scandinavian dramatists. And the crucial linkman who brought the Irish revolution into contact with the historical experience and values of Scandinavia was the Anglo-Irish genius, George Bernard Shaw.

In Shaw's case, a book on Ibsen launched his sparkling literary career. Shaw published the *Quintessence of Ibsenism* in 1891, and his first play followed the next year. Shaw was introduced to Ibsen by William Archer, Ibsen's translator and champion in England; Archer was a drama critic on the *World* and Shaw was the music critic on the same periodical, and together they worked to help each other, and ultimately Ireland, by promoting the iconoclastic modernism of the Scandinavians. Shaw had read and knew well fifteen of Ibsen's plays, and directed 1/64 of his immense letter writing energy (which ran to a total of 877 pages in his collected letters) to discoursing on Ibsen themes between 1874 and 1897. When, in 1898, the British theatre celebrated Ibsen's 70th birthday, Shaw wrote up the celebrations in the *Saturday Review*.[10] Shaw's work on Ibsen also inspired the black sheep of the Anglo-Irish, Oscar Wilde. Wilde made an illuminating comment on the Irish frame of mind, telling Shaw that his 'little book' on Ibsen and Ibsenism was such a delight that he constantly took it up, always finding it stimulating and interesting. England, added Wilde, 'is the land of intellectual fogs but you have done much to clear the air: we are both Celtic'.[11] Wilde continued his admiration for Scandinavian letters in prison, asking for August Strindberg's latest works, and for two plays of Ibsen, *Little Eyolf* and *John Gabriel Borkman*,[12] to be purchased for him to read when he was released. Wilde knew *Hedda Gabler* well enough to quote its last words 'people don't do these things'.[13]

Wilde's enthusiasm led nowhere and had no effect. In Shaw's case, however, the Scandinavian signposts were illuminated and others took up the message.[14] And Shaw was prepared to tread where few at first were keen to follow, into the heat of August Strindberg's inferno in Stockholm. Shaw sought out Strindberg in his flat in July 1908 on William Archer's behalf, hoping that he could talk Strindberg into letting Archer translate his works, which had never been produced professionally on the English stage. J. T. Grein announced the production of Justin Huntly M'Carthy's translation of *The Father* by the Independent Theatre in 1891, but it was not presented. As Shaw could not read Swedish and knew Strindberg's work only through German translations, the meeting with Strindberg was not a success.

Shaw flooded the room with energetic eloquence in a 'fearful lingo', half French, half German, but Strindberg stopped the conversation by saying that Archer was not in sympathy with him. Shaw gallantly replied that Archer was not in sympathy with Ibsen either, but added that he was 'accessible to poetry'. Whereupon Strindberg took out his watch and said in German 'At two o'clock I am going to be sick'. The visitors accepted this delicate intimation and withdrew.[15] Shaw gave up, but not before he had urged Strindberg to allow an English production, despite the fact that the only suitable theatre was a favourite with the innocent bourgeoisie and their daughters, who (preferring *Peter Pan*) would have flown home stricken at the very first moment of *Miss Julie*.[16]

Ibsen's message was primarily political and acceptable to the Irish mind. Eleanor Marx took part in a private reading of *A Doll's House* (at which Bernard Shaw, as he put it, 'impersonated' Krogstad) and (badly) translated *The Wild Duck*. Although Ibsen dealt in such works as *Ghosts* with taboo themes such as syphilis (and Havelock Ellis wrote an introduction to one of his works), the plays of Ibsen were mild compared with the outrageous immorality of Strindberg. While Marx was acceptable in Dublin, Freud was not, and Strindberg remained a closed book even to the avant-garde like James Joyce.

Like Shaw, James Joyce first made his literary mark with a study of Ibsen. There were not superlatives enough for Joyce to express his admiration for the Norwegian dramatist. Joyce's first published work was a review of Ibsen's play, *When We Dead Awaken*. It appeared in the *Fortnightly Review* in April 1900, while Joyce was a student. Joyce was to graduate at the Royal University with a BA degree in 1902, but the College authorities (so he believed) had their hearts set on preventing him earning his living as a medical practitioner and thus having the income and the leisure to produce literary masterpieces. Joyce resolved to shift to Paris and support himself as an English teacher, while reading for a medical degree at the University. A large part of his undergraduate notoriety stemmed from his enthusiasm for Ibsen. The fashionable undergraduate cause was the Irish Literary Theatre, but Joyce regarded it as provincial and spent his first literary energy laboriously lauding Ibsen.

Indeed it is scarcely possible to exaggerate the influence of Ibsen on Joyce. As a precocious rebel, Joyce's review of *When We Dead Awaken* was accepted by W. L. Courtney, for the *Fortnightly Review*, where it fell under the eye of William Archer. Archer forwarded the review to Ibsen, and Ibsen sent forty words of thanks to his well-wisher Joyce through

Archer. Joyce's life was changed forever. In a touching
letter, Joyce thanked Archer for his kindness, adding that
he was 'a young Irishman, eighteen years old, and the words
of Ibsen I shall keep in my heart all my life'.[17]

It is interesting to note that Irish writers 1886-1925
were, like Ibsen before them, largely expatriate, and preferred to develop their treatment of Irish themes in the
tranquillity of self-imposed exile in a larger market area
unaffected by Dublin's provincialism. Joyce, for example,
although he wrote voluminous letters in Italian, German and
French, and lived in romantic Paris, Zurich and Trieste, was
obsessed by such remembrances as whether the Star of the Sea
Church had ivy on its seafront, whether there were trees in
Leahy's terrace at the side, what were the steps leading
down to the beach? Like Ibsen's character Tesman, Joyce
(writing from Trieste) asked his aunt these questions. And
in the same letter in which he told her that his play *Exiles*
had been translated into Swedish, and that the American
censor had burnt the magazine *Little Review* publishing
Ulysses, he asked her for 'tittletattle' about the Hollis
Street Maternity Hospital.[18]

Of course, not all Irish literary figures knew or cared
about Ibsen, and naturally not all of the revolutionary
leaders in such a polyglot amalgam of nationalist forces as
the Gaelic League, the Gaelic Athletic Association, the
Irish Parliamentary Party, the Irish Republican Brotherhood,
the Irish Citizens' Army and the Irish Volunteers were
interested in European literature and its meaning. James
Connolly (so far as I have been able to discover) had never
heard of Ibsen or Strindberg. Sir Roger Casement knew
nothing of Norway and Finland's struggle for independence.
Eamon de Valera (who at least lived to see the Finnish civil
war) did not ponder on its meaning. Arthur Griffith was my-
opic and concentrated exclusively on the Austro-Hungarian
Empire: dual monarchy and the lessons of history were found
in warmer climates from Scandinavia. In prison, Constance
Markievicz once dreamed about Norway (although she thought
that it might have been northern Germany) but Ibsen,
Strindberg and the Norwegian and Finnish independence movements never entered her waking consciousness.

The case was otherwise with W. B. Yeats, one of the central figures of the Irish national romantic movement.
Yeats's attitude to Ibsen was at first summed up by his
comments on *A Doll's House*, a production he saw at the age
of twenty-four, and subsequently recalled as follows

> ... somebody had given me a seat for the gallery. In the
> middle of the first act, while the heroine was asking for

macaroons, a middle-aged washer-woman who sat in front of me stood up and said to the little boy at her side, 'Tommy, if you promise to go home straight we will go now'; and at the end of the play, as I wandered through the entrance hall, I heard an elderly critic murmur, 'A series of conversations terminated by an accident.' I was divided in mind. I hated the play; what was it but Carolus Duran, Bastien-Lepage, Huxley and Tyndall all over again? I resented being invited to admire dialogue so close to modern educated speech that music and style were impossible.

'Art is art because it is not nature', I kept repeating to myself, but how could I take the same side with critic and washer-woman? As time passed Ibsen became in my mind the chosen author of very clever young journalists, who, condemned to their treadmill of abstraction, hated music and style; and yet neither I nor my generation could escape him because, though we and he had not the same friends, we had the same enemies. I bought his collected works in Mr. Archer's translation out of my thirty shillings a week and carried them to and fro, upon my journeys to Ireland and Sligo . . . .'.[19]

By the beginning of the twentieth century Yeats's attitude to Ibsen had become more critical. The common enemies remained. Yeats wrote poetry (which was not used) for Ellen Terry's production of *The Vikings at Helgeland* in 1903,[20] and saw a production of *Lady Ingar of Östrät* in 1905,[21] but in general Ibsen was regarded by him as commercial, commonplace and business-minded. Yeats criticised Ibsen's works as lacking the suggestion of dreams and any clear thought or emotion about the old life.[22]

Yeats himself was anything but commercial, commonplace and business-minded, but not even the oblique literary censorship imposed by the great artist's physical presence and ubiquitous example could obliterate Ibsen's message. One could take the actors in Yeats's productions as being representative of those men in Ireland who believed in the need for a new awakening in Irish consciousness and demanded personal liberation as a parallel commitment to the national revolution. If they did not actually belong to a banned organisation, or a national group apart from Yeats's circle of actors, they were nevertheless certain to have either joined in the Easter Rising or voted Sinn Fein afterwards. And in a remarkable way Yeats had the gift of creating interest in drama in breasts hitherto unsensitised. Once the spark was kindled, however, it often burned out of control in what might be called the Caliban syndrome. In 1902 W. B.

Yeats used 'Ibsenite' as a pejorative adjective and considered that 'the accursed Norwegian cloud' ought to be avoided. To help sweep Ibsen out of the box-offices, and to produce a dream-like antidote, Yeats produced his own *Kathleen ni Hoolihan* and AE's *Deirdre* to enthusiastic audiences. It fell in with his dramatic theories to use amateur casts. After all, if the drama was designed to show how Ireland was enslaved by the British and that the common people and their commonplace lives were the only hope of national resurrection, then the commonplace people ought to be able to get across the poetry of Ireland's dramatists, without the barrier of theatrical careerism between them and their audience. Sincerity of performance demanded sincerity in the performers. Some of the actors were so sincere that they, in touching moments, brought Yeats copies of their own (unpublished) works for advice. One of them, who was an agricultural labourer, came to Yeats to read a play of his own compositon about the United Irish League. Yeats at first was puzzled and did not recognise the style as his, or that of AE. For the work was written in the mode of the only dramatist the agricultural labourer had ever actually read - Henrik Ibsen.[23] Something, thought Yeats, 'must come out of all this energy and delight in high things'.

The Irish romantic nationalists of the middle class have long been known to have been cultivated and educated. The Irish revolution was a white-collar rising, by men inspired by political theory, with a cerebral base that they had learned in their schools and universities. It could not be killed by kindness, any more than good administration of Norway would stop the demand for the removal of the mark of the union from the Swedish-Norwegian flag. If the middle classes in Ireland had no *Kalevala* and no folk songs, they did at least have *Kathleen ni Hoolihan* and *Deirdre*. But more important, the blue collar substrata also read books and plays, and if the British secret service had taken the trouble to find out that agricultural labourers came home from their meetings of the United Irish League, and curled up by the peat fire with the latest play by Ibsen, they may have thrown in the towel sooner.

Action moved from thought with Patrick Pearse, who, in a climactic moment, stepped out in front of the Post Office in 1916 to read aloud the proclamation of the provisional Government of the Irish Republic. Pearse was a great admirer of Henrik Ibsen. In 1906 he paid tribute to the old troll whom he hailed as 'one who showed the world what the "little" nations can do'.[24] Ten years later, shortly before he was executed for his beliefs (and after the date was set for the Rising) Pearse linked Norwegian and Irish history together by writing and publishing the pamphlet *Ghosts*. He acknowledged his debt to Ibsen for the title, and in his *Ghosts* reviewed the separatist tradition in Ireland, describing Tone, Davis, Mitchel, Lalor and Parnell as 'ghosts' with a body of teaching.[25]

The Irish revolution, which began a decisive phase in 1886 with Gladstone's first Home Rule Bill, and ended with partition an accomplished fact in 1925, was a complex phenomenon in which the themes of art and politics were inextricably bound. If Cuchulain stalked through the post office in Easter 1916, so did *Peer Gynt*. And the Anglo-Irish, who brought the *Wild Duck* to the land of the wild geese, put him there.

NOTES

1. K. Spindler, *Gun Running for Casement in the Easter Rebellion, 1916* (London, 1921) p. 17.
2. Two thousand Finns enlisted in the Kaiser's army to fight against Russia under the 'Hunter Regiment' banner as the 27th Royal Prussian Light Infantry. Jean Sibelius composed a march in their honour (wisely anonymously). The decision to send German troops to Finland was made at a conference of the German military and political command on 13 February 1918. German troops occupied Åland in March 1918, and the Baltic division arrived in April, the German Government regarded the small matter of a division as a very profitable investment.
3. Scandinavian scholars have long studied Irish culture. See S. B. Liljegren, *Irish Studies in Sweden* (Stockholm, 1961); *The Irish Element in the Valley of Fear* (Stockholm, 1964); S. Nejdefors-Frisk, *George Moore's Naturalistic Prose* (Stockholm, 1952). The University of Uppsala, in particular, has a long tradition of Celtic studies. See also, on a modern note, P. Gill, *Moral Judgements of Violence among Irish and Swedish Adolescents* (Göteborg, 1979).
4. N. Mansergh, *The Irish Question*, 3rd edn (London, 1975) p. 81.
5. A. Griffith, *The Resurrection of Hungary: A Parallel for Ireland* (Dublin, 1904).
6. *Lloyds Shipping Register*, 12 Sept. 1905.
7. The Anglo-Irish played a role in Ireland analogous to that of the Swedish-Finns during the Finnish struggle for independence. J. L. Runeberg, *Tales of Ensign Stål*,

Elias Lönnrot with his collection of the *Kalevala*, Jean Sibelius, P. E. Svinhufund, Marshal Gustaf Mannerheim and General Hannes Ignatius all showed how the plantation caste contributed a vein of steel to the independence movement.

8. By article 6 of the Treaty of Brest-Litovsk, Russia agreed to stop agitation against the Government and the public institutions of Finland. Red Guards immediately left Finland and the Åland islands. Early in 1918 P. E. Svinhufund concluded agreements with the Germans which would have made Finland a German state had Germany won the war. The Finnish Government offered Friedrich Karl, Prince of Hessen, the Finnish Crown once the Civil War was over.
9. I am indebted to Professor MacDonagh for this information.
10. *Saturday Review*, 26 Mar. 1898.
11. Wilde to Shaw, 23 Feb. 1893, *Selected Letters of Oscar Wilde*, ed. R. Hart-Davis (London, 1962) p. 332.
12. Wilde to R. Ross, 6 Apr. [1897], *Letters*, p. 522.
13. Wilde to More Adey, 8 Mar. 1897, *Letters*, p. 421.
14. For a bitter, ironic and iconoclastic Irish comment on the influence of Scandinavian letters see S. O'Casey, 'Dramatis Personae Ibsenisensis', *American Spectator* (New York, July 1933), quoted in S. O'Casey, *Blasts and Benedictions: Articles and Stories*, ed. R. Ayling (London, 1967) pp. 46-50. J. M. Synge, on the other hand, was an Ibsen enthusiast.
15. Shaw to W. Archer 16 July 1908, *Bernard Shaw Collected Letters 1898-1910*, ed. D. H. Laurence (London, 1972) p. 802.
16. Shaw to A. Strindberg, 16 Mar. 1910, *Collected Letters*, p. 908.
17. Joyce to W. Archer, 28 Apr. 1900, *Selected Letters of James Joyce*, ed. R. Ellmann (London, 1975) vol. i, p.6.
18. J. Joyce to Josephine Murray [Feb. 1920], *Selected Letters*, p. 248.
19. W. B. Yeats, 'The Trembling of the Veil, The Tragic Generation', *Autobiographies* (London, 1961) pp. 279-80.
20. Yeats to Lady Gregory [Apr. 1903], *The Letters of W. B. Yeats*, ed. A. Wade (London, 1954) p. 398.
21. Yeats to Florence Farr [Jan. 1906], *Letters*, p. 467.
22. Yeats to Frank Fay, 28 Aug. [1904], *Letters*, p. 441.
23. Yeats to Henry Newbolt, 5 Apr. 1902, *Letters*, p. 370.
24. P. Pearse, *'An Claidheamh Soluis'*, 2 June 1906; R. D. Edwards, *Patrick Pearse, the Triumph of Failure* (London, 1977) p. 92.
25. Pearse, *Ghosts*, 25 Dec. 1915; *Patrick Pearse*, pp. 252-4.

11 The Priest in Politics: the Case of Conscription
PAURIC TRAVERS

At the end of March 1918, when the seriousness of the German offensive on the Western Front became known, the War Cabinet decided to extend conscription to Ireland. The preoccupation with events in France was such that the Cabinet disregarded the almost unanimous advice of its Irish advisers, preferring the more optimistic advice of the military, especially Field Marshal Lord French. A 'dual policy' of granting Home Rule in exchange for conscription was inaugurated and French sent to Ireland to enforce it.

The new military service bill passed all its stages by 18 April, but, as the Cabinet had been warned, Irish opinion was not placated by the promise of Home Rule. The Irish Parliamentary Party withdrew from the House of Commons in protest against conscription and joined forces with the leaders of Sinn Fein and the Irish Labour movement in a vigorous anti-conscription campaign. Faced with strong opposition and the threat of violent resistance, the Government was quickly forced to the conclusion that neither conscription nor Home Rule were practical. A new voluntary recruitment campaign was initiated and the Irish Government was happy to concentrate on restoring order.

As in Australia, much of the significance of the Irish conscription crisis derives from the intervention of the Catholic Church. It not only gave its imprimatur to the anti-conscription movement but became involved in that movement at almost all levels. Clerical involvement in Irish politics was not new or even a recent phenomenon. Rarely, however, was its manifestation so overt or controversial. Not since the days of O'Connell had Catholic Ireland been so united. Church and political leaders effectively coalesced in the anti-conscription movement, thus guaranteeing its success.

The English press (with some exceptions), senior Government ministers (ditto) and most Ulster Unionists saw the crisis as confirmation of the inherent 'disloyalty' of the Catholic Church. Strangely enough, the traditional nationalist interpretation of the affair has tended to confirm this view, as it saw the Church's intervention as evidence of an emphatic move, within the hierarchy, away from the constitutional and towards the physical force nationalists. Sinn Fein certainly gained considerably from the apparent seal of approval given by the bishops. Whether that was what the bishops intended is another matter.

The part played by the Church needs to be considered on a number of levels. The rationale behind its involvement must be explained and its contribution to the ultimate success of the movement evaluated. The implications of its attitude are controversial and require clarification. The internal politics of the Church played a part, but the question does not stop there. Neither the fortunes of Sinn Fein nor the Irish Party were independent of the Church and, on this occasion, clerical intervention produced shock waves which affected Anglo-Irish relations as a whole.[1]

For all their reputation as powerful manipulators of Irish politics, the Catholic bishops were not often overtly active on the political scene in the period immediately preceding 1918. The 'showdown' with Parnell was followed by a relative hiatus. When the education issue was defused, they reverted, with some notable exceptions, to taking a watching brief. Cardinal Logue was opposed to anything other than occasional intervention, and the once dominant Archbishop Walsh drastically curtailed his political pronouncements.

Even the First World War failed to produce a concerted response from the Catholic Church in Ireland. Its attitude was a microcosm of nationalist Ireland generally, and it developed along a roughly similar course. A small minority voiced their opposition to the war but the majority response was, as a police report of late 1914 testified, one of 'general support'.[2] Nevertheless, this support was passive rather than active, and markedly cautious. The Church as a whole did not give any sustained lead to its flock. The Pope's neutrality and traditional suspicion of England tempered a natural sympathy for Catholic Belgium.

The tactless recruiting methods of the War Office, a protracted dispute on the question of Catholic chaplains and the formation of the coalition government, which included 'implacable enemies of Ireland', all helped to increase this suspicion. When it was announced that Edward Carson would be a member of the coalition, Bishop Fogarty of Killaloe, for long a supporter of the Irish Party, wrote to John Redmond

> Home Rule is dead and buried and Ireland is without a National Party or National Press. The 'Freeman' is but a

government organ, and the National Party but an Imperial instrument.

What the future has in store for us, God knows; I suppose conscription, with a bloody feud between people and soldiers.[3]

By April 1916, the police were reporting that the clergy as a body were 'lukewarm' on the subject of recruiting.[4] This trend can only have been compounded by the executions and the partition negotiations of 1916.

The reaction of the bishops to the proposal to extend compulsory military service to Ireland was swift and uncompromising. On 9 April 1918, some hours before Lloyd George announced his intentions, the standing committee of the hierarchy discussed the matter. The statement which followed was unashamedly based as much in the political as in the spiritual field and left no doubt as to the hierarchy's position. It asserted that any effort to enforce conscription without the consent of the people was completely unjustifiable and would not succeed. The bishops then proceeded to make a strong condemnation of the Government's record especially with regard to Home Rule:

Had the government in any reasonable time given Ireland the benefit of the principles which are declared to be at stake in the war by the concession of a full measure of self government there would have been no occasion for contemplating forced levies from her now. What between mismanagement and mischief making, this country has already been deplorably upset, and it would be a fatal mistake, surpassing all the worst blunders of the past four years, to furnish a telling plea now for desperate courses by an attempt to enforce conscription. With all the responsibility that attaches to our pastoral office, we feel bound to warn the government against entering upon a policy so disastrous to the public interest and to all order, public and private.[5]

The timing of the meeting is important. The Irish Convention had completed its sittings with much success. Even the Irish Party had been unable to agree on a joint report, and three of the four Catholic bishops who were members of the Convention had voted in favour of the minority nationalist report while the Irish Party had split on the issue.[6] John

Redmond was dead and John Dillon, the new chairman of the Parliamentary Party, had not yet had an opportunity to regroup his forces. With continued fragmentation possible, the rumours that Lloyd George was considering Irish conscription took on a more menacing air. The bishops obviously felt that the matter was best not left within the realm of party politics.

Significantly, the first authoritative suggestion that an anti-conscription pledge should be initiated was made by the administrator of Logue's own parish. Rev. Joseph Brady arranged a series of meetings in Armagh, for Sunday 14 April, to start 'a solemn league and covenant' against conscription.[7] Obviously, Brady's model was the Ulster Covenant of 1914 though he was careful to point out that the methods employed to resist conscription would not be those sanctioned by Carson's covenant. Instead, he outlined what was essentially Logue's position, that the 'Constitutional Weapon of Passive Resistance, employed so successfully by thousands of conscientous objectors in England, Scotland and Wales for years recently' would be 'quite sufficient' and that they had 'the highest theological authority' for its use.[8] Logue, absent due to Confirmation commitments, sent a message supporting the pledge which committed those who took it to 'passive resistance in every shape and form'. Brady's actions, approved if not actually enjoined by Logue, suggest that the Church, from quite early on, was willing to play an active role in the crisis. It is also interesting that though Logue clearly prescribed passive resistance only, Brady ventured that other weapons might be decided on by their leaders later on, a speculation of which his archbishop would not have approved.

At about the same time, Cardinal Logue summoned a special meeting of the hierarchy to be held at Maynooth on 18 April. The immediate reason for the meeting was the proposed liability of the clergy to conscription. Though this proposal was dropped, clerical students remained liable, so the first part of the meeting was spent discussing this provision. It was decided that all clerical students due for ordination should be ordained immediately while the remainder should be sent home.

When Cardinal Logue telegraphed Archbishop Walsh, informing him that the meeting was to take place, he observed that the whole country expected general action by the bishops.[9] Thus, it was likely that that aspect would also be discussed. Walsh, too, was conscious of the need for leadership. He wrote to the national press condemning the dual policy and decrying the fact that although numerous anti-conscription resolutions had been passed, there had been no instructions as to what practical steps might be taken to resist.[10] De Valera, leader of Sinn Fein, had met his secretary, Father Curran, the previous Friday and apparently told him that the Volunteers intended to offer physical resistance to conscription. Walsh was certainly unhappy with 'the negative approach that was inherent in the phrase "passive resistance"'[11] but there is little to suggest that he was in general agreement with de Valera as is sometimes suggested.[12]

On the morning of the Mansion House Conference, the gathering of the rival nationalist leaders, who were to organise the resistance to conscription, de Valera did call on Walsh and discussed the anti-conscription pledge which he intended to propose at the Conference. This was undoubtedly a shrewd move on his part as it out-manoeuvred those at the Conference who were likely to object to the terms of the pledge. De Valera used this single meeting with Walsh to give the impression that he wielded more influence with Church leaders than he then had, thus adding to his own respectability and that of Sinn Fein.[13]

Walsh denied that he and de Valera were close. In fact, during the crisis he showed himself quite critical of some of de Valera's actions and, ironically, his relations with Dillon improved. (He told him that he took a 'decidedly more sympathetic view' of the Irish Party since his election to the chairmanship.)[14] The main aim of Walsh's letter to the press would seem to have been to encourage the emergence of a national leadership to direct the anti-conscription campaign. Active preparations would be necessary, even for passive resistance.[15]

The widespread desire for firm national leadership resulted in the meeting of all the major nationalist figures at the Mansion House in Dublin on the same day as the Maynooth meeting. De Valera had persuaded Walsh to get the bishops to delay any decision concerning conscription until they had heard from the Conference, which, in the event, sent a delegation to Maynooth.[16] There, each member of the delegation addressed the assembled bishops. [17] The Lord Mayor of Dublin, Laurence O'Neill who was chairman of the Mansion House Conference, asked for their spiritual help and prayers. Mr de Valera, however, asked for a strong stand from the bishops and was again insistent that nothing be said which would limit the freedom of the Volunteers, who would fight conscription, if imposed, regardless of what they might decide. Passive resistance, as envisaged by Cardinal Logue and others, would, he argued, be useless. Physical resistance was justifiable and would be offered and it was better that the Government should know this in

advance. This latter argument was appealing because it held
the promise that a little brinkmanship might persuade the
Government to back down. Another factor which must have
influenced the bishops was the agreement of the political
leaders. Dillon, who spoke after de Valera, strongly supported the pledge suggested by the delegation though he had
opposed it at the Mansion House.[18] Like the bishops, his
most immediate fear was that rash action by the Volunteers
might spark off an outbreak.

Broadly speaking, there were, within the hierarchy, two
schools of thought on national politics. On one side were
people such as Dr Fogarty of Killaloe and Dr Hallinan of
Limerick, both of whom were increasingly critical of the
Irish Party and sympathetic to Sinn Fein. On the other side
were people such as Bishop O'Donnell of Raphoe who still remained loyal to the Party. Walsh was certainly closer to the
former position. As for Logue, though disinterested in party
politics, he was conservative by nature and had an intense
dislike of Sinn Fein. However, to approach the Maynooth
meeting in this light may be misleading. By these criteria, the crucial decision was the approval, by the
hierarchy, of de Valera's pledge, which promised resistance
'by the most effective means at our disposal'. Clearly this
involved a shift of emphasis on their part. But the shift
was more tactical than ideological and the following weeks
proved that it was more apparent than real.

By accepting a purposely ambiguous pledge, the bishops
left themselves open to the criticism that, by failing to
specify the means of resistance, they gave the Volunteers a
carte blanche. Yet this, once again, ignores the reality of
the situation as outlined to the meeting by de Valera. On
all sides, it was felt that only a united opposition could
be successful. If there was disunity, the Government was
less likely to proceed. If it did proceed, then the pledge
seemed to rule out blood-sacrifices on the lines of 1916.

The response of the bishops more than satisfied the delegation from the Mansion House Conference. Following their
meeting, the hierarchy announced that a public Mass of
intercession would be held in every church in Ireland on the
following Sunday to 'avert the scourge of conscription'. At
these Masses it was to be announced that public meetings
would be held later that day for the purpose of administering the anti-conscription pledge. The clergy were also
requested to announce that a collection would be held at all
church gates, at the earliest suitable date, 'for the
purpose of supplying the means to resist the imposition of
compulsory military service'. A separate statement, signed
by all the bishops, was also issued, condemning conscription

without consent as 'an oppressive and inhuman law' and justifying all resistance 'consonant with the law of God'.
Having thus given the Volunteers what they wanted, the bishops, almost as an after-thought, added a reminder that there was 'a higher Power which controls the affairs of men' and that he would be 'conciliated' by 'strict allegiance to the Divine Law', by more earnest attention to their religious duties and by fervent and persevering prayer. A National Novena in honour of our Lady of Lourdes was announced, to secure general and domestic peace. Finally the heads of all families were exhorted to have the Rosary recited daily to protect the 'spiritual and temporal welfare of our beloved country' and to 'bring us safe through this crisis of unparalleled gravity'.[19] With such an impressive array of adversaries ranged against it, it is not surprising that the Government quickly had second thoughts.

The stand taken by the bishops met with strong condemnation from the Unionist press in England and Ireland. In England, the subsequent debate on Irish conscription centred to a large extent on the defiance of the Catholic bishops. The attitude of the Pope to the war had always been a matter for distaste to some Englishmen and it was now hinted that the inspiration for Ireland's revolt had come from Rome. A concerted 'no popery' campaign was conducted in some quarters and even the more moderate of the Tory newspapers felt that the Pope should intervene to bring the Irish bishops to heel. *The Times, Star, Morning Post, Daily Express, Spectator* and *Observer* all roundly condemned the bishops.[20] When accused of instigating a 'no popery' campaign, the editor of *The Times* retorted that the decision as to whether there was to be such a campaign rested with the Catholic hierarchy: if the bishops continued to challenge the imperial Parliament, there would be one. In a subsequent editorial, he argued that the bishops' action had 'shaken to the foundations the whole edifice of religious toleration in these islands'.[21] J. L. Garvin in the *Observer* was even more vociferous. He wrote,

The Catholic bishops have gone the length of denying in principle and practice the supremacy of the Imperial Parliament on that very point of common service and defence which is most vital of all. It touches the very existence of these islands. On this there is no possibility of compromise with the Irish bishops. The intolerable pretensions, into which the secret anti-ally bias of so many of their body has led them, must be faced by the whole power of the State and must be beaten.[22]

The Government itself was divided on the significance of the bishops' intervention. H. E. Duke, the Chief Secretary, and his successor Edward Shortt, felt that it would have a moderating effect, a view shared by Arthur Balfour, the Foreign Secretary.[23] Even James Campbell, the Irish Lord Chief Justice, was inclined to accept that the presence of the bishops in the anti-conscription campaign meant that there was less likelihood of bloodshed.[24] Others took a less tolerant view. Lord Curzon, a member of the War Cabinet, repeatedly condemned what he called the 'rebellion' of the Irish Church. Lord French told the Prime Minister on the day after the Maynooth meeting that the bishops and the Irish Party were preaching 'absolute rebellion' and later reported that the Church had taken 'the entire lead in this business'.[25] Even more significantly, Walter Long, who was soon to become responsible for Irish affairs in the Cabinet, classified the actions of the bishops as a 'declaration of war on the King's government'.[26]

Strangely enough, Lloyd George was among the most critical of the Church's stand. Perhaps, as Stephen Gwynn suggested, the Welsh Baptist thought he was fighting the European power of Rome.[27] Whatever the reason, Lloyd George increasingly justified going ahead with conscription, not on the grounds of military necessity - ostensibly the reason it had been suggested in the first place - but on the grounds that the authority of the imperial Parliament over Ireland, and the authority of the State over the Church, would have to be asserted. Though Duke insisted that the intervention of the bishops made conscription impossible, the demands of practical politics were being overruled by the demands of principle. It was clear that the crisis was damaging the Irish Party and giving a boost to Sinn Fein, and, more ominously, the Irish Volunteers and the IRB. But Lloyd George, though admitting that it was questionable whether the Cabinet should have raised the issue at that time, argued that once raised, it had to be 'boldly faced'.[28]

Of course, not all politicians saw the Church as challenging the imperial Parliament. Lloyd George's preoccupation with the Church may partly have been an effort to mobilise non-conformist opinion in England in support of his Irish policy. If so, he was not totally successful. The *Westminster Gazette*, for instance, dismissed the 'no popery' campaign as a 'stunt'. It commented:

The measure of the mess Mr Lloyd George has landed us in

by his headlong policy in Ireland is the necessity by which he feels bound to appeal to religious intolerance, a particularly dangerous cry in the north of Ireland. The idea that the Vatican has ordered the Catholic Bishops to oppose Conscription is absurd.[29]

In general, the sentiments expressed in the *Gazette* were echoed by the Asquithian wing of the Liberal Party. Rather than impede the war-effort, they had abstained when the question of Irish conscription had come before Parliament, but they insisted that the only policy which could be successful was one which faced the realities of the Irish situation. There was no use condemning the Irish bishops. 'Indeed,' ventured the *Manchester Guardian*, 'there is every indication that the Catholic Church is acting not as an incendiary, but as a restraining force and we trust it will continue on this path.'[30]

The importance that the Government as a whole attached to the opposition of the bishops is evident from the efforts that the Foreign Office made to have the Pope restrain them. On the suggestion of Austen Chamberlain, Mr Balfour, the Foreign Secretary, was instructed to notify Count de Salis, British representative to the Holy See, of all cases of improper interference by the Irish priesthood in secular affairs.[31] A dossier of such cases was later passed on to a papal representative. The reaction must have been a disappointment to the Government. When Cardinal Logue was invited to comment, he explained that such cases were not representative of the clergy as a whole; and the only response from the Pope himself was a letter to the Irish bishops, in August, inviting them to act with caution and moderation.[32] The semi-official Vatican organ *Corriere d'Italia* was less guarded. It explained

> The Holy See has always left the episcopacy of each country free to take what attitude it might think best in the internal affairs of its country. Thus, whatever Cardinal Logue may consider it expedient to do about conscription in Ireland cannot affect the impartiality or neutrality of the Vatican in this war, nor can it be considered a violation of the policy consistently followed since the war began.[33]

The strong reaction, in England, to the intervention of the Church attracted a lot of attention in Ireland and produced a debate on the more philosopical and theological aspects of the question in some circles. However most of the bishops were reluctant to go beyond the line espoused in their statement after the Maynooth meeting when conscription was characterised as 'an oppressive and inhuman law'. The right of resistance to unjust laws had long been an accepted part of Catholic doctrine, so this was used to justify the bishops' stand. Bishop Finnegan of Kilmore, preaching at Cavan Cathedral, gave the official view of the hierarchy: for a law to be binding on the conscience, it had to be just; conscription was unjust.[34]

What made the position of the bishops controversial and ambiguous was the basis on which they decided that conscription was unjust. Their joint statement cited lack of consent and the 'historic relations' between the two countries. But the same argument could equally well be used to resist all laws passed by the imperial Parliament. Neither the hierarchy nor the Irish Party were prepared to openly deny the right of the imperial Parliament to legislate for Ireland except in this specific case. Thus they stopped short of the outright repudiation of Westminster which Sinn Fein desired and the Unionists condemned. However the logical outcome of an argument based on Irish separateness and the need for consent would be to do just that.

The *Irish Catholic* tried to stifle criticism on this point by arguing that 'nothing was to be gained from calling into question the right of the British Parliament to pass laws binding on Ireland. It was only the right to impose conscription which was been challenged'.[35] Those of the bishops who tried to come to terms with the apparent inconsistency were forced to argue that there was something unique about conscription which made it different from other laws which were unpopular in Ireland. Speaking at Ballinasloe, Dr Gilmartin, Bishop of Clonfert, argued that conscription was 'an invasion of the fundamental rights of the nation'. Ireland, he said, was a distinct nation: geographically, economically and socially. The Act of Union had been imposed by corrupt means. If, in practice, the people had accepted it, it was to avoid anarchy.[36]

Dr McRory, Bishop of Down and Connor, was even more succinct. The opposition of the hierarchy, he said

> . . . was and is based on the principle that if a nation has any rights at all, it has the right to say when and why it shall shed its blood, and also on the ground that no power has any moral right to coerce young Irishmen to fight in the alleged interests of freedom until they have been allowed to enjoy freedom for themselves.[37]

What the bishops saw as subtlety, the 'purists' on both sides rejected as inconsistency. Sinn Fein, the Unionists and some Lloyd George Liberals agreed that what was involved was a complete repudiation of the imperial Parliament. It was as such that they welcomed or condemned it, though even the more radical bishops carefully avoided such a clear-cut interpretation of their position.

Some of the bishops adduced 'practical' reasons why conscription was unjust and unhuman. They voiced fairly widely held fears about the spiritual well-being of Irish conscripts dying in France without the sacraments and about the effect such a drain of manhood would have on the community at home. For instance, having argued that, because of English misrule, Ireland had barely a sufficient population to perpetuate the race, Dr Gilmartin announced that conscription 'would leave our fields without workers, would leave our girls without husbands, would leave our colleges without students, would perhaps complete the decay which the last few years have partially arrested'.[38] Bishop Browne of Cloyne foresaw economic, social and cultural ruin if conscription was implemented; and in a message to a protest meeting at Fermoy he echoed Dr Gilmartin's sentiments:

> It is appalling to contemplate the suffering and desolation which would necessarily follow the drifting away of the manhood of the country - famine stricken homes, our industries and trade, already stunted by an unsympathetic government, completely paralysed, the growing crops wasted for want of hands to reap the fruit, unrest and disorder everywhere.[39]

The fear that conscription would lead to unrest, disorder and ultimately chaos, more than anything else lay behind the involvement of the bishops. Their theoretical justifications were a defence and not a cause of that involvement and they were more concerned to channel resistance than to create it. A study of a cross-section of their speeches bears this out. Before the first meeting of the Mansion House Conference, these speeches had as their central theme the message that no action should be taken until the political leaders met. Once the Conference came into being, the message repeatedly propagated by the bishops was that resistance should follow the lines to be advised by the Conference, that unity was essential and that any one engaging in isolated outbreaks was an enemy of the people. For instance, at a Confirmation ceremony in Clones, Cardinal Logue promised that if the rules promulgated by the political leaders were followed there would be no disturbances. He condemned spasmodic outbreaks and warned the young men that, though they were bound by God's law and civil law to oppose conscription, they should not take the matter into their own hands or get into any 'foolish movement'. He cautioned them, in particular, to guard against secret societies, take the advice of their bishops, do nothing rash and take instructions only from duly recognised leaders.[40]

Logue was worried lest the anti-conscription campaign should be manipulated by Sinn Fein or the IRB to engineer another rising. During the crisis he told a reporter from the *Manchester Guardian* that he had always been opposed to Sinn Fein and still was.[41] Nevertheless, with the exception of his explicit references to secret societies, the tone and general content of his address were reproduced in the speeches of his colleagues. In fact, their speeches are all so similar that it seems likely that they decided in advance on the line to be taken. Even the more radical bishops invariably included appeals for prudence.

All of the bishops agreed that conscription should be resisted by every means 'consonant with the law of God', but no significant debate resulted on what that phrase entailed. The political leaders were to decide on the 'most effective means' and the long delay on the part of the Mansion House Conference in producing practical proposals facilitated a general evasion of the issue. There was much militant rhetoric and talk of 'firm uncompromising resistance' in the speeches of the bishops which admirably matched the mood of the people. It also concealed a marked lack of definition.

Among the more forthright was Logue himself. He declared his strong opposition to physical resistance and contended that they were not pledged in the agitation to do anything violent. He remained convinced that only passive resistance could be successful.[42] Without the benefit of hindsight, very few people would have argued that a military struggle against the might of the British Empire could have been anything other than a failure. In a speech directed as much at the Mansion House Conference as at his congregation, Dr Foley, Bishop of Kildare, spelled out what many may have been thinking. He asked his audience to observe that

> the bishops did not proceed to determine what forms of resistance would be consonant with the law of God; they [the bishops] knew that the right of resistance might be exercised at a time or in a place or in a manner in which useless slaughter would be the result, and they naturally left it to the political leaders to decide what particular means would be 'the most effective at their disposal'.

> Their leaders would not recommend any means of resistance of the effectiveness of which they were not reasonably

assured.[43]

Involvement of the Church in the conscription crisis was not confined to the bishops. The parish clergy followed their lead by denouncing compulsory service, by organising the taking of the anti-conscription pledge – generally at church-gate meetings – and the collection of the defence fund, and by acting as the main officers on the local defence committees, which were usually set up under their auspices. The arrangements for the pledge, defence fund and local committees varied considerably throughout the country but the most common feature was the involvement of the clergy.

Not surprisingly, those who saw the hierarchy as the instigators of Irish recalcitrance interpreted the actions of the local clergy as being part of the same conspiracy. The post-1916 period saw a noticeable radicalisation in the views of many of the younger clergy. It was to contain this that Cardinal Logue had issued his well-known pastoral in November 1917 warning against a 'mischievous' and 'Utopian agitation in favour of an appeal to the Peace Conference and the establishment of an Irish Republic'. The conscription crisis provided the more political of the clergy with a ready-made outlet for their energies. The dossier of seditious speeches by priests, compiled by Arthur Samuels, Solicitor General for Ireland, certainly contained some colourful material. In Virginia, County Cavan, Father Gaffney PP was reported to have told his congregation at Sunday Mass that, if men in uniform attempted to enforce conscription, they would be justified in shooting them. In Letterkenny, Dr McGinley PP was said to have urged the people to resort to passive resistance only when every revolver was empty. In a memorandum on the organisation of Irish resistance to conscription, Duke, the Chief Secretary, reported that the Roman Catholic priests were foremost among the advocates of resistance and that, in some cases, bloodshed was looked for. Priests in Antrim, Tyrone, Cavan, Donegal, Meath, Westmeath, Wexford, Kerry, Tipperary, Galway and Sligo were said to have declared their determination 'to join their parishioners and resist to the death'. Duke was of the opinion, however, that such cases were not typical and that passive resistance was generally prescribed.[44]

The Government's Irish advisers were more worried about the influence that the clergy could exercise over the RIC. In the absence of a national register, the RIC would have been essential to the successful implementation of conscription, with the result that the force came under a good deal of pressure not to have anything to do with it.

The Inspector General of the RIC expressed grave fears about the effect of the pressure on the younger officers, especially in outlying areas. An extreme example of the sort of pressure they were under was Eyries, County Cork where the local curate, Gerald Dennehy told a church-gate meeting that police who assisted in imposing conscription would be excommunicated and those who killed them would be blessed by God. Canon Hayes PP, Ballylongford, was more subtle, as befitted a parish priest. He called on police and soldiers of Irish blood to lay down their arms rather than go against their Church. The Chief Secretary advised the Cabinet that the fears about the reliability of the police were another reason to think again about conscription.[45]

In general, the local clergy, like the bishops, had a unifying effect on the movement against conscription. The Mansion House Conference had stipulated that local anti-conscription committees should be representative of all local bodies and that the local clergy should be represented. The chairmanship of the committees almost invariably fell to the parish priests, who tended to be more conservative than their curates. The Irish Party, whose organisation had fallen into disuse in many areas, benefited from this and were keen to have as many senior clergy as possible represented on local defence committees.

The outstanding example was a long dispute in Belfast as to how the parish and regional committees should be constituted. Understandably, the United Irish League proposed that parish priests should automatically be members of both. Sinn Fein, on the other hand, proposed to limit the number of parish priests or regional committees and to balance their presence on the parish committees by also giving membership to all the curates in each parish. A three-day conference failed to resolve the issue.

Belfast was still an Irish Party stronghold, but there was similar evidence from elsewhere. Father Varden PP, Ballinasloe, assured John Dillon that he retained the support of all the parish priests in the archdiocese of Tuam and the only support for Sinn Fein came from a small number of junior clergy.[46] Dillon acknowledged that the conservatism of the parish priests helped his party. When he declared that it was impossible to over-estimate the Church's service in placing its organisation at the disposal of the anti-conscription movement, he was probably referring in part to their help in ensuring that the parish committees would not be completely dominated by Sinn Fein.[47]

The bishops saw their involvement in the anti-conscription campaign as inevitable. Nevertheless, it was not an involvement many of them relished. The virulent 'no popery' campaign emphasised the delicacy of their position. When the immediate danger of conscription lessened, they were content to fade into the background and resume a watching brief. As early as the end of April, Cardinal Logue wrote to Archbishop Walsh: 'I am going round on Confirmations, and have beautiful weather, thank God. I would be alright if the politicians and the no-popery letter writers would leave me in peace'.[48] Walsh, too, was feeling ill at ease. He had been made one of the trustees of the National Defence Fund, but the position was largely honorary. He was removed from the day to day administration of the fund and very often did not know what was going on. When local committees wrongly sent money directly to him, he admitted that he knew nothing about the correct procedure.[49] When the National Aid Committee, the republican welfare organisation, was given control of the administration of relief to victims of conscription, he lost his patience and demanded that the conditions under which the fund was to be administered be laid down before any money was touched. He complained to Dillon

> Things are becoming less and less satisfactory. I am overflooded with questions about the arrangements regarding the funds and it is humiliating to have to say that I know nothing whatever about them. This, of course, is an impossible position for a trustee.

> The announcement in this mornings papers seems to make matters more perplexing still. It seems to imply that funds are to be handed over by trustees to be disbursed by persons of whom the trustees know nothing.[50]

The East Cavan by-election marked the withdrawal of the hierarchy from the centre of the stage. When Sinn Fein nominated Arthur Griffith, hopes for a continued 'national front' vanished. With the approval of Cardinal Logue, Bishop Finnegan, in whose diocese the constituency lay, tried publicly and privately to arrange a compromise, but none was forthcoming. Dillon appealed to Archbishop Walsh to use his influence with Griffith and de Valera. Walsh declined on the grounds that he did not know Griffith and had met de Valera only once. He did, however, write to the Lord Mayor of Dublin telling him very forcibly that if the Manison House Conference could not agree on a compromise the sooner it 'wound up' the better.[51] The strong view the hierarchy took of the contested election was again emphasised when Father O'Flanagan, acting President of Sinn Fein, was suspended by Dr Coyne of Elphin for speaking at a meeting in Cavan without seeking the permission of the local parish

priest. None the less, Griffith had strong clerical support
in the constituency, so much so that Dillon described the
eventual result as a victory for the priests,[52] who were
probably less willing than the bishops to withdraw from the
political arena.

The reassertion of party differences gave the hierarchy an
added reason to avoid further controversy. The immediate
threat of conscription receded when the Government announced
a new voluntary recruiting campaign in May, in an effort to
get itself off the hook. Indeed, for a time, some members of
the Irish Government tried to placate the bishops and win
them over with concessions. This appeasement included the
appointing of well-known Catholics to some vacant legal
positions.[53] It culminated in the appointment as Under
Secretary of James MacMahon, a native of Armagh, whose main
qualification for the job was that he was reputedly in close
contact with the hierarchy.[54] At the end of June, Lord
French met Cardinal Logue but his overtures did not prove
very fruitful and French soon became disillusioned. Though
friendly in his attitude, Logue could not and would not
compromise on the question of conscription. When an emissary
was dispatched to 'sound' prominent Irishmen, he found Logue
conciliatory but firm. He reported that Logue

> over and over again emphasised the fact that he had gone
> into this business in order to restrain the people from
> violence. The Church has increased it's power with the
> people by taking up the popular side, and he affected to
> be much disappointed at the attacks made on him in the
> House of Commons and *The Times*, and that the people on
> this side did not see that the Church's action was
> intended entirely to prevent the outbreak of a revolution,
> and restrain violence. He was adamant so far as his
> present action with regard to conscription was concerned.
> He would not, however, put any obstacle in the way of
> voluntary enlistment, though he would not help it. . . .
> His attitude with regard to the Austrians was sympathetic,
> but he is pro Ally, not pro Entente.[55]

The intervention of the Church in the anti-conscription
campaign had the effect of a cementing agent which bonded
diverse elements together. Faced with the prospect of
Catholic nationalist Ireland united in complete determination to resist conscription, the Government had to back
down. The unlikely alliance of Sinn Fein and the Irish Party
would hardly have lasted even the length it did were it not

for the bishops. They provided not just moral legitimacy for the anti-conscription campaign but a whole infra-structure for resistance. The influence of the Church permeated the official anti-conscription movement to such an extent as to guarantee that cautious voices would be heard to balance more impulsive counsel. Had they not intervened, things might have been very different. Be that as it may, their intervention also seemed to prove, once again, that nationalism and Catholicism were synonomous. That lesson was certainly drawn in England and in Ulster.

By sanctioning the campaign, the bishops helped to give Sinn Fein a respectability which it did not previously have. Though the crisis did not herald a permanent shift in the hierarchy's position, it is arguable that the *status quo ante* could not be completely restored. Obviously, the hierarchy was not a monolithic body. Like Irish society as a whole, it was comprised of people of varying political views. (The same, incidentally, was true of the priests.) But it would be a mistake to try to explain the role of bishops simply by reference to their supposed place in a narrow and very fluid political spectrum. When they decided to throw their weight behind the anti-conscription movement, they did so not only because they believed that conscription was wrong, but also because they believed that, without their intervention, chaos and disorder would result. It was that, more than anything, which persuaded them to risk the accusation of unwarranted political interference.

NOTES

1. A shorter version of this paper was delivered at an Irish Ecclesiastical History Conference in Dublin, in 1978, under the title 'The Church and the Conscription Crisis'. In Ireland, unlike Australia, remarkably little work has been done on the role of the Church in resisting conscription. David Miller's *Church, State and Nation in Ireland 1898-1921* (Dublin, 1973) provides a background narrative for the period as a whole. On conscription itself, it is rather disappointing and provides little original detail or comment. Much more challenging is Tomas O'Fiaich's 'The Irish Bishops and Conscription' *(Capuchin Annual,* 1968, pp. 351-68), which tackles the vital question of the importance to be attached to the imprimatur given by the bishops to the Mansion House Conference. Some of the conclusions are questionable and it is unfootnoted, but the article

is invaluable.
2. Miller, *Church, State and Nation in Ireland*, p. 311.
3. Fogarty to Redmond, 3 June 1915 (NLI, Redmond Papers, ms 15, 188).
4. Miller, *Church, State and Nation in Ireland*, p. 312.
5. *Freeman's Journal*, 10 Apr. 1918. The members of the standing committee were Cardinal Logue, Archbishops Walsh (Dublin) and Harty (Cashel), and Bishops O'Donnell (Raphoe), O'Dea (Galway), Kelly (Ross), Browne (Cloyne), Foley (Kildare and Leighlin) and McRory (Dromore).
6. Archbishop Harty, Bishop O'Donnell and Bishop McRory voted for the minority nationalist report. Bishop Kelly missed the final sessions through illness, see *Report of Proceedings of Irish Convention* (Dublin, 1918).
7. *Freeman's Journal*, 13 Apr. 1918.
8. *Irish Independent*, 18 Apr. 1918.
9. Logue to Walsh, 13 Apr. 1918 (Dublin Diocesan Archives, Walsh Papers, 379/7).
10. *Irish Independent*, 16 Apr. 1918.
11. O'Fiaich, 'The Irish Bishops and Conscription', pp. 355-6.
12. See, for example, Miller, *Church, State and Nation in Ireland*, p. 404. The suggestion, in the official Irish biography of de Valera, that he may have met Walsh on the previous Friday is incorrect (P. O'Fiannachta and T. P. O'Neill, *de Valera* (Dublin, 1968) p. 105). See Walsh to Dillon, 24 Apr. 1918 (TCD, Dillon Papers, Walsh Correspondence, 95).
13. When Walsh died, de Valera referred to the invaluable help and guidance he had given him during the conscription crisis. O'Fiaich takes Walsh's letter to the press to mean that he was not happy about the 'negative approach inherent in the phrase "passive resistance" '. He cites as corroboration the fact that de Valera told Walsh's secretary the previous Friday that the Volunteers intended to offer active resistance to conscription, including the use of force if necessary, and Walsh's letter criticising the Irish Party during the Longford by-election of 1917. O'Fiaich is thus suggesting that Walsh's aim was to rally support for the Volunteers (O'Fiaich, 'The Irish Bishops and Conscription', pp. 354-5). This interpretation is also to be found in O'Fiannachta and O'Neill, *de Valera*, p. 105, where it is suggested that the letter, inspired by de Valera's conversation with Curran, was intended to foster active as opposed to passive resistance.

14. Walsh to Dillon, 22 Apr. 1918 (Dillon Papers, Walsh Correspondence, 94).
15. It should be noted that the phrases 'active resistance' or 'active preparations' did not always mean violent resistance. Logue, for instance, was in favour of 'active resistance' but opposed to violent resistance. He told de Valera at the Maynooth meeting that when he spoke of passive resistance, he did not mean they should lie down and let people walk over them. See, William O'Brien, *Forth the Banners Go* (Dublin, 1969) pp. 165-6.
16. D. Macardle, *The Irish Republic* (Dublin, 1937) p. 250.
17. O'Fiannachta and O'Neill, *de Valera*, p. 106; O'Brien, *Forth the Banners Go*, p. 165. There is no official record of the proceedings available. A few personal accounts survive among which there is little or no dispute as to what transpired. O'Fiaich gives the best summary based as it is on the recollections of the participants. The delegation consisted of de Valera, Dillon, Healy, O'Brien and the Lord Mayor of Dublin, Laurence O'Neill.
18. O'Fiannachta and O'Neill, *de Valera*, p. 107; O'Fiaich, 'The Irish Bishops and Conscription', pp. 356-7; O'Brien, *Forth the Banners Go*, p. 166.
19. *Irish News*, 19 Apr. 1918. The phrase justifying all resistance 'consonant with the law of God' was suggested by Dr Fogarty and agreed to by the politicians (O'Fiaich, 'The Irish Bishops and Conscription', p. 337).
20. *Irish Independent*, 25 Apr. 1918.
21. *The Times*, 25 and 27 Apr. 1918.
22. *Observer*, 28 Apr. 1918. Garvin was, of course, of Irish parentage and had once been both a Catholic and a Nationalist.
23. *Daily Chronicle*, 29 Apr. 1918; memorandum from Duke to the Cabinet on the anti-conscription campaign, 21 Apr. 1918 (PRO, Cab. 24/49, G.T. 4302).
24. Campbell to Bonar Law, 23 Apr. 1918 (House of Lords Records Office, Bonar Law Papers, 83/2/24).
25. French to Lloyd George, 19 and 23 Apr. 1918 (HLRO, Lloyd George Papers, F/48/6/8-9).
26. Long to Bonar Law, 27 Apr. 1918 (Bonar Law Papers, 83/2/32).
27. Gwynn to W. G. S. Adams, 7 May 1918 (Lloyd George Papers, F/63/2/34).
28. War Cabinet, 397, 23 Apr. 1918 (Cab. 23/4).
29. *Westminster Gazette*, 29 Apr. 1918.
30. *Manchester Guardian*, 27 Apr. 1918.

31. War Cabinet, 406, 7 May 1918 (Cab. 23/6).
32. Miller, *Church, State and Nation in Ireland*, p. 406; O'Fiaich, 'The Irish Bishops and Conscription', p. 363.
33. *Freeman's Journal*, 27 Apr. 1918.
34. An article by Father Peter Finlay, Professor of Catholic Theology at the National University in the Summer edition of *Studies* ('The Doctrinal Authority of the Bishops', *Studies* (Summer 1918) pp. 193-209) outlined what was probably the official interpretation of the basis of the bishops' stand. In the same month, Dr Peter Coffey (writing in the *Irish Ecclesiastical Record*, pp. 483-98) put the more republican case. The ambiguity of both is outlined in Dr Walter MacDonald, *Some Ethical Questions of Peace and War* (1919) pp. 145-57.
35. *Irish Catholic*, 19 Apr. 1918.
36. *Freeman's Journal*, 24 Apr. 1918.
37. *Irish News*, 29 Apr. 1918.
38. *Freeman's Journal*, 24 Apr. 1918.
39. Ibid., 25 and 30 Apr. 1918.
40. Ibid., 25 Apr. 1918.
41. *Manchester Guardian*, 30 Apr. 1918.
42. Ibid.; *Freeman's Journal*, 22 Apr. 1918.
43. *Freeman's Journal*, 26 Apr. 1918.
44. Samuels to Lloyd George, 2 May 1918 (Lloyd George Papers, F/44/9/2); memorandum by Duke, 18 Apr. 1918 (Cab. 24/48, G.T. 4272).
45. Ibid.; Inspector General's (weekly) Report on 'Public Feeling in Ireland' for the week ending 20 Apr. 1918 (Cab. 24/49, G.T. 4326); report by French to the Cabinet, 19 Apr. 1918 (Cab. 1/26, File 12).
46. Sean MacAlain (secretary of Sinn Fein Divisional Executive in Belfast) to Dillon, 30 May 1918 (Dillon Papers); Varden to Dillon, 28 May 1918 (Dillon Papers). Varden was probably not a good judge of the support for Sinn Fein among the curates.
47. *Freeman's Journal*, 6 May 1918. It is significant that the Volunteers insisted on working independently of the parish committees.
48. Logue to Walsh, 29 Apr. 1918 (Walsh Papers, 379/6).
49. See, for example, Canon Lennon PP, Gorey to Walsh, 14 May 1918 and Father Curran to Lennon, n.d. (Walsh Papers, 379/7).
50. Walsh to Dillon, 25 Apr. 1918 (Dillon Papers, Walsh Correspondence, 96).
51. Walsh to Dillon, 24 Apr. 1918 (Dillon Papers, Walsh Correspondence, 95).
52. T. M. Healy, *Letters and Leaders of My Day* (London,

1928) vol. ii, p. 597; Dillon to O'Connor, 17 June 1918 (Dillon Papers, O'Connor Correspondence, 496).
53. Justice James O'Connor was appointed to the Court of Appeal despite the objections of James Campbell, the new Lord Chancellor, and Walter Long. O'Connor had been considered for the post of Lord Chief Justice but after strong objections from Campbell and Long, the post went to Justice Moloney who was also a Catholic (Campbell to Bonar Law, 3 July 1918, Bonar Law Papers, 83/5/2); French to Lloyd George, 6 July 1918 (Lloyd George Papers, F/48/6/15).
54. Campbell to Bonar Law, ibid.; French to Lloyd George, 12 Oct. 1918 (Lloyd George Papers, F/48/6/20).
55. 'Report on Present State of Ireland Especially with Reference to Conscription', written by the Duke of Atholl and forwarded to Lloyd George on the suggestion of Lord Milner, 29 Apr. 1918. (Lloyd George Papers, F/94/3/45).

12 The Irish Republican Brotherhood in Australia: the 1918 Internments

PATRICK O'FARRELL

On 17 June 1918, seven members of the Irish National Association, which had been founded in Sydney in July 1915, were arrested and detained on the ground that they were members of what the acting Prime Minister, Mr Watt, described as 'an Australian division of an organisation known as the Irish Republican Brotherhood' which 'had been secretly and systematically organised, and its object was the establishment of an Irish republic independent of Britain'.

Did the Irish Republican Brotherhood, the Fenian Brotherhood, architect and conspiratorial instigator of the Easter 1916 rebellion in Ireland, really exist in Australia? Was there here a unit of that secret Irish army?[2]

The arrests of June 1918 were made under special regulations of the War Precautions Act, regulations gazetted by the Commonwealth on 28 March 1918. These were directed against what was called 'Sinn Fein' and any advocacy of the independence of Ireland. In addition to prohibiting the advocacy of disloyalty, or hostility to the British Empire – or its dismemberment – the regulations also declared it an offence to wear or display any badge, flag, banner or symbol associated with 'the movement known as Sinn Fein', and gave the Minister powers to authorise the entering, search and closure of premises associated, in his opinion, with such activities.

The very general terms of this regulation, its use of the description 'Sinn Fein', and its timing, all point to significant aspects of Government motivation, and information, in regard to Irish matters. The Easter 1916 rebellion in Ireland had become commonly known as the Sinn Fein rebellion. The use of this term in the regulation points to the very superficial state of official knowledge at this time, nearly two years later. In fact the regulation was informed essentially by the kind of general anti-Irish suspicion and hostility that pervaded the utterances of the Prime Minister, W. M. Hughes, in which denunciations of IWW plotting and Sinn Fein disloyalty were commonly paired: the

IWW and Sinn Fein were twin bogeys whose detailed content or actual reality was too repulsive to contemplate.

If the looseness of its wording is a general indication, the timing of the regulation makes particularly clear its *ad hoc* political contrivance. Its specific impetus seems to have come from events in Melbourne. The St Patrick's Day procession of 16 March 1918, with Dr Mannix its central figure, a float depicting the 'martyrs of the Easter rising', and Sinn Fein banners much in evidence, brought loyalist reaction to Mannix and the Irish Question to a pitch of fury. Particularly provocative was Mannix's alleged failure to acknowledge the playing of the National Anthem, and his vigorously pro-Irish oration to a cheering multitude. In response, on Thursday 21 March, 'Loyalist Melbourne rose in protest against Daniel Mannix'. A Town Hall rally was decided on, and organised by Herbert Brookes and Dr Leeper, warden of Trinity College of the University of Melbourne. In the midst of preparations, Brookes had an idea which ultimately was to result in catching, not Dr Mannix as intended, but the IRB. To use his own words, 'inspired by a sudden thought, I rang the Prime Minister, Mr W. M. Hughes, with whom I was on a friendly footing, and told him of the meeting that was to take place, and asked him if he would be prepared to receive a deputation from that meeting urging him to proclaim Sinn Fein as a disloyal organisation. He agreed.' The meeting of protest against the 'ugly traitor in our midst' took place, an enormous and highly excited deputation sought out Hughes in the Federal offices nearby, and he agreed publicly amidst great cheering, to proscribe Sinn Fein as an illegal organisation.

The following Monday, 25 March, three days before the appropriate regulations were gazetted, military and civilian detectives in Sydney raided the homes of members of the local Irish National Association - notably its President, John Sheehy, its founder and Secretary, Albert Dryer, and Dryer's mother, Mrs Mary Weber who lived in Lithgow. Various books, letters and documents were seized.

Whether or not, as Dryer believed, the Irish National Association had been under police surveillance since its formation in 1915, it was the natural first target, once Hughes had determined on action against 'Sinn Fein'. Even before the 1916 rebellion the INA had a radical nationalist complexion. On 24 April 1916 the INA's monthly ceilidh dancing was abandoned 'in sympathy with the patriots who lost their lives (being murdered after the Irish insurrection) to satisfy the blood lust of the champion of small nations'. Its support for the rebellion and Irish independence predated and was more extreme than that of Dr Mannix. It was also more vulnerable and isolated in that it was relatively small – though the 1200 members it had in Sydney in 1918 was not insignificant – though rather more in that its membership was largely working class, and in that its radicalism separated it from, indeed put it at odds with, the traditional and powerful Home Rule, Australian-Irish organisations and personages. Its Irish republicanism was public and flagrant: it was the logical place to start to release the frustrated anti-Irish feelings of which Mannix was the particular focus. To take action against Mannix directly and immediately was obviously too dangerous and potentially disruptive in the climate of the time. But there seems little doubt that the authorities had their hopes: perhaps the records of the leaders of the INA would reveal that the prominent and the powerful had incriminated themselves irrevocably, and the evidence merely awaited seizure. In fact, such hopeful thinking was not absurd. Mannix was the INA's idol. He had been approached for support on several occasions and a copy of a letter to him was among those seized in later raids on INA members. But whether from caution or other reason, Mannix had not responded and could in no way be connected with the INA.

The homes of Dryer and others were raided on 25 March. Yet it was not until 23 and 24 May that the Sydney offices of the INA were entered by police and documents seized – a delay of two months. On 24 and 25 May further raids and seizure of materials took place at the homes of eleven INA members in Sydney, four in Melbourne and one in Brisbane. Then, after a few days' more delay, Dryer was called before a stipendary magistrate and interrogated, in camera, in regard to the INA, the existence of 'Sinn Fein' in Australia, and Irish activities generally. He was also asked if he would enlist, to which he replied that he would fight to defend Australia itself, but not otherwise. These procedures, and the sequence of events then and later, suggest that Dryer himself – the central figure in the INA – had by care and cleverness, succeeded in frustrating and confusing the authorities. He had given little, if anything, away.

The raids of 24 and 25 May altered the situation, not dramatically, but sufficiently to sustain Government action. On 17 June, after nearly a month to ponder the new seizures, and three months after the initial raids in March, seven members of the INA were arrested and interned in Darlinghurst Gaol, Sydney. On 19 June these arrests were announced by the acting Prime Minister, Mr Watt. He declined to give the names of those arrested: they were not made public for a fortnight. He referred to the discovery of an Australian division of the IRB using the INA as a cloak, to those arrested as 'ringleaders in this conspiracy', to 'sinister attempts . . . made by republican extremists' and declared 'Part of the plan of the organisation was to enrol volunteers, who were to be despatched from Australia to America, and thence to Ireland to aid an armed revolution. The organisation in America was in touch with Germany and money for hostile purposes was remitted from Australia.' Watt also indicated that 'For the fuller information of the people, and the interests of justice' a public enquiry would be held, presided over by a judge - and that there was no occasion for alarm. The terms of this announcement were obviously such that the judicial procedures were superfluous, so far as assumption of guilt was concerned: the Government had already determined the matter and an enquiry could merely demonstrate its rectitude. From the point of Watt's announcement the Government required the IRB to exist and exist it would - a compulsion which the detainees and those who defended them ignored, or at least pretended to ignore, for a variety of purposes. For the detainees, postulated membership of a revolutionary secret society required them to deny it, or at least demand it be proved; for their professional and respectable legal defenders the latter applied, with the additional incentive that such an Irish organisation in Australia was repugnant and inconceivable in terms of their approach to Australian society.

If the Government had expected horror and alarm to follow Watt's sensational revelations - and they were hardly phrased to induce the calm for which he called - it was disappointed. The arrests served to unify the Irish Australian community in strong support of the detainees and in the belief that the charges were persecuting fabrications. A defence fund was launched. Archbishop Mannix called for Irish solidarity in support of the detainees and gave five guineas to the fund. Labour politicians, led by Frank Brennan and Frank Tudor, demanded a full trial, and not an enquiry. Leading Irish Catholic lawyers volunteered their defence services free. Yet there was a tinge of insecurity and restraint in this response, a certain lack of conviction. It was necessary to defend the Irish Catholic community against its traducers and enemies, but the charges were very serious, and what if they were true?

The judicial enquiry was held before Mr Justice Harvey in Sydney from 8 to 30 August 1918. Those detained were Albert Thomas Dryer, Edmund McSweeney, Michael McGing and William McGuinness, all of Sydney; Maurice Dalton and Frank McKeown of Melbourne, and Thomas Fitzgerald of Brisbane. All except Dryer were Irish born. They were defended by Frank Brennan MP and Messrs Mack and McTiernan, instructed by the leading

Sydney firm of Collins and Mulholland. Justice Harvey accepted the essence of the Crown case, but not its more extreme conjectures. The tone of his report was remarkably mild, given the possible implications of some of the evidence and the hysteria endemic at the time. On some of the individual cases he suggested there was slight or only very general evidence linking them with the IRB. Not surprisingly, the Government confirmed all detentions. Six of the prisoners were released on 19 December 1918: Dryer was held until 11 February 1919.

Judge Harvey's report dealt individually with those detained, using the case of Dryer as a foundation for his reconstruction of the history of the IRB in Australia: writing in 1956, Dr Dryer described the report as containing the 'salient facts' and it is so treated in the following discussion, supplemented by other information.

The Judge found that Dryer, founder of the INA, a clerk in the Customs Department, had at the beginning of August 1916 been 'enrolled as sub-centre of the first New South Wales sub-circle of the Irish Republican Brotherhood'. This secret organisation, based in America, had not existed formally in Australia prior to 1916, though there were a number of men here who had been members of old circles elsewhere. Australian branches adopted the organisation and ritual of the American IRB, Clan na Gael, headed by John Devoy, which had strong German connections. Judge Harvey's report took the - correct - view that the IRB was central to the Easter Rising, and emphasised the role of the Irish rebels' German connections via America - again correct, if excessively stressed.

From the evidence before him (mainly seized correspondence), Harvey held that the Australian IRB was begun in Melbourne in 1916 by Maurice Dalton and John Doran. Dalton, then aged seventy-three and an old age pensioner, professed to be an old IRB member and to have taken part in the Fenian rebellion in Ireland in 1867. An unashamed apostle of violent Irish rebellion, Dalton had founded the INA in Melbourne. He had become associated with John Doran, a young man of Irish origin and possibly both American and English backgrounds. Doran was the key but absent figure in the inquiry. Apparently deserting from a ship, by 1910 he was an influential member of the Melbourne Shipwrights Union, and prominent in the Gaelic League of Victoria. Although remaining a shadowy figure, the impression remains of a restless aggressive adventurer, perhaps a poseur, intelligent and able, but irresponsible and conspiratorial by nature. Doran and Dalton founded an IRB branch in Melbourne, with Doran, typically, it might seem, later confessing an 'incomplete knowledge' of the system of IRB organisation.

On 8 July 1916 Doran sailed to Sydney where he spent two months organising the IRB there. Two sub-circles of ten men each were formed, Dryer and McSweeney prominent in one, McGuinness and McGing in the other. Before sailing on - as a deckhand - to San Francisco, Doran visited Brisbane to found the IRB there, with Fitzgerald the initial member. All this he reported by letter to Dalton in Melbourne and Devoy in America in communications which were in part open if general information, part Gaelic, part a crude invisible ink method, and part a simple code which described the growth of the IRB in terms of the progress of some business enterprise. Some of this inept conspiratorial correspondence - including the names of the Sydney IRB members conveyed in invisible ink but described as a dancing class - was seized from the elderly and careless Dalton.

Following Doran's departure for the USA, Dryer took over responsibility for extending the organisation in Sydney - to about fifty it seems by November 1916. In America Doran established contact with Devoy and brought the Australian organisation into communication with him and Clan na Gael - and Ireland via that route. Harvey assumed from circumstantial evidence that some secret informal means was used to maintain contact between Australia and America: in fact Irish seamen on the Pacific run (particularly the brothers Matthew and Andrew Organ) conducted a covert postal service for both letters and prohibited Irish revolutionary literature. In October 1917, in one of Doran's letters, reference had been made to Australian money for Irish arms to be purchased in Germany via America: in December 1917 Dryer forwarded £20 to Doran in San Francisco. Judge Harvey was satisfied that Dryer was central to the organisation and was anti-British, indeed pro-German to the extent that this served Ireland's interests. This seems a fair judgement of fact, later confirmed by Dryer, and not made with animus. Indeed Harvey had a clear insight into Dryer's remarkable character. When, referring to Dryer, his counsel said that 'there were men who became obsessed with ideas about reform. Dryer in that sense perhaps lived in a world of his own', the Judge interposed 'An enthusiast and an idealist'.

Harvey judged Edmund McSweeney to have been as deeply involved in the conspiracy as Dryer. He had been IRB Treasurer and may have had an English IRB background. Michael McGing he believed to have been not very influential in the IRB though active and prominent in the INA. Here Harvey revealed an ambivalence inherent in the situation: he swung between carefully distinguishing between the IRB and an innocent INA, and the assumption that the INA was a sympathetic front organisation which the IRB members exploited for secret seditious purposes.

In Harvey's opinion, William McGuinness was also a dual IRB - INA activist though more deeply involved than McGing. Indeed McGing was merely an expert exponent of Irish dancing. But unknown to Harvey, McGuinness had genuine, recent and impeccable IRB expertise. Born in Belfast in 1889, he had become closely associated with Bulmer Hobson, and was sworn into the IRB in Belfast in 1906. He had met the famous Fenian O'Donovan Rossa and Roger Casement: Sean MacDermott, one of the 1916 leaders, was a friend. He had come to Sydney in 1912 and joined the INA as soon as he heard of its formation. At the enquiry, the press described him as 'Irish of the intellectual type . . . . An earnest, alert young man.' McGuinness hardly featured in the enquiry - in fact he was the group's personal link with key personalities in the 1916 Rising.

Of Dalton's guilt Harvey had no doubt: this old rebel had boasted proudly in his correspondence that he had initiated the Australian IRB. He had provided Doran with credentials to the American IRB. In the wake of the IWW arson trials in Sydney, Dalton possessed a recipe for the IWW 'five dope', called a 'recipe for a severe cold'. Nor was there any doubt about Thomas Fitzgerald, the Brisbane bookseller, who appears to have been *the* Brisbane IRB.

Frank McKeown, a Melbourne bricklayer, could not be directly connected with the IRB. Against this, he had resigned as Secretary of the Melbourne INA because it was insufficiently Irish. And he had sent a postcard to Fitzgerald which, when translated from the Gaelic, (he was a Gaelic enthusiast) read 'To h. . . with the King'. But Harvey regarded evidence of his IRB membership as 'very slight'.

Harvey's summing up was that none of the interned men had had any direct connection with the enemy: such little as they had had been via America. But they had collected money which was used to purchase arms from Germany and they had used the INA as a front and cover, though there was no evidence its ordinary members were aware of this. He concluded by remarking that he had depended almost entirely on documentary evidence. The accused had not elected to give evidence: they had neither defended nor explained themselves.

No wonder. The documents revealed only the milder part of the story. In 1916-17 the Sydney IRB had established a secret military training camp in the Blue Mountains. They had no arms, and service was to be in Ireland itself. But in the hysterical anti-Irish climate of the time, any exposure of such arrangements to train men to fight against Britain seems likely to have led to what the Government at one stage contemplated – a charge of high treason against Dryer. Would he have become another Roger Casement? Seen in this light, the possibilities of the case for serious consequences become most interesting, as does its actual conduct.

From Dryer's private writing in the 1950s, it is evident – indeed he explicitly states – that he, Dalton, McGuinness, McSweeney and Fitzgerald were members of the IRB. By omission one may assume that McKeown and McGing were not, though at no stage did any of the internees deny such membership. The formal status of such membership may be obscure, though McGuinness and Dalton seem certainly to have been members in Ireland and McSweeney may have been. There is also the undoubted fact the IRB had historical roots in Australia of which John Devoy was well aware: when an international Revolutionary Directory was established in 1877 to conduct relations between Clan na Gael and the IRB in Ireland it had one Australian member. As late as 1924, Devoy was to blame difficulty of communications for rendering Australian participation a dead letter. What is certain is that at least five of the accused believed themselves to belong to the IRB, at least in spirit, to a degree which transcends the precise question of whether they took oaths and of what kind, and the validity of their membership. Just as the Government in its search for a scapegoat on which to vent its anti-Mannix spleen needed the IRB to exist, so did certain Australian Irishmen. Their hopes and dreams for Ireland took form in affirmation of the IRB and in its practical consequences – secret revolutionary conspiracy and indeed military training. The whole matter – like so much of Irish history – takes place in that blurred and twilight world between myth and reality, between dream and nightmare. And marvellously clever and apt, that is how those accused chose to depict themselves at the enquiry, to exploit the possibilities of the charges being seen as utter fantasy or complete farce.

Justice Harvey's low key and essentially sympathetic handling of the case invites careful scrutiny. His report explicitly averts both to his powers to compel witnesses to testify, and to his deliberate decision not to call any. Given what lay beneath the surface of the case, and with Mannix in the wings stating that his heart and soul were with the detainees, it was a happy choice. A persecuting, vigorously conducted and exhaustive enquiry might have been a step towards that unspeakable but menacing phantom that privately haunted some serious minds – the spectre of civil war. Certainly, had it been pursued differently the case could have fed, on both sides, the plot theses which centered around the existence of Sinn Fein in Australia - theses of sedition and revolution on the one hand, repression and persecution on the other.

Harvey damped down the Crown case. That case raised the possibility of charges of treason, pounced on references to Mannix, referred to the supply of arms, and even to the possibility of smuggling out of Australia men who wanted to fight for Ireland. Harvey pursued none of this, and none of it surfaced in his report. One reason for this may be sound and informed political common sense - the decision to avoid exacerbating tension. Another may have been that he had been given, and according to Mrs Dryer had his eyes opened by, Francis P. Jones *History of the Sinn Fein Movement and the Irish Rebellion of 1916*. It was also evident in the enquiry proceedings that he had read at least some of the confiscated Irish revolutionary publications. Or simply, he understood Ireland's case. But it also seems possible, indeed likely from his interpolated comments, that he was deceived by the minimising tactics of the defence, masterminded by Dryer, which exploited the inherently unlikely nature of a conspiracy which had in fact gone well beyond what the Crown alleged.

Albert Dryer was a man of high intelligence and considerable resource: he was also utterly dedicated to the cause of Irish independence although he was Australian born and was never to even visit Ireland. From a primary education he had put himself through night school, and then Sydney University, completing a BA in 1913: later he was to secure qualifications from Sydney Technical College, and eventually he graduated and practised in medicine. As an openly declared extremist in Irish affairs, Dryer was early aware that his activities were under some form of surveillance. In March 1917 he complained formally to the Postmaster General, with righteous indignation, that his mail within Australia was being opened. His evasive action took several and intelligent forms. His overseas mail went via Irish seamen as couriers. A copy of a letter apparently addressed to Doran in San Francisco indicates a more devious ploy. In it Dryer denounces the Hun, expresses disagreement with Dr Mannix, criticises Sinn Fein, refers disparagingly to the labour movement, and claims (twice) that he is thinking of enlisting - the reverse of all his real beliefs but expressed sufficiently naturally to be plausible. As the judicial proceedings revealed, the authorities were intercepting and photographing his mail and this letter seems designed to neutralise the indiscreet stageiness of Doran's open communications: Doran's open letters from the USA creaked of conspiracy. How many of these fabrications Dryer fed the censors is unknown, but it could be that the confusion created by their existence - or the (correct) assumption that Dryer kept copies of these loyal effusions as a hedge against prosecution - led to the incident of Dryer being interrogated by a magistrate about whether he would enlist, and stopped the authorities short of a treason charge.

Another device Dryer exploited, for outgoing mail, was the use of Win-the-War envelopes, which passed the censor unopened. For incoming mail he used an alias, in two forms - the obvious Arthur J. Drury at his own address, but also Miss Alice Drury at an address in Annandale. Dryer's internal correspondence was carefully phrased and designed to be relatively innocuous if intercepted. The real overseas mail went by hand, and what was seized seems likely to have been only a small trace of that. Briefly, the members of the Australian IRB were not incompetent fools. The points of weakness were Doran, writing carelessly from the freedom of America, and the elderly and brazen Dalton, who kept letters he should have destroyed.

But the military training camp, at Govett's Leap in the Blue Mountains remained an undiscovered secret. It was nothing large or elaborate. The surviving photographs show only a group of five, and Dryer himself outside a tent. A sketch map gives its location. The interested few had no arms, only enthusiasm to fight for Ireland - and the hope (it seems less than a detailed plan) that it might be possible to get aboard a ship, perhaps meeting it at sea, bound for the USA, and thence to Ireland. Doran was to follow up this possibility in America, and wrote to Dryer about it. Nor was this simply romantic fantasy: in November 1916 the boxer Les Darcy and a companion paid £75 each to stow away to America. Significantly, their ship was of the same Luckenbach line Doran proposed, but Dryer lost touch with him. Dryer's 'brother in arms' Matthew Organ scoured San Francisco for Doran, failing to find him at the addresses Dryer had supplied: all he unearthed was a story that Doran, after four months on the run, had been arrested for pro-German conspiracy. In fact, in the very month of the Sydney enquiry, Doran, in the guise of a fictitious cousin of Dryer's, sent him (as Arthur J. Drury) a postcard from Alaska using the usual business code jargon to convey the news that he was then out of touch with the southern Clan na Gael.

The realities of the case may be interpreted now as minor, as unfulfilled hopes and dreams, foolish games. Yet there is no doubting the utter seriousness of those involved and the strength of their determination to do something for Ireland

if they could. And there is no doubt of the cleverness of
the defence which Dryer meticulously constructed and handed
to his lawyers. He sought to depict the charges as absurd,
ludicrous, figments of the imagination and not proved by the
evidence. The major stumbling blocks were the evidence re-
lating to Doran and Dalton, and this was disposed of by
trying to represent the accused as innocent simpletons and
game-players. So, according to Mr Mack 'there was nothing
that did not smack of Tom Sawyer and Huckleberry Finn. The
invisible writing was a mere schoolboy trick.' To suggest
conspiracy was absurd. Dalton was a talkative old story-
teller. Doran 'played on these simple-minded men to get
money. He was a confidence man.' Indeed the whole business
'was purely Irish imagination. They deceived themselves into
thinking they were doing something for the sake of Ireland. . . . It was a mere tongue war they wished to wage' -
to which Judge Harvey added, with devastating percipience,
'Unfortunately, this sort of thing led to Easter Week.'

It was a good try, ingenious and to a degree successful.
What relatively little had emerged had been ridiculed and
diminished, even though the Crown had a much better case
than it knew. In detention, the internees remained unrepentant and conspiratorial. An Irishman, Lieutenant Rickwood,
was in charge of the gaol: he was kind and sympathetic - too
sympathetic, for he was eventually disciplined for his
indulgence of the prisoners: he smuggled in visitors. Dryer
had a camera smuggled in to take a picture of the detainees
for sale as a publicity postcard. One attempt to smuggle in
a code kit was intercepted, but it seems that a later effort
went undetected. The detainees found themselves confined
with another Irishman, unknown to them: they assumed him to
be an informer, planted in the hope they would incriminate
themselves.

The authorities recognised, in their own way, Dryer's
degree of success in out-smarting them. He was detained two
months longer than the others and handed his dismissal from
the Customs Department the day before his release. He spent
the next twenty years looking for secure employment: engaged
in 1915, he did not marry until 1933.

So, nothing much came of it, save anguish for Dryer -
another potential turning point at which traditional Australian history failed to turn, hardly even worth a derisory
footnote, at best a remote and muffled echo of big events
elsewhere, at worst a pathetic and irrelevant Irish joke.

So it seems. And this being so, how could it be otherwise?
Easily enough. For what had happened was the victory of
expectations of normality over the reality of what had
actually taken place. The earth-bound forces of probability,

solid common sense, and the leaden myth of Australian social harmony, carried too much weight to allow such wild dreams, such deep passion, such divergent idealism to actually exist - although they did. The suppression took place with the conspirators' active connivance, assisted by the unimaginative incompetance of the authorities: having accidentally, in pursuit of Mannix, discovered a real plot, the Government hardly took it seriously itself.

Those accused took it very seriously indeed. Their deliberate decision to remain silent and to ridicule themselves through their own lawyers was not an attempt to avoid punishment, but an endeavour to protect their plot and their cause. From that point of view it is fair to ask if those tactics were correct, that is, most efficacious, no matter what the personal cost. Whatever of that, it is what they actually did, most cleverly, and got away with. But what might have made real history - no mere footnote - in the explosive, divided and hate-filled Australia of 1918 was the strident and proud disclosure, of which those detained were perfectly capable had their tactics been otherwise, that dedicated Irish plotting was indeed afoot, and that there existed the determined nucleus, however tiny, of a secret Irish army.

NOTES

1. The substance of this paper will form a chapter of the author's forthcoming general study, *The Irish in Australian History*.
2. Save for contemporary newspaper reports, and Rohan Rivett, *Australian Citizen: Herbert Brookes 1867-1963* (Melbourne, 1965) this paper is based in the main on the papers of Dr Albert Dryer, which will, eventually, be available in the National Library, Canberra. I am grateful to the late Mrs Elizabeth Dryer, not only for access to her husband's papers, but for a long friendship in which she confirmed and added to the story, not only in conversation, and comments on the documentation, but in a personal correspondence valuable for its reminiscence, its unique historical content, and its human warmth.

13 Grafting Ireland onto Australia: some Literary Attempts
GERARD WINDSOR

A title such as this, that makes any mention of Irish-Australian literary mergers, raises a spectre that I want to lay immediately. I am thinking of that will-o'-the-wisp, the Irish character in the Australian landscape. I know that hunting the Irish element in the Australian character, and in Australian writing, has been a practice much honoured in the observance.[1] I do not wish to condemn the activity; it can be an invigorating and fruitful sport, but it can also be beset by so much circular argument and gratuitous assumption, that I want to make a definite, initial distinction between it and what I intend to do in this paper.

I am not interested in supposedly Irish traits or moods in Australian writing, and their origins, either for the sake of proving the feelings from the sources or vice versa. I want to start from a much more prosaic fact. I have been struck by the number of Australian writers, at work between the 1890s and 1921, who turned quite explicitly to Ireland for subject matter. Let me qualify this general statement. I have in mind seven writers, all of them minor, and two at least only peripherally writers. They were not a literary movement or coterie in any sense at all, although some of them must have known one another. What links them is solely their Irish interest. It varies from an occasional nostalgic nod towards Ireland from some of them to absorbing central interest in Ireland or Irish people from others. Again, some of the writers try to make Australian sense of their Irish interest: for others there is a complete dichotomy which does not seem to concern them at all. Their success as literature, admittedly a relative success, seems to be linked to the degree of this effort they make in accommodating Ireland to Australia.

I am proposing, albeit tentatively, that this literary interest in Ireland was something unique in Australia. Many of the opinions and feelings about Ireland are not particularly significant, but the group's very existence seems to have no parallel at all. The writers were all permanent residents of Australia, one of them even born here, and, although four of them were born in Ireland, they had more or less willingly chosen to make Australia their home. (I must admit the 'more or less willingly': there is a sense in which the demands of consumption or a missionary vocation cannot be refused.) But the point remains; Ireland fascinated Australian writers as no other country of origin did. Or, even more strikingly, Ireland or the Irish personality had in the minds of these writers a significant relevance for Australia that no other nation or national character was seen to be offering.

My *septem pro Hibernia*, in the order I shall discuss them, are Maurice O'Reilly, W. J. Lockington, Bernard McElhill, Victor Daley, David McKee Wright, Thomas E. Spencer, and Patrick Hartigan (John O'Brien). They are all men, not surprisingly perhaps when their common subject matter is so invariably regarded as a woman. I am not going to discuss the writers chronologically. Time or Irish events do not seem to impose any pattern, except that events may have brought the series to a close. The last book appeared in November 1921, the month before the signing of the Anglo-Irish Treaty. After that date the phenomenon of Australian literary interest in Ireland seems to have disappeared. The likelihood of course, as Patrick O'Farrell has suggested, is that from 1922 Australians, and writers amongst them, lost their interest in Ireland. An Ireland torn by civil war was not the Ireland the poets had imagined. Australian literary interest in Free State and Republican Ireland has been nil.

With a proper sense of priorities I want to discuss first of all two priests - briefly Father Maurice O'Reilly and then at slightly greater length Father William Lockington. Father O'Reilly was born at Cobh in 1866, went to Australia in 1892 and died there in 1933.[2] He is best known for his Rectorship of St John's College within the University of Sydney and for his Sydney championship of the Mannix position on conscription. But in 1920 he published in London a volume, in green boards, dedicated to his mother, and decorated with a gilt monogram of shamrocks, but entitled quite simply *Poems*.[3] The book contains in fact quite a number of verses well worthy of preservation. They range from lightly done whimsical pieces such as 'My First Grey Hair' to clear-eyed Australiana set-pieces like 'The Anzacs', a poem that could be the model for that song, much beloved of Liam Clancy and Irish dance bands a few years ago, 'And the Band Played Waltzing Matilda'. But scattered throughout are the Irish poems. The stance is one of defiant nationalism. The last stanza of 'Ireland and Empire Day' goes:

> We will rejoice when our beloved land
> Shall in her glory 'mid the peoples stand,
> As she was erst - a nation once again;
> Then summon us to mirth and jubilee
> For all your victories by land and sea,
> But not till then -
> Never till then! [4]

And in 'St Patrick's Day' O'Reilly calls for a curiously English gesture to honour the Irish heroes . . .

> Hats off! O brothers of Irish blood,
> Poured out in many a crimson flood,
>   On many a distant strand!
> Heirs of the knightly thoughts of old,
> Sprung from sires of heroic mould,
>   Valiant of heart and hand;
> Hats off ! for we speak of the sainted dead,
> The men who dared - the men who bled
>   For the Irish Faith and Land! [5]

It is all fairly conventional sentiment, but none the less heartfelt on O'Reilly's part. He describes himself as 'The Exile of the South' and his 'home-sick heart' flying to 'a green isle out in the far nor'-west', so that his final comment on his two loyalties is:

> We prize the men of the Southland so,
>   For the grasp of their kindly hand;
> For a freedom as wide as the ocean's flow,
> For the welcome with which they have sought to show
>   That theirs was no foreign strand;
> Till we almost acclaimed it 'home' - but, no,
>   It is not our own dear land. [6]

What is worth noting is that Maurice O'Reilly's commitment to Ireland is a full-bloodedly political allegiance. His interest in Catholic Ireland is present, but it is secondary.

This stance sets him apart from his clerical colleague, the Jesuit Father William Lockington. Lockington was a New Zealander, born in 1871, who decided at the age of twenty-five to become a priest. He crossed to Australia, and soon thereafter to Ireland for most of his studies. He had spells in Jersey, Lancashire and New York, but spent about ten years in Ireland, mainly in Limerick and Tullabeg, and returned to Australia late in 1913. He proceeded to become Superior of the Jesuits there and died in 1948. His first book was published in both London and New York in 1920. It was entitled *The Soul of Ireland*, [7] and is appallingly unreadable. It was also published in green boards, a somewhat deeper green than Maurice O'Reilly's, and dedicated to the 'mother of the mothers of Ireland'. The theme of the book is simple. Ireland's soul is Catholicism; understand that and you understand Ireland. This viewpoint leads to what can only be described as highly novel interpretations of Irish history. One passage for example would give Toynbee quite a shock:

> The march of nations is not a slow struggle upwards from barbarism to high ideals, as some would have us believe; but, too often, is a blinded descent from honor and greatness to barbarism, because of lost ideals. It is not evolution from the mythical 'caveman' upwards, but a succession of degrading fallings from the high estate in which man was placed by God. With feet clogged by the clay of earth, and eyes blinded by the mists of earth, as those without compass or helm, nations have blundered aimlessly down to nothingness.
>
> As the student of the history of mankind stands amazed at the almost cyclic regularity of the recurrence of these falls, he cannot but be struck by one notable and almost unique exception to what seems a universal law. That exception is Ireland. As he unrolls the pages of the centuries, pages that tell of the passing of empires and the shattering of civilization, of the discovery of new worlds, of new languages, of new beliefs, of dark epochs when the tide of ignorance flowed full and fast and barbarism threatened to rule supreme, he sees that Ireland has ever held a level course, unmoved and confident in every crisis. While others fall in helpless ruin, he sees that nation for 1,400 years steadily progressing and never declining. The secret of her splendid strength is to be found in her heroic devotion to the ideals given to her by St. Patrick, and a comprehension of these is essential for him who would read aright her history. In giving Ireland the Catholic faith, St. Patrick gave her the perfect way through which to attain these ideals.[8]

The portrayal of Ireland's steady progress for 1400 years could certainly be a challenge to some adventurous Irish historian. The rest of the book is an equally imaginary, highly rhetorical depiction of the Irish people at prayer and at virtue. The chapter headings say it all: 'Christmas in Ireland', 'Month of Mary', 'Corpus Christi in Ireland', 'The Nuns of Ireland', 'Soggarth Aroon', 'Mothers of

Ireland', 'Martyrdom of Ireland', 'Triumph of Ireland'. The book's 182 pages allow no relief from the breathless, bombastic wishful-thinking, the vague and completely unfounded generalisations, and the fatuously pious imaginings. But the message is clear: Ireland has Catholicism, it is therefore blessed beyond all other nations. Therefore, if you want to be similarly blessed, you know where the secret lies. Father Lockington does not bother with pointing the lesson to any particular countries, least of all to his native New Zealand, or the Australia he was living in and where his life's work lay. As he journeyed and worked up and down the east coast of Australia, the land of his dreams, ideals, and spiritual allegiance was Ireland.

The phenomenon was more, I think, than that classic experience of the colonials' thinking and speaking of the mother country as 'home'. Such nostalgia lacks the proselytising devotion of Father Lockington as well as his readiness to detail and hymn the superior virtues of the luminary, beneficent other land.

My third writer, Bernard McElhill is a particular problem. He published in Melbourne in 1893 a volume entitled *National Songs of Australia : Bush Poems and Digging Adventures. Dramas, etc.* [9] He was Ulster born, and in spite of the title of his book, the first poem in it is entitled 'The Brook', the fourth is a lament for 'Father Thomas Burke', the celebrated Irish Dominican preacher, and an Irish element remains strong throughout the volume. Arguably the most memorable writing is the Preface where McElhill immediately informs the reader:

> I suffer from pulmonary phthisis; my literary progress has been marred by the disease; no writing has been accomplished since my twenty-seventh year; and much has been tried when little should have been attempted. No more need be added to certify that better advantages might have produced better results.

This suggests that McElhill died in Australia, but he regarded himself as a spiritual exile. A lyric, entitled 'Erin', is described as going to the tune of 'The Last Rose of Summer':

> Tho' destined for ever
>   Thy hills ne'er to see,
> Yet still, dearest Erin,
>   My heart yearns for thee! [10]

But McElhill's most interesting Irish/Australian reflections are in his slightly more dramatic poems. He has a tableauesque piece, 'By The Camp Fire',[11] set on the goldfields, where an Irishman, a Scotsman, a sailor, a Spaniard and an Australian all rise up and sing some ditty. It is a gauche piece, but it has several curious features. There is almost universal praise of Australia; it has been the flower of the sailor's travels, the place where the Scotsman's happiest days have been spent, and so on. The one exception is Pat Quigley, the Irishman. Pat is the only member of the party who merits a name, or any personality. He is a hayseed of the most stupid variety.

> The lasses all laughed at the sight of Pat Quigley,
> And, still as they grinned, my affection grew stout;
> Some comical colleens would call me Pat Ugly,
> For I was the dickens to pull them about.
>
> Ochone! how I sigh for the sight of old Gorkin,
> Where green valleys stretch, and where bright rivers
>   flow!
> I'll ne'er be contented, whate'er be my fortune,
> Till back to the hills of old Ireland I go.

Literary conventions would normally suggest Hibernophilia would stand condemned merely by being espoused by someone of this cloddish disposition. But McElhill seems incapable of rising even to this level of sophistication; he has not got to first base in integrating or making sense of his various national loyalties. The weakness is illustrated by his charmingly illogical way of assigning tunes to the ditties these diggers utter. The Scotsman starts his piece: 'I came frae Inverness . . .' Immediately above this McElhill has written simply, 'Tune: - "God Save Ireland" '. And for the sailor's song starting, 'I claim not a home; I was born on the billows . . .', the tune is 'Dear Harp of My Country'.

McElhill in fact carries his confusion even further. He is quite ambivalent about his native land and fellow countrymen. If Pat Quigley shows traces of the classic Irish joke figure, we get the fully fleshed individual in another poem.

> My name is Gillhooly from Cork,
>   An Irishman born, do ye moin';
> I sailed to Australia for work,
>   And, faith sir, they treated me foin. [12]

Gillhooly is lazy and stupid, but still professing the love for old Blarney that it appears we are supposed to take seriously. Yet there is a further quality that I think important. At first sight Gillhooly is a variation on the classic new chum. But not really. He in fact fits in extremely well. In spite of his 'begorra' and his incompetence, starting to muster at six when he should have finished at four, his shrewdness is all too evident, and it is giving him a good life. He suits this Australian landscape only too well.

A far more sophisticated portrait of the Irish clown is drawn elsewhere by the recognised poet Victor Daley. This writer, undoubtedly the most competent of those I discuss, is the stock piece of evidence for any talk about an Australian Celtic twilight. But insofar as wistful velleities, pale lovers, nostalgic sighs, fairy murmurs, and the rest of it are present in his work, I am not interested in them. As with the other writers, it is only Daley's direct references to Ireland and Irish people that concern me. He was born at Navan in 1858, went to England at about the age of fourteen and to Australia when he was twenty. Only one volume of verse was published in his lifetime. It is in the two posthumous volumes that we find some moves towards a definition of Ireland's place in Australia. Daley defines the green-coloured spectacles of his kin.

> A homely-looking folk they are, these people of my kin;
> Their hands are hard as horse-shoes, but their hearts come through the skin;
> They are all right well-connected in this land of Arcady;
> And if your name's not Hogan here it must be Hegarty . . .
>
> They love the land they live in, all these folk that I esteem —
> But the land they left behind them is an everlasting dream.
> Old Michael Cleary said to me — his age is seventy seven —
> 'There's no place like Australia, barrin' Ireland and Heaven'.[13]

But in spite of this affectionate laughter Daley himself speaks of meeting 'my colleen dear' who tells him 'I am your own Ireland', and he ends another poem:

> O, if I were young and free,
>   With wealth at my command,
> I would give it all to be
>   Once more in Ireland.[14]

It is difficult to know whether this is anything more than conventional nostalgia. Daley died in Sydney in 1905 after a career of notable devotion to Australian causes. In fact his espousal of Australia's independence was particularly fierce, and one of his finest poems, 'When London Calls', is a bitter attack on Britain's cultural imperialism. But the ironic fact is that the pseudonym he adopted for this poem and his other light or satirical pieces was not Australian, much less Aboriginal, but in fact Irish, 'Creeve Roe', Red Branch. Somehow, being an Australian poet under an Irish banner was *not* a form of the split and cringing cultural personality. No anomaly seems to have struck Daley. There seems to have been an implicit assumption that obeisance to Ireland involved no disloyalty to Australia. Britain took you away from Australia; Ireland did not. But why this should have been so does not seem to have been a question that occurred to Daley.

Once only in his poetic opus does he appear to have found it necessary to make a choice between the two nations. This is in the marvellous comic poem 'The Glorious Twelfth at Jindabye'; it deserves a more exalted place in the Australian recital repertoire. It concludes:

There are bonds of blood and marriage now these ancient foes between,
And the Orange is inextricably mingled with the Green:
And that this broad, kindly feeling should increase in coming time
Is the wish for Green and Orange of the writer of this rhyme.[15]

The poem is appropriately dated '1898'. It is worth noting that even when the old evils are dissipated on the Australian air, the Irish virtues are retained and clearly admired. Loyalty, a strong clan and family spirit, wittiness, and big-hearted conviviality are enthusiastically portrayed in a way that looks forward to the poems of 'John O'Brien'.

The vision of the blending of the Orange and the Green recurs in another poet's work. But this time Australia plays no part in the alchemy. David McKee Wright's 1918 volume of verse, *An Irish Heart*,[16] is a curious oddity of Australian literature.

Wright was born in County Down in 1869, taken to England at the age of seven and to New Zealand at the age of seventeen. His father was a Congregationalist minister and Wright himself studied for the cloth, but eventually turned to journalism instead. In 1909 he went to Sydney and remained there till his death in 1928. His importance to Australian literature is that he was offered and accepted the editorship of *The Bulletin*, the citadel of the distinctively national note in Australian literature. He had himself published a few pamphlets of verse in New Zealand, but his major production - and only Australian volume - was *An Irish Heart*. It is a bemusing piece of work to have appeared in Australia, particularly at that date. It too appeared in green boards, and had a border of shamrock vine!

It is about Ireland, and then again it is not. The verse is undistinguished to the point of being bad, and its central fault is that it gives to airy nothings a name - Ireland - but absolutely no sense of local habitation at all. It strikes a vapidly romantic note, a washed-out echo of Yeatsian juvenilia. We know that the setting is Ireland because we have Pegeens and Noras and fiddlers and beggars and Dannys, but the national delineation goes no further. There is no Irish landscape, no working of Irish mythology. Yet outrageously diluted mythology underlies the whole approach. There are any number of fairies, little people, nymphs, lustrous or occasionally white arms, red lips and kisses. (Wright is exceedingly oral.) There is the occasional non-Irish touch; a poem called 'The Wave' is a dream of a nymph on a barrier reef, and there is another poem entitled 'Hellas at Watson's Bay'.

> At Watson's Bay the sun is fair,
>   The sea is blue;
> I find Athene standing there
>   When I find you;[17]

The romantic urge leads Wright to this kind of pastiche every time. A poem entitled 'The Holy Piper' tells how St Padraig expelled the snakes from Ireland, but the deed is done because a snake fatally bites 'O'Brien's daughter' - whoever O'Brien, or his daughter, is - although we *are* told 'Surely she was very fair / With a red rose in her hair'![18]

When all this is said, however, Wright is centrally, if monotonously, singing the praises of Ireland. It is an obsession, not without its comic results. He has an outrageous pun in a romantic lyric which opens: 'The Young Day combs his yellow hair / On the mountains of Morn's Desire.' [19] Wright never points to any specific virtues in his Ireland that makes the country unique or supreme - as Father Lockington does - but his adulation, and desire that it should be shared, is extreme. He has a sonnet entitled simply 'Ireland'.

> A green and purple island of the sea,
> A red and very bitter story told,

Flecked with the jewel-tales set deep in gold,
And aching with the pride of memory.
A stalwart people straining to be free;
Yet in their bondage rich to have and hold
More than broad Freedom's ample robes may fold
Of all that fills the soul's fine treasury.

Be still, my dream, my purpose and my love,
O Island of White Saints and happy things
Set to a mournful cadence in the west -
Green graves below, a sorrowing mist above -
Yet with a voice that down the ages sings
Till men who never knew thee hold thee best![20]

His crystal ball promises even more than this universal homage. The centre-piece of the book is a long poem entitled 'Dark Rosaleen', which, as he says, 'is the accepted translation of *Roisin Dubh*, one of the mystic names for the Spirit of Ireland'. It is roughly a series of love poems in which the beloved is this spirit of Ireland. And she will beneficently exert her power as the spirit of friendship and harmony. Wright sees a triumphant future. His poem ends:

Put the horn to your mouth,
   Blow over land and sea.
For the North will kiss the South
   A kiss full and free.[[21]

Needless to say this vision of the North kissing the South was rather premature.
Only once does Wright move towards an interesting idea. The third poem of 'Dark Rosaleen' begins each stanza with the words 'This is my country', and then describes what is presumably an Irish psychological landscape. The last stanza goes:

This is my country: wherever God goes walking
   Down the clear, windy ways,
And the quiet people that were and are are talking
   Of great things and great days;
For you are there, with the flower of Hope in your hand;
   And always the glad tears start
   Deep in the heart of my heart,
And I seem to understand
That the world is Ireland.[22]

I take the point to be that the poet's mind has been broadened to see that the spirit of Ireland is not confined to one little green isle. Ireland can be found anywhere. But breakthrough in generosity and expansiveness though this may be, it really emphasises Wright's basic point. 'Wherever God goes walking' and other noble things happen, it is because Dark Rosaleen is there. Ireland is the yardstick for the blessed state, and the existence of any blessedness is due, somehow, to the presence of Ireland.

This is all very extravagant, and Wright is anything but convincing. But the very extravagance is what makes the phenomenon worth noting. Here is this colonial, twice over, plainly besotted at the age of forty-nine by a country he left when he was seven. And the context of his infatuation makes it all the more weird. *An Irish Heart* was published early in 1918. After the Easter Rising of 1916 and the conscription debates in Australia in 1916 and 1917, it was a time when the open espousal of Irish sentiments was rather a liability. And they were particularly ironic coming from a literary editor of the violently pro-conscription, anti-clerical *Bulletin*. Just about the only safe feature that Wright displayed was an outlook that was non-sectarian in the extreme. The one virtue of his attenuated Ireland was that she had no denominational features at all.

Lockington said that Ireland was God's own country. Wright agreed that it was, and suggested that its spirit might actually flourish elsewhere. But neither of them did anything about trying to fit that spirit into Australia, the country they had chosen, more or less, to live in.

Other writers did. McElhill and Daley made some kind of a gesture in that direction. A rather more substantial attempt was made by Thomas Edward Spencer. He was an Englishman, born in 1845, who travelled to Australia for a brief visit when he was eighteen, and returned and settled there in 1875. He wrote three volumes of verse, mainly humorous ballads interspersed with love lyrics of a kind, and 'How McDougall Topped the Score' deservedly remains his best known work. He surpasses himself in it; elsewhere his sense of narrative and climactic effect is poor. In addition Spencer wrote three books of humorous prose, *The Surprising Adventures of Mrs Bridget McSweeney*, [23] *A Spring Cleaning and Other Stories by Mrs. Bridget McSweeney* [24] and *That Droll Lady: Being the Further Adventures of Mrs Bridget McSweeney*.[25] These appeared respectively in 1906, 1908 and 1911, the year after Spencer's death. This rapid, regular production suggests the adventures were popular and only curtailed by Spencer's decease. This impression is reinforced in the third book where Mrs McSweeney thinks of herself as a celebrity and bumps into people who have read all about her, and are delighted to meet her in the flesh.

Mrs McSweeney is an Irish lady of indeterminate age, but large size, living in Sydney. She has a husband called Pat, and the twins, called Pat and Mike. They live in a terrace in, I suspect, the environs of Surry Hills, and Pat has an unspecified job that seems to be unskilled white-collar. Mrs McSweeney's adventures follow a formalised, predictable pattern. She is visited by her neighbour, Mrs Moloney, who asks to hear about Bridget's latest outing. The latter obliges. These outings cover every form of respectable amusement available in Edwardian Sydney. So the episodes go under such titles as 'Mrs McS. goes to the Zoo . . . to Manly . . . to the Botanic Gardens . . . to Paddy's Market . . . to Killara (which is a picnic) . . . visits the Wombeyan Caves'. Misfortune is always in attendance; various forms of falling over, falling about, impairment of costume, unwise consumption of liquor, gallantries from strangers, which turn out to be victimisation by con men, and improper dalliance by Pat, the husband. Mrs McSweeney is vain, vulgar, tasteless and gossipy. Her description of a new hat is a fair example of her style. 'You didn't see me new chanticlere hat? It has, or I mane it had, a full-sized bantam roosther on tops, red poppies all round, a big tartan bow at the back, and forget-me-nots undherneath. Oh, it was a poem.'[26] She goes to the zoo and becomes too intimate with an eagle which savages the rooster. 'I shtraightened me hat the best way I could, but it was like Kitty Rooney when she arrived in America, it had lost its characther.' It was Spencer's clear assumption that this highly Irish lady had an individual kind of virtue, and that it was worth fitting her into an Australian context. But of course it was as a figure of fun rather than as any source of spiritual strength or example.

In brief she is classical stage Irish. She is constantly going back in thought to 'the land of me girlhood'. So, for example, the weather one day 'minds me of the toime whin I was a gurrul, chasin' the pigs out of the potato field on me father's farrum at Ballyragin'.[27] But she does not really have any practical, day to day interest in Ireland. She has adopted Australia completely. One episode, 'Mrs McSweeney on Home Rule',[28] says it all:

'And do you think Home Rule is a good thing?' I says.
'Of course I do,' says he. 'Do you think Father Donovan ud talk like that if it wasn't?'
'And suppose whin there's Home Rule they can't agree?' says I.
'Well, thin, thim that can't agree can go to the divil,' he says. 'There are thim that rule and thim that have to be ruled, and the shtrongest must have their way. But

don't talk to me,' he says, 'for the roof of me head is flappin' up and down,' he says.

'Well,' says I, ''tis toime for you to get up and go to wurruk.'

'I can't go to-day, Biddy,' he says, groanin'. 'Sind young Pat down to till thim I have the rheumatiz,' he says.

'I'll do no such thing,' I says. 'You'll get up and go to your wurruk like a daycent man. Home Rule will not kape your wife and family.'

'I can't raise me head from the pillow,' he says.

'I'll raise it for you,' says I, and I tuk him be the hair and shuk him.

'Holy murdher!' he says, 'let me go. You are shakin' me brains to a pulp,' he says.

'Well, get up,' says I.

'I'll do as I like in me own house,' says he. 'Go away and lave me in pace.'

'Do you belave in Home Rule?' says I.

'I do,' he says. 'I'll belave in anything if you'll let me alone.'

'Thin if you belave in Home Rule,' I says, 'up you get, for I'm the ruler of this home.'

When I say that Mrs McS. is stage Irish I want to add one qualification. Spencer writes continually about non-native-born Australians - generally disparagingly. His many portraits of Germans in Australia - interesting as this was the decade before the First World War - invariably portray them as incompetent fools, speaking unintelligible English to boot. Anyone whose native tongue is not English is a rogue or an idiot, Scotsmen appear fitfully (and they are thoroughly acceptable) but the rest of the world seems to be made up of the Irish. And Spencer likes them. In spite of Mrs McS.'s catalogue of short-comings he clearly likes her. And the curious thing is, it seems to me, that for all her stage-Irishness, she is not alien in Australia. In fact the round of activities that constitute her adventures show just how acclimatised, how at home, how thoroughly Australian she is. The truth seems to be that Spencer wanted to write about Australians, about people who were essentially likeable, but who had colour and amusement value as well - and time and again he found himself coming up with Irish characters.

The last of my septet was also interested in the portrayal - without ridicule but with plenty of humour - of average Australians. And again he found the Irish element all-important to that character. This was the priest Patrick Hartigan who was born in Australia, at Yass, in 1879 and died at Lewisham in 1952. He published one book of verse, *Around The Boree Log*,[29] during his lifetime. This was in November 1921 and he wrote it under the name of 'John O'Brien'. He had written and published about a dozen poems prior to 1921 when Angus and Robertson invited him to publish a book with them. He handed the care of his Narrandera parish over to a curate and between February and June of 1921 wrote about another thirty-four poems. He wanted the book to take the title of one of his pieces, 'The Little Irish Mother'. Angus and Robertson did not like it, and so he wrote an introductory poem, 'Around The Boree Log' and gave the volume that name. In view of the times – this was the climax of the Anglo-Irish war – Angus and Robertson's reader asked him to change the title 'The Little Irish Mother' to 'The Little British Mother'. Hartigan stuck to his guns.[30]

Such a change would have made nonsense of the whole volume. It is a collection of ballads celebrating the life of the Catholic Irish-Australian rural community – usually of the generation of Hartigan's own childhood, so that there is a strong nostalgic note throughout. It is clearly a world written about with intimate and affectionate knowledge, but behind it is the sort of thesis so crassly enunciated by Lockington in the previous year. Catholic faith is the supreme gift, Ireland has accepted that gift most fully and fruitfully, therefore imitate Ireland in all things and you can not go far wrong. This by now is a truism of Irish-Australian history, but Hartigan's espousal of the position was somewhat more sophisticated.

In so many ways he presents an Irish, or Irish-derived community. Other national groups do not exist. One poem, 'Sittin' Be the Wall',[31] describes old-timers at a dance. Everyone mentioned has an Irish name: Johnnsie Connor, Paddy Gleeson, Ned McCarthy, Kitty Dooner, Jerry Toohey, Grogan, Hogan, McGeadie, Bridgie Hardy, Timsie Brady, Deegan, Matt Driscoll, Mary Leary. Throughout the poems traditional Irish virtues, above all piety and the sense of family and community, are hymned over and over. Some times his descriptions of the Irish in Australia – which is certainly what they are – become indistinguishable from the Irish in Ireland. Many of his poems were republished in Ireland. From there one of his best-known poems, 'The Trimmin's on the Rosary' found its way into the pages of *The Boston Pilot* in 1942. The paper assured its readers this was the story of the recitation of the Rosary in an Irish home. There was no mention of its Australian origins.

But in fact John O'Brien's whole emphasis was on the blending of the Irish virtues into the Australian scene and character. The construction of Australia was what he was interested in, even if he did think the Irish did it best. The *loci classici* are 'The Little Irish Mother':

> There's a Little Irish Mother that a lonely vigil keeps
>   In the settler's hut where seldom stranger comes,
> Watching by the home-made cradle where one more Australian sleeps
>   While the breezes whisper weird things to the gums,
> Where the settlers battle gamely, beaten down to rise again,
>   And the brave bush wives the toil and silence share,
> Where the nation is a-building in the hearts of splendid men -
>   There's a Little Irish Mother always there.[32]

and 'St Patrick's Day', where the display of green fervour leads the poet to conclude, 'Never yet were men more loyal to the holy ties that bind them, / And the love they gave their country made me conscious of my own'.[33] The title of the last poem in *Around the Boree Log* is, significantly, 'Come, Sing Australian Songs to Me'.

A clerical commentator in 1933 summed up John O'Brien's achievement.

> The humour, the sentiment, the homely phrase, and deep feeling, and above all the characters remind us of the ballad poetry of old Ireland. It is indeed Ireland transplanted to Australia. The piety, the simple faith, the humour are Irish but the flowers, the trees, the birds, the bush, the whole surroundings are Australian, and from the happy blending of the power and energy of the youthful Australian spirit with that of the ancient traditions, customs and religion of Ireland, we have the Irish-Australian, a type distinct among the peoples of the earth.[34]

This seems reasonable, but in fact it does not go far enough. There is a curious irony about the work of John O'Brien. His world is strikingly narrow. His community of Irish-Australian Catholics have no such thing as an Anglo-Saxon or a Protestant neighbour. O'Brien does not even envisage the nightmare of the wholesale mixed marriages that are the triumphant climax of Daley's 'Glorious Twelfth at Jindabye'. There is nothing pluralistic or ecumenical about O'Brien's world at all. Yet, by some oddity of the Australian character, his appeal has been too wide to leave him in the category of a merely denominational writer.

Around the Boree Log has been the verse success story in Australian publishing history, at last count somewhat ahead of its old rival, *The Sentimental Bloke*. Why? The most plausible reason, it seems to me, is that O'Brien portrayed not just the Irish-Australian type, but in fact quite simply the Australian type. In the tradition of, but even more strikingly than, Gilhooly from Cork, and Mrs Bridget McSweeney, the Caseys and the Hanrahans and the lad from Tangmalangaloo were genuine Australian types, in fact the touchstone Australian types. If a writer wanted to portray the real Australian, either he made him so dinkum that all traces of foreign origins were obliterated - and so we have The Bloke and Dad and Dave - or he made him an Irishman.

This personality profile seems to have been the one really positive, and the unique, result of Australian literary interest in Ireland. Harking back to other countries did happen, but it was far more fitful and resulted in no positive grafting. W. C. Wentworth, long before, had spoken of Australia as 'a new Britannia in the southern seas',[35] but this merely meant that Australia would take Britain's place when the old country was clapped out. There was no catalogue of British virtues that would turn Australia into a replica Britannia. Will Ogilvie, out from Scotland for twelve years in Australia, wrote 'To a Bunch of Heather': 'Can it be like me you're ailing / For a sight of mountain moorland, little exile from the blue?'[36] But this was no more than nostalgia, a sentiment the 'Irish' poets were unloading continually. Far from trying to make Australian sense of Scotland, Ogilvie gave up the colonies and went home.

Yet when Ireland's unique recurrence in Australian writing is admitted, a question that has to be asked is whether it gave quality to the literature. The answer must be no. The reason lies in the focus, or the elements, of the perspective taken on Ireland. And that consisted in either Irish piety or Irish nostalgic appeal or some form of the Irish stage personality. The material, that is, was rather poverty-stricken. It was in stark contrast to the kind of material that produced the flowering of literature in Ireland during the same period. In Australia not one feature was reproduced of that pattern of influences that Professor Lyons, for example, sees at work in Ireland - a small closely knit group influenced by 'theosophy, occultism and magic, Irish fairy-tales and folklore, the Celtic sagas, geography and politics'.[37] In comparison the Australian larder for a concoction of 'Irish' literature was quite threadbare. It was a decidedly sentimental and pious old Kathleen that Australia tried to deal with. By the time

Ireland's cultural new look had been put on and had been advertised as far afield as Australia, Ireland had disqualified herself on other grounds from further Australian interest. And in any case by then Australia was starting to discover its own folklore and sagas. Ireland's newly discovered ones were irrelevant. It was as R. D. Fitzgerald, the poet, wrote of his Irish grandfather's real estate transaction:

>   We sever
> worn threads. It was more than a business affair:
> he bought my grandfather's house forever
> did Donovan of the Square.
>
> The choice made and the new land entered,
> not for a day but for days to be,
> what next but to grasp this life that centred
> in the south? The north had been sunk at sea.
> Ireland, the last of it, passed from view
> to another's trust. I cede my share,
> and hope he died as rich as a Jew –
> Pat Donovan of the Square.[38]

NOTES

1. For example Zora Cross, *An Introduction to the Study of Australian Literature* (Sydney, 1922); Brian Elliott, 'The Celtic Twilight in Australia', *Australian Quarterly*, vol. xiii (Dec. 1941) pp. 61-70; Vincent Buckley, 'Identity – Invention or Discovery?', *Quadrant*, vol. xxiv (Aug. 1980) pp. 12-19.
2. F. D. King, *Memories of Maurice O'Reilly C.M.* (Bathurst, 1953).
3. Maurice O'Reilly, *Poems* (London, n.d. 1920?).
4. Ibid., p. 20.
5. Ibid., p. 81.
6. Ibid., p. 37.
7. W. J. Lockington, *The Soul of Ireland* (New York, 1920), with an introduction by G. K. Chesterton.
8. Ibid., pp. 136-7.
9. Bernard McElhill, *National Songs of Australia: Bush Poems and Digging Adventures. Dramas, etc.* (Melbourne, 1983).
10. Ibid., p. 71.
11. Ibid., pp. 36-43.
12. Ibid., p. 52.

13. Victor J. Daley, 'In Arcady', *Wine and Roses* (Sydney, 1911), pp. 130-1.
14. Ibid., 'Mavourneen', p. 110 and 'An Old Tune', p. 117.
15. Muir Holburn and Marjorie Pizer (eds), *Creeve Roe: Poetry by Victor Daley* (Sydney, 1947) pp. 95-100.
16. David McKee Wright, *An Irish Heart* (Sydney, 1918).
17. Ibid., p. 62.
18. Ibid., p. 19.
19. Ibid., p. 4.
20. Ibid., p. 60.
21. Ibid., p. 135.
22. Ibid., p. 119.
23. *The Surprising Adventures of Mrs Bridget McSweeney* (Sydney, 1906).
24. *A Spring Cleaning and Other Stories by Mrs Bridget McSweeney* (Sydney, 1908).
25. *That Droll Lady: Being the Further Adventures of Mrs Bridget McSweeney* (Sydney, 1911).
26. Ibid., p. 31.
27. *A Spring Cleaning*, p. 231.
28. Ibid., pp. 308-13.
29. John O'Brien (Patrick Hartigan), *Around The Boree Log And Other Verses* (Sydney, 1921).
30. For detail on Father Hartigan I am indebted to his nephew, literary executor and biographer, Father Frank Mecham.
31. John O'Brien, *The Parish of St Mel's and Other Verses* (Sydney, 1954) p. 100.
32. *Boree Log*, p. 7.
33. Ibid., p. 116.
34. Michael Henry, *Manly*, vol. iv (1933) pp. 188-9.
35. In, for example, Walter Murdoch and Alan Mulgan (eds), *A Book of Australian and New Zealand Verse* (Oxford, 1950).
36. Will H. Ogilvie, *Fair Girls and Gray Horses: With Other Verses* (Sydney, 1958) pp. 131-2.
37. F. S. L. Lyons, *Ireland since the Famine*, 2nd edn (London, 1973) p. 234.
38. R. D. Fitzgerald, 'Transaction', *Forty Years' Poems* (Sydney, 1965) pp. 111-12.

14 Yeats and the Anglo-Irish Twilight

F. S. L. LYONS

Of all the clichés that cluster round the name of W. B. Yeats his identification with the Celtic twilight is perhaps the most familiar and the most persistent. In later years he became impatient with the label and strove to shake it off, but that it stuck to him so closely was largely his own doing. After all, had he not invested largely in a supernatural world over which eventually he seemed to assume almost proprietary rights? And did he not as early as 1893 gather his knowledge of fairy-tales and folklore into a book which he actually called *The Celtic Twilight?* And had he not accustomed his readers to recognise that grey, ghostly twilight as the hour before dawn, when 'this world and the other draw near'?[1] Since Yeats never lost his passionate belief in the supernatural, though it became more various and sophisticated as he grew older, it is understandable that the connection with the Celtic twilight should continue for many people to be the hallmark by which he is most easily recognisable. In actual fact, of course, he passed through many revolutions of thought and of technique during his long life and at the end of it - in the two decades of the 1920s and the 1930s - he was far more preoccupied with what I have called the Anglo-Irish twilight than with the Celtic twilight. The change of emphasis was fundamental to his evolution as a poet, but it was also a response to the political upheaval which had transformed Ireland in his own lifetime. In this chapter therefore, I shall be dealing both with a chapter in Yeats's intellectual biography and with an episode in the history of his country.

The term 'Anglo-Irish twilight' clearly needs to be defined, but so too perhaps do the Anglo-Irish themselves. The very name 'Anglo-Irish' only began to come into fashion during the nineteenth century. In the narrow literary sense it was used mainly to describe writings on Irish themes by Irishmen in the English language. It also carried much broader cultural, social, religious and political implications. Essentially, the Anglo-Irish were the descendants of those who had conquered and colonised the country from Norman times down to the end of the seventeenth century and who dominated it for two hundred years thereafter[2]. For such people, the idea that they represented an alien strain in the Irish racial amalgam would have been unacceptable, indeed nearly incomprehensible. Let one of them, H. A. Law, testify from a time, 1929, when, as we shall see, twilight had almost become nightfall:

> . . . whom do we mean by the Anglo-Irish? Note that the name was not chosen by those of whom I speak. *They* have been content, and commonly proud, to call themselves simply 'Irish'. But that word has of late been so much used as a synonym for 'Gaelic' that, for the sake of clearness and convenience, some distinction had to be made in speaking of one particular body of Irish citizens. . . . Endless exceptions must be made; but for our present purpose it may be assumed that the typical Anglo-Irishman is Protestant in faith, has some connection with the landowning class as it existed from the end of the seventeenth century to the end of the nineteenth century, and cherishes family traditions of service to the Crown of these islands.[3]

This definition serves well enough except that it omits the stratum to which Yeats himself belonged. For although there was a landed connection - his father contrived to be a minor absentee landlord as well as an impoverished painter - on both sides of his family the poet was descended from a middle class which in his case contained professional people (mainly clergymen) as well as merchants and sea-captains. This Protestant middle class was never very large, but it was important out of proportion to its numbers, for not only did it take a major share of public appointments and private enterprise, but it also dominated the Anglo-Irish intellect, such as it was.

When Yeats was born in 1865 the Anglo-Irish were already on the defensive. Their Golden Age, the eighteenth century, when they ruled Ireland as 'the Protestant nation' was far behind them. The abolition of the Irish Parliament in 1800 and the establishment of the political and economic union with Britain, which was to last until 1921, made their dependence upon British power more obvious and they dwindled from an 'Ascendancy' into a 'Garrison'. With increasing alienation went increasing vulnerability. After the rise of Catholic nationalism under O'Connell, later transmuted into Parnell's Home Rule movement, their political base was undermined. Then the Anglican Church establishment was overthrown. Finally, the landlord class, weakened by the Great Famine of the 1840s and by foreign competition, was battered by the land agitation and by acts of Parliament into accepting the break-up of their estates and the transformation of their tenants into small, conservative, tight-fisted farmers. Outwardly and precariously, it is true, Irish society remained deferential until the First World War and the Big House was still in many localities the centre of authority and style. Yet, with the onset of the Gaelic revival in and after the 1890s, and with the re-emergence of militant republicanism in the early 1900s, a new Ireland was unmistakably in the making and to this the Protestant Anglo-Irish must conform or be excluded.

Exclusion at first seemed the more likely fate. Blow after blow fell upon them in rapid succession. First, their physical presence was reduced by the death of so many of their sons in the 1914-18 war. Next, the war with Britain between 1919 and 1921 exposed their lives and their houses to destruction. Then, the partition of the country cut them off from the Protestant majority in north-east Ulster. Finally, the establishment of the Irish Free State as a self-governing dominion, after a further perilous episode of civil conflict, left them utterly isolated and, as a tiny minority of five per cent of the population, at the mercy of those whom they had ruled for centuries. Now, truly, their twilight had begun.

But one must not exaggerate. The new Irish Government was bent on demonstrating its tolerance, and they were given initially sixteen out of the thirty nominated seats in the Senate, the Upper House of the legislature; among the fourteen others also there were several, including Yeats, who, although by no means Unionists, belonged to and were to speak for the Anglo-Irish tradition.[4] Nevertheless, the future seemed dark enough. Not only were senators individually threatened and several of their houses burnt during the Civil War, but even when quieter times came there were other more insidious dangers. The new State embodied the ideals of the renascent nationalism of the men of 1916 in which the emphasis was laid on the Gaelic and Catholic heritage of the Irish people. The effect of this upon the Anglo-Irish minority was to drive them into a sullen and fearful estrangement. This was all the more tragic because in the generation before 1914 there had seemed for a moment the possibility of achieving a fusion of the Gaelic and the Anglo-Irish traditions. This had been a prime object of the founders of the Irish Literary Theatre out of which the Abbey Theatre had evolved. The dominant figures in that enterprise - Yeats and Lady Gregory and Synge - had all shared the passionate belief that it would be possible so to use the rich resources of Irish fairy-tale and folklore and heroic legend to create an Irish literature in the English language that might be of European significance.

The early battles which Yeats fought to achieve what he called 'unity of culture' in Ireland are not my present theme, but they do relate in two main ways to his involvement with the Anglo-Irish twilight of the 1920s and 1930s. First, although this effort towards reconciliation did create a famous theatre, it was many years before it became a popular success and then only because it moved away from Yeats's intentions towards its own kind of realism. Yeats was caught in a cross-fire from unionists and nationalists. The unionists distrusted him partly because they were not interested in and did not understand either his art or his ideals, but still more because as an 'advanced' nationalist whose tutors had been Maud Gonne and the Fenian, John O'Leary, he was suspect as a traitor to his caste. Nationalists, on the other hand, distrusted him partly because they could never be quite sure that he really had deserted his caste, and partly because their theory of culture was quite different from his. Yeats believed not only that both traditions deserved to be cherished, but that the art resulting from their coming together must be the expression of each writer's own perception of life. His critics, however, always obsessed by the need to assert an Irish identity in the face of overwhelming English influence, thought that art's highest necessity must be to serve a cause and that the writer must be demonstrably national, or indeed, nationalist. Yeats would have none of this. Writing in 1904, when struggling against mounting criticism of Synge and of the theatre, he defined national literature as 'the work of writers who are moulded by influences that are moulding their country, and who write out of so deep a life that they are accepted there in the end . . .' And, arguing against the inherent provincialism of Irish life, he added: 'No nation, since the beginning of history, has ever drawn all its life out of itself. . . . If Ireland is about to produce a literature that is important to her, it must be the result of the influences that flow in upon the mind of an educated Irishman today. . . . Gaelic can hardly fail to do a portion of the work, but one cannot say whether it may not be some French or German writer who will do most to make him an articulate man.'[5]

The second point about Yeats's early confrontation with his critics was that he increasingly came to identify them with the Irish urban middle class which took a reductive view of what he was doing when it paid him any attention at all. His enemies were mostly, though not wholly, Catholic and they roused his anger partly because of their subservience to the simple pieties enjoined upon them by their priests. As he wrote in 'September 1913':

> What need you, being come to sense,
> But fumble in a greasy till
> And add the halfpence to the pence
> And prayer to shivering prayer, until
> You have dried the marrow from the bone?[6]

But also, of course, they infuriated him by their philistine rejection of the arts. This reached a climax when Lady Gregory's nephew, Hugh Lane, withdrew his offer to give his collection of modern French painting to Dublin, because not enough money was raised to provide a suitable gallery and because he and his pictures were subject to scurrilous abuse. This produced in Yeats the bitter irony of 'To a Shade' where he summons the ghost of Parnell to observe the fate of Lane who, like Parnell himself, had been overthrown by the Dublin entrepreneur, William Martin Murphy, the epitome of Catholic bourgeois nationalism:

>   A man
> Of your own passionate serving kind who had brought
> In his full hands what, had they only known,
> Had given their children's children loftier thought,
> Sweeter emotion, working in their veins
> Like gentle blood, has been driven from the place,
> And insult heaped upon him for his pains,
> And for his open-handedness, disgrace;
> Your enemy, an old foul mouth, had set
> The pack upon him.[7]

The aristocratic disdain which marks these and other poems of the period was, however, the product of something more fundamental than a need to shock the bourgeoisie. From about the beginning of the century several influences had been combining to move him away from the simple-minded revolutionary nationalism of his impetuous youth. For one thing, he was getting older. Also, Maud Gonne's marriage in 1903 to John MacBride for the time being shattered his political compass, though in fact for several years before that he had been acutely aware of the damage that over-involvement in politics was doing to his development as a poet. Undoubtedly, this awareness was intensified by his friendship with Lady Gregory, which was to last from 1896 to 1932 and which was to make of Coole Park (her home) the focus of many of his musings upon aristocracy and the Anglo-Irish civilisation handed down from the eighteenth century.

He was influenced also by his reading, itself to a considerable degree shaped for him by his new friends. Thus it was in 1902 that the Irish American John Quinn introduced him to Nietzsche, who interested him immediately, as he once remarked, 'as a counteractive to the spread of democratic vulgarity'.[8] In 1907, Lady Gregory opened his eyes to Castiglione's *The Courtier*, and that summer took him on a tour to Italy which excited his imagination about the exceptional world of the Renaissance.[9] From Castiglione he took the idea of *sprezzatura*, the ability to do all things with ease or nonchalance which separates the aristocrat (as it might be Lady Gregory's son Robert, for example) from the parvenu. Perhaps also his meeting with Ezra Pound in 1909 and their close collaboration between 1912 and 1914 worked in the same direction, for Pound had a similar contempt for the public and 'popular art' in general.

His recoil from Ireland in and around 1913 was never, even at its worst, a recoil from Irish themes, but the recoil itself was reversed by the Easter Rising of 1916. It moved him deeply after an initial shock of horror, when he thought it had destroyed his own life's work, which, as we shall see, in a sense it had done.[10] Not only did his poem 'Easter 1916' retract much of the bitterness of 'September 1913', but he began to yearn to strike roots in the country. Before the year 1916 was out he bought the semi-ruined Tower at Ballylee, not far from Coole Park, which was to become for him not merely a summer residence but one of his most potent symbols. The next year he married Georgie Hyde-Lees and with the birth of his two children in 1919 and 1921 the need to end his nomadic existence became more urgent. In 1922, therefore, he came home to Dublin.

The Yeats who thus returned to Ireland, who entered the Senate and who shortly afterwards received the Nobel Prize, was already one of the best-known Irishmen of his time. But he was, as always, an unpredictable force. During the years of the war and its aftermath many currents of thought had been colliding in his mind. He had begun to adumbrate that semi-philosophical, semi-fanciful and wholly individual 'system' which in 1925 he published as *A Vision*. But though this was both an attempt to round out his thought and to offer a view of history that would transcend the flux and reflux of contemporary chaos, he had been more closely touched by that chaos than perhaps he knew. It was a European as well as an Irish condition, which presented itself to him partly as a threat of communism and partly, in more apocalyptic terms, as the general violence which accompanied the fall of one civilisation and opened the way for the next. The inherent conservatism of his mind, which his father had long ago identified, now began to assert itself.[11] 'What I want,' he had written to his old friend AE (George Russell) in April 1919, 'is that Ireland be kept from giving itself (under the influence of its lunatic faculty of going against everything which it believes England to affirm) to Marxian revolution. . . . I consider the Marxian criterion of values as in this age the spearhead of materialism and leading to inevitable murder.'[12]

As it happened, he was wrong about the possible engulfment of Ireland by Marxism. What was at issue between 1919 and 1921, and again in the Civil War of 1922-3, was the old struggle for an independent republic. For Yeats this posed something of a dilemma. His own youthful politics had been republican and to the end of his days he would cherish a sentimental attachment to Fenianism, but at this stage of his evolution he had come to see the restoration of order as the prime necessity. 'Out of all this murder and rapine,' he asserted in May 1922, 'will come not a demagogic but an authoritative government.'[13] 'Everywhere,' he wrote a few months later, 'one notices a drift towards Conservatism, perhaps towards Autocracy. . . . We are entering on the final and most dreadful stage. Perhaps there is nothing so dangerous to a modern state, when politics take the place of theology, as a bunch of martyrs. A bunch of martyrs (1916) were the bomb and we are living in the explosion.'[14] And in November: 'We are preparing here, behind our screen of bombs and smoke, a return to conservative politics as elsewhere in Europe. . . . The Ireland that reacts from the present disorder is turning its eyes towards individualist Italy.'[15]

A few weeks later he took his seat in the Senate which he was to hold from 1922 until 1928. Although always liable to take a highly individual line, he attached himself to a group of ex-Unionists led by the distiller, Andrew Jameson, an old friend of his father.[16] As a confirmed outsider, he knew a minority when he saw one. And this was recognisably *his* minority - his by birth, by religion, by common cultural tradition. Yet, as he soon found, it was unwise to press the identification too closely. Politically, he was moving to the right while they were moving to the left and their contact with each other was not much more than that of ships that pass in the night. They were bent on survival, on protecting their diminished caste from expropriation or worse, and on influencing Government so far as they could by co-operation with the new regime. Moreover, these Senate representatives of the old order had little interest in Yeats's aesthetic ideas and no understanding of the concept of unity of culture for which he was about to make his last stand. The Anglo-Irish, as an actuality as opposed to a symbol, had always been a disappointment to him in their arrogant noon; they were to be no less a disappointment in their submissive twilight.

This did not prevent him from being an attentive and intermittently effective Senator. Although he never really mastered the rules of procedure, he played his part in committee work, took a leading role in choosing the design of the new Irish coinage, pleaded the case for the preservation of Irish manuscripts, demanded (vainly) the establishment of an academy of the arts such as he had seen in Stockholm when he received his Nobel Prize, and made substantial contributions on such matters as copyright law, the Lane pictures and Irish secondary schools. His record of attendance was consistently good and his interventions in debate were more numerous than those of the average Senator up to 1925. Thereafter, increasing fatigue and the realisation that the Government was paying less attention to the Senate, led him to speak much less often and on a more limited range of topics.[17]

The impact he made on the Senate was to Yeats himself a matter of secondary importance. Membership of that body, the advertisement and respect it gave him, was significant only to the extent that it provided him with a platform from which to carry on the main business of his public life which, as he saw it, was to lead opinion towards the recognition of the fact that independence without unity of culture, without willing acceptance of all traditions, was a vain achievement. 'The old Ireland is dead,' he said in a speech outside the Senate in 1923, 'an Ireland that had its own idealism, its own principles, its own sentiments, which produced some good oratory and much self-sacrifice. . . . A new Ireland is beginning, with a new idealism - an idealism of power, patience and economy.'[18] To see how this doctrine of reconciliation fared we have to look more closely at the situation he found on his return to Ireland and at how his own thought developed in the light of that situation.

As I have suggested, it was a situation in which the tide was running strongly in favour of the assertion of an Irish identity which would be both Gaelic and Catholic. Gaelicism was to be achieved by the encouragement of the Irish language by all possible means including its insertion into the educational system on a compulsory basis. Catholicism was to be strengthened, so far as the State could strengthen it, by the enactment of legislation on divorce, birth-control and censorship which assumed that public morality was in effect Catholic morality. Against this tide the

Anglo-Irish had few enough defences. A handful of the same people who had worked with Yeats in the years before 1914 to bring about a fusion of cultures took up once more the same struggle though in vastly more difficult circumstances. Chief among them were Sir Horace Plunkett, AE, John Eglinton, Lady Gregory (through the Abbey Theatre) and Yeats himself. Their battle was a mainly literary one and was fought chiefly in the columns of the *Irish Statesman*, a weekly paper founded in 1919 by Plunkett and edited by AE. After about a year, it was forced to close, but Plunkett refounded it in 1923 with the same editor who conducted it with great courage and brilliance until its final closure in 1930. With a boldness born perhaps of desperation AE and his contributors, especially John Eglinton, tried to assert two propositions. One was that the Anglo-Irish had to come to terms with the regime and accept that the independent Irish nation was an inescapable and permanent fact. The other was that this offered them perhaps their best opportunity since the eighteenth century, and certainly their last, of playing an influential part in the shaping of the new nation. 'The true destiny of Ireland,' Eglinton proclaimed, 'is to be a composite nationality.'[19] And to moderate Anglo-Irish people, he said, 'Irish nationality is a unifying influence, which must continue to proceed from them as it originated amongst them.'[20]

This was at best a dubious reading of Irish history, for the Irish nationality of the eighteenth century to which Eglinton looked back so fondly had been the limited, exclusive preserve of the Protestant Ascendancy. There was no possibility that the newly independent Catholic nation would concede Eglinton's grandiose demand that the Anglo-Irish should exert once more their traditional leadership. On the contrary, the reaction of the now dominant Gaelic-Catholic majority was, first, to insist that the Irish language was the essential badge of nationality; second, to deny the existence of the Anglo-Irish as a separate tradition; and finally to ensure, as the legislation of the State increasingly made clear, that there would be no privileged position for the minority. Personally they would receive the most generous tolerance, their lives and their property would be protected against anyone who sought to destroy either, but the concept of society that would prevail, the criteria of liberty that alone would be acceptable, would be defined by Catholic and nationalist values.[21]

Thus the lines of battle had been firmly drawn even before Yeats had returned to Ireland. Indeed, with hindsight, one could say that the battle had already been fought and lost by his Anglo-Irish allies. With one part of his mind Yeats was probably aware of this and in 1919 had written despondently to a friend, 'We are reeling back into the middle ages, without growing more picturesque.'[22] He was unhappy about the Abbey, which had become disconcertingly popular instead of the esoteric theatre of his early dreams, and still more unhappy about the fusion of cultures. To Lady Gregory he wrote in that same year that while they had no doubt created a People's Theatre, 'its success has been to me a discouragement and a defeat.'[23] And about the same time, in the essay, 'If I were Four and Twenty', he reflected the disillusionment of the old man he had begun to dread becoming. 'If I were not four and fifty,' he wrote, 'with no settled habit but the writing of verse, rheumatic, indolent, discouraged, and about to move to the Far East, I would begin another epoch by recommending to the nation a new doctrine, that of unity of being.'[24]

Yet this world-weariness was deceptive. He did not move to the Far East (though there *had* been an offer of a university post in Tokyo), and his energy, both in his life and in his work, seemed undiminished. Looking back nearly ten years later he gave the impression that in that dawn of independence it had been bliss to be alive. The Government by its mere existence, he wrote, 'delivered us from obsession'. 'No sooner was it established, the civil war behind it, than the musician, the artist, the dramatist, the poet, the student, found — perhaps for the first time — that he could give his whole heart to his work.'[25] As for himself, the change was magical and momentous:

> Freedom from obsession brought me a transformation akin to a religious conversion. I had thought much of my fellow-workers, Synge, Lady Gregory, Lane — but had seen nothing of Protestant Ireland as a whole but its faults, had carried through my projects in face of its indifference, had fed my imagination upon the legends of the Catholic villages or upon medieval Irish poetry: but now my affection turned to my own people, to my own ancestors, to the books they had read. It seemed we had a part to play at last that might find us allies everywhere, for we alone had not to assume in public discussion of all great issues that we could find in St Mark or St Matthew a shorthand report of the words of Christ attested before a magistrate.[26]

This was a statement of profound significance, perhaps all the more so since Yeats seems not to have grasped the full implications of what he was saying. By turning away from the traditional and mainly peasant sources of his youthful work

and back, as he said, 'to my own people', he was opening the
door to a duality rather than a unity of culture. It would
be some time before he realised this; indeed, he may never
have allowed himself to realise it completely. But if, as I
believe, the last two decades of his life marked a decisive
defeat for his ideal of cultural fusion, we shall find a
large part, though not the whole, of the reason for this in
his highly subjective interpretation of the eighteenth century - 'that one Irish century,' as he put it, 'that escaped
from darkness and confusion.'[27]

Essentially, it was an interpretation based upon his reading of Swift, Berkeley and Burke, with side-glances at
Goldsmith and Grattan.[28] 'My son,' he wrote in 1930,
' . . . when told that Italy excelled in painting, England
in poetry, Germany in music, asked in what Ireland excelled,
and was told that Ireland must not be judged like other
nations because it had only just won back its freedom. I may
suggest to him, if I live long enough, that the thought of
Swift, enlarged and enriched by Burke, saddled and bitted
reality, and that materialism was hamstrung by Berkeley and
ancient wisdom brought back; that modern Europe has known no
men more powerful.'[29]

By such hyperbole, one is tempted to say, Yeats proved his
own quintessential Irishness, but these lofty claims have to
be viewed against the degradation of the Anglo-Irish in his
own day. To see those famous men as European, even world
figures, was to have the sense of belonging to a great tradition, and to belong to it was a challenge to prolong it.
Thus, the eighteenth century gave Yeats models and symbols
which provided him with the basis for rethinking his attitude not only to Ireland, but to the world at large. At
bottom, his new heroes stood for the aristocracy of intellect, they were all, he thought, men who had fought against
the barbarism and chaos of their age, just as Yeats felt
impelled to do in his own day. Especially, they could be
recruited into his private war against the levelling and
vulgar tendencies of the modern world which he equated with
the rise of English Whiggery. 'Whence came our thought?'
asks one of the Seven Sages in the poem of that name. 'From
four great minds that hated Whiggery,' answers another. And
yet another sums it up:

>   Whether they knew or not,
> Goldsmith and Burke, Swift and the Bishop of Cloyne
> All hated Whiggery; but what is Whiggery?
> A levelling, rancorous, rational sort of mind
> That never looked out of the eye of a saint
> Or out of drunkard's eye.

And the seventh sage surely speaks for Yeats himself:

> All's Whiggery now,
> But we old men are massed against the world.[30]

From each of his chief allies (leaving Goldsmith aside) he took something for his armoury. From Berkeley's philosophy he found support for the unending struggle against the world of abstraction and measurement which had come in with Newton and Locke and which heralded the mechanical world of the industrial revolution:

> Locke sank into a swoon;
> The Garden died;
> God took the spinning-jenny
> Out of his side.[31]

Or, as he put it more brutally, 'Descartes, Locke and Newton took away the world and gave us its excrement instead, Berkeley restored the world.'[32] Moreover, it was as an Irishman that he did it. When he selected the three or four propositions of English materialism and asserted that 'we Irish do not hold with this', he was making a declaration of independence. 'That,' said Yeats, 'was the birth of the national intellect and it caused the defeat . . . of English materialism, the Irish Salamis.'[33]

From Swift he derived a view of human liberty which, while combining compassion with indignation, was fundamentally pessimistic. And Yeats could quote with evident approval Swift's own maxim: 'I should think that the saying *vox populi, vox dei* ought to be understood of the universal bent and current of a people, not of the bare majority of a few representatives, which is often procured by little art, and great industry and application; wherein those who engage in the pursuits of malice and revenge are much more sedulous than such as would prevent them.'[34] And it was from Swift also that Yeats learned that the perfect balance in a State was of the One, the Few and the Many - that is, the executive, the possessors of wealth or talent who identify their lives with the life of the State, and the masses who join whoever will bribe them most. Sooner or later the balance was sure to break down and then would follow tyranny, at first of the Few or the Many, but ultimately of the One.[35] 'All civilisations,' commented Yeats, 'must end in some such way, for the Many obsessed by emotion create a multitude of religious sects but give themselves at last to some one master of bribes and flatteries and sink into the ignoble tranquillity of servitude.'[36] And he felt that Swift had

all too clearly foreseen the difficulties of giving
responsibility or a voice to those who cannot judge of their
acts and their consequences. 'Swift thought,' he wrote in
his 1930 diary, 'that we set free a multitude of private
interests to overbear all who by privilege of station,
genius or training, possessed the public mind, and thereby
at last created a situation that had no issue but despotism. . . . I think of Swift's own life, of the letter where
he describes his love of this man and that, and his hatred
of all classes and professions. I remember his epitaph and
understand that the liberty he served was that of intellect,
not liberty for the masses but for those who could make it
visible.'[37]

The conservative, indeed anti-democratic, drift of this is
unmistakable and it was only strengthened by Yeats's study
of Burke, with his repeated warnings about the dangers of
innovation and revolution, his scorn for political abstractions, his insistence to have in government intelligent and
able men well endowed with property. And Yeats marked in his
own copy of James Prior's life of Burke two of the great
man's aphorisms. 'Permit me then . . . to tell you what the
freedom is that I love. It is not solitary, unconnected,
individual, selfish liberty. It is social freedom.' And
again: 'But the liberty, the only liberty I mean, is a
liberty connected with order.'[38]

Not less important to Yeats was Burke's doctrine of
continuity. 'A nation,' Burke had said in a passage in
Appeal from the New to the Old Whigs, which Yeats carefully
marked, 'is not only an idea of local extent . . . but it is
an idea of continuity which extends in time as well as in
numbers and in space. And this is a choice not of one day,
or one set of people, not a tumultuary and giddy choice; it
is a deliberate election of ages and of generations . . . .'[39] For this continuity Burke chose the oak
tree as his symbol and Yeats gratefully seized upon it, both
because it conveyed the idea of historic growth and because
it could be used to discredit numerical democracy. Hence the
tribute paid in 'Blood and the Moon':

And haughtier-headed Burke that proved the State a tree,
That this unconquerable labyrinth of the birds, century
  after century,
Cast but dead leaves to mathematical equality.[40]

Most of all, Burke was for Yeats the man who sought to
roll back European anarchy in the shape of the French Revolution.[41] But that anarchic tide threatened always to rise
again and with the Bolshevik triumph in Russia Yeats felt

the first premonitions of a new deluge. Sometimes this led him to the verge of the ludicrous when at a meeting in Trinity College he turned fiercely on an inoffensive Labour leader demanding to know whether organised labour was seeking revolutionary allies to bring about a dictatorship of the proletariat.[42] Against this threat he was ready to propose a movement from democracy towards authority. Thus, in February 1924, he took advantage of a Dublin production of Paul Claudel's play, *L'Otage*, to link the writer's name with that of Mussolini and to see in both of them a portent of authoritative rule. 'When I was under thirty,' he wrote, 'it would seem an incredible dream that 20,000 Italians, drawn from the mass of the people, would applaud a politician for talking of the "decomposing body of liberty".' And like the good Burkean he was, he added: 'Everything seems to show that the centrifugal movement which began with the Encyclopaedists and produced the French Revolution . . . has worked itself out to the end.' 'When the democratic movement was in its beginning Burke opposed it . . . and what he did vainly when the movement was in its sunrise, Peguy and Claudel have done in poems and plays in its sunset.' 'Authoritative rule is certainly coming,' he proclaimed, 'I see the same tendency here in Ireland . . . What else can chaos produce . . . ?'[43]

These tendencies in his thought - authoritarian, aristocratic, looking back towards a highly individual view of the eighteenth century - prepared the way for the famous outburst in the Senate in 1925 which at one and the same time announced his Anglo-Irish allegiance and increased his personal isolation. In February the Senate was asked to discuss the framing of a Standing Order which would make it impossible to introduce a bill for divorce *a vinculo matrimonii* (that is, complete divorce with liberty to remarry). That was ruled out but the issue came up for debate in June when the Senate passed a resolution that a Standing Order be framed by which divorce bills must receive a first reading in each House before being proceeded with by the Senate; this, of course, was tantamount to ensuring the complete exclusion of such bills.

When the matter was first raised in February, Yeats was ready with a speech, not then delivered, but soon afterwards published in the *Irish Statesman*. Part of it was a reasonable exposition of the unhappiness caused to families where divorce was impossible, and part made a point still relevant today, that it was useless to speak of reunification with the Protestant north, if such an obviously Catholic piece of legislation were to become part of the law of the land. But he entered on more dangerous ground when he accused the

Government of breaking the religious truce in Ireland and fomenting a quarrel. 'Fanaticism having won this victory,' he said, '. . . will make other attempts upon the liberty of minorities. I want those minorities to resist, and their resistance may do an overwhelming service to this country, they may become the centre of its creative intellect and the pivot of its unity.'[44]

This resistance he took upon himself when the debate came on in June. He was excited, overheated and altogether at his most pugnacious. What gave greatest offence at the time no doubt was his attack upon the Roman Catholic Church which he saw as the driving force behind the new law. 'You are to legislate on purely theological grounds and you are to force your theology on persons who are not of your religion.' And why stop there? Would there not, he asked prophetically, soon be a move towards censorship of literature? 'Once you attempt legislation on religious grounds you open the way for every kind of intolerance and for every kind of religious persecution.' True, divorce had also been condemned by the Protestant Bishop of Meath, but Protestant bishops, Yeats remarked contemptuously, influenced no votes. 'It is one of the glories of the church in which I was born that we have put our bishops in their places in discussions requiring legislation.' In any event, to deny divorce was not going to prevent separation of husband and wife when their relationship became intolerable. 'You are going to invite men and women in the prime of life to accept for the rest of their existence the law of the cloisters. Do you think you are going to succeed in what the entire of Europe has failed to do for the last 2,000 years?' Then, after an ironic digression on the hypocrisy of forbidding divorce when the three principal statues in the centre of Dublin - those of O'Connell, Nelson and Parnell - were all of known adulterers, Yeats came to the passage in which arrogantly but yet magnificently he joined his cause to the Anglo-Irish tradition as he saw it:

I think it is tragic that within three years of this country gaining its independence we should be discussing a measure which a minority of this nation considers to be grossly oppressive. I am proud to consider myself a typical man of that minority. We against whom you have done this thing are no petty people. We are one of the great stocks of Europe. We are the people of Burke; we are the people of Grattan; we are the people of Swift, the people of Emmet, the people of Parnell. We have created the most of the modern literature of this country. We have created the best of its political intelligence. Yet I do not altogether regret what has happened. . . . You have defined our position and given us a popular following. If we have not lost our stamina then your victory will be brief, and your defeat final, and when it comes this nation may be transformed.[45]

It was an astonishing outburst and its effect was almost wholly disastrous. His speech had been interrupted many times and the outraged reception it got outside the Senate was entirely predictable. Even the *Irish Times*, then the mouthpiece of the Anglo-Irish minority, while lamenting the denial of liberty to the minority which the prohibition of divorce entailed, censured his 'hurtful and aggressive remarks'. 'Attacks on the bishops of two churches – "in one red burial blent" – will not induce the philosophic frame of mind in any class of electors or legislators.' 'A poet may sing of broken hearts,' it added sententiously, 'but the task of mending the bruised hearts that seek relief from tragic wedlock in the Free State needs qualities of steadiness and compromise that are found more often in plainer men.'[46]

For Yeats all this was beside the point. The primary need was to fight fanaticism and intolerance wherever they appeared. If this meant a collision with Catholic bourgeois nationalism, or even with his own people, then that was unfortunate, but it was none the less essential if independence of mind was to be preserved in the country. And if that independence could only be achieved at the price of unity of culture then there was not much doubt about how he would go. True, for some time longer he struggled to maintain a balance between the two traditions. Thus, in a remarkable article, 'The Child and the State', in the *Irish Statesman* in December 1925, he pleaded for a more imaginative education which would draw upon both Gaelic and Anglo-Irish sources. 'In Gaelic literature we have something that the English-speaking countries have never possessed – a great folk literature. We have in Berkeley and in Burke a philosophy on which it is possible to base the whole life of a nation.' 'Feed the immature imagination upon that old folk life, and the mature intellect upon Berkeley and the great modern idealist philosophy created by his influence upon Burke who restored to political thought its sense of history, and Ireland is reborn, potent, armed and wise.'[47] In his diary for 1930 he was still hoping against hope for the final consummation: 'Preserve that which is living', he wrote, 'and help the two Irelands, Gaelic Ireland and Anglo-Ireland, so to unite that neither shall shed its pride.'[48] And in 1932, resourceful and energetic as ever, he took a major part in the foundation of the Irish Academy of Letters; initially designed more to protect artistic freedom than to foster unity of culture, it nevertheless included representatives of the two traditions and was a notable example of Yeats's power to influence those who were much younger than himself and whose background was very different from his.

But these were brave gestures in face of a darkening scene. The impulse towards conformity on the basis of Catholic morality enforced by Church and State, or by a public opinion which upheld Church and State, was very strong and Yeats constantly found himself locked in controversy. This, while as always the breath of life to him, tended to lead him into extreme positions where even the Anglo-Irish were not always prepared to follow him. Sometimes, admittedly, he invited trouble. Thus in 1924 he had encouraged a group of young men to launch a paper, *To-morrow* designed to shock the bourgeoisie, which it did so effectively that it closed after two issues. Yeats apparently wrote, but did not sign, a 'manifesto' for the first issue which asserted: 'We are Catholics, but of the school of Pope Julius the Second and of the Medicean Popes, who ordered Michelangelo and Raphael to paint upon the walls of the Vatican, and upon the ceiling of the Sistine Chapel . . . the reconciliation of Galilee and Parnassus. . . . We proclaim that we can forgive the sinner but abhor the atheist, and that we count among atheists bad writers and bishops of all denominations. . . . What devout man can read the pastorals of our hierarchy without horror at a style rancid, coarse and vague, like that of the daily papers?'[49] A little over a year later, when writing ostensibly to condemn the attempted suppression in Ireland of the 'Cherry Tree Carol', he used the failure of the magazine *To-morrow* (it collapsed because it printed a story by Lennox Robinson alleged to be blasphemous) to hammer home the point he was really concerned to make. 'We are quick to hate and slow to love . . . ', he said. 'To some extent Ireland but shows in an acute form the European problem and must seek a remedy where the best minds of Europe seek it - in audacity of speculation and creation.'[50]

'Audacity' - that was indeed the keynote of Yeats's activity in these years, and it was as necessary in the world of art as in the world of speculation. In 1926, for example, he had to fight his last great battle in the theatre, a battle essentially the same as the one he had fought in the early years of the century. Then it had been on behalf of Synge; now it was on behalf of Sean O'Casey, whose play *The Plough and the Stars* dared to lay the realities of the Dublin slums alongside the myths which had already gathered round the men of 1916. When a full-scale riot stopped the play Yeats went on stage to chastise the audience. 'You have disgraced yourselves again. Is this to be the ever-recurring celebration of the arrival of Irish genius? Synge first and then O'Casey. . . . From such a scene in this theatre went forth the fame of Synge. Equally the fame of O'Casey is born here tonight. This is his apotheosis.'[51] O'Casey himself looked on, impressed but also appalled. 'For the first time in his life', he recorded, 'Sean felt a surge of hatred for Cathleen ni Houlihan sweeping over him. He saw now that one who had the walk of a queen could be a bitch at times . . . she had hounded Parnell to death; she had yelled and torn at Yeats, at Synge, and now she was doing the same to him. Sean went home feeling no way exalted by his apotheosis.'[52]

It was far otherwise with Yeats. A few days later he took up with relish the various charges which had been made against the Abbey and its directors - that it was a minority cult, that it could never be national, that it habitually used the English language, that its dialect English was an invention, above all that the directors were 'stout Cromwellians'. He had no difficulty in rejecting the specific accusations but he seized joyfully on the epithet. 'We Cromwellian directors,' he said, 'laid down this principle twenty-five years ago and have not departed from it: never to accept or reject a play because of its opinions.' And he went on to make the point that was uppermost in his mind in all these quarrels, that the excellence of the few would never be representative of the many. 'Of one thing we may be quite certain; at no time . . . does an intellectual movement express a whole people, or anybody but those who are built into it as a victim was long ago built into the foundation of a bridge. Sometimes, if those few people are great enough . . . they give their character to the people.'[53]

But for this to occur Irish writers had to have access to their public and Irish readers had to have access to world literature. Yet in 1928 appeared the Censorship of Publications Bill which, when passed into law in 1929, ensured that neither of these things would happen. Although aimed primarily at obscene literature and at literature advocating artificial birth control, the new law set up a board of censors which would have power to exclude virtually any literature which it regarded as objectionable, a power used so extensively that in the decades to come many masterworks not only of Irish but of European and American authors were barred to Irish readers.

True to form, Yeats regarded this as simply an extension of his arch-enemy, 'fanaticism'. Under the old regime, he said, 'we were helots and where you have the helot there the zealot reigns unchallenged. And our zealots' idea of establishing the kingdom of God upon earth is to make Ireland an island of moral cowards.'[54] He had left the Senate before the bill was debated there, but he published in the *Irish Statesman* two articles which were the gist of what he would have said. Essentially, he made three points. The first was very much his own concern (though in fact it did not happen) that a literary censorship could easily become a stage censorship, which, had it existed thirty years earlier, would have made his theatre movement impossible. His second objection was the classical Protestant one. Why should Catholic morals be imposed upon non-Catholic people? The Government was forbidden to favour one religion above another and now, he maintained, they were in breach of the fundamental law of the State. And finally, in Ireland, the tide of change could no longer be turned back. The protagonists of the censorship did not understand, he said, that you cannot unscramble eggs, 'that every country passing out of automatism passes through demoralization, and that it has no choice but to go on into intelligence.'[55]

Yeats was not alone in this fight, nor indeed was it only an Anglo-Irish concern. The imposition of the censorship was fiercely attacked by many people from many standpoints, though it is certainly fair to say that both in the press - especially in the *Irish Statesman* - and in the legislature the remnants of the Anglo-Irish intelligentsia were in the thick of the fray. With their predictable defeat ended the last concerted effort of the minority to maintain its values and what it believed to be its rights in an increasingly alien world. Within the next few years many familiar landmarks were to disappear and some new and ominous ones were to emerge. In 1930 the *Irish Statesman* ceased publication. In 1931 the Cork writer, Daniel Corkery, published *Synge and Anglo-Irish Literature*, the most sustained attack yet made on the whole concept of an Anglo-Irish culture and in its day highly influential. In 1932 de Valera, whom Yeats had hitherto regarded with grave suspicion, came to power. In that year also Lady Gregory died and in Dublin the Eucharistic Congress marked the apex of Catholic triumphalism. In 1933 a special tax was laid on foreign newspapers. In 1935 the importation of contraceptives was forbidden by law. And in that year AE died in exile in Bournemouth. In 1937 the new constitution established a virtual republic in the twenty-six counties, restated the political objective of a united Ireland, and embodied the Catholic social thinking of the previous two decades.

The thrust towards the Gaelic and Catholic view of nationality seems unmistakable. Of the great figures of the renaissance only Yeats survived. Where did he stand? The question is not easy to answer. On the one hand, failing health kept him out of Ireland for long periods and he was no longer the ubiquitous and overpowering presence he once had been. On the other hand, there were phases - especially after a successful operation in 1934 - when his energy blazed with all its old fire and many critics have seen the poems and some of the plays that he wrote in the 1930s as being among his most splendid achievements.

Nevertheless, they were the achievements of a man who was very clearly going his own way and retreating into 'the Anglo-Irish solitude'. His public influence, indeed, was more than ever to be divisive. The tendency towards authoritarianism, which he had observed ten years earlier, became more pronounced during the years of economic depression and Ireland did not escape. There arose a movement which, if not absolutely Fascist, was Fascist in its inclinations. It came into being partly to protect politicians of the right against violence from the IRA which it was feared (erroneously) might not be contained by de Valera's Government. Soon there emerged a leader, a dismissed chief of police, General O'Duffy, and with him the usual paraphernalia of marchings, salutes and uniforms, in this case the 'Blueshirts' by which name the new organisation was generally known. Given that there already was in Ireland considerable respect for the Italian version of the corporative state, and that there existed there as elsewhere a nucleus of discontented ex-servicemen, the possibility of an extreme right-wing coup came very close in 1933. That this did not happen was partly because the Government kept its nerve, partly because Ireland was more strongly attached to democracy than its opponents believed, but most of all because O'Duffy was a bumbling incompetent, wholly lacking in charisma. The slogan suggested for his followers, 'Hail O'Duffy', was something less than mesmeric; the man himself was no Mussolini, much less a Hitler, and by 1934 the danger, such as it was, had passed.[56]

On all this excitement Yeats cast a speculative eye. In fact he did more. He met the organisers of the movement and tried his hand at writing some marching songs for the Blueshirts. But his enthusiasm was brief and the songs were altered to make them even more unsingable than they had been originally. This reaction may partly have been due to a conference Yeats had with O'Duffy. It was, Yeats wrote to a friend, to have been an occasion for him to 'talk my antidemocratic philosophy'. But there was no meeting of minds, perhaps because O'Duffy had not much mind to meet. The general's personality seems to have disappointed the poet, while the poet's philosophy, we may assume, was doubtless caviare to the general.[57] But the reason for Yeats's disenchantment goes deeper. He was, as we know, anti-Communist, authoritarian and attracted towards certain aspects of Fascist thought. He was, however, primarily a believer in aristocratic excellence, in the 'despotism of the educated classes',[58] as he called it, and was not interested in the minutiae of party warfare.[59] Therefore, though his letters for a few months breathed the hectic excitement of a possible return to the arena, this subsided very quickly.[60] As he wrote to Ethel Mannin a few years later, 'Do not try to make a politician of me, even in Ireland I shall never I think be that again - as my sense of reality deepens, and I think it does with age, my horror at the cruelty of governments grows greater. . . . Communist, Fascist, nationalist, clerical, anti-clerical, are all responsible according to the number of their victims.'[61] And when O'Duffy took a legion to Spain to fight for Franco, Yeats drew back in horror from this evidence of Catholic Fascism in action. 'I am convinced', he wrote, 'that if the Spanish war goes on, or if [it] ceases and O'Duffy's volunteers return heroes, my "pagan" institutions, the Theatre, the Academy, will be fighting for their lives against combined Catholic and Gaelic bigotry.'[62]

This did not mean that Yeats became in his old age any less extreme in his opinions. It means rather that in his last poems and plays, and in the fierce tirade of his final prose work *On the Boiler*, he concerned himself rather with the themes which seemed to him to have far greater urgency than contemporary politics. They were themes of love and loneliness, of old age and death, of the general crisis of civilisation, above all, and abiding through all, themes of Ireland and of the part his special people had played in its history. And just as there were many themes, so there were many moods and tones - sometimes elegiac, sometimes enraged, sometimes tragic, sometimes full of joy, but always a turning towards life, a passion to confront it and to achieve dignity when the end came.

Believing that the movement of history was cyclical, and that the soul of man lived many lives, Yeats could face with equanimity his own passing, the end of the Anglo-Irish order, and the eclipse of civilisation as he had known it. And all omens notwithstanding, he could still believe that if Ireland turned from the cult of numbers to the excellence of the few, its future would be assured. 'We have,' he said in a last echo of his divorce speech, 'as good blood as there is in Europe. Berkeley, Swift, Burke, Grattan, Augusta Gregory, Synge, Kevin O'Higgins are the true Irish people,

and there is nothing too hard for such as these. If the
Catholic names are few [in fact, only one] history will soon
fill the gap.'[63]

Yet, at the end of his life the gap still yawned and the
unity of culture he had dreamed of seemed no more than an
historical curiosity. Watching his Anglo-Irish people dwindle and perish, Yeats had two duties towards them to perform
in his last years. The first was to celebrate them with affection and pride. And here, as in 'Coole Park and Ballylee,
1931', Lady Gregory's name led all the rest as he watched
her dying of cancer before his eyes:

> Sound of a stick upon the floor, a sound
> From somebody that toils from chair to chair;
> Beloved books that famous hands have bound,
> Old marble heads, old pictures everywhere;
> Great rooms where travelled men and children found
> Content or joy; a last inheritor
> Where none has reigned that lacked a name and fame
> Or out of folly into folly came.[64]

And in 'The Municipal Gallery Revisited', she and her
nephew, Hugh Lane, were joined with Synge in the litany of
his friends:

> You that would judge me, do not judge alone
> This book or that, come to this hallowed place
> Where my friends' portraits hang and look thereon;
> Ireland's history in their lineaments trace;
> Think where man's glory most begins and ends,
> And say my glory was I had such friends.[65]

Yeats's second duty was to dismiss these friends into the
dark without sentiment and without compromise. He could do
this the more stoically because he believed that out of the
chaos that lay ahead, however long it might last, a new order would come:

> When I stand upon O'Connell Bridge in the half-light [he
> wrote in 1937] and notice that discordant architecture,
> all those electric signs, where modern heterogeneity has
> taken physical form, a vague hatred comes up out of my own
> dark and I am certain that wherever in Europe there are
> minds strong enough to lead others the same vague hatred
> rises; in four or five or in less generations this hatred
> will have issued in violence and imposed some rule of kindred. I cannot know the nature of that rule, for its

opposite fills the light; all I can do to bring it nearer is to intensify my hatred.[66]

This hatred was the same sacred rage with which for most of his life he had opposed the filthy modern tide, as he called it, of democratic and materialist vulgarity and which in his last two decades had led him to create an Anglo-Irish ideal which, no doubt, had little enough connection with historical reality, but which became his symbol of aristocratic excellence. Yet hatred, as he half admitted to Dorothy Wellesley, was perhaps the wrong word. 'You say that we must not hate,' he wrote. 'You are right, but we may, and sometimes must, be indignant and speak it. Hatred is a kind of "passive suffering", but indignation is a kind of joy. "When I am told that somebody is my brother Protestant," said Swift, "I remember that the rat is a fellow-creature"; that seems to me a joyous saying. We that are joyous need not be afraid to denounce.'[67]

Here, surely, we are close to the centre of the labyrinth. 'A poet writes always of his personal life, in his finest work out of its tragedy, whatever it be . . . ', he said in 1937. And he recalled a saying of Lady Gregory's, 'Tragedy must be a joy to the man who dies.'[68] And thus, as he made ready for the end, what breathes through his last poems is a sense of tragic joy coupled with an affirmation of his always indomitable will:

What matter though numb nightmare ride on top,
And blood and mire the sensitive body stain?
What matter? Heave no sigh, let no tear drop,
A greater, a more gracious time has gone;
For painted forms or boxes of make-up
In ancient tombs I sighed, but not again;
What matter? Out of cavern comes a voice,
And all it knows is that one word 'Rejoice'![69]

NOTES

1. *Uncollected Prose by W. B. Yeats*, ed. John P. Frayne (London, 1970) vol. i, p. 173 (hereafter cited as *Uncollected Prose*). See also M. C. Flannery, *Yeats and Magic* (Gerrards Cross, Bucks, 1977) pp. 66-7.
2. J. C. Beckett, *The Anglo-Irish Tradition* (London, 1976) p. 11.
3. *Irish Statesman*, 17 Aug. 1929.
4. Donal O'Sullivan, *The Irish Free State and its Senate*

(London, 1940) pp. 90-1.
5. W. B. Yeats, *Explorations*, paperback edn (New York, 1973) pp. 155-6, 157-8.
6. W. B. Yeats, *Collected Poems* (London, 1950) pp. 120-1.
7. Ibid., p. 123.
8. A. Zwerdling, *Yeats and the Heroic Ideal* (New York, 1965) p. 20 and source there cited.
9. For this dating, which is later than the 1903 or 1904 often cited by Yeats scholars, see Daniel A. Harris, *Yeats, Coole Park and Ballylee* (Baltimore and London, 1974) p. 5, n. 22.
10. In a letter to Lady Gregory (11 May 1916) he wrote: 'I am trying to write a poem on the men executed - "terrible beauty has been born again". . . . I had no idea that any public event could so deeply move me - and I am very despondent about the future. At the moment I feel that all the work of years has been overturned, all the bringing together of classes, all the freeing of Irish literature and criticism from politics' (*The Letters of W. B. Yeats*, ed. Allan Wade (London, 1954) pp. 612-13; hereafter cited as *Letters*).
11. Richard Ellmann, *Yeats: the Man and the Masks* paperback edn (London, 1961) pp. 181-2.
12. *Letters*, p. 656.
13. Ibid., pp. 681-2.
14. Ibid., p. 690.
15. Ibid., p. 693.
16. J. M. Hone, 'Yeats as a Political Philosopher', in *London Mercury* (March 1939) p. 494.
17. *The Senate Speeches of W. B. Yeats*, ed. Donald R. Pearce (London, 1961) *passim*. See also W. B. Stanford, 'Yeats in the Irish Senate', in *Review of English Literature*, vol. iv (July 1963) pp. 71-80; and David Fitzpatrick, 'W. B. Yeats in Seanad Eireann', in Robert O'Driscoll and Lorna Reynolds (eds), *Yeats and the Theatre* (London, 1975) pp. 159-75.
18. *Irish Times*, 25 Aug. 1923. This was a speech in support of the candidature of an ex-Unionist, Bryan Cooper, for the Dail.
19. *Irish Statesman*, 27 Dec. 1919.
20. *Irish Statesman*, 29 Nov. 1919.
21. For the contemporary argument, see F. S. L. Lyons, *Culture and Anarchy in Ireland, 1890-1939* (Oxford, 1979) pp. 105-12, 147-69.
22. *Letters*, p. 658.
23. *Explorations*, p. 250.
24. Ibid., p. 280.
25. *Uncollected Poems by W. B. Yeats*, ed. John P. Frayne

and Colter Jackson (London, 1975), vol. ii, p. 488 (hereafter cited as *Uncollected Poems*).
26. Ibid., vol. ii, pp. 488-9.
27. *Explorations*, p. 345.
28. In what follows I am indebted to the work of various scholars, notably Donald Torchiana, *W. B. Yeats and Georgian Ireland* (Evanston, Ill., 1966); Thomas R. Whitaker, *Yeats Dialogue with History*, especially ch. ix (Chapel Hill, NC 1964 edn); Douglas N. Archibald, 'The Words upon the Window-pane and Yeats's Encounter with Swift', in O'Driscoll and Reynolds (eds), *Yeats and the Theatre*, pp. 176-214.
29. *Explorations*, pp. 297-8.
30. *Collected Poems*, p. 272.
31. Ibid., p. 240.
32. *Explorations*, p. 325.
33. Ibid., pp. 333-4.
34. Ibid., p. 357.
35. He derived this idea from Swift's *A Discourse of the Contests and Discussions between the Nobles and the Commons in Athens and Rome* (1701).
36. *Explorations*, p. 352. Elsewhere, however, in his 1930 diary, Yeats records that he thought Swift's explanation too simple, by which he seems to have meant that it did not accord with Yeats's own theory of history. Influenced this time by Coleridge, he wrote that 'civilisation is driven to its final phase not by the jealousy and egotism of the many . . . but by "pure thought", "reason", what my System calls "spirit" and "celestial body", by that which makes all places and persons alike' (ibid., p. 316).
37. Ibid., p. 315.
38. Donald A. Torchiana, *W. B. Yeats and Georgian Ireland*, p. 170, n. 7.
39. Ibid., p. 193.
40. *Collected Poems*, p. 268.
41. Torchiana, *Yeats and Georgian Ireland*, p. 201.
42. *Irish Times*, 30 Jan. 1919.
43. *Uncollected Prose*, vol. ii, pp. 434-5.
44. Ibid., vol. ii, pp. 449-52.
45. *Senate Speeches*, p. 99.
46. *Irish Times*, 12 June 1925.
47. *Uncollected Poems*, vol. ii, pp. 458-9.
48. *Explorations*, p. 337.
49. *Uncollected Prose*, vol. ii, pp. 438-9. The editors of this volume note that Richard Ellmann's attribution of this article to Yeats (*Yeats: the Man and the Masks*, pp. 249-51) was confirmed by Mrs Yeats. At the time,

however, Yeats himself was cautious. In a letter to Olivia Shakespear of 21 June 1924 he wrote that he had heard that certain young men were about to publish a review. 'I said to one of them, "Why not found yourselves on the doctrine of the immortality of the soul, most bishops and all bad writers being obviously atheists." I heard no more till last night when I received a kind of deputation. They had adopted my suggestion and were suppressed by the printers for blasphemy' (*Letters*, pp. 705-6). My own feeling, like that of Richard Ellman, and even apart from Mrs Yeats's authority, is that the rhetoric of the article is exactly that used by Yeats in moments of high excitement.

50. *Uncollected Prose*, vol. ii, p. 465. This essay had to be published in *The Dial*, since AE feared for the existence of the *Irish Statesman* if it appeared there.
51. *Irish Times* and *Irish Independent*, 12 Feb. 1926.
52. Sean O'Casey, *Autobiographies*, paperback edn (London, 1963) vol. ii, pp. 150-1.
53. *Uncollected Prose*, vol. ii, pp. 465-70.
54. *Manchester Guardian*, 22 Aug. 1928; *Irish Independent*, 23 Aug. 1928.
55. *Uncollected Prose*, vol. ii, pp. 477-80, 480-5. The quotations (p. 484) are from the second of two articles, 'The Irish Censorship'.
56. For the Blueshirt movement see D. Thornley, 'The Blueshirts', in F. MacManus (ed.), *The Years of the Great Test, 1926-39* (Cork, 1967) pp. 42-54; also Maurice Manning, *The Blueshirts* (Dublin, 1970) *passim*.
57. *Letters*, pp. 812-13.
58. For example, twice in his 1930 diary, *Explorations*, pp. 308, 325.
59. For a critical view of this episode, see C. Cruise O'Brien, 'Passion and Cunning: an Essay on the Politics of W. B. Yeats', in A. Norman Jeffares and K. G. W. Cross (eds), *In Excited Reverie* (London, 1965), especially pp. 252-65. But see the attack upon Dr Cruise O'Brien's essay by Patrick Cosgrave, 'Yeats, Fascism and Conor O'Brien', in *London Magazine*, vol. vii (July 1967) pp. 22-41, and the more measured response of Mary Carden, 'The Few and the Many: an examination of W. B. Yeats's Politics', in *Studies* (Spring, 1969) pp. 60-2. More recently there has been a more detailed and, in the main, convincing refutation of the O'Brien essay in Elizabeth Cullingford, *Yeats, Ireland and Fascism* (London, 1981) especially chs 11 and 12.

60. *Letters*, pp. 808-9, 811-12, 812-13, 813-14, 814-15.
61. Ibid., pp. 850-1.
62. Ibid., p. 885.
63. *Explorations*, p. 442.
64. *Collected Poems*, p. 276.
65. Ibid., p. 370.
66. W. B. Yeats, *Essays and Introductions* (London, 1961) p. 526.
67. *Letters*, p. 876.
68. *Essays and Introductions*, pp. 509, 523.
69. *Collected Poems*, p. 337.

15 The Anglo-Irish and the Historians, 1830–1980

G. C. BOLTON

Who were the Anglo-Irish? According to Professor J. C. Beckett 'It is essentially a historian's term':

> Grattan and his Protestant contemporaries never doubted that they were Irishmen, without any qualifications. . . . But by the time of Grattan's death, in 1820, a shift of opinion was already evident; and it became more sharply marked during the next generation. The change was noted by one of the powerful Beresford family, which had dominated much of Irish political life in the later eighteenth century. 'When I was a boy', he said, '"the Irish people" meant the Protestants; now it means the Roman Catholics.'[1]

Anthony Malcolmson makes the same point in another way: 'The term "Anglo-Irish Ascendancy" is a historian's term, which can be defined as the historian chooses. . . .'[2] For many historians the term has specific reference to the dominant social and political elite of the eighteenth-century: a central network of perhaps five hundred families, with a wider penumbra of small Protestant tradesmen and farmers, lapsed Catholics, and minorities such as Huguenots and Quakers from whom the inner cousinhood recruited new blood. Of course, ever since the twelfth century there was a process of ethnic fusion between the native Irish and the successive waves of interlopers coming from England to establish political suzerainty: the Norman Irish, the Old English of the sixteenth and seventeenth centuries, and finally the Georgian Ascendancy. Malcolmson goes on to point out, following a hint given by Lecky, that during the debates on the Catholic Relief Bills of 1792 and 1793 public men such as Henry Grattan and Richard Burke were using the phrase 'Protestant Ascendancy' as a new term requiring definition. According to the *Oxford English Dictionary* the first use of the term 'Anglo-Irish' is dated at 1792, though the context is not given.[3] The first illustration given of the use of the term comes from a work entitled *Popular Songs of Ireland*, published in 1839 by the antiquary Thomas Crofton Croker. Significantly enough it reads: 'The Anglo-

Irish settlers degenerated', thus circulating one of the most persistent stereotypes about them.

Following this weight of authority I shall deal in this chapter principally with the changing image of the eighteenth-century Anglo-Irish in the historiography of the nineteenth and twentieth centuries. Of course, to a large extent their reputation has fluctuated with the evolution of Irish nationalism. The Home Rule party and its predecessors looked back to the Parliament of 1782 as the aborted prototype of an independent Irish legislature, and this made for favourable assessments of the class and generation which produced Henry Grattan and John Foster. The Gaelic revival of the late nineteenth and early twentieth centuries raised doubts about the national authenticity of those Irish who shared neither the religion nor the ethnic origins of the Catholic majority, and as Professor Beckett has observed, 'It was in response to this narrower and more exclusive nationalism that the term "Anglo-Irish". . . acquired general currency.'[4]

As well as fluctuating with changing concepts of nationalism, interpretations of the Anglo-Irish role in history also varied with changing concepts of colonialism. Like the eighteenth-century Americans the Anglo-Irish defined themselves as a separate interest-group through disputes with the metropolitan power. Like the Americans they could be seen as colonial rebels moving through these disputes to a new nationalism. But unlike the Americans their capacity for defiance was limited through fear of invasion or rebellion; and unlike the Americans they were greatly outnumbered by a population of longer occupancy. In perceiving themselves as no longer English it was open to them to assimilate with the Celtic Irish, but from a metropolitan English point of view such assimilation could be seen as an example of the degenerative effects of a frontier environment on a colonising people. In either case the history of the Anglo-Irish could be read as a model for more far-flung settlements in the overseas British Empire. Historians' interpretations of the Anglo-Irish would also fluctuate according to the questions which contemporaries were asking about Britain's imperial role in general.

Historians also provide the raw materials for myths. In the same decade that Crofton Croker offered his disparaging comment on the Anglo-Irish two works appeared which were to crystallise later stereotypes. In 1839 Henry Grattan junior published the first of the five volumes of his father's *Life and Letters*. [5] Reinforced by the citation of much original correspondence, this work presented the idealised picture of Grattan's Parliament as a brilliant gathering of eloquent

THE ANGLO-IRISH AND THE HISTORIANS, 1830-1980   241

and constructive legislators, snuffed out by a Union effected by parliamentary corruption.

A more powerful piece of mythmaking was generated by Sir Jonah Barrington. One of the last survivors of Grattan's Parliament, Barrington had not been one of its most distinguished ornaments. Born in 1760, he sat in the Irish House of Commons from 1790 to 1800, and became a judge of the Admiralty Court in 1798. As a Queen's County man his connections were with Sir John Parnell, the anti-Unionist Chancellor of the Exchequer, and through him with the Speaker, Foster. He became a vociferous anti-Unionist and somewhat notorious letter of cats out of bags, and perhaps for this reason was not deprived of his post with other anti-Unionists. Instead he remained in office until 1830, when his deficiencies became too great for even the easy-going standards of the Irish judiciary. He was dismissed, and went to live in Paris. At various stages since 1809 he had been publishing his reminiscences, and between 1827 and his death in 1835 three volumes made their appearance: *Historic Anecdotes and Secret Memoirs of Ireland*, *Personal Sketches of his Own Times*, and *The Rise and Fall of the Irish Nation*. (*Historic Anecdotes* first appeared between 1809 and 1813. It lacked several of the juicier stories in the later edition, presumably because the subjects of them were still alive to contradict them.)

Barrington was an amusing and dramatic writer unimpeded by a pedantic respect for facts, and his account of the allegedly corrupt practices in the passing of the Act of Union probably left a stronger impression on later generations even than Henry Grattan junior. The old rogue was taken more seriously after his death than he was living. He was reprinted in 1869, 1887 and 1917, each of them times when nationalist propaganda was on the offensive. He could be cited as an eye-witness to British perfidy; but he was also a witness to the 'good old days gone by', validating the fictional stereotypes of Edgeworth and Lever and transforming the eighteenth century into a Golden Age which might console contemporaries in the same way as Englishmen from time to time praised the pristine Anglo-Saxons before the coming of the Norman yoke. In Barrington's idealised picture the eighteenth century became a model of social harmony:

At the Great House all disputes among the tenants were then settled - quarrels reconciled - old debts arbitrated; a kind Irish landlord reigned despotic in the ardent affections of his tenantry, their pride and pleasure being to obey and support him. But there existed a happy reciprocity of interests...[6]

This reciprocity of interests was far-reaching:

> The Catholic and the Protestant at the same time lived in habits of great harmony; they harboured no animosities or indisposition towards each other; the one governed without opposition, the other submitted without resistance, and the Catholic clergy had every inclination to retain their flocks within proper limits, and found no difficulty in effecting that object.[7]

Although subsequent historians were well aware of Barrington's drawbacks as a trustworthy eye-witness he was one of the few published sources on the social history of the late eighteenth century, he was lively and readable, and they all used him. Froude and Lecky cited him in footnotes; and from him Yeats drew some of the raw material that went into a poem such as 'The Tower':

> Beyond that ridge lived Mrs French, and once
> When every silver candlestick or sconce
> Lit up the dark mahogany and the wine,
> A serving-man, that could divine
> That most respected lady's every wish,
> Ran and with the garden shears
> Clipped an insolent farmer's ears
> And brought them in a little covered dish.

That was a story which Barrington told about his own grandmother; and it was partly from Barrington too that Yeats drew the concept of the Anglo-Irish as a race having

> The pride of people that were
> Bound neither to Cause nor to State,
> Neither to slaves that were spat on,
> Nor to the tyrants that spat,
> The people of Burke and of Grattan
> That gave, though free to refuse. . . .[8]

Suspect history and an infelicitous rhyme; but they go on to a superb conclusion. Thus the rearguard defender of the Anglo-Irish went for his materials to that durable mythmaker Barrington nearly a century after his death.

Even Friedrich Engels, writing to Marx in 1856, was not immune to the panache of the Anglo-Irish: 'Of mixed blood, mostly tall, strong handsome chaps, they all wear enormous moustaches under colossal Roman noses, give themselves the fake military airs of retired colonels, travel around the country after all sorts of pleasures, and if one makes an inquiry, they haven't a penny, are laden with debts, and live in dread of the Encumbered Estates Court.'[9] Marx in his lecture of December 1867 to the London German Workers' Educational Association saw ethnic assimilation as a precondition of the formation of classes among the Irish. According to the notes taken by one of his hearers:

> . . . over 50 per cent of the English descendants in Ulster have remained Catholic. The people were driven into the arms of the Catholic clergy, who thus became powerful. All that the English government succeeded in doing was to plant an aristocracy in Ireland. The towns built by the English have become Irish. That is why there are so many English names among the Fenians.[10]

This is as garbled as most lecture notes, but it is clear that Marx spoke of the division between Anglo- and Celtic Irish as giving way through assimilation to a class-based divergence between landlords and tenants.

In Marx's own notes the term 'Anglo-Irish' occurs three times: once, when he refers to the early eighteenth century as a period of 'struggle between the Anglo-Irish colony and the Irish Nation' — but later states that the 'English incomers were absorbed into the Irish people and Catholicised'; once under 1783, 'Equal rights for the Anglo-Irish Parliament'; and once in speaking of the Act of Union: 'By the Legislature [*sic*] and Customs Union of Britain and Ireland closed the struggle between the Anglo-Irish and the English.'[11] Marx saw the Anglo-Irish and their middlemen as being replaced by, after the famine, 'English capitalists, insurance societies, etc.' The Anglo-Irish were either eliminated or absorbed into the common Irish stock. It was their capitalist supplanters whom Marx saw as the landlords whose overthrow was a necessary preliminary to the overthrow of the English ruling classes.

But for many years the views of Marx and Engels were of negligible importance in Irish historiography. Instead the generation who had been enthusiasts for the Young Ireland movement in the 1840s and were writing Irish history in the 1860s were grappling with the question of how Ireland's Protestant minority could be incorporated into a wider Irish nationalism. D'Arcy McGee, in his *History of Ireland* published in 1868 deplored the 'ascendancy party' as 'an exclusive caste' grasping 'the rights and freedoms which belong to an entire people'; but he also saw them as providing the cutting edge of leadership in the nationalist cause, starting with Jonathan Swift who 'laid the foundations of his own and his country's patriotism, among the educated middle-class of the Irish capital'.[12]

More systematically John Mitchel identified as one of his themes 'the origin of a Colonial Nationality among the English of Ireland'. He traced the development of a distinctive national self-concept among the Anglo-Irish to the commercial policies of the early eighteenth century, which he saw as intended to teach 'the Irish Protestant Ascendancy . . . that it was the mere agent of the English empire'.[13] Swift's view of himself as 'an Englishman in Ireland' could be contrasted to his younger contemporary Bishop Berkeley's description of himself as an 'Irishman' in the *Querist* of 1735. By the close of the eighteenth century, wrote Mitchel:

> . . . there had lately been formed gradually a marked Irish character even among the Protestant colonists, before the eve of Independence, and still more notably since that time. Gentlemen born in this country and all whose interests and associations were here, no longer called themselves Englishmen born in Ireland, as Swift had done . . .

After making reference to the powerful assimilating influence of the native Irish, he added:

> The formation of this modern composite Irish character is of course attributable to the gradual amalgamation of the privileged Protestant colonists with the *converted* Irish who had from time to time conformed to the established church. . . . In truth it had become very difficult to determine the ethnological distinction between the inhabitants of this island.[14]

As might be expected of an apologist for American slaveholding Mitchel rejected any idea of an analogy between the condition of the Irish and that of the American blacks or any other people held in subordination by an alien minority on the grounds of race. He upheld the status of the Irish as a distinctive European nationality, in no way diminished by a capacity for assimilation.

Starting from the same premises, another contemporary historian could draw very different conclusions. 'From a combination of causes,' wrote James Anthony Froude in 1872, 'some creditable to them, some other than creditable – the Irish Celts possess on their own soil a power greater than any other known family of mankind, of assimilating those who venture among them to their own image.'[15] For Froude this meant that the Irish environment was perilous for English settlers, since prolonged exposure to it led to degeneracy of the original stock. Of the eighteenth-century Anglo-Irish he wrote:

> Those who were really Protestant retained, for a generation or two, their distinguishing character; but, like the Normans before them, they assimilated themselves to their adopted element, as the fish takes the color of the gravel on which he lies; and the race of Irish gentry, which acquired so marked a notoriety in the last century, began gradually to shape itself; a race noted, among many characteristics, especially for this, that they hated labor as heartily as the Irish of earlier centuries. Every one who could subsist in idleness set himself up for a gentleman.[16]

The sources of Froude's bias are well known. In reaction from the Tractarian movement he was suspiciously and dogmatically anti-Catholic. From Carlyle and Kingsley came the notion of the Anglo-Saxons as entitled through their achievements to the favour of providence and the exercise of moral and political leadership throughout the world. Knowing Ireland from before and after the Famine, and having written on Tudor policy in Ireland, he could not resist the temptation of applying his beliefs to a study of seventeenth- and eighteenth-century Ireland. In part he wanted to counter the Gladstonian liberalism which had already led to Disestablishment. But he was also influenced by his interest in colonial questions.

As a partisan of Governor Eyre in the Jamaica controversy of 1865 he upheld the right of a metropolitan power to suppress popular dissent. He was also fascinated by the propensity of colonists to be modified by a frontier environment, assuming like many contemporaries that any change from the metropolitan original must be for the worse. Thus in 1861, after research in the archives at Simancas he declared himself 'a convert . . . to the Spanish of the sixteenth century. They were as noble a people as ever lived'.[17] But in *Oceana* he comments on the degeneracy of the Spanish in Latin America as an example to be avoided by the colonising English.[18] The tendency to fall away from the standards of metropolitan England could be countered by the vigorous encouragement of emigration. Implicitly Froude saw the initiative for colonial policy, for good or ill, as depending on the mother-country rather than on any independent sources within the colonies.

Holding these views, Froude was inclined to attribute what he saw as Ireland's stagnation during the eighteenth century to Britain's selfish commercial policies. By discriminating against most of Ireland's export industries, she was largely responsible for the deterioration of the Anglo-Irish:

> The puritan spirit of the seventeenth century settlers was dying out. The industrial spirit which should have taken its place had been forbidden to grow. A majority of the landowners were lounging in England or abroad . . . and the ruling race so painfully planted, to hold and civilise Ireland into a Protestant country, degenerated into the politicians of 1782, and the heroes of the memoirs of Sir Jonah Barrington.[19]

Setting aside Froude's cheerful assumption that civilisation and Protestantism are identical, this interpretation also begged the question of how 'the politicians of 1782' contrived to secure the repeal of many of their grievances. Froude's interpretation hardly belongs to the highest order of historical explanation:

> The Americans were pointing the way to redress, setting the example of resistance, and creating an opportunity. A great occasion raises common men to a level above their own. Accident, or the circumstances of the country, had created in Ireland at this time a knot of gentlemen whose abilities and whose character would anywhere have marked them for distinction.[20]

Having conceded this morsel of praise to the Anglo-Irish Froude reverted to his customary form, finding little to praise in any of the leading figures in Grattan's Parliament except for John Fitzgibbon, Earl of Clare. Of him Froude wrote: 'There had grown out of the Irish race by some freak of nature a man who had no personal object of his own . . . [and] detested anarchy.'[21] Even in his rare moments of praise Froude could not refrain from sneering at the Irish. Yet his final conclusion was unequivocal. 'England, not the gentry, was to blame for the condition of Irish society. . . . It would have been better and happier by far had England never confiscated the lands of the Irish, had she governed Ireland as she governs India, and never attempted to force upon her a landed gentry of alien blood.'[22] It is not entirely surprising that *'The English in Ireland* is reputed to have been Parnell's favourite book. It made him, he said, a Home Ruler because it exposed the iniquities of the English government.'[23]

Froude's provocative thrusts at the Irish stimulated quick responses from a number of critics, including Mitchel; but the ultimate rejoinder is usually considered to be the five-volume *History of Ireland in the Eighteenth Century*, by W. E. H. Lecky, originally published between 1878 and 1890 as part of a longer work, but subsequently in 1892 issued separately. Like Froude, Lecky based his analysis on an extensive search of archives in Dublin and London, but where Froude mainly sought after atrocity stories which illustrated the barbarity and ineptitude of the Irish, Lecky was much more systematic about tracing the socio-economic background of eighteenth-century Ireland. Like Froude, Lecky deplored the political influence of Catholicism, but his language was more temperate. Like Froude, Lecky admitted that the effect of the Union had been to diminish the political influence of the Anglo-Irish in the short term and their social status in the longer term; but he deplored the loss of their influence. Lecky had particular sympathy for Grattan's idealism and for Foster's astute grasp of commerce, and praised the men who made the constitution of 1782 as the model of a responsible conservative elite.

I follow Donal McCartney in seeing Lecky as evolving from a temperate nationalist to a repudiater of democracy and Home Rule.[24] In the last year of his life, 1903, he set out his views in an introduction to a revised edition of his early work, *Leaders of Public Opinion in Ireland*. Here he denied any real analogy between 'a Parliament representing in the highest degree the loyalty, the property, and especially the landed property of Ireland, and an ultrademocratic and land league Parliament . . .', and asserted, in words which could easily be mistaken for Froude's: 'They are probably not wrong who believe that the worst result of the Union has been that it has dragged Ireland into a plane of democracy for which it is utterly and manifestly unfit.'[25] After the intemperate strictures of Froude, Lecky restored the standing of the eighteenth-century Anglo-Irish as an integral part of the dominant Irish nationalist myth. Curiously, Lecky was much closer to Froude than was often credited. Like Froude he believed that the appropriate role for the Anglo-Irish was that of a beneficent ruling elite, and like Froude he held that metropolitan British policy was the main cause for their failure to develop that role. In light of this failure both saw metropolitan British rule as preferable to any alternative, and neither sympathised with modern democratic nationalism. It was just that Lecky was much less vehement about the ill effects of prolonged exposure to the Irish environment.

The surprising thing is that Lecky's aristrocrat Unionist nostalgia prevailed among most of the historians of the next generation, many of whom went well beyond him in their espousal of Home Rule. In an anthology of 1888 edited by the

Parnellite, R. Barry O'Brien, the chapter on Grattan's Parliament by George Sigerson praises Anglo-Irish political achievement.[26] George O'Brien's *Economic History of Ireland in the Eighteenth Century* spelt out the virtues of Irish economic nationalism as fostered by Grattan's Parliament. Even Swift MacNeill, who portrayed the Act of Union as evidence of the corruptibility of the Ascendancy, declared that he aimed 'to encourage and foster a zeal for the systematic study of Mr Lecky's writings on Irish history which will in itself be an epoch in the reader's intellectual life'.[27] MacNeill's critique was but a re-hash of Barrington seen through the late nineteenth-century's misunderstanding of the conventions of eighteenth-century politics.

Between 1886 and 1916 there was a curious discrepancy between the Irish social and political scene - the domination of the Catholic-backed Home Rule party, the rise of the Gaelic League - and the survival of the Anglo-Irish influence among Irish historians. To the extent that any work of history in those years fuelled an advanced nationalist consciousness, credit must be given to Alice Stopford Green's classic refutation of the myth of Irish cultural and economic backwardness; but this stopped short at the sixteenth century.[28] Possibly the role of the later Anglo-Irish was becoming an irrelevant issue. James Connolly's writings, intent on reconciling Marxist economic theory with Catholic practice, hardly spared a glance for the Ascendancy. On the other hand the assimilation of the Anglo-Irish into nationalist historiography could be plentifully illustrated by the numerous articles and books written around 1900 to emphasise the Irish role in the creation of the British Empire.[29] In such studies Anglo- and Celtic Irish were lumped as part of an honourable and beneficial contribution by Irish nation-builders who shared the imperial achievement. There was no hint of fellow-feeling with the colonised and no rejection of the Anglo-Irish as authentic Irish.

Coincidentally with their loss of social and political importance the Anglo-Irish played a dominant role in the literary movement of the late nineteenth century. As Professor Beckett says:

The romanticism that was already dying in Western Europe still survived in Ireland; and it influenced, one might also say dictated, both their choice of material and the use they made of it. For the most part, their poems, plays and stories either deal with myth and legend or present a picture of peasant society that is hardly nearer to the realities of everyday life as it was lived in the Ireland of the time . . .[30]

To this one would add that the romanticism is no more surprising than the identification with a portrait of peasant society from the deferential, pre-Famine Ireland of the past. The self-concept which the Anglo-Irish had of themselves was largely created for them by historians and mythmakers looking back to the late eighteenth century, to the period when Grattan and his contemporaries felt able to assert their identity with their fellow-Irish in an imprecise rhetoric steeped in romantic nationalism. It was not until the 1920s that a scholar of any substance in Daniel Corkery argued for the persistence of a superior Gaelic tradition into the eighteenth century and dismissed the Parliament of that time as 'a noisy sideshow'.[31]

After the events of 1916-22 there seems to have been even less incentive for historians to re-examine the Anglo-Irish. Possibly this was partly due to the myth - still prevalent when I began to work in the field in the mid-1950s - that much valuable archival material had been destroyed during the Troubles, so that few sources could be added to the State papers which Lecky had already worked over so magisterially. Possibly the prevailing temper of the ruling authorities in both Dublin and Belfast made it more comfortable for historians to work within existing orthodoxies rather than to disturb the past with revaluations. Perhaps reflecting a post-1918 growth in awareness of the problems of colonialism, a number of writers glanced at a comparison between eighteenth-century Ireland and the slave economies of America and the West Indies. A standard text published in 1921 asserted: 'The Protestants developed the vices of slave-owners, becoming idle, dissipated, and neglectful of their duties. The Catholic population grew, as a serf population always does grow, cringing, shifty, untruthful.'[32] The implications of such a comparison were nowhere deeply explored.

It was not until 1944 that a perceptibly fresh eye was turned on eighteenth-century Ireland, when R. B. McDowell initiated his long and productive career with the publication of *Irish Public Opinion 1750-1800*. [33] This would have been a notable piece of work if it had done no more than indicate the potential of contemporary newspapers as source material. It also marked the first serious attempt to cut the Ascendancy loose from the old stereotypes, and to show the ruling elite of the eighteenth century interacting with a background of literate public opinion and engaged actively and consistently in the reconciliation of conflicting interest-groups, all of them responsive to the prevailing currents of European political thought.

One might have expected an increase in Marxist interpretations of Irish history, but they were few. From between the wars, I have found only an essay by Elinor Burns[34] arguing that because landowners in Ireland were the garrison of a foreign ruling class who were also hindering the growth of an Irish bourgeoisie, the nationalist movement from the late eighteenth to the middle of the nineteenth century could be seen as an alliance between the bourgeoisie and the peasantry; which was all very well as a hypothesis but required a definition of the bourgeoisie elastic enough to include Wolfe Tone, Lord Edward Fitzgerald, Henry Grattan, Robert Emmet and Daniel O'Connell. In 1947 T. A. Jackson in *Ireland Her Own* used the language of class, but almost entirely to belittle the religious factor in Irish nationalism. Class solidarity, he wrote, led Protestant landowners to collaborate with their Catholic neighbours 'in evading all the more offensive personal restrictions of the Castle';[35] and he added à *propos* Grattan's Parliament, 'The champions of the "colony" against the English government no more thought of themselves as "Gaels" when they called themselves "Irish" than Benjamin Franklin or George Washington identified themselves with the Sioux or the Iroquois when they called themselves "Americans".'[36]

Jackson's anti-Catholic populism had few followers in later historiography. A more substantial picture of Ireland as the colonial economic satellite of metropolitan England was presented in 1951 by Erich Strauss.[37] Strauss was subsequently to write a useful and perceptive biography of Sir William Petty, but his earlier book took the Marxist argument no further than the old master himself had got in the 1860s, and the Ascendancy gentry were seen mainly as an ineffective *rentier* class succumbing to the more dynamic purposes of English industrial capitalism. The book seems to have had singularly little impact: I can find no review of it in *Irish Historical Studies*, the *Times Literary Supplement*, the *New Statesman and Nation*, the *English Historical Review* or *History*; and the *American Historical Review* dismissed it with a perfunctory sneer at its Marxist bias. (It was, after all, the heyday of Senator McCarthy.)

Greater attention greeted the appearance in 1952 of the first volume of Vincent Harlow's *Founding of the Second British Empire*. [38] This sprawling but seminal work – 'almost a masterpiece' as Richard Pares described it – explored the interaction of English and Irish political and economic policy in the late eighteenth century in greater detail than any writer since Lecky. Harlow's thesis sought to show how at the time of the American Revolution British colonial policy was shifting from the possession of colonies as tied sources of primary produce and markets for British exports. Instead a looser pattern of trade was preferred, based on sea power and the possession of strategic entrepots. Seen in that light, Britain's bestowal of greater economic and political autonomy on Ireland was not simply a concession wrested in the heat of the American Revolution, but part of a longer-term shift in strategy; and it was no coincidence that Harlow's hero was the Earl of Shelburne, County Kerry landowner as well as British Minister. In turn, Harlow's approach stressed the role of the Anglo-Irish as ruling colonial minority, both as constructive architects of Irish economic growth, but also as reactionary opponents of the Irish masses whose pretensions were growing partly in consequence of this economic growth.

A few years later in 1957 Richard Koebner was to analyse successive editions of Grattan's speeches to see how his concept of Irish nationality was modified between 1780 and after 1800. Where his earlier speeches demanded Ireland's autonomy as a political kingdom his revised versions placed that autonomy in subordination to the wider interests of the British Empire - one is almost tempted to say of a British Commonwealth of Nations.[39] This may mean that Grattan was reflecting a shift in the attitude of his generation of Anglo-Irish, but it may also reflect the altered, but still optimistic view which historians in the 1950s shared about the adaptability of the British Empire.

This view of Ireland as one of a number of case-histories in a pluralistic British Commonwealth of Nations made for a cooler and more dispassionate attitude in studies of eighteenth-century Irish politics and administration published during the 1960s. E. M. Johnston and G. C. Bolton showed how English forms and institutions were adapted to the needs of the late eighteenth-century Irish polity.[40] A little later F. G. James produced a study of the neglected first half of the eighteenth century, integrating Ireland in the 'Atlantic Civilisation', and particularly with the contemporary growth of constitutional and commercial practice in North America and the West Indies.[41] Meanwhile L. M. Cullen's seminal studies of Irish trade and economy in the eighteenth century placed the Anglo-Irish in a fresh perspective by showing them as part of a network of economic relationships far more subtle and complex than the classic picture of a simple exploitative *rentier* class.[42]

Debate on the Irish past was sharpened as the Ulster situation deteriorated after 1968. Religion was found to be as intractably powerful as ever in provoking Irishmen to kill and maim other Irishmen. L. J. McCaffrey in 1968, while claiming that 'the Irish played a role in British history from 1800 to 1922 similar to that of the Negro in American history', also stressed that 'In Ireland religion symbolised all the interests that distinguished a defensive, parasitic aristocracy from the ambitious and aggressive peasant masses.'[43] Patrick O'Farrell in 1971 went further in suggesting that most historians risked over-emphasising political and economic factors in Irish conflict to the detriment of the religious component. He knocked away a central prop of the Lecky tradition:

> Lecky makes the error, typically English in its politicality and its nineteenth-century assumptions, that the significance of religion in the Irish situation was that it marked the class barrier between democracy (or rather rabble) and gentry . . .[44]

Nor was O'Farrell much impressed with the historic role of the Anglo-Irish, whom he characterised as:

> . . . an intermediate group, neither Irish nor English. (The negative catches this situation better than the positive form - *both* Irish and English.) This group was not of a normal colonial type. Its American equivalents had strong popular support, its Indian equivalents had close ties to the mother country. The Old English, or Anglo-Irish were alien to both populace and mother country, and were distrusted by both. Lacking secure roots in either its old country or its new, this group tended towards restlessness and irresponsibility.[45]

It is only at this final dismissive phrase that doubts stir. 'Restlessness and irresponsibility' are hardly verdicts that one would apply to John Beresford or John Foster. They are however proper epithets for the hard-riding, hard-drinking, debt-ridden squireens described by Jonah Barrington. Their retention by one of the ablest contemporary historians is a salutary reminder of how the Protestant Ascendancy appeared from the Catholic underside.

A different verdict on the Anglo-Irish was given by J. C. Beckett in 1976.[46] Beckett's study of the Anglo-Irish tradition was also concerned to repudiate the kind of reverse discrimination which would condemn the Anglo-Irish as less truly Irish than the Gaelic majority, and he placed great stress on their contribution to Irish literature, while conceding their limitations of imagination. But he added a new note in assessing their political role, a note which could only have been struck in the aftermath of the decolonisation of the British Empire. The Anglo-Irish, Beckett argued, made their last and one of their most valuable contributions to Ireland as mediators between the metropolitan Government and the emerging new nation. Seen in this light, the Irish Convention of 1917-18 assumes a new importance as a valiant last-ditch attempt to hold together the Home Rulers and the Ulster Unionists. A small enlightened Anglo-Irish group could be seen as the one faction capable of exercising the necessary mediatory skills; and their lack of success may have been a question of timing rather than inevitability. Beckett concedes that this may be an over-optimistic view, but for a scholar writing after seven dreary years of renewed conflict in Ulster it was understandable that he should cherish this hope:

> But the Anglo-Irish, though now stripped of political influence and dwindling, in all appearance, towards a painless extinction, still survive; and, while they survive, they may even yet be able to make a healing contribution to the tormented politics of their country. Their double experience, of power and the loss of power, has bred in them a wisdom and a breadth of outlook that Ireland needs and cannot find. They stand for comprehension, instead of uniformity; for a frank acceptance of the fact that Ireland and Great Britain have so much in common that total separation can be to the advantage of neither; for a grateful recognition of the debt that Ireland owes to the cultural influence of England.[47]

This concept of the benign influence of a former ruling caste surviving the loss of effective power has its precedents in the recent history of the British Empire: the English-born Cabinet Ministers who stayed on in East Africa after independence; perhaps even in Australia the widespread belief that the judiciary, the professions, and the academic world are enhanced by some surviving vestiges of British tradition. In the context of the current situation in Northern Ireland, it may be over-hopeful to expect that all would acknowledge a debt to the cultural influence of England; but it is a not ignoble aspiration.

At all events, Beckett's influence is evident in the work of those who have followed him in regarding the Anglo-Irish as a fit topic for historical revision. Among his graduate students Patrick Buckland in 1972 developed the theme of the Anglo-Irish as achieving their moment of greatest political self-consciousness not in the eighteenth century but in the rearguard action of the southern Unionists between 1885 and 1921.[48] Buckland took a less optimistic view of the outcome of those years, considering that they ended with a disappointing but understandable abdication of political responsibilities by the Anglo-Irish, and reversion to 'localism and apathy'. W. B. Yeats's memorable speech in the Senate in 1925 - 'We are no petty people. We are one of the great stocks of Europe' - can be seen as the last blaze of the Anglo-Irish flame before political extinction.

A similar portrait of the Anglo-Irish as rearguard, this time in the eighteenth century, was given by another of Beckett's school, Anthony Malcolmson's *John Foster: the Politics of the Anglo-Irish Ascendancy*.[49] Part of this book is simply a detailed study of the techniques by which a prominent Ascendancy family built up a local following in its county, and part looks at Foster's contribution to Irish economic policy, but there is also a strongly recurrent theme about the role of the Anglo-Irish. Malcolmson sees them as united in a loveless marriage of convenience with the British Government, and Foster as a beleaguered partisan of his class fighting a delaying action against the twin threats of Catholic populism and a sell-out by Westminster. It is difficult not to sense a parallel with the garrison mentality of the Stormont politicians of the 1970s, though Malcolmson is too good a historian to force the parallel explicitly. Instead he contents himself with observing that:

> The really important distinction between the politics of the Anglo-Irish Ascendancy and contemporary British politics was the difference in the intensity of conviction which such major matters of policy and principle [as parliamentary reform and Catholic Emancipation] evoked.[50]

Perhaps his most revealing hint about the isolation of the Anglo-Irish is contained in an almost throwaway comment about Foster's performance as a politician after the Union at Westminster:

> . . . his aggressive (and audible) provincialism remained - Wilberforce, who had met him before the Union, called him 'Mr *Spaker*', and Chief Secretary Wickham commented in 1802 that the British Opposition had been 'more astonished at the strength of Mr Foster's brogue than convinced by his arguments'.[51]

Their very accents fated the Protestant Ascendancy to be classified irrevocably as Irish.

Perhaps the time has now come when the role of the Anglo-Irish is a question which needs no further attention as such. Historians such as Beckett, James and Malcolmson have given a sufficiently ample picture of the Anglo-Irish in action during the eighteenth century to eradicate at last the picturesque caricatures bequeathed by Jonah Barrington. Professor MacDonagh's work on the administrative machinery of Ireland in the late eighteenth and early nineteenth centuries is not only likely to establish the case for Ireland's ruling class as competent and constructive administrators; it may also show them as pioneers in many of the techniques of administration, notably in the use of the State as entrepreneur, which would later be adapted for use in Canada and Australasia. Professor McDowell's *magnum opus* on late eighteenth-century Ireland published in 1979 is remarkable for its capacity to present a many-sided picture of Irish political and social history without lapsing into any of the old stereotypes of Irish historiography.[52] In his Ford lectures for 1978, Professor Lyons has similarly integrated the Anglo-Irish culture of the nineteenth century into the wider theme of dissolving patterns of European order and hierarchy.[53] Both works show qualities of objectivity and span which perhaps could only be approached after the passing of the Anglo-Irish. Both are a felicitous testimony to the continuing durability of that pivot of Anglo-Irish culture, Trinity College, Dublin.

NOTES

1. J. C. Beckett, *The Anglo-Irish Tradition* (London, 1975) p. 10.
2. A. P. W. Malcolmson, *John Foster: the Politics of the Anglo-Irish Ascendancy* (Oxford, 1978) p. 352.
3. The term 'Anglo-Irish' failed to gain admission to the twelve-volume *Oxford English Dictionary* and has to be sought in the *Supplement* of 1972. Professor Beckett informs me that the term may be found in a late mediaeval Latin source.
4. Beckett, *The Anglo-Irish Tradition*, p. 10.
5. H. Grattan, *Memoirs of the Life and Times of Rt Hon Henry Grattan, by his Son* (London, 1839-46) 5 vols.
6. J. Barrington, *Personal Sketches of his Own Times*, vol. i (London, 1827) pp. 5-6.
7. J. Barrington, *The Rise and Fall of the Irish Nation* (London, 1833) p. 20.
8. W. B. Yeats, *Collected Poems*, 2nd edn (London, 1950) pp. 218-225. 'The Tower' was written about the time of Yeats's notable speech in the Senate of the Irish Free State in defence of the Anglo-Irish. See note 48.
9. Friedrich Engels to Karl Marx, 23 May 1856, in K. Marx and F. Engels, *Ireland and the Irish Question* (Moscow,

1971) p. 85. See also N. Mansergh, *The Irish Question 1840-1921* (London, 1965) ch. iii.
10. Marx and Engels, *Ireland and the Irish Question*, pp. 140-1.
11. Ibid., pp. 126-39.
12. D. McGee, *History of Ireland* (Glasgow, 1868) vol. ii, p. 210.
13. J. Mitchel, *History of Ireland from the Treaty of Limerick to the Present Time* (Glasgow, 1869) p. 29.
14. Ibid., p. 177.
15. J. A. Froude, *The English in Ireland* (New York, 1873) vol. i, p. 21.
16. Ibid., p. 280.
17. W. H. Dunn, *James Anthony Froude: a Biography 1857-1894* (Oxford, 1963) p. 295.
18. J. A. Froude, *Oceana*, Silver Library edn (London, 1898) p. 335.
19. Froude, *The English in Ireland*, vol. i, p. 513.
20. Ibid., vol. ii, p. 197.
21. Ibid., vol. ii, p. 391.
22. Ibid., vol. iii, p. 469.
23. H. Paul, *The Life of Froude* (London, 1905) p. 241.
24. D. McCartney, 'Lecky's Leaders of Public Opinion in Ireland', *Irish Historical Studies*, vol. xiv (1964) pp. 119-41. See also J. J. Auchmuty, *Lecky* (Dublin, 1945).
25. W. E. H. Lecky, *Leaders of Public Opinion in Ireland* (London, 1903) pp. xiii-xiv.
26. R. B. O'Brien, *Two Centuries of Irish History* (Dublin, 1888); G. Sigerson, *The Last Independent Parliament of Ireland* (Dublin, 1918); G. A. T. O'Brien, *Economic History of Ireland in the Eighteenth Century* (Dublin and London, 1918).
27. J. G. S. MacNeill, *The Constitutional and Parliamentary History of Ireland till the Union* (London, 1917): see also *Titled Corruption* (London, 1894).
28. A. S. Green, *The Making of Ireland and its Undoing 1200-1600* (London, 1908). I am indebted to Professor Patrick O'Farrell for this point.
29. J. A. Knowles, OSA, 'What the Irish have done for Australia', *New Ireland Review*, vol. xx (1903) pp. 169-82; H. Heinrick, *The Irish in England and Scotland* (Dublin, 1904); E. O'Donnell, *The Irish Abroad: a Record of the Achievements of Wanderers from Ireland* (London, 1915) especially ch. xiv.
30. Beckett, *The Anglo-Irish Tradition*, pp. 140-1.
31. D. Corkery, *The Hidden Ireland* (Cork, 1925); *Synge and Anglo-Irish Literature* (Cork, 1931).

32. M. Hayden and G. Moonen, *Short History of the Irish People* (Dublin, 1921); quoted in T. A. Jackson, *Ireland Her Own* (London, 1947) pp. 68-9. Another example may be found in P. Guedella, *The Duke* (London, 1931) pp. 1-4.
33. R. B. McDowell, *Irish Public Opinion 1750-1800* (London, 1944).
34. E. Burns, *British Imperialism in Ireland* (Dublin, 1931) p. 10.
35. Jackson, *Ireland Her Own*, pp. 68-9.
36. Ibid., pp. 82-3.
37. E. Strauss, *Irish Nationalism and English Democracy* (London, 1951).
38. V.T. Harlow, *The Founding of the Second British Empire*, vol. i (London, 1952).
39. R. Koebner, 'The Early Speeches of Henry Grattan', *Bulletin of the Institute of Historical Research*, vol. xxx (1957) pp. 102-14; *Empire* (Cambridge, 1961) ch. vi.
40. E. M. Johnston, *Great Britain and Ireland, 1760-1800* (Edinburgh, 1963); G. C. Bolton, *The Passing of the Irish Act of Union* (Oxford, 1966).
41. F. G. James, *Ireland in the Empire* (Cambridge, Mass., 1973) p. 312.
42. L. M. Cullen, *An Economic History of Ireland Since 1660* (London, 1972); 'Irish Economic History: Fact and Myth', in L.M. Cullen (ed.), *The Formation of the Irish Economy* (Cork, 1969); 'Problems in the Interpretation and Revision of 18th Century Irish History', *Transactions of the Royal Historical Society*, ser. v, vol. xvii (1967) pp. 1-22.
43. L. J. McCaffrey, *The Irish Question, 1800-1922* (Lexington, 1968) p. 7 and p. 2.
44. P. O'Farrell, *Ireland's English Question: Anglo-Irish Relations 1534-1970* (London, 1971) pp. 63-4.
45. Ibid., p. 17.
46. Beckett, *The Anglo-Irish Tradition*.
47. Ibid., pp. 152-3.
48. P. Buckland, *The Anglo-Irish and the New Ireland* (Dublin, 1972) p. 300. See also F. S. L. Lyons, 'the Minority Problem in the 26 Counties', in F. MacManus, *The Years of the Great Test, 1926-39* (Cork, 1967) pp. 92-103.
49. Malcolmson, *John Foster*.
50. Ibid., p. xxiii.
51. Ibid., p. 432.
52. R. B. McDowell, *Ireland in the Age of Imperialism and Revolution, 1760-1801* (Oxford, 1979).
53. F. S. L. Lyons, *Culture and Anarchy in Ireland 1890-1939* (Oxford, 1979) especially chs. 2-3.

16 Poetry and the Avoidance of Nationalism

VINCENT BUCKLEY

The 'nationalism' of my title is an all-Ireland nationalism: not necessarily conterminous with the republican separatist nationalism of Wolfe Tone and of his varied descendants, but certainly including it as a centre of power exerting a strong inward pull. Nor do I intend the definition to be a merely political one, or to be equated with the stated (or supposed) policies of any group or party: it is enough that it be a strong emotional disposition, or habit of mind, or social or political intention.

At the same time, it would be merely confusing and self-defeating to try to oversee all the other viewpoints which have been from time to time offered as versions of nationalism within Ireland, if not precisely Irish nationalism: I mean British imperialism, Ulster Ascendancy loyalism, Paisleyism, and so on; I also mean restrictive Gaelic nationalism, and Catholic nationalism.

Now, an all-Ireland nationalism, of whatever sort, takes form and support in an Ireland which is not united, whose disunity is enforced by acts of a parliament which is not Irish, and in which various efforts have been and are being made to bring about unity. A poetry of nationalist feeling, if it existed, would have some relation to those facts, and would in some sense push against this state of affairs. It might include some protest against institutions devised to prevent the desired Ireland from coming into being, some protest against the particular injustices created by the regime, a sense of some groups as persecuted, and perhaps even some interest in and sense of particular acts of heroism in military, political or cultural operations conducted against the regime. It would not need to be jingoistic poetry, or factional poetry, or republican manifestoes in verse; personally I have no interest in any of those kinds.

I assume that we cannot expect any poet to project his view of the present into the future in such a way as to delineate solutions to intractable problems. We might, however, expect more realism and less impressionism than we are accustomed to getting at the moment. We might also be surprised at the lack of 'protest', or of what I might call an adversary note, in the poetry. I do not demand, desiderate, or even request it; but I am surprised at its relative absence.

There is no doubt that myths of nationality and of struggle still live in the Irish psyche; and it is natural to assume that they will exist also in poetry, which is the most myth-saturated of all the artistic forms. The assumption would be that (a) poets continue to be stimulated, motivated by such myths, (b) they respond to the stimulus by adopting extreme nationalist positions in their poetry, and (c) even where this response is not overt, it may still be polemical and full of hostilities. As to (c), covert responses are hard to detect, and nothing can be built on them, although Conor Cruise O'Brien and others try to build something very damaging on a few lines by Seamus Heaney. As to the other two stages of assumption, if for example there were evidence for (a) but not for (b), we should then be faced with a new problem of definition: we should have to ask why the stimulus was diverted or not responded to. My own view is that there is no evidence for (b), very little for (c), and that whatever evidence there is for (a) would require so much parenthesis in its unravelling as to be almost useless for building a case about Irish poets.

And, especially, *against* them; for there is a seldom stated accusation associated with these assumptions: that the poets have contributed to the violence which nourishes them; insofar as that accusation can gain some currency, either in Irish intellectual circles or in the reading publics of England and North America, it will have the effect of pushing the poets not just away from subjects already taboo, but also from contiguous areas, for example from all questions of mass injustice, or torture, or clandestine military operations. Thus a poet who would never dream of supporting the Provisional IRA is psyched into not writing his poem on Tom Barry, or on SAS technology, or on the psychology of the H-Block prisoners; he is knocked off the ball. Further, the atmosphere thus created is extended to make it seem natural to prohibit large classes of people from commenting on national affairs on the national radio and television. Literary criticism too may be a technique of thought control.

Dr O'Brien makes his influential statement or accusation quite early.[1] The occasion is his review of Heaney's *North*. He cites Heaney's poetically unremarkable lines about a girl who has been tarred and feathered ('Punishment') and comments:

'Betraying' . . . 'exact' . . . 'revenge'. . . . The poet

here appears as part of his people's assumption that, since the girl has been punished by the IRA, she must indeed be guilty: a double assumption - that she did, in fact, inform on the IRA and that informing on the IRA is a crime.

There *is* a double assumption, but it is made not by Heaney but by O'Brien - that Heaney says something he does not say, and that saying it is reprehensible. Heaney's real sin is in saying that he 'would understand' a form of behaviour from which he clearly recoils and to which his attitude cannot fairly be called even ambivalent.

But, then, O'Brien sees Heaney as representing, both instinctively and deliberately, a nationalist bias and preoccupation which place him on one side, and against others, in a defined political conflict. It is not that he is pressing for nationalist *solutions*, but that he is following a nationalist fault line. 'His upbringing and experience have given him some cogent reasons to feel that one side *is* worse than the other, and his poems have to reflect this.'[2] (Notice the note of predetermination or of political will in that 'have'.) So complete is Heaney's identification with the Catholic 'side' that he sees Ulster Protestants as 'inherently hostile and frightening . . . a matter of muzzles, masks and eyes'. He is in fact programmed by history to do this, for whereas 'Yeats was free to try, and did splendidly try, or try on, different relations to the tragedy, Heaney's relation to a deeper tragedy is fixed and pre-ordained.'[3]

I think this an unusually subjective reading of *North*, a volume whose tensions seem to me of a different kind and to come from different sources, as I shall try to illustrate later. What is interesting, as indicating the actual ruling pressures of literary opinion, is what has happened to O'Brien's sharp objection to 'Punishment'; I have seen three further objections to this poem, each quoting its closing lines; clearly many critics are uneasy about their own otherwise easy approval of Heaney. One commentator, Ciaran Carson, echoes O'Brien's suggestion that Heaney is too nationalist, and converts it into the suggestion that he is virtually a propagandist: 'Heaney seems to have moved - unwillingly, perhaps - from being a writer with the gift of precision, to become the laureate of violence - a mythmaker, an anthropologist of ritual killing, an apologist for the situation, in the last resort, a mystifier.'[4] If I am right, there is something hostile and unstable about the critical situation. I shall further argue that a similar hostility and instability apply to the creative situation.

Denis Donoghue may seem to offer support for O'Brien's

views in his lecture 'Now and in Ireland: The Literature of Trouble';[5] but he does not: not entirely. It is in fact possible to read him in two diverging ways; and that is characteristic of almost all the material with which we are dealing. Donoghue stresses that poetry 'has been provoked in one way or another by passionate intensities in the North of Ireland since 1968 . . .', but he knows that the violence goes a lot further back; 'the history of Ireland has been taught, especially in Catholic schools, as a story of national feeling expressing itself in virtually every generation since the eighteenth century as a revolutionary act to drive the English out of Ireland'; and, despite the new and somewhat problematic revisionism in Irish historiography, that version of history lives on.

It seems that here we are getting hints at a cause-effect relationship, in which what is taught in schools *causes* literary responses to violence, and perhaps even the violence itself. Yet, 'in one way or another . . .': well, we may want to ask in a given case, in the case of Kinsella or Heaney for example, *what* way? Donoghue partly mystifies the issue. For he goes on, after an effective reference to Cathleen Ni Houlihan,

> It is well known that much of modern Irish literature has been provoked by violence, and that images of war very soon acquire a symbolic aura in this country. Our traditions are histrionic and oratorical. The themes of Irish literature are few: if we list children, isolation, religion and politics, we come nearly to the end of them. . . .
> It is simple fact that Yeats, O'Casey, and a dozen writers up to Francis Stuart, Brian Friel and Seamus Heaney have been aggravated by Irish politics to the point of turning their aggravation into verse and prose. . . .
> The cult of violence is never far away from Irish feeling. . . .
> But he [Yeats] was afraid that his poetry would stop if conflict stopped within himself; the grappling of opposites kept his art in force. This motive is still active in Irish poetry, but on the whole our poets have been turning their rhymes toward some form of transcendence. Heaney is the most telling poet in this respect, and the success of *North* makes his case exemplary.

Donoghue's article has been widely received as an authoritative claim that Irish poetry in this century is too concerned to celebrate violence, too nationalist in intention, and has been turned that way by a deliberate education policy. He has only himself to blame for this misreading; for he goes some way toward assimilating Heaney to the psychological position which he attributes to Yeats, who was, in any case, not a product of the education policy of which Donoghue is speaking. This assimilation of Heaney to Yeats is a further mistake, in my opinion. In fact, it is only if Yeats's late poetry is your chief evidence that you can make the case about violence mentioned above. For most other Irish poets, the nearness of violence, in the schoolroom, in the streets, in the newspapers, and above all in the imagination, produces a poetry which, far from being positively nationalist, is either opposed to or evasive and ambivalent about any national aims. Further, while it may hold on to conflict, advert to it, even show fascination with it, it hardly ever analyses it or prescribes it.

O'Brien's and Carson's (probably hostile) statement of a view gets some support from the confused or regretful remarks of those who are not *prima facie* hostile to national feeling. So Peter Costello stresses the way in which 'Republican feelings were kept alive in nineteenth-century Ireland' by songs and stories, which were also used for this purpose in his own boyhood, so now 'once again history is repeating itself, and young people are throwing themselves into the madness of a discredited Republicanism, knowing only a history of poses and postures and lies'.[6] He cites Bernadette Devlin's childhood attraction to the poetry of Patrick Pearse;[7] he lists members of the Civil War generation of writers who had 'fought in the Troubles' or had 'written in support of Irish nationalist ideas';[8] and he insists that 'the character of the isolated hero, and the deeds of the outlaw band of fighting men, whether of Cuchulain or Pearse, the Fianna or the IRA, continue to fascinate the Irish imagination, as we shall see in the course of this history of the revolution and the literature it inspired.'[9]

My unscholarly assembling of isolated quotations does, I think, convey the impression that many readers would take from Costello's book: that the impulses active in poetry between 1916 and 1923 are still active, so that the allegiance of much of the poetry of the past four decades is nationalist in the sense that it supports political initiatives. My case is that this is conspicuously not true, and that the citing of Bernadette Devlin's childhood is merely mystifying, so far as poetry is concerned. Further, and I do find this astonishing, no important modern Irish poetry is concerned with 'the character of the isolated hero' or 'the deeds of the outlaw band of fighting men'. I know of no poem for General Tom Barry or for the H-Block prisoners, for example.

These may strike some of you as bizarre suggestions for poetic themes. They are in fact not offered as suggestions at all; my interest at this point is to ask you to re-focus your attention to the actual things which are half-hidden by such abstractions as 'nationalism', 'terrorism', and so on; and I think that, if we can manage this turn in focus sharply enough, we may see what our automatic expectations *are* and that they are not being met. Surely a Martian or an anthropologist, confronted with the Irish poetry of the past decades, would say, 'But where are all the fire-breathing poetic Irish whom we have been told of so often, and against whom Dr O'Brien wants to protect us? Where are the protesters? Where is the generosity of imagination to bring conflicting interests and images together in a dialectic which *may* lead to reconciliation?' The answer is, nowhere. There is no Yeats, no Blake. The latter would have had no hesitation in writing about the H-Block prisoners, had he felt like it.

Such suggestions as Costello's arise in the course of attempts to understand a situation which is complex and puzzling; and there is certainly some preoccupation with violence to be understood. In an attempt to give a diagnosis of 'Ulster terrorism' (within which he does not appear to include Government terrorism) Richard Kearney nominates as his fourth perspective the 'Mythological'.[10] Ulster terrorists are driven by myths, of a sort that associates the motif of periodic recurrence with the motif of bloodsacrifice.

The myths in question are highly literary; they are carried in modern times by Pearse and, for a brief few months, by Yeats ('The Rose Tree'); they are 'histrionic and oratorical' in style; they are probably internalised in the thinking of some present-day IRA and IRSP members, though not, certainly, of all. I doubt if they much affect the thinking of the manifold groups of loyalist terrorists; and I doubt if the SAS has ever heard of them. Still, as Kearney says, they are influential among some contemporary terrorists. They are not influential on poets, who react to them as to a dangerous taboo, and whose motive is not to think that thought.

The poets have passed their own law in the place where it matters — in the instinctive imagination. They will not touch blood-sacrifice, even as a subject. What does fascinate them is death, funerals, detritus and failure. The mode is pretty consistently that of irony or elegy rather than of heroism or romance. Epic and romance stand in the background, almost totally obscured, among the ancient memories to which the irony applies.

It is interesting, quite in parenthesis, that the withdrawal from motifs of mystical heroism occurred also among the poets of 1916, among whom I may perhaps include Francis Ledwidge. It is true also of Thomas MacDonagh. Where Plunkett and Pearse associate their own shedding of blood with the wounds of Christ as well as those of Cuchulain, MacDonagh does not; and Ledwidge's own lament for MacDonagh, and his more general lament, 'The Blackbirds', while they certainly advert to traditional republican motifs, of the Poor Old Woman, and the Dark Cow, are in total effect elegaic lyrics of the gentlest kind:

> But when the Dark Cow leaves the moor,
> And pastures poor with greedy weeds,
> Perhaps he'll hear her low at morn
> Lifting her horn in pleasant meads.
> ('Thomas MacDonagh')
> But in the lonely hush of eve
> Weeping I grieve the silent bills.
> I heard the Poor Old Woman say
> In Derry of the little hills.
> ('The Blackbirds')

It is also worth saying that Pearse's own poetry is not dominated by motifs of blood-sacrifice, but contains also a form of irredentist triumphalism which does not necessarily depend on such motifs. He was not a mere fantasist; he was a soldier, and he was concerned ultimately with victory. So

> And I say to my people's masters: Beware,
> Beware of the thing that is coming, beware
>   of the risen people,
> Who shall take what ye would not give. . . .
> ('The Rebel')

and

> O King that was born
> To set bondsmen free,
> In the coming battle,
> Help the Gael!
>   ('Christmas 1915')

a reasonable enough request at a time when much greater warring forces throughout the world were not only asking that God be on their side, but boasting that He already was. Yet it was not the ideology of 'the risen people' and the embattled Gael that inspired Yeats to his poems of 1916.

POETRY AND THE AVOIDANCE OF NATIONALISM 265

Although he seems at moments to suggest that revolutionary violence is desirable, really his theme is its inevitability. 'The Rose Tree', after all, quotes Pearse and Connolly, not their living followers; and 'Sixteen Dead Men' argues a political case:

> You say that we should still the land
> Till Germany's overcome;
> But who is there to argue that
> Now Pearse is deaf and dumb?
> And is their logic to outweigh
> MacDonagh's bony thumb?

The view is calculating rather than triumphalist; yet it is a nationalist assertion for all that. Like the note of Pearse's poetry, it is never struck again.

If we focus on the events of the past twelve years, we may think that poets have been shocked or anaesthetised into evasiveness by the sheer violence and uncertainty of the situation. Yet it is true that they were just as equivocal or unforthcoming for most of the previous four decades. This is not because the Irish muse, being lyrical, does not take to rougher diet, or because there were not crises worthy of a vigorous pen. To take the second point, there was the complex crisis of the 1930s, the 'emergency' of the war years, the republican campaign of 1956-62, the beginning of which coincided with a massive movement of unemployed. None of these was subjected to poetic treatment of any quality. Nor were the events of 1966, the year of the celebrations of Easter 1916, with *Mise Eire*, TV reconstructions of the Rising, a splendid revival of traditional music, and of course, the extremist backlash in the north, with Paisley's campaigns and the Malvern Street murders. None of this produced any creative commentary in poetry of a sort which might be held to advance present nationalist aspirations.

Still on this point, it might be thought that this, a century of extreme subjectivity, is not a century for political poetry. But the facts show otherwise; it is. Those very decades saw much pressure on poets to write protest poetry. Understandably, Vietnam was a great subject for Australian poets, as for American. But before that there had been the spate of poems in English on the Hungarian rising and its aftermath; after it there were the poems on Biafra and Bangla Desh; now there is a spate of poems on whales and dolphins. I do not mock this; I have written in three of these causes. The point I make is that it is conventional, it is expected, to protest and to affirm there; it is conventional, expected, not to protest or to affirm in the matter of Ireland. And if, going to the sources, one looks at the 1950s anthologies of Hungarian and Polish poetry, one sees that there they not only spoke, they were of one mind. The Irish poets marched at Newry after Bloody Sunday; but only Thomas Kinsella and Seamus Deane wrote of the massacre. One might suspect a pressure in the intellectual environment *against* involvement, that is, in tacit support of the *status quo ante* or whatever is left of it.

As to the first of my two points, it should not be thought that the Irish muse is lyrical and disinclined for asperity. Satirical and polemical attitudes are often struck, and quite specific targets often nominated. This is true of Kavanagh's 'The Great Hunger' as well as several of his shorter poems, of the greater part of Clarke's later poetry, and even of Kinsella at more than one stage of his development. Lesser poets are insistently, not to say obtrusively, sardonic in their view of the world, which is to say, of the society closest to hand. But in all cases their attack is on the state of social conscience, hypocrisy in public life, the oppressive nature of Catholic regulations and mores, and certain social and psychological workings in the life of the countryman. In some cases, there is a hint that the disillusionment encompasses a disappointment in the failure of revolutionary idealism (of 'the national ideal'), but this is seldom made a primary theme. We are justified in taking the implication that there is belief in the viability of republican policies. Consider the striking case of Clarke:

> *The Trial of Robert Emmet*
> *to be re-enacted*
> *at Green Street Courthouse*
> *for An Tostal, 1956*

Sentence the lot and hurry them away,
The court must now be cleared, batten and spot
Swung up with rope and ladder, lighting-plot
Rehearsed. No need of drop-scene for the play
To-night: bench, box and bar in well-mixed ray
Make do. Though countless miscreants have got
A life-term here, and some, the scaffold knot,
Forget the cells our safety fills by day.
See British greed and tyranny defied
Once more by that freethinker in the dock
And sigh because his epitaph remains
Unwritten. Cheer revolution by the clock
And lastly – badge and holy medal guide
Your cars home, hooting through our dirtiest lanes.

It is a method of attack that replicates something of the spirit of the middle Yeats, and Paudeen is again the target; but Clarke has advanced historically beyond the perspective of Yeats. For him, the revolutionary gesture, once made, is negated by the celebratory uses to which the forces of respectability put it. The implication is that the national ideal has been irretrievably sabotaged, by its champions.

We may compare this bitter treatment with the more openly romantic nostalgia of Padraic Fallon:

The Young Fenians

They looked so good;
They were the coloured lithographs
Of Murat, Bernadotte and Ney
And the little Corsican.
Mars had made them from our dead
And given to each his martial head . . .

Flags flew from our every word;
The new names rang from litanies,
Saviours each one;
They were the eagles in the morning sun;
A country rising from its knees
To upset all the histories.

Fallon's political intention may be obscure. But these are Fenians, the quintessential national revolutionaries. In his approach to them Fallon, also reliant on Yeats, is more concerned with romantic gesture, movement and appearance than with present political possibilities – or betrayals. And whereas his poem is eloquent, what has it to do, really, with the savage endurance of the Fenian leaders, or of their latter-day followers?

The whole question of active nationalism, inside and outside poetry, revives of course in the post-Lemass years, of which those from 1968 to the present are the most anguished. Prose reflections on Irishness, non-Irishness, and dual-Irishness, are endless, and so is the market for them. They have their equivalents in poetry; but of most of these I would agree with the poet James Liddy:

An effect of a decade's cycle of violence in Ulster has been an undermining of Yeats' nationalist assumptions. . . . Southern Irish poets are now in turn becoming counter-analytic, editing and sometimes censoring this cultural tradition.[11]

Much of the emotional turmoil has to do not with identity (who we are) but with self-specification (what to say of ourselves). This anguish about the audience gets even into the anthology *The Wearing of the Black*, edited by Padraic Fiacc, from which some of the misreadings of recent Irish poetry are derived. Fiacc's own poetry shows a fascination with violence, and so does much in his anthology. At the same time, implicit in the blood-glisten is the question how all this will appear to others, and how we poets will appear in the midst of it. A peculiar engrossed self-consciousness is the mode, and in part the subject.

In Fiacc, this self-consciousness amounts to bitterness; in John Montague it amounts to a desire to put together, whatever the labour, the sections of the ancestral life that have been divided up by history as well as by oppression. This has been his task the whole of his writing life. He situates the present (conceived not as event but as landscape) in the context of personal past, family past, the middle past of (the usurper's) history, and the antique past of prehistory. Fragments, items of all these pasts run together to form a new *gestalt* - which is to say, a new poem - sequence - and then move apart, to form different combinations. Montague's aim is compositional, his mode frequently elegaic; but he does not arrange his world so as to achieve a polemical effect. His political views, whatever they may be, are not present as a forming motive in the poetry. What he achieves is indicated with great poignancy by one of his own titles, 'Like Dolmens Round My Childhood The Old People'. Poetically speaking, *those* are his politics.

Or half of them; for his most substantial work *The Rough Field*, is concerned to bring the usurped land of the sixteenth century into close touch with the despoiled land of the present. In this, he passes initially through a Belfast where a more immediate politics rule, and in which it must have been tempting for him to release his own counter-aggressions. But he does not. He is travelling home; and home is County Tyrone, O'Neill country, where he will set himself for the rest of the long sequence to recover the feel of his family as a whole, of its individual members, of its neighbours (those human dolmens), and of the 'lost tradition' of Gaeldom.

There is a wealth of reference in this poetry; and at every point we are aware of the pressure of the present on it; as of the pressure of the past into the present. Yet Montague is writing laterally, as it were. The most moving section is perhaps *The Fault*, which has to do with his dead father, 'a Northern Republican', who was

> right to choose a Brooklyn slum
> rather than a half-life in this
> by-passed and dying place,

though Montague recognises the likeness between father and son:

> When I am angry, sick or tired
> A line on my forehead pulses,
> The line on my left temple
> Opened by an old car accident.
> My father had the same scar
> In the same place, as if
> The same fault ran through
> Us both; anger, impatience,
> A stress born of violence.

It is not until the section, *A New Siege*, dedicated to Bernadette Devlin, that the violence of the present is confronted. The author calls it 'an historical meditation', but its method is filmic, a kind of staccato documentary. Such a mode is often chosen for poetry that deals with armed conflict. It lends itself to partiality and propaganda, because it is so easily able to direct the reader's (the viewer's) attention to item on item whose importance is presumed, and does not have to be argued for.

Montague's treatment is scrupulously melancholy, and attains a balance by sheer tone. This is set by the opening lines

> Once again, it happens;
> like an old Troubles film
> run for the last time.

One is conscious of care in the assembling of fragments, so that, except in the case of his own family, the poet does not have to commit himself to a note of personally felt protest or to any hint of policy. Whenever injustice comes in sight, the tone becomes impersonally lamenting. I feel this is deliberate policy; and Montague's well-known habit of re-writing and re-assembling strengthens this sense.

Heaney is a fascinating case; he is not really a republican, nor a political poet; and the poems, from *North* onward, in which he has dealt with the killing politics of the six counties owe more to Robert Lowell than to Patrick Pearse. His own self-descriptions make this clear. In an unpublished interview with Helen O'Shea he acknowledges a debt to Corkery and to John Montague for his awareness of 'a Gaelic hinterland', but goes on to say that 'my people, if I can use that proud, biblical phrase, had very little conscious sense of Gaelic tradition, and what was important to them, certainly, was the ritual of the Catholic Church. Mind you, there was strong resistance to the Unionist and the British presence and 'hegemony', as they would say. But that was more old-style Nationalist, than it was pure early Gaelic.' 'Old-style Nationalist'; that is, not republican or irredentist. He confesses then that he wanted the good opinion of the English literary world, and adds:

> Now, often I'm tempted to write a brutally simple thing, 'Troops Out!' or 'H Block', you know: 'Give them political status!' And you could write that with some force, and it would have some force as a writing, because of the context out of which it springs. But I think that it would, might, disable the overall drift of your work, finally, and it might disable you, too: it might disable me.[12]

And so he does not do it. Although he sometimes 'puts the prejudices and Catholic resentments to work', he does so with some obliquity. The poetic facts bear out the self-image he presents in the interview. For example, neither of his first two books concerns itself with northern injustice or violence at all; his third volume, *Wintering Out*, is chiefly devoted to other themes, although it was published in 1972, four years after the first police assaults in Derry. Only one poem, 'The Other Side', seems to demand comment in political terms, for the more interesting 'Tollund Man' is quite abstract, if shocking, in its references to political violence. 'The Other Side' is about neighbourliness between rural Catholics and Protestants; the tone is affectionate and aggravated; the motto might be Robert Frost's 'Good fences make good neighbours'. This landscape has no fences but foreignness. The Protestant farmer neighbour, amusingly sententious and hence foreign, indeed a little challenging about Catholicism, is in fact a lonely man. Heaney stresses this, yet stresses also a certain sterility in his mental world.

> His brain was a whitewashed kitchen
> hung with texts, swept tidy
> as the body o' the kirk.
>
> Then sometimes when the rosary was dragging
> mournfully on in the kitchen
> we would hear his step round the gable

> though not until after the litany
> would the knock come to the door
> and the casual whistle strike up
>
> on the doorstep. 'A right-looking night,'
> he might say, 'I was dandering by
> and says I, I might as well call.'

But this is in no way political, and it is Heaney's Catholicism, not his nationalism, however old-style, that is in play.

In *North* (1975), the case becomes far too complicated to deal with here. I shall merely cite examples. 'Funeral Rites' presents images of that central Irish social occasion, simply remarking

> Now as news comes in
> of each neighbourly murder
> we pine for ceremony,
> customary rhythms:

The much-maligned 'Punishment' in fact lays irony on irony, very conscious of its own procedures. The sentence which so inflamed Dr O'Brien is in fact balanced beautifully across the poem with another sentence about a long dead girl killed in a pagan ritual: so we have

> Little adulteress

to balance

> your betraying sisters

and Heaney makes the same judgment about his own voyeurism in relation to the old and to the new atrocity:

> My poor scapegoat,
>
> I almost love you
> but would have cast, I know,
> the stones of silence.

If he can say that to the ancient girl sacrifice, he is even more driven to accuse himself of weakness in the later case

> I who stood dumb
> when your betraying sisters,
> cauled in tar,

wept by the railings,

who would connive
in civilized outrage
yet understand the exact
and tribal, intimate revenge.

The point is not their 'betraying' (whatever that was), but his dumbness.

A third poem, 'Ocean's Love To Ireland', is both political and evasive. It makes contorted and unclear reference to Raleigh's complicity in the infamous massacre at Smerwick in 1580; yet the tropes are self-consciously joky, and the poem has little relevance to present discontents. 'Act of Union' is even more posed, although the nationalist resentment briefly shows through.

The 'politics', however, are almost entirely in Part II, in 'Whatever You Say, Say Nothing', and 'Singing School'. They are, to be blunt, the politics not of a freedom fighter but of a participant commentator: a little reminiscent of Norman Mailer, as well as Lowell. The main drive is towards commentary, and the poet as speaker is placed into the poem chiefly in the commentator role. Mostly, his cry is 'I am the man, I suffered, I was *not* exactly there'. Savage comment is directed not just at the intrusive journalists but at the group or caste that Heaney actually represents, the socially mobile northern Catholics: 'We're on the make / As ever' '. . . fork-tongued on the border bit', 'The liberal papist note sounds hollow . . .', 'Sanctioned, old, elaborate retorts'.

There is passion in 'Whatever You Say, Say Nothing', and a desire that the log-jam of the authoritarian, suspicious, manipulative State be broken. But there is no intention to take part in that process; and a large part of the passion in this honest, clumsy, representative poem comes from self-distrust, and works in self-accusation. By comparison, 'Singing School' is varied and good-humoured, if with an underlying desperation.

The desperation has to do with roles chosen, declined, threatening and involuntary. He writes of what he did not choose (his national and religious identity) and of what he cannot now choose (a creative political participation in the agony of his people). There is a splendid vignette of repressive power in 'A Constable Calls', the standard image of 'Orange Drums' in the poem of that name, and various examples of authority misused or politics as brute force. Yet the basis of the sequence is a self-pondering, in which Heaney, however representative his background, is seen not as a representative but as an impotently solitary figure:

> While the Constabulary covered the mob
> Firing into the Falls, I was suffering
> Only the bullying sun of Madrid. . . .
>
> 'Go back,' one said, 'try to touch the people.'
> Another conjured Lorca from his hill.
> We sat through death counts and bullfight reports
> On the television, celebrities
> Arrived from where the real thing still happened.
>
> I retreated to the cool of the Prado.
> Goya's 'Shootings of the Third of May'
> Covered a wall . . .
> ('Summer 1969')

And, later, retired further from Belfast, to life in Wicklow,

>   a wood-kerne,
> Escaped from the massacre,
> Taking protective colouring
> From bole and bark, feeling
> Every wind that blows,

he sits or wanders, asking himself about the nature of

> My responsible *tristia*.
> For what? For the ear? For the people?
> For what is said behind-backs?

'Neither internee nor informer', he is now 'an inner emigre'.

This highly intelligent self-focussing certainly concerns a political situation, but it refracts that through the prism of a constantly turning self which, in the process, becomes the central subject. It also, of course, presents the political situation, to which the speaker is palpitatingly responsive. Part of his awareness, however, is that he is not, and never can be, politically committed; he is doomed to be an outsider to the agony and the disorder which engage his guilt, but not his action. In one sense it is political poetry, in that it exposes fragments of a political reality; and the viewpoint from which he does so is, I suppose, nationalist. In another sense, it is apolitical, anti-political poetry, because its centre of attention is a self whose own burden is that it finds political action impossible; further, it implicitly counsels this finding as the one that most clearly fits the facts.

In the light of all that, the judgement that Heaney is a propagandist is preposterous, and is calculated to increase his guilt and self-consciousness to no creative purpose whatever. It could, of course, affect his sense of the attitudes available to and proper for him. I hope it fails to do that.

Seamus Deane's politics are well known, for he is in a sense a public intellectual as well as a poet, often called on for analysis of the Irish situation. His provenance, as a man of republican and working class background, is also no secret. Like Kinsella, he responded openly to the shootings of Bloody Sunday. His poem appears as number six in a sequence of *Fourteen Elegies*. It has that curious abstractness and indirectness of emotion which are so common in Irish poetry, and which sort so oddly with an emphasis on the epiphanic image. Not until near the end of the poem is a note of personal terror struck, and then it is no note of protest, exactly:

> Let us bury the corpses.
> Fast. Death is our future
>
> And now is our past.
> There are new children
> In the gaunt houses.
> Their eyes are fused.
> Youth has gone out
> Like a light. Only the insects
> Grovel for life, their strange heads
> Twitching. No one kills them
> Anymore. This is the honeymoon
> Of the cockroach, the small
> Spiderless eternity of the fly.

In this 'elegy', by far the most particularised and gripping lines are those on the insects.

In a sense, Deane, as a highly sensitive native of Derry city, is at a stage beyond protest; for him, street warfare is nightmare and conflagration, not spectacle; the first observable violence is that done to the unemployed and the exploited. Military conflict is, from one point of view, a war superimposed upon a war. Work wrong and death from violence belong to the one order of reality. Thus, I feel that his finest poems on the north are those written on the death of his father, poems which are ostensibly not about politics at all. In such poems the personal is not merely the focus for, it is the summation of, the general fate; and injustice is so much assumed that it is unnecessary to make much of it. Loss and nightmare are another matter. I would expect them to remain a permanent part of Deane's poetic consciousness.

Thomas Kinsella's place in the pattern goes back beyond anyone else's, except perhaps Montague's. By no means a political poet in any usual sense, and lacking most of the time in any nationalist motivation, he has throughout his life conducted a careful venture, which aims at visionary revelation rather than commentary. Four times in his career has he moved into the role of commentator on 'political' affairs. The first was in 'A Country Walk', in *Downstream* (1962); the second was in the title-poem of *Nightwalker* (1968); the third was in *Butcher's Dozen* (1972), written after the Derry massacre; and the fourth was in the recent *The Messenger*, concerned with his father's lifelong left-wing activism.

Of these the last concerns my present theme only because it shows that Kinsella's background was not nationalist in the ordinary sense, and in fact opposed the activites of certain 'nationalist' elites: Kinsella's patent sympathy for his father's position may have something to do with his own usual detachment from politics, which would be, in his father's terms, compromised by opportunism. Of *Butcher's Dozen*, all that needs to be said has already been said by the author, in his notes to *Fifteen Dead*, in which the pamphlet is reprinted. He makes neither claim nor apology for the poem, and is amusingly unrepentant in his rehearsal of certain relevant facts. It is worth guessing, however, that this work and his continued attitude to it are in part responsible for the weak reception Kinsella's poetry now receives in Britain. But, written in shock and protest, it is extraneous to his life's work, and needs no further comment here.

The two earlier cases are most interesting, and they exemplify my position. They are also very early (pre-Troubles) cases of what James Liddy contends for, a passionate revision of standard nationalist claims, and a hostile analysis of State *mores*.

Kinsella's visionary concentration, when it is applied to history, is applied directly from the present, and in terms of landscape; this or that spot is where the thing happened, whether it be something from the prehistory of the sagas, or eight hundred or two hundred or forty years ago. That is, unlike Montague, whose history is of the books, and is therefore concerned with crucial events and with the dramatic demeanour of princelings and others, Kinsella elicits a history of the grass. He directs his gaze, even physically, to the bare place which can be re-peopled only in terms of feeling, not of chronicle. Kinsella, a most passionate poet, has feeling in abundance. Thus, in 'A Country Walk', the well known lines

> Around the corner, in an open square,
> I came upon the sombre monuments
> That bear their names: MacDonagh and McBride,
> Merchants; Connolly's Commercial Arms. . . .

are spoken not in cheap derogation of the ordinary (for the heroes in question always *were* ordinary, during their lives, as Yeats pointed out) but in order to return him from the lucid hallucinations of history to his stolid self. The hallucinations, or active conjurings, were of deaths in battle, in the Civil War, in 1798, in the Cromwellian and in the Norman massacres, and in the mythic conflicts of saga. Despite an eloquent tone and movement, Kinsella attributes no grandeur to any of these events; they move between monstrous and poignant reflection:

> There, the day that Christ hung dying, twin
> Brothers armed in hate on either side;
> The day darkened but they moved to meet
> With crossed swords under a dread eclipse
> And mingled their bowels at the saga's end

Just so, two thousand years later,

> Brother met brother in a modern light.
> They turned the bloody corner, knelt and killed. . . .

and, just so, with the only personal reference,

> There the first Normans massacred my fathers . . .

It is the eloquence of cycle and of doom, hidden yet strangely perceptible to the poet's eye in the field's grass itself. A revision of standard nationalism, indeed. Yet in no way oriented to British or to any other approval: Kinsella's superego in his own.

Six years later, the superego drives him to a passion of distaste for how 'nationalist' Ireland has developed. We must remember that the years under attack are the Lemass years, the years of affluence and commercial confidence. Foreign investment thrives; the poet in his role as civil servant has to assist it. The investors are German:

The wakeful Twins

>   Bruder and Schwester
> Two young Germans I had in this morning
> Wanting to transfer investment income;
> The sister a business figurehead, her brother
> Otterfaced, with exasperated smiles
> Assuming - pressing until he achieved - response.
> Handclasp; I do not exist; I cannot take
> My eyes from their pallor. A red glare
> Plays on their faces, livid with little splashes
> Of blazing fat. The oven door closes.

Once again, it is hallucination, of a poet-servant trapped in the administration of his country's (anti-national) fiscal policies. The target is not the Germans, but those policies. The poet's reaction to both is part of his opening lament: 'I only know things seem and are not good.'

The malaise is exemplified in the story of The Wedding Group: revolutionary leaders, 'makers of modern Ireland', who in fact fell into mortal, hypocritical, comic enmity: The Groom, The Best Man, The Fox, and their three ladies. 'A tragic tale' which soon devolves into 'a tragicomical tale':

> And look, over here, in the same quarter,
> The Two Executioners - Groom and Weasel -
> '77' burning into each brow;
> And look, the vivid Weasel there again,
> Dancing crookbacked under the Player King. . . .

These are images of the destruction of national unity - indeed, of ordinary decency and honour. By their acts these founding anti-heroes created the behaviour which their successors now find most seemly.

I repeat that the subject of this passionate and sardonic taste is not Seamus Deane's beleaguered and impoverished Derry, rotted with sectarian injustice, but the new, affluent southern Ireland, guided towards wealth by men already wealthy. Kinsella sees it as a process of national betrayal by a combination of fiscal policy, clerical authoritarianism, popular self-deception, opportunism, and commercial style. The poet revises the national ideology because, as he sees the matter, its proponents have already sabotaged it. That is, Kinsella has no interest in the question of how outsiders will see developments in Ireland (historically, the processes which he excoriates were much admired outside the country); he is interested in what has become of the national psyche.

If the view of the Irish poets as a purposive group roaring with national afflatus turns out to be wrong (in fact, almost a paranoid fantasy), what, then, appears to be the case? Here we are in the area of at best reasonable guesswork, and although I realise that explanations as well as descriptions may be called for, I cannot offer more than guesses.

First, then, I hazard that, except for Yeats, republican poetry has not survived the Civil War. In Yeats's work, a nostalgic yet powerful irredentism came again in the 1930s, but the poems which it produced were nothing like his poems associated with Easter 1916, and they did not set off other poets of any quality. Over those decades, so formative for Ireland, her poets have been in a state of perpetual revisionism. They have drawn with surprising persistence on 'the past' for images, perspectives, exemplars, and spurs to irony, but in real political terms, these moves were little more than manoeuvrings before a superego which was, in effect, British.

I further suggest that there has been general and extreme self-consciousness about the very value of a national ideal. This has been produced by pressure from British reference points and from Irish vocational elites, who wished to stress their individuality, but not if it meant their losing acceptance by those British reference points. But there is neither support for a continuing revolution nor unequivocal regret at its lapse. Irish poetry is concerned neither with the possibility nor with the failure of national uprising. And it is surprising that injustice on a national scale should have received so little of the magnanimous attention we might have expected.

NOTES

1. 'A Slow North-East Wind', *Listener*, 25 Sept. 1975, pp. 404-5.
2. Ibid.
3. Ibid.
4. 'Escaped from the Massacre', *The Honest Ulsterman*, no. 50 (Winter 1975).
5. 'Now and in Ireland: the Literature of Trouble', *Hibernia*, 11 May 1978, pp. 16-17.
6. P. Costello, *The Heart Grown Brutal* (Dublin, 1977) p. 292.
7. Ibid., p. 73.
8. Ibid., p. 186.

9. Ibid., p. 6.
10. 'Myth and Terror', *The Crane Bag*, vol. ii (1978). It is worth saying that one critic who does not indulge in this narrowing focus is Terence Brown, a northern Protestant whose *Northern Voices* (Dublin, 1975) is perhaps the most subtle account of the tensions at work in the poetry as distinct from other places.
11. James Liddy, 'Ulster Poets and the Protestant Muse', *Eire-Ireland*, vol. xiv (Summer 1979) p. 118.
12. Interview of 10 Jan. 1979, as yet unpublished.

Index

Abbey Theatre, 114, 130, 214, 221, 229
Abercorn, Lord, 17
Abernethy, Rev. John, 29
Abrams, M. H., 133
Adelaide, 73-4
Advocate, 63
AE, see also Russell George, 138, 145, 158, 218, 220
Afghanistan, 90, 91
Alcala, college at, 20
Alexander I, 152
Alexander II, 150
All Saints' Day, 41
All Saints' Eve, 22
America, 3, 9, 10, 11, 59, 80, 90, 99 n30, 205, 246, 250-1, 259, 265
   IRB in, 185-190 *passim*, 191
Amnesty Association, 72
Anglican Church
   in England, 27
   in Ireland, 14-5, 17, 18-21, 27, 35-6, 213
Angus & Robertson, 207
Archer, William, 154-6, 157
Åsen, Ivar, 151
Athlone, fairs in, 46-7
Augustine, St, of Hippo, 30
Augustinian College, Lisbon, 20
Australia
   British tradition in, 253
   conscription, 161, 177 n1
   Duffy's descendants in, 63
   Duffy's views on, 57
   IRB in, 185-90
   migration to, 84

St Patrick's Day
   celebrations 1887, 1888, 72-81
   sport in, 105, 106, 116 n4, 121 n56
   writers, 194-209
Austrian Netherlands, 19
Austro-Hungarian Empire, 150, 156

Bacon, Francis, 24
Balfour, Arthur, 168-9
Balkans, 87-8
Barrington, Sir Jonah, 241-2, 246, 248, 252, 255
Barrow, John, 44
Beckett, J. C., 239, 240, 252-4
Beckett, Samuel, 146
Beerbohm, Max, 124
Belfast, 174, 249, 268
Belfast Reading Society, 34
Belfast Society, 29
Belgium, 145, 162
Beltane, 22
Beresford, John, 239, 252
Bergen Theatre, 151
Berkeley, George, Bishop of Cloyne, 24-5, 30, 222-3, 227, 232, 244
Bessborough, Lady, 15
Bjersby, Birgit (Bramsback), 142
Black, Joseph, 24
Blake, R. T., 107
Blasters, 33
Bloody Sunday, 109, 266, 274
Blueshirts, 231

Blunt, Wilfrid Scawen, 78, 79
Bolton, G. C., 251
Bordeaux, College at, 20
Boru, Brian, 77
Boulter, Hugh, Archbishop of Armagh, 15, 21, 27-8
Boyle, Robert, 24
Brady, Rev. Joseph, 164
Bray, Thomas, Archbishop of Cashel, 46
Bramwell, John, Bishop of Derry, Archbishop of Armagh, 25
Brennan, Frank, 185
Brisbane
  INA in, 184
  IRB in, 185, 187, 188
  St Patrick's Day in, 72-4
Bristol, 11
British Empire, 172, 182, 250-1, 252-3
  Irish-American attitudes to, 88-90
  Irish attitudes to, 83-98
  Ireland's relationship to, 150
  Irish role in creation of, 248
Brookes, Herbert, 183
Brooke, Charlotte, 137
Browne, Robert, Bishop of Cloyne, 171, 178 n5
Brown, Terence, 279 n10
Brown, Thomas, 90
Bryce, Viscount James, 66
Buckland, Patrick, 253
Bulletin, 201, 204
Burke, Edmund, 1-13, 17, 222, 224-5, 226, 227, 232, 242
  Anglo-Irish relations, 2-4
  anxiety about Irish executive in 1790s, 10
  Catholic question, 1, 2-7, 12
  Church and State, 17
  differences from other Protestants, 4
  early background, 1, 4-5
  Irish demands for legislative independence, 6-8
  North American colonies compared with Ireland, 10-12
  party considerations, 7-8
  reform of Irish parliamentary system, 6
Burke, Peter, 41-2, 45
Burke, Richard, 239
Burns, Elinor, 250
Butler, Joseph, Bishop of Durham, 27
Butt, Isaac, 83, 84-8, 92, 95-6,

Calvin, John, 30
Campbell, James, 168
Canada, 3, 64, 84, 255
Carleton, William, 23, 44-5, 49-50
Carlyle, Thomas, 58, 62, 132-3, 245
Carnarvon, Lord, 65
Carnival, 41-2, 45
Carpenter, John, Archbishop of Dublin, 23
Carr, T., Archbishop of Melbourne, 77
Carson, Ciaran, 260
Carson, Edward, 12, 162, 164
Case, T. B., 153
Casement, Roger, 125, 149, 156, 188-9
Casimir, 150
Castiglione, G. B., 217
Catholic Church
  in France, 30
  in Ireland, 270: challenging popular festivals, 43, 46, 47; on conscription issue, 161-77
  W. B. Yeats' attack on, 226

INDEX

Catholic Confederates, 6, 9
Cavan East, by-election, 175
Cavell, Edith, 126
Cawley, W. P., 79
Celtic Times, 113
Chamberlain, Austen, 169
Champion, 113
Charlemont, Lord, 28
'Cherry Tree Carol', 228
Chesterton, G. K., 124
Civil War, 214, 218, 262, 276, 278
  its effect on the GAA, 109, 111
Clan Na Gael, 88, 90-1, 92, 186-7, 189, 191
Clancy, Liam, 195
Clare, Lord, 10, 246
Clarke, Austin, 137, 266-7
Clarke, Samuel, 26-7, 28-9
Clausen, Fritz, 153
Clayton, Robert, Bishop of Killala, Cork and Clogher, 27-8
Clayton, Charlotte (Lady Sundon), 28
Clifford, W., 110
Coleridge, S. T., 236 n36
Collins & Mulholland, 186
Comte, Auguste, 133
Condorcet, Marquis de, 34
Confederacy, 57
Conloch, 137, 139
Connolly, James, 140, 156, 265, 276
Coole Park, 216, 233
Cooper, Bryan, 235 n18
Corkery, Daniel, 135 n2, 230, 249, 269
Corporation of Dublin, 122
Costello, Peter, 143, 262-3
Courtney, W. L., 155
Coyne, Bernard, Bishop of Elphin, 175
Croke, T., Archbishop of Cashel, 72, 105, 117 n11
Croke Park, 110, 112, 118 n20
Croker, Thomas Crofton, 43-4, 45-6, 239-40
Cuchulain, 123, 137-9, 142-5, 159, 262, 264
Cullen, L. M., 251
Cullen, Paul, Cardinal, 60
Cuppe, Pierre, 32
Curran, Rev., 165, 178 n13
Curzon, Lord, 168

Daley, Victor, 195, 200-1, 204, 208
Dalkey Hill, 123
Dalton, Maurice, 186-9, 192
Darcy, Les, 191
Davins of Deerpark, 112
Davis, Richard, 83
Davis, Thomas, 48, 56, 57, 77, 159
Davitt, Michael, 84, 93-4, 105, 117 n11
De Salis, Count, 169
De Valera, Eamon, 110, 165-6, 175, 178 ns12 and 13, 230-1
De Vere, Aubrey Thomas, 137
Deane, Seamus, 266, 274-5, 277
Denmark, 151
Dennehy, Rev. Gerald, 174
Derry, 270, 274-5, 277
Derry, bishopric, 18, 27, 28
Descartes, Rene, 25-6, 30, 223
Devlin, Bernadette, 262, 269
Devoy, John, 90-1, 94-5, 110
Dicey, A. V., 65
Dillon, John, 57, 165-6, 174-6
Dollard, Rev., 114
Donnelly, Terence, Bishop of Derry, 15
Donnybrook Fair, 43, 47
Donoghue, Denis, 261-2
Doran, John, 186-7, 190-2
Doyle, Canon, 67
Drury, Arthur J., 191

Dryer, Albert, 183-93 n2
Dublin University, 15-16, 20, 25, 28
Duffy, Charles Gavan, 48, 56-68, 77, 119 n22
Duke, H. E., 168, 173

Easter Rising, 125, 149, 157, 158, 159, 182-3, 186, 192, 204, 217, 218, 265, 266, 278
Edinburgh, Duke of, 61
Eglinton, John, 220
Ellis, Havelock, 155
Ellmann, Richard, 236 n49
Emmet, Robert, 34, 71, 79, 117 n11, 226, 250, 266
Engels, Friedrich, 242-3
Eyre, Edward John, 245
Eyries, County Cork, 174

Fallon, Padraic, 267
Fenians, 49-50, 61, 71-2, 76, 106-7, 109, 117 n15, 182, 186, 218, 243, 267
American, 88, 89, 91, 97
Ferguson, Sir Samuel, 137
Fiacc, Padraic, 268
Fianna, 262
Finland, 149-53, 156, 159 n2
Finegan, Patrick, Bishop of Kilmore, 170, 175
Fitzgerald, Dick, 112
Fitzgerald, Lord Edward, 250
Fitzgerald, Nicholas, 78
Fitzgerald, R. D., 210
Fitzgerald, Thomas, 187, 188-9
Fitzgibbon, John, Earl of Clare, 246
Fogarty, Michael, Bishop of Killaloe, 162, 166
Foley, Patrick, Bishop of Kildare and Leighlin, 172, 178 n5
Ford, Patrick, 88-90, 92, 96-7
Foster, John, 240, 241, 247, 252, 254
France, 4, 14, 26, 34, 42, 63, 125, 138, 145, 161
theological developments in, 30-2
Franciscan College, Prague, 19-20
Franco, General F., 232
Freehill, Francis Bede, 78
Freeman's Journal, 88
Freemasons, 34
French, Lord, 161, 168, 176
French Revolution, 1, 5, 12, 35, 150, 224-5
Freud, Sigmund, 155
Friedrich Karl, Prince of Hessen, 160 n8
Friel, Brian, 261
Frost, Robert, 270
Froude, James Anthony, 244-7

Gael, 113
Gaelic Athlete, 113
Gaelic Athletic Association (GAA), 49, 51, 71, 104-16, 157
political role, 106-11
organisation of modern sport, 111-2
Gaelic League, 107-8, 119 n23, 157, 248
of Victoria, 186
Gaelic Sunday, 108
Gaffney, Rev., 173
Garvin, J. L., 95, 167
Geneva, 16
Germany, 138, 159 n2, 161, 185, 186, 187, 188, 222, 265
Gibson, Edmund, Bishop of London, 26-8
Gilmartin, Thomas, Archbishop of Tuam, 170-1
Gladstone, W. E., 64, 65, 66, 72, 78, 89, 95, 103 n106, 159
Goldsmith, L., 222, 223
Goltz, General Von Der, 149

Good Confessor, 21
Gonne, Maud, 215, 216
Gore-Booth, Eva, 137
Gougane Barra, Co. Cork, 43-4, 45-6
Govett's Leap, Australia, 191
Grattan, Henry, 1, 6-7, 9, 15, 17-8, 70, 222, 226, 232, 239-40, 241, 242, 246-9, 250-1
Green, Alice Stopford, 248
Gregory, Lady, 123, 134, 138, 214, 216, 217, 220, 221, 233, 234, 235 n10
Grein, J. T., 154
Greig, Edvard, 151
Griffith, Arthur, 83, 98, 150, 156, 175-6
Gwynn, Stephen, 168

Hallinan, Denis, Bishop of Limerick, 166
Hall, S. C. and A. M., 40-1, 46
Harlow, Vincent, 250-1
Harris, John, 75
Hartigan, Patrick (John O'Brien), 195, 206-9
Harty, John, Archbishop of Cashel, 178 ns 5 and 6
Harvey, Justice John Musgrave, 185-90, 192
Hawthorne, Nathaniel, 75
Hayes, Canon, 174
Healy, John, Archbishop of Tuam, 179 n17
Healy, T. M., 102 n92
Heaney, Seamus, 259-62, 271-4
Helsinki, 152
Henry, Mitchell, 86
Hervey, Frederick Augustus, Bishop of Cloyne and Derry, 28
Hibernian Society, 73, 75-7 *passim*
Higinbotham, George, 61
Hoadley, Benjamin, Bishop of Bangor, Hereford, Salisbury and Winchester, 26-8, 38 n49
Hoadley, John, Bishop of Ferns, Archbishop of Dublin and Armagh, 27
Hobbes, Thomas, 25
Hobson, Bulmer, 188
Hort, Josiah, Archbishop of Tuam, 15
Hughes, W. M., 182
Huguenots, 16, 26, 30, 239
Hull, Eleanor, 138
Hulme, T. E., 133
Hume, David, 30, 35
Hungary, 150, 265-6
Hutcheson, Francis, 24, 30, 35
Huxley, Aldous, 128, 157
Hyde-Lees, Georgie, 217

Ibsen, Henrik, 151, 154-9 *passim*
Imperial Federation League, 65
India, 3, 86, 89-90, 92-8 *passim*, 246, 252
Inglis, Henry, 45, 54 n43
Industrial Workers of the World (IWW), 182, 188
Irish Republican Army (IRA), 231, 259-60, 262, 263
Irish Academy of Letters, 228
Irish Amateur Athletic Association, 106
Irish Citizens' Army, 156
Irish Evicted Tenants Fund, 73-4
Irish Literary Theatre, 155, 214
Irish National Association, 182-4
Irish National Brotherhood, 107
Irish National League, 70, 73, 74, 78, 94
Irish National Literary Society, 125
Irish Olympic, 110
Irish Party, 162-3, 165-6, 168, 170, 174, 176

Irish Players, 134
Irish Republican Brotherhood
   (IRB), 72, 104, 105-7,
   156, 168, 182-3, 184-9,
   191
Irish Statesman, 220
Irish Republican Socialist
   Party (IRSP), 263
Irish World, 88-90, 94
Italy, 42, 150, 217-18, 222,
   225

Jackson, T. A., 250
Jamaica, 245
James, F. G., 251, 254
James, 1st Duke of Leinster,
   34
Jameson, Andrew, 218
Jansenius, Cornelius, Dutch
   Bishop of Ypres, 30
Johnston, Denis, 142
Johnston, E. M., 251
Jones, Francis P., 190
Jorgensen, Alfred, 153
Joseph II, Emperor of Austria,
   19
Joyce, James, 135, 151, 155-6

Kavanagh, Patrick, 145, 266
Kearney, Richard, 263
Kearney, Dr, 20
Kelly, Denis, Bishop of Ross,
   178 n6
Kennedy, Rev. John, 19
Keogh, John, 2
Kickham, Charles, 50
Kilkenny College, 25
King, William, Archbishop of
   Dublin, 15, 20-1, 27, 38
   n50
Kinsella, Thomas, 144, 261,
   266, 274-7, 300-4
Koebner, Richard, 251
Kohl, J. G., 47-8
Krause, David, 126

Land League, 93, 102 n88
Lane, Hugh, 216, 219, 221, 233

Law, H. A., 213
Lecky, W. E. H., 239, 242,
   247-8, 249, 250, 252
Ledwidge, Francis, 145, 264
Leeper, Alexander, 183
Lemass, Sean F., 276
Lens, Peter, 33
Liddy, James, 267, 275
Liebniz, Gottfried Wilhelm
   von, 25-6
Lloyd George, David, 163-4,
   168-9, 171
Locke, John, 25, 30, 223
Lockington, Rev. William, 195,
   196-8, 202, 204, 207
Logue, Cardinal, 162, 164,
   166-71, 172-3, 175-6,
   178 n5
Lombard College, 20, 32-3
Long, Walter, 168
Lough, Derg, 54 n43
Louvain, college at, 19
Lowell, Robert, 269, 272
Lylehill, 18
Lynch, Rev. Nicholas, 33
Lyons, F. S. L., 83, 209,
   255

MacBride, John, 216
MacCarthy, Denis Florence,
   137
MacDermott, Sean, 188
MacDonagh, Oliver, 255
MacDonagh, Thomas, 142, 264,
   276
Mack, Sidney, 185, 192
Mackey, 'Tyler', 112
MacLua, B., 109
MacMahon, James, 176
MacNeill, John Swift (Eoin),
   248
MacPherson, J., 137
Madden, R. R., 33
Malcolmson, Anthony, 239,
   254-5
Mannix, Daniel, Archbishop of
   Melbourne, 183-5, 190,
   193, 195

INDEX

Mansergh, Nicholas, 83, 84, 97, 149–50
Mansion House Conference, 165–7, 171–2, 174, 175, 177 n1
Mant, R., 22
Marcuse, Herbert, 144
Markievicz, Constance, 150, 156
Marsh, Francis, Archbishop of Dublin, 20
Marx, Eleanor, 155
Marx, Karl, 218, 242–3
Mathew, Rev. Theobald, 40–1, 47–8, 49
May Day, 41, 42
May Eve, 22
Maynooth, 35
  April 1918 meeting at, 164–7, 168, 170, 179 n15
McCaffrey, L. J., 83, 85, 251
McCarthy, D., 110
McCartney, Donal, 247
McCormack, John, 110
McDowell, R. B., 249, 255
McElhill, Bernard, 195, 198–200, 204
McFadden, Rev., 78
McGee, T. D., 64, 243
McGing, Michael, 185–9
McGinley, Dr, 173
McGuinness, John, 78–9
McGuiness, William, 185–9
McKeown, Frank, 185, 188–9
McMullen, L., 153
McRory, Joseph, Bishop of Dromore, 170, 178 n5
McSweeney, Edmund, 185–6, 187, 189
McTiernan, Edward, 185
Meagher, Thomas Francis, 49
Melbourne, 56, 58, 65, 183–4, 186–7, 188, 198
  St Patrick's Day in, 75, 76–8
Meslier, Jean, 32
Midsummer's Eve, 22, 41, 42
Militaire Philosophe, le, 32

Millen, General F. F., 90–1
Miller, David, 46
Mitchel, John, 57, 97, 159, 244, 246
Moloney, Justice Thomas Francis, 181 n53
Molyneux, William, 25
Montague, John, 268–9, 294–6, 302
Moran, Patrick Francis, Archbishop of Sydney, 78
Moravians, 16
Morley, Viscount (John), 79
Morris, William, 133
Munch, P. A., 151
Murdoch, Iris, 141
Murphy, William Martin, 216
Mussolini, B., 225, 231
M'Carthy, Justin Huntley, 154

Naoroji, Dadabhai, 95
Napoleon, 150, 152
Nation, 56, 57–8, 66, 77, 87
National Aid Committee, 175
National Defence Fund, 175
Nesbitt, Nathaniel, 17
Newenham, Thomas, 44
Newry, 266
Newton, Isaac, 24, 25, 26, 223
Nietzsche, F., 217
Nolan, Edward, Bishop of Kildare and Leighlin, 44
North, Lord, 7, 11
Norway, 149–51, 156, 158
Nowlan, John, 107, 118 n20

Ogilvie, Will, 209
Organ, Andrew, 187
Organ, Matthew, 187, 191
Orr, James, 34
O'Brien, Conor Cruise, 83, 259–63, 271
O'Brien, John, Bishop of Cloyne, 20
O'Brien, William Smith, 57, 74, 78, 87, 96
O'Casey, Sean, 126, 134, 140, 228–9, 261

INDEX

O'Connell, Daniel, 47, 49, 57, 69-70, 161, 213, 226, 233, 250
O'Connor, Arthur, 34, 78
O'Connor, Frank, 145
O'Connor, Justice James, 181 n53
O'Curry, Eugene, 138
O'Dea, Thomas, Bishop of Galway, 178 n5
O'Donnell, Frank Hugh, 91-4, 102 n92
O'Donnell, Patrick, Bishop of Raphoe, 166, 178 n5
O'Donovan, John, 46
O'Duffy, Eimar, 144
O'Duffy, Eoin, 109, 153, 231-2
O'Farrell, Patrick, 83, 113-4, 195, 252
O'Flanagan, Rev., 175
O'Grady, Standish James, 138, 145
O'Halloran, Sylvester, 138
O'Higgins, Kevin, 232
O'Leary, John, 215
O'Loghlen, Colman, 77-8
O'Neill Daunt, W. J., 86, 96
O'Neill, Laurence, 165, 179 n17
O'Neill, Owen Roe, 77
O'Reilly, Maurice, 195-6, 197
O'Shanassy, John, 59, 61
O'Toole, L. J., 109, 118 n20

Paine, Thomas, 34
Paisley, Rev. Ian, 258, 265
Palatines, German, 16
Papacy, 20, 61, 162, 167, 169, 228
Paris, University of, 32
Parnell, Charles Stewart, 66, 70, 71, 83, 85, 91, 92, 95-7, 107, 117 n11, 125, 159, 162, 213, 216, 226, 229, 246
 Duffy's views on, 66
 on Home Rule, 70
 on imperial connection, 85, 91, 92
Parnell, Sir John, 241
Pearse, Patrick, 137, 139-43, 158, 262-5, 269
Pearson, C. H., 63
Petty, William, 250
Piaget, Jean, 143
Piers, Richard, Bishop of Waterford, 15
Pitt, William, 8, 10
Plunket, Benjamin John, Protestant Bishop of Meath, 226
Plunkett, Horace, 220, 264
Pound, Ezra, 217
Prague,
 colleges at, 19
 Archbishop of, 20
Presbyterian Church in Ireland, 16, 18-9, 22
Presbytery of Antrim, 16, 18, 29
Presbytery of Glasgow, 29

Quakers, 16, 239
Quisling, V., 153

Ranjitsinhji, Prince, 110
Redmond, John, 97, 107, 162, 164
Reid, J. S., 33
Reid, Thomas, 35
Revolutionary Directory, 189
Ribbonmen, 50
Richardson, Rev. John, 21
Richer, Edmund, 31
Rickwood, Lieut., 192
Ripon, Lord, 65
Robinson, Lennox, 228
Rossa, J. O'Donovan, 188
Royal Irish Constabulary, 41, 118 n17, 173-4
Rundle, Thomas, Bishop of Derry, 27-8
Ruskin, William, 133
Russell, George, see also AE,

Russell, George – *contd.*
123, 138, 158, 220
Russell, Thomas, 34
Russia, 87, 90-1, 126, 149-53, 159 n2, 160 n8, 224

Salisbury, Lord, 84, 87
Samhain, 22
Samuels, Arthur, 173, 180 n44
Scandinavia, 42, 150-5, 156, 159 n3, 160 n14
Scotland, 5, 9, 14, 16, 24, 35, 59, 75, 164, 206
Shackleton, Abraham, 5
Shaftesbury, 3rd Earl of, 25, 30
Shakespear, Olivia, 237 n49
Shanahan of Kilfinane, 112
Shaw, G. B., 122-35, 144, 154-5
Sheehy, John, 183
Shelburne, Earl of, 251
Sheppard, Oliver, 137
Shortt, Edward, 168
Sigerson, George, 248
Simmons, James, 146
Simson, Rev. John, 28-9
Sinn Fein, 98, 151, 157, 161, 165-6, 170-1, 172, 174, 175-7, 182-5, 190
Smith, Adam, 30
Society of Jesus, 30
South Africa, 92, 93, 97
Spencer, Thomas E., 195, 204-6
Spindler, Karl, 149
Spinoza, Benedictus de, 26
St Bartholomew's Day, 42-3
St Enda, 142
St John's Day, 42
St John's Eve, 22, 45
St John's Well, 23
St Patrick's Day, 72-81, 183, 196, 208
St Patrick's Eve, 74
St Patrick's Societies, 73, 77
St Patrick's Well, 22-3

Stack, Austin, 109
Stephen, Mr Justice A., 78
Stephens, James, 72, 145
Stockholm, 153, 154, 159 n3, 219
Strauss, Erich, 250
Strindberg, August, 154-6
Stuart, Francis, 144, 261
Sullivans, A. M., D. B. and T. D., 71
Svinhufund, P. E., 159-60 n7, 160 n8
Sweden, 150, 152
Sweetman, Nicholas, Bishop of Ferns, 19
Swift, Jonathan, 6, 15, 222-4, 226, 232, 234, 243
Sydney, 58, 65, 72-6, 78-9, 134, 182-9, 191-2, 195, 201-2, 205
Syme, David, 61
Synge, J. M., 123-4, 134, 137, 144, 160 n14, 214-5, 221, 228-9, 232-3
Synod of Ulster, 16, 18, 21, 29, 33

Tailteann Games, 110
Talbot, Lord, 27
Tara, 49
Telltown, Co. Meath, 46
Tenant League, 57, 60
Terry, Ellen, 157
Thompson, William Irwin, 143
Thornley, David, 85
Tocqueville, A. de, 44
Toland, John, 25-6, 33
Tomorrow, 228
Tone, Wolfe, 34, 159, 250, 258
Toohey, James, 79
Trinity College, Dublin, 28, 61, 225, 255
Troy, John Thomas, Bishop of Ossory, Archbishop of Dublin, 18, 33
Tullamore, 74, 79

Ukraine, 150

INDEX

Ulster, 18, 29, 35, 146, 177, 198, 214, 243, 253, 258, 260, 263, 267
Ulster Covenant, 164
Ulster Unionists, 161, 253
Unionists, 167, 170, 214, 235 n18, 247, 254, 270
United Irish League, 158, 174
United Irish Societies, in Australia, 73
United Irishmen, 34, 150

Varden, Rev., 174, 180 n46
Victoria, 56-7, 60-2, 65-6, 72-4, 77-8
Volunteers, 6, 108, 156, 165-7, 168, 178 n13

Wakefield, E., 22, 47
Wales, 106, 112, 164
Wall, Mervyn, 141
Walpole, Robert, 27
Walsh, J. J., 107, 110, 118 n20
Walsh, William, Archbishop of Dublin, 162, 164-7, 175, 178 ns 5 and 13
Walsh of Portnascully, 112
War of Independence, affect on GAA, 109

Warburton, William, Bishop of Gloucester, 27
Watt, William, 182, 185
Webb, Alfred, 94-5, 97
Weber, Mary, 183
Wellesley, Dorothy, 234
Wentworth, W. C., 209
Wergeland, Henrik, 151
Werner, Heinz, 143
Wesley, John, 16, 28, 35
West Indies, 249, 251
Westminster Confession of Faith, 29
Wexford Rising of 1798, 71
Whigs, 7, 11, 224
Wilde, Oscar, 123-4, 154
Wilde, William, 40-1, 47
Wilson, Angus, 134
Windisch, W., 138
Wright, David McKee, 195, 201-4

Yeats, W. B., 123-4, 129, 134, 139, 142-4, 145, 156-8, 202, 212-38, 242, 254, 260-3, 264, 267, 276, 278
Young Irelanders, 47-9, 56, 58, 59, 71, 76-7, 78, 267